Xcode® 5

D0851512

Xcode® 5

Richard Wentk

WILEY

Xcode® 5

Published by
John Wiley & Sons, Inc.
10475 Crosspoint Blvd.
Indianapolis, IN 46256
www.wiley.com

Copyright © 2014 by John Wiley & Sons, Inc., Indianapolis, Indiana

Published by John Wiley & Sons, Inc., Indianapolis, Indiana

Published simultaneously in Canada

ISBN: 978-1-118-83433-6

Manufactured in the United States of America

10 9 8 7 6 5 4 3 2 1

For general information on our other products and services or to obtain technical support, please contact our Customer Care Department within the U.S. at (877) 762-2974, outside the U.S. at (317) 572-3993 or fax (317) 572-4002.

Library of Congress Control Number: 2013956856

For Jan

About the Author

Richard Wentk is one of the U.K.'s most reliable technology writers, with more than ten years of experience as a developer and more than fifteen years in publishing. He covers Apple products and developments for *Macworld* and *MacFormat* magazines and writes about technology, creativity, and business strategy for titles such as *Computer Arts* and *Future Music*. As a trainer and former professional Apple developer returning now to development on the iPhone and OS X, he is uniquely able to clarify the key points of the development process, explain how to avoid pitfalls and bear traps, and emphasize key benefits and creative possibilities. He lives online but also has a home in Wiltshire, England. For details of apps and other book projects, visit `www.zettaboom.com`.

Credits

Acquisitions Editor
Aaron Black

Project Editor
Martin V. Minner

Technical Editor
Brad Miller

Copy Editor
Gwenette Gaddis

Director, Content Development & Assembly
Robyn Siesky

Vice President and Executive Group Publisher
Richard Swadley

Contents

Preface

Having become comfortable with Xcode 4, I was curious about the changes that Apple would make in Xcode 5. Some, such as the removal of the old GCC toolchain and its replacement with an all-LLVM compiler and debugger, were expected. Others, such as further simplification of the permission profiling and app submission process, were very welcome.

Xcode 5's designers have continued to simplify app development and make it more accessible to the public. There is no doubt that the App Store has been a phenomenal success, with millions of contributions from both professional and amateur developers. The latter have proven that Xcode works as intended. Starting with little or no software experience, they have developed and sold apps to an international market. Even if the quality is variable, the sheer number of apps proves that app development isn't quite the mystery it once was.

As Apple moves into new markets, the number of newcomers continues to grow. So the first goal of this book is to introduce the key features of Xcode 5 for those who are just getting started. Newcomers should begin at the front of the book and work their way through it in order. The sequence of the earlier chapters is designed to be a practical primer for Xcode development, not just a list of features and changes.

A second goal is to highlight important changes, and introduce some of the more complex features in more detail. Many newcomers use Xcode in a simple click-bang way, missing out on the power and flexibility hidden under the surface. The less-obvious features are easy to skip, but exploring them can open up new possibilities for testing, debugging, project management, and build control.

Some tools, such as Instruments, have further hidden layers of their own that would require a further book the size of this one to explore fully. Others, such as bots, are new in Xcode 5. Still others, including details of the build system, have been expanded in this edition, with extra notes about the challenges developers can encounter when trying to integrate code from projects built in other environments.

Because space is limited, this book doesn't dig into every feature to the deepest possible level. But new Xcode 5 users and experienced Xcode 5 users should find creative inspiration here, as well as a good store of tips and techniques that can push them through the essentials of basic development and into the deeper possibilities of managed testing and build design.

Every author works hard to make his or her books as helpful as possible. Comments and feedback are welcome at `xcodedr@zettaboom.com`.

Acknowledgments

Although book publishing has become digital, book writing hasn't. A book continues to be a team effort.

My thanks go to acquisitions editor Aaron Black for making the project happen and to project editor Martin V. Minner for his continuing support and extended patience. Sincere thanks are also due to the rest of the team at Wiley for their hard work behind the scenes, especially technical editor Brad Miller, whose feedback and comments were invaluable.

Personal gratitude is due to Annette, Alexa, and Hilary, who all contributed more than they know.

Software development has become a communal activity, and particular appreciation is due to the countless bloggers, experimenters, developers, and problem-solvers on the web whose generosity and creativity have made so much possible in so many ways.

Finally, love as always to Team HGA. I couldn't have written it without you.

Introduction

This book is about developing iOS and Mac projects using the Xcode 5 development tool-chain. You'll find this book useful if you have experience with Cocoa or Cocoa Touch and have used Xcode 4 in the past or if you have worked with other development environments and are curious about how to work productively with Xcode 5.

This isn't a book about languages or frameworks, and the only loose prerequisite is some basic experience with a C-family language. You'll get the most from it if you download and install Xcode 5 for yourself, work through the examples, and experiment with it as you read.

If you're new to Apple development, you may also want to read the *Objective-C, iOS,* and *Cocoa* Developer Reference titles. A few framework features are mentioned in the text. You don't need to be familiar with them to use this book successfully, but you do need to understand how to learn about them using the built-in documentation before you can develop iOS and Mac apps that can be sold through the App Store.

Chapter 1 looks back briefly at previous Mac development tools and introduces some of the core differences between Xcode 4 and Xcode 5. It introduces the essential elements of the Xcode UI and explains how it's possible to create iOS and OS X projects.

Chapter 2 explains how to choose a Mac for development, how to sign up as a paid developer, and how to install and customize Xcode. It's a feature of Xcode development that while the installation process is simple, it has hidden options that are easy to miss. Also, there are important differences between installing a single version of Xcode and using multiple versions across multiple platforms to develop commercial apps while also experimenting with beta OS code.

Chapter 3 introduces the Xcode templates. It demonstrates how you can use the templates to get started with app development, but also explores some of the more specialized templates available for both iOS and OS X projects, and it explains how you can create files that can work as templates for your own projects.

Chapter 4 looks in more detail at the editor features, including the navigator panels that collect project information in a single switchable pane. This chapter explores the many project navigation features and support tools in Xcode 5 and introduces timesaving features in the enhanced code editor.

Chapter 5 explains how to organize and manage files and projects. It examines groups in the project navigator, demonstrates how to add and remove files from a project, and explains how to add Apple frameworks to a project.

Chapter 6 is a guide to the Apple Documentation built into Xcode. Apple has structured the Documentation in specific ways, and you'll progress more quickly and with less effort if you understand what this means in practice. Understanding and using the Documentation and searching it in Xcode are key skills. Don't skip this chapter, even if you already have experience in other environments.

Chapter 7 introduces the key features of Interface Builder and explains how you can use IB to build complete applications, because IB isn't just for interfaces. It introduces storyboards and nib files, and explains how to build a simple iOS app that responds to a button tap.

Chapter 8 explores IB in more detail. It shows you how to set up constraints to automate UI layout across multiple devices and resolutions, and how to get started with storyboards. It also explains how to localize your project so it can support foreign languages.

Chapter 9 takes a closer look at the timesaving features in Xcode, including the structure management tools that can help you move sections of code to their most appropriate location, manage indentation intelligently, and add or remove comment blocks. This chapter also introduces code completion and explains how you can customize the code snippet and code completion macros with your own most-used blocks of code.

Chapter 10 introduces the Xcode Organizer, a multi-purpose tool for managing supporting files and other project information that doesn't belong in the code editor. It introduces device provisioning and profiles and explains how you can manage your test devices.

Chapter 11 is a comprehensive introduction to the Xcode provisioning process, which is necessary for device testing, beta distribution, and App Store distribution for both iOS and OS X projects. It takes you step by step through the provisioning process and explains the principles of provisioning so you can understand what certificates, identities, and profiles do and why they're necessary.

Chapter 12 introduces the Xcode build system. It introduces project and target build settings and explains the relationship between them. It also looks in detail at build setting management, explaining how you can use build configurations and the new schemes feature to create flexible, multi-target builds for more complex projects.

Chapter 13 goes deeper into the app development process. It introduces a list of common and useful build customizations, takes you step by step through the different build processes needed for iOS App Store, iOS Ad Hoc, and OS X App Store builds. It also explains how you can use Xcode to submit projects to the App Store. Finally, it introduces the internals of the build system and explains how you can use custom scripting in the build phases and build rules to satisfy almost any build requirement.

Chapter 14 goes deeper into the build system. It explains how you can incorporate code and libraries from external sources, including open-source projects. It includes a practical demonstration of building a simple library as an Xcode workspace and includes notes about possible strategies for more complex projects.

Chapter 15 explores the version control features. It introduces the different ways in which you can manage project versions in Xcode and illustrates their strengths and weaknesses. It ends with a practical example of using Xcode with the GitHub collaborative online code repository and explains how GitHub can be used for solo and group projects.

Chapter 16 introduces the Xcode debugger. It explores the different ways in which you can view and use console, and it demonstrates how you can add, remove, and manage breakpoints; view variables; and monitor them as they change.

Chapter 17 explores Instruments and demonstrates how you can use them to profile almost any aspect of your code, including memory use, performance, and impact on the surrounding system. It includes a profiling example that demonstrates how you can use Instruments to check for memory leaks.

Chapter 18 introduces the Unit Test features and explains how you can use them to create and check automated test cases in your code, to help you guarantee that when you make changes to existing code, it continues to function as it should. It also demonstrates how to set up Xcode 5's bots to support continuous integration, so your projects can produce a daily build automatically, with comprehensive reporting of build and test issues.

Appendix A lists the extra tools built into Xcode, such as the printer simulator, accessibility inspector, file merge tool, and application loader.

Appendix B lists the extra tools and utilities you can download from Apple's developer support library.

Appendix C introduces Xcode's CoreData and plist editing features.

Code appears `in a monospaced font`. Items you type **appear in bold.**

Projects and examples were developed with various versions of Xcode 5 and 5.1, from the first developer releases to the final GM seed, on OS X 10.9.0 to 10.9.2. Apple continually updates Xcode, so graphics and features may differ slightly from the illustrations and feature descriptions in this book.

Supporting code is available on the book's website at `www.wiley.com/go/xcode5`. See the readme there for the most recent system and software requirements. Code is supplied as-is with no warranty and can be used in both commercial and private Cocoa projects, but may not be sold or repackaged as tutorial material.

Getting Started with Xcode 5

 In This Part

Introducing Xcode 5

X code is Apple's free suite of developer tools; it is used to create applications for iOS mobile devices and for Mac OS X. Xcode 5, shown in Figure 1.1, is the most recent version.

Developer tools are complex, and Xcode has always tried to hide much of that complexity from novice developers. You can use Xcode in a very simple click-to-build way, but this simplicity can be misleading. Many developers never explore Xcode's more advanced features and never discover how they can use them to save time, solve problems, or extend their projects with original and creative features.

Xcode also includes an unexpectedly enormous selection of helper applications and developer tools. A complete guide to every element in Xcode would require a shelf of books. This book concentrates on beginner- and intermediate-level features, but it also includes hints and pointers for advanced developers.

Understanding the History of Mac Development Tools

In This Chapter

Understanding the history of Mac development tools

Moving to Xcode 5

Comparing iOS and OS X development

Before OS X, Apple's IDE (Integrated Development Environment) was MPW (Macintosh Programmer's Workshop). MPW is no longer supported, but can still be found on the Internet Archive, as shown in Figure 1.2.

MPW competed with a commercial development system called CodeWarrior. Both were expensive, and many would-be developers were put off by the initial start-up costs.

Looking back at early IDEs

CodeWarrior was based on the Metrowerks C compiler and environment. It smoothed the transition from the 68k processors to the PowerPC and helped make the new PowerPC Macs a success. As an IDE, CodeWarrior provided complete support for the PowerPC architecture; MPW took longer to catch up with Apple's own new hardware. CodeWarrior also compiled code more quickly than MPW and created faster and more efficient binaries.

Figure 1.1

Xcode 5 is a significant refresh of the radical changes introduced in Xcode 4.

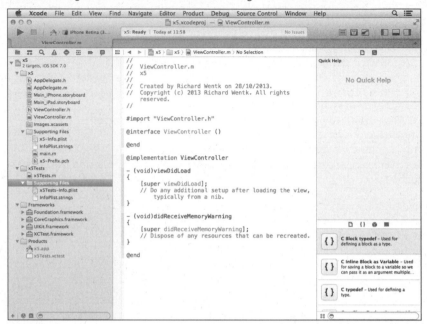

Figure 1.2

The MPW IDE is no longer available from Apple, but users of antique Macs can still download it from other sites.

NOTE

Early versions of MPW were famous for their error messages, which included "We already did this function," "This array has no size, and that's bad," and "Call me paranoid, but finding '/*' inside this comment makes me suspicious." Later Apple IDEs reverted to more traditional messages.

Developing Xcode

With the move to OS X, Apple decided to retain control over the developer environment. An IDE called Project Builder had been developed as part of the NeXTStep project. A free copy of Project Builder was bundled with every copy of OS X. In Fall 2003, an updated and enhanced version was shipped and named Xcode 1.0.

Xcode has been updated with every major new release of OS X. Xcode 2.0 shipped with OS X 10.4 "Tiger." It included improved documentation, better support for Java, and the Quartz Composer visual programming tool, which is described in more detail in Appendix B.

Xcode 3 shipped with OS X 10.5 "Leopard" and introduced improved debugging tools. Xcode 3.1 added support for early versions of iOS.

Xcode 3.2 is shown in Figure 1.3 and was released with OS X 10.6 "Snow Leopard." Prior to this release, Apple supplied separate builds of Xcode for iOS and OS X development. With version 3.2, Xcode became a unified development environment that could target both platforms. This widened the developer base, but it also made Xcode more difficult to download. The Mac version was around 800GB. The combined version is typically around 3GB.

Figure 1.3

The Xcode 3 IDE was productive but limited by obvious UI inefficiencies, such as poor support for editing multiple files simultaneously.

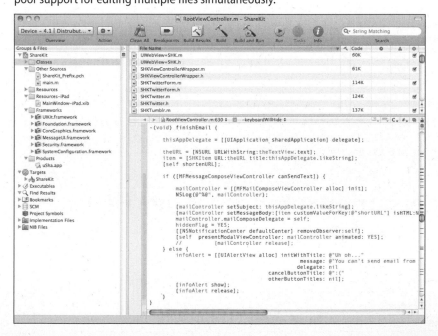

Alternatives to Xcode

Xcode is optimized for visual development of Objective-C and Cocoa projects. In practice, this means the Cocoa and Cocoa Touch libraries and documentation are tightly integrated into Xcode. Xcode 5 supports Objective-C++, which allows developers to mix C++, C, and Objective-C code, with some limitations. For example, the C++ and Objective-C class hierarchies are independent and do not allow cross-inheritance.

For details of mixing and interfacing Objective-C and C++, search online for Chapter 13 of "The Objective-C 2.0 Programming Language"—a document originally written and distributed by Apple, but now available only from other sites.

If you are used to developing in a different environment, you may feel that Xcode works in ways that don't match your requirements. If you plan to create windowed applications with official Apple UI elements, building Objective-C and Cocoa code in Xcode is likely to be your most efficient choice. If you prefer to create UNIX applications with command line or X11 features, you may prefer an alternative.

Although OS X is based on Darwin/POSIX rather than Linux, it's relatively easy to create a cross-platform application core that can be extended with platform-specific features. It's possible to use Xcode from the command line in Terminal with your own make files (build management and configuration files). If you're used to GCC and GDB on other platforms, you can run them directly from the command line, bypassing most of Xcode's features.

Java and C/C++ developers may prefer the free Eclipse IDE available at `www.eclipse.org`. Eclipse can be extended with a C/C++ IDE. Cocoa isn't supported, but Java and mixed development are.

For multi-platform support, Mono remains an option. Mono compiles C# rather than Objective-C or C++, but it's designed to support cross-platform output, running similar code on Windows, OS X, iPhone, Android, and Linux platforms. Mono also supports ASP.NET web projects.

MonoMac and MonoTouch versions include bindings to key OS X and iOS APIs. A version for Android is also available. The main IDE is called MonoDevelop and is available at `monodevelop.com`. Although Mono has obvious advantages, Apple's support for the competing platform isn't reliably enthusiastic. At times, Apple has barred from the App Store apps developed in languages other than C, Objective-C, and C++. But some MonoTouch applications have been approved for sale. Mono may be a better choice for developers coming from a C# and Windows background who don't want to learn a completely new language.

Game developers should explore the ever-increasing number of cross-platform game libraries and development environments that support iOS and OS X. Examples include Unity, Sparrow, Citrus, and cocos2D. The state of game development changes continuously. For the most recent details, search online for "iOS game engine" and "OS X game engine," adding other platforms—Android or others—as needed.

CAUTION

Strong Java support was a feature of earlier Xcode versions, but that has been downgraded in recent releases. Apple has moved Xcode toward supporting C-family development, including C, Objective-C, C++, and Objective-C++. These are now the officially supported languages for iOS and OS X development.

Understanding Xcode 5's Key Features

For developers who are beginning Xcode, Xcode 5 includes the following features:

- A project navigator that lists and groups related project files
- File and project templates for both OS X and iOS projects

- A code editor that includes static code checking, code completion, and dynamic hints and tips
- A visual UI design tool called *Interface Builder,* also known as IB, which can prototype visual interfaces, but can also be used to manage and preload other application objects
- Further integrated editors for class management and for Apple's Core Data database framework
- A debugger that supports expressions and conditional breakpoints
- Support for direct access to various online code repositories
- A minimal but useful *iPhone Simulator* that runs iOS applications on a Mac
- A collection of *Instruments*—tools that can profile speeds, monitor memory allocations, and report other key features of code as it runs
- Support for both visual development and low-level command-line compilation
- A selection of further helper applications

CROSS-REFERENCE

For a list of helper tools and applications, see Appendixes A and B.

Xcode doesn't support or include the following:

- **Editors for graphics, sounds, fonts, 3D objects, or other media types:** External editors must be used.
- **Built-in support for languages other than C, C++, and Objective-C:** You can extend Xcode to work with other languages, but Xcode is optimized for C-family development. (This does not include C#.)
- **Development tools for other operating systems:** OS X is similar enough to BSD UNIX to allow for some code sharing. But Xcode cannot be used to develop applications for Windows, Android, or Linux, or for web languages such as Perl and PHP.
- **Unlocked open development for iOS:** Applications for iOS hardware must be code signed and linked to a time-limited certificate. In practice, this means that even if you use Xcode, own an iPhone, and are a registered developer, your own applications will cease to run after the time-limited certificate expires.
- **Development on non-Apple platforms:** Currently, Xcode requires a Mac running a recent copy of OS X.

NOTE

Rumors come and go of a merger, or at least a relationship, between Xcode and Microsoft's Visual Studio development tools. At the time of this writing, a merger seems almost impossibly unlikely.

Code changes in Xcode 5

Xcode 5 includes some significant changes to Objective-C. Older code still compiles, but you can use some new time-savers when writing new code.

The first change is that ivars are now optional. If you declare properties in the usual way, you should not need to add corresponding ivars—the compiler generates them automatically.

You can also save time with a new autosynthesize feature. `@synthesize` directives are now optional. Xcode can add `@synthesize` directives automatically.

This new feature has a catch—you need to add an underscore in front of autosynthesized property names. For clarity and compatibility, you may want to continue using explicit directives.

Moving to Xcode 5

Xcode 5 simplifies and expands many of the features in Xcode 4. Many developer tasks are repetitive chores that have become embedded in the development process for historical reasons. Developer tools typically assume a workflow and mindset that date back to the very earliest days of computing, more than half a century ago.

The designers of Xcode 5 have continued to rethink these assumptions and tried to automate chores where possible. Compiler technology has also improved, and Xcode 5 no longer supports the GNU compiler and debugger; it works exclusively with a newer compiler toolchain called LLVM.

Compared to Xcode 4, Xcode 5 has a number of improvements:

- **Simplified and automated configuration:** Xcode 5 makes it easier to manage devices, teams, and development certificates. It also includes built-in tools for setting up apps for test- and runtime-access of Apple services such as iCloud, Passbook, and Game Center.
- **Enhanced testing:** A new Test Navigator supports simplified development and management of unit tests.
- **Continuous integration bots:** When used with OS X Server for OS X Mavericks, developers can create "bot'" that build apps, check and test them, and distribute them automatically to beta testers.
- **Improved layout tools:** The old nib file system has been integrated into screen-oriented storyboards, which simplify UI (User Interface) development. Each screen includes auto-layout features that make it easier to produce layouts that work with different screen resolutions, aspect ratios, and orientations.
- **Simplified asset management:** Icons, launch screens, and other art can be collected and compressed into a single Asset Catalog file.

- **Improved debugging:** Gauges show CPU, memory, and other resource requirements, including energy use. A new visual debugger based on the LLDB engine makes debugging information easier to read. A Quick Look preview tool can show images, web pages, documents, and even Bezier curves in memory.

- **Simplified source control:** Branch management is streamlined, and you can choose to host and manage repositories locally, on OS X Server for OS X Mavericks, or on an external Git server.

CAUTION

If you load a project made with an older version of Xcode into Xcode 5, you sometimes see an error message reporting a "Missing SDK." There is an easy fix for this. For details, see "Selecting the Base SDK" near the beginning of Chapter 13.

NOTE

Xcode 5 is backward compatible with Xcode 3 and Xcode 4. You can load Xcode 3.x and 4.x projects, and you should be able to build them, after making any necessary updates to the code to make it compatible with the newest SDKs.

Introducing the Xcode 5 editor

The features of the editor are described in more detail in Chapter 3, but this chapter includes a simple orientation for impatient developers who are new to Xcode.

Xcode 5 gathers every feature into a single window with multiple work areas and panes. The active areas can be shown, hidden, split, or resized as needed. Every Xcode feature, including Interface Builder (IB) and the debugger, can appear in this window. Features can be hidden when you're not using them. You can also create your own *workspaces* to save and restore complete window layouts.

TIP

Xcode 5 is more productive with a larger monitor. You can have a console/debugger, editor, file list, and IB open simultaneously in tiled panes. With a large monitor, these panes become large enough to be truly useful without scrolling, resizing, or switching.

At the top of window, the toolbar area includes a summary panel that displays project status. This gives progress updates as a project builds and displays a count of warnings and errors after each build. The toolbar has been simplified. Only build/run and stop buttons are available.

Working with tabs

Xcode 5 uses *tabs*—editor sub-windows that work like the tabs in a browser, allowing single-click switching between selected files, as shown in Figure 1.4. With tabs, you can add your choice of files to the tab bar as you work and then save the tab bar with the project. You can also remove files from the tab bar when you are no longer working on them.

TIP

In Xcode 5, you can show/hide the Navigator area at the left of the window and the Utilities window at the right independently for each tab.

Figure 1.4

The tab bar appears under the main toolbar near the top of the Xcode 5 window.

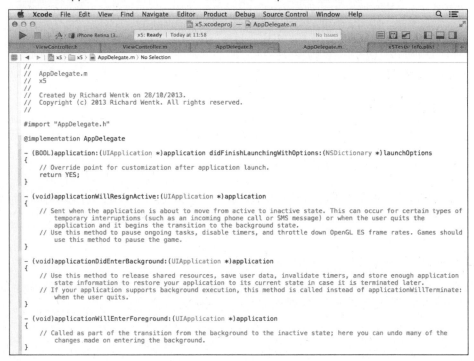

TIP

Tabs save the current cursor position, so you can use them to switch quickly between different sections of the same file. It's often useful to open multiple tabs that show the most significant methods or functions in a file.

Working with multiple windows

Not every developer is enthusiastic about single-window development. Fortunately, you can open multiple windows into a single project and select a different collection of editors and features in each window. A key goal is flexibility; you can arrange your workspace how you want it, with the features you want to see. As shown in Figure 1.5, you can still "tear off" a separate floating window to edit a single file by double-clicking the file.

Selecting and navigating files

Xcode 5 includes a hierarchical *navigation bar* that generates a menu tree from your project files, listing the files and symbols. As shown in Figure 1.6, you can select any file almost instantly. In fact, you can select any symbol in any file, for quick access to definitions and documentation.

Figure 1.5

In Xcode 5, you can still float individual files from a project in separate windows. But there are usually more efficient ways to work.

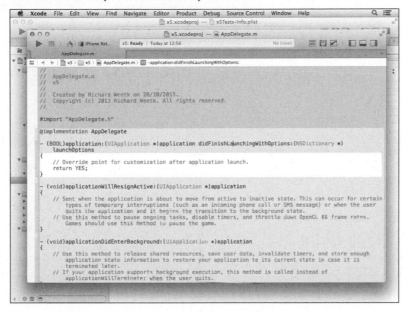

Figure 1.6

The navigation bar (*jump bar*) drastically speeds up access to any file in your project, by presenting them all in a single unified menu tree.

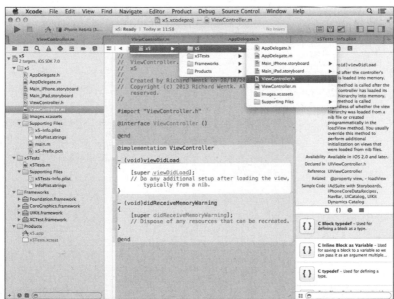

You can also select files in a more traditional Finder-like way using Xcode 5's Project Navigator. But as shown in Figure 1.7, you can access files in yet another way, through a separate menu that lists other relevant items, including header files, includes, related classes, and categories. Click the icon to the left of the left-pointing arrow to view this menu. It lists related files, including superclasses and subclasses, protocols, and includes.

Figure 1.7

At the left of the navigation bar, a separate menu shows files and items that are more loosely related to the currently selected file.

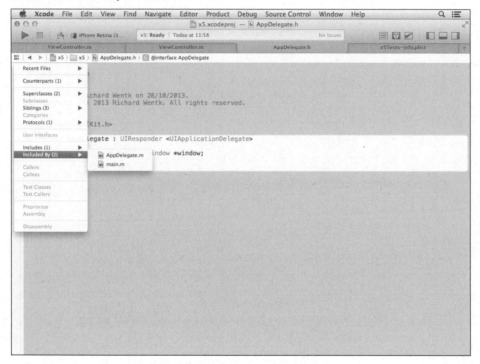

Using Counterparts

Xcode 5 uses an *Assistant View* to show related files in split windows. When you select a file for editing, Assistant makes an informed guess about a useful counterpart and displays it automatically. By default, this means that selecting a header file displays the implementation file in the second pane, and vice versa, as shown in Figure 1.8.

Figure 1.8

The button for selecting the Assistant option is in the grouping at the top right and looks like a waiter's dinner jacket with a bow tie. It splits the editor into two panes and automatically displays a counterpart file whenever a file is selected.

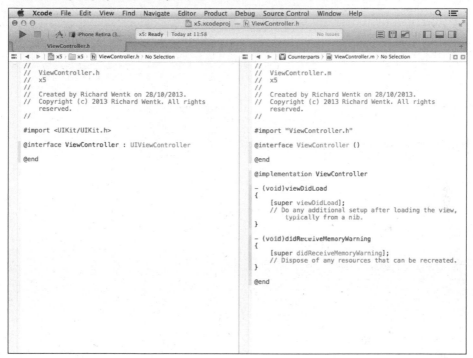

TIP

In Xcode 5, you can customize the behavior of the Assistant. You can split the pane as in Xcode 4, open a new editor pane, open a new window, or open a new tab for the counterpart. See the Navigation tab in Xcode ⇨ Preferences. You can also set up double-clicks so they open a new tab or a new pane.

This feature is one of the most useful timesavers in Xcode 5. You can also manually select a counterpart or other file using a new contextual right-click menu, as shown in Figure 1.9.

Figure 1.9

You can change the behavior of Assistant to select a specific type of counterpart file, which can include an object's superclass as well as its headers and includes. This is useful for newcomers who may not be aware that Cocoa and other OS X headers are available in Xcode and can be used as a reference.

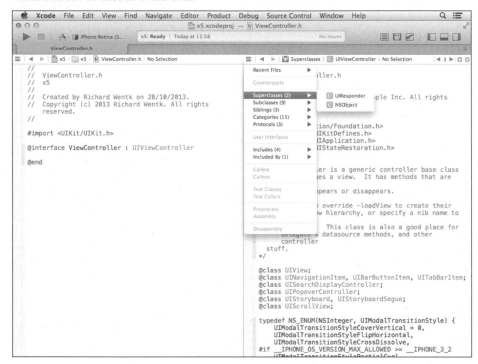

Working with Interface Builder

Interface Builder, Apple's UI development tool, is built into Xcode 5, and the UI layout process is closely integrated with associated code. One of the key Xcode development skills is learning how to link UI objects to the code that manages their behavior. In Xcode, you do this by control-dragging a line from a UI object to a view controller and telling Xcode to insert some skeleton definitions for the associated code, as shown in Figure 1.10.

Xcode inserts appropriate code for you in both the header file and the implementation. It also synthesizes outlet variables automatically. For detailed examples of creating links between outlets, actions, and IB objects, see Chapters 7 and 8.

Figure 1.10

This powerful timesaving feature inserts outlet code automatically in Xcode 5.

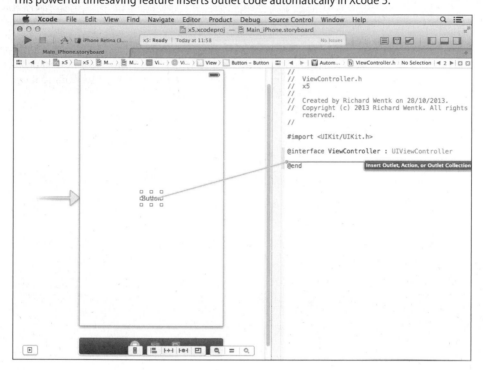

CAUTION

In Xcode 5, iOS projects use storyboards for UI design, and OS X projects use the older nib file format. Although the technologies are different, the linking process used for both is very similar.

Exploring code and file management

Xcode 5 includes two panes at the left and the right that can be revealed or hidden as needed, using a pair of buttons near the top right of the toolbar. The left pane, known as the *navigation pane*, lists various elements in a project. This includes a list of groups and files, as shown in Figure 1.11. But the pane can also list symbols, search tools, log listings, build issues, breakpoints, debugging information, and unit tests.

The pane on the right is the *utilities pane*. This pane gathers miscellaneous information; for example, IB's inspector panes appear here. It also shows build target and localization information, links to documentation, and file locations. When you select a file, the contents of this pane are updated automatically.

The utilities pane includes an optional Library sub-pane that can display file templates, standard code snippets, standard system objects that include both UI and data classes, and project media files. You can hide the Library sub-pane by dragging it down or reveal it by pulling it up.

Figure 1.11

The left and right panes in Xcode 5 display ancillary information and manage optional features that may not be needed while editing.

The Code Snippet feature in the Library is shown in Figure 1.12. It's often useful to reuse the same code between projects, and the Code Snippet makes it easy to do this. To add code to a project, drag it from the library and drop it in the editor window. You also can view a preview of each snippet by selecting it before dragging. By default, this pane includes a small selection of standard snippets, but you can extend it indefinitely by adding your own. For more details, see Chapter 9.

Figure 1.12

The Code Snippets feature makes it easy to reuse code. You can add custom snippets of your own.

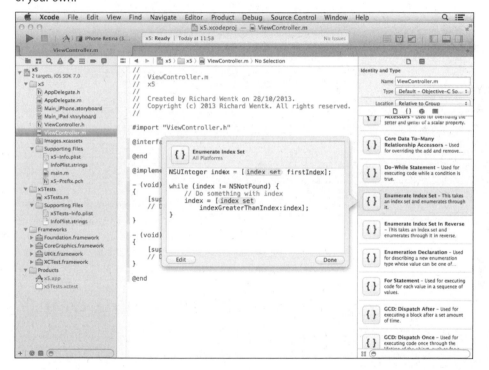

Exploring the debugger

As shown in Figure 1.13, the debugger appears in a new pane at the bottom of the editor window. To reveal it, select View ⇨ Show Debugger Area. Both console output and debugger output appear in this area. You can choose to view either or both by clicking the new buttons that appear at the top right of the area. The debugger now supports multi-threaded debugging. You can set breakpoints by clicking in the gutter area to the left of the editor.

Figure 1.13

The debugger area appears in a pane in the main window, although for convenience you may decide to launch it in a separate window. On a smaller monitor, the debugging and console area can feel cramped.

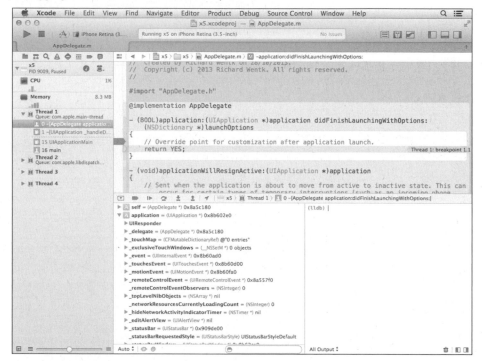

Comparing iOS and OS X Development

Although Xcode supports OS X and iOS development equally and it can be used to develop apps for both the iOS and Mac App Stores, there are significant differences between the two platforms.

Developing for OS X

OS X development in Xcode 5 can be build-and-go, or you can choose to develop apps for the OS X App Store. Build-and-go development is unrestricted. You can create applications that run in a debugging environment on your own Mac and package them as applications that you can run independently, sell from a website, or prepare for network distribution.

Optionally, you can *sign* them, so that OS X recognizes you as a registered developer when users try to install them. This is not obligatory, but it eliminates a warning message that may confuse users and discourage them from installing your application.

You can also create Mac apps for the App Store, which has its own separate distribution system. App Store apps must be signed and are installed automatically after purchase.

Figure 1.14 shows a simple OS X application using a template as a starting point.

Figure 1.14

You can create a very simple OS X application using a template as a starting point and adding a text label in IB. The application runs in its own window and replaces the OS X menu bar (not shown here). Although it appears to run independently, it is in fact controlled by Xcode and can be debugged while it's running.

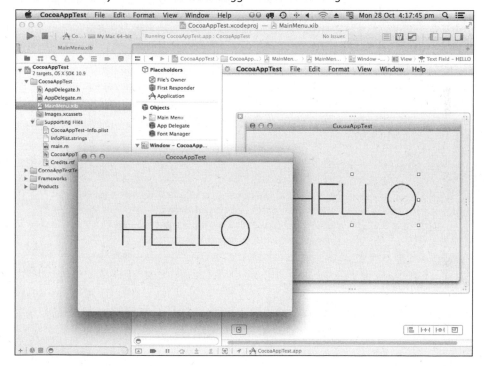

NOTE

Xcode doesn't include network deployment features, but it does create application binaries that can be handed to network deployment tools.

CAUTION

Xcode 5 currently supports development of 64-bit applications for OS X 10.8 and 10.9. If you want to build 32-bit applications for OS X 10.6 or create universal binaries for older versions of OS X, you need an early version of Xcode 4.

Developing for iOS

iOS development is more complicated than OS X development. Development is controlled by *provisioning,* an Apple-generated security control, which is built into Xcode and manages access to hardware testing and App Store distribution.

iPhone, iPod touch, and iPad platforms all use iOS, but these platforms are significantly different and may not always run the same version of iOS. Even when they do run the same version, not all hardware features and UI options are available on every device, and each device family now includes a wide range of display resolutions.

In extreme cases, conditional code is required to check which device an app is running on and which version of iOS it supports. Code paths may need to be selected accordingly with manual checks at runtime.

The Xcode Simulator, shown in Figure 1.15, includes separate iPhone and iPad testing options, with a selection of different resolutions and runtime environments. You can emulate GPS locations and journeys to a limited extent, but realistic emulation of hardware features such as the accelerometer and gyro is not available. All but the very simplest commercial apps should be tested on real hardware.

Figure 1.15

You can create a very simple iOS app and test it in the Simulator. The Simulator is best considered an educational rather than a production environment. It's adequate for apps with simple text and graphics, but it doesn't fully implement the GPS, accelerometer, gyroscope, or other hardware options in iOS devices.

NOTE

The Simulator in Xcode 3 and 4 included attractive graphic versions of iPhone and iPad hardware. Xcode 5 does not continue this tradition. The Simulator displays graphics in a plain window.

The extra requirements of provisioning and multi-platform support can make iOS development feel challenging and complex. A further complication is the need to produce high-quality supporting graphics and screen designs for maximum buyer impact in the App Store.

To date, Apple's beta cycle for iOS has been more aggressive than for OS X, and it's usual to have a new beta preview of iOS available almost as soon as the most recent version has been made public. Beta development requires a parallel version of Xcode and beta firmware for every test device. It may also require an updated version of iTunes and OS X.

So although the iPhone and iPad are simpler than a Mac, and app code can be much simpler, you should allow extra time to work for projects to support all the different possible targets, versions, and security options. You should also allow further time to develop attractive UI designs that work on all available screen resolutions and orientations.

Xcode 5 does not automate these options. The new layout tools can produce working multi-resolution UI designs, but the design process remains complicated. Developing and testing a universal iOS app—a single app that can run on an iPhone, an iPod, and an iPad, with support for all screen resolutions—remains a challenge.

OS X and iOS cross-development

In theory, you can migrate projects between platforms. In practice, Cocoa on OS X and Cocoa Touch on iOS have so many differences that dual-platform development of a non-trivial application is either challenging or unrealistic.

Currently iOS and OS X applications have distinct markets and partially distinct distribution models. Although a few applications have appeared on both—social networking tools and games are the most popular choices—Xcode does little to simplify the development of multi-platform projects.

The development workflow is almost completely distinct. The two platforms have these features:

- **A separate collection of classes for UI design and for data management:** Many of the more creative and sophisticated classes in OS X are either absent or only partially implemented in iOS.

- **A separate testing and debugging environment:** iOS applications can run in a Simulator or on a hardware device. OS X applications run in a debugging sandbox.

- **A different but converging core programming model:** iOS supports multi-tasking with some limitations and restricts access to the device file system. OS X supports a wider range of multi-tasking options and offers less restricted access to files, but you can build in restrictions if you choose to.

● **Separate documentation suites:** iOS and OS X have separate collections of documentation and distinct source code examples.

● **Different accelerated graphics frameworks:** OS X implements OpenGL in full; iOS implements the simpler OpenGL ES framework.

● **Different project templates for separate bare-bones starter application sketches:** iOS includes a set of templates for simple UI-driven handset apps. OS X includes a more complex collection of templates that support the development of plug-ins, screen savers, and other libraries.

● **A partially distinct set of supported instruments for testing:** Limited overlap exists, but some instruments remain unique to each platform.

Apple's Model-View-Controller design pattern implies that applications should keep UI designs, UI management code, and underlying data collections distinct. OS X includes controller classes that make it easier to manage data and create UIs to work with it. Most of these classes are absent in iOS. This makes it difficult to use MVC effectively when attempting dual-platform development.

If you plan to develop across platforms, try to package the underlying data model into its own collection of classes. You may be able to reuse these classes without major changes. Keep UI and UI management code elsewhere.

Generally, combined iOS and OS X remains possible but difficult. It's more realistic to think of Xcode 5 as two separate development environments with a common frontend than as a single unified environment designed to produce code for either platform.

Summary

Xcode 4 was a dramatic reinvention of Xcode 3, but Xcode 5 is more of a slipstream update with fixes, consolidations, and minor changes. It's cleaner and simpler than Xcode 4, and it should be easier to work with. But a few key features have been moved or even removed. Expect a short period of readjustment, but no significant shocks.

Getting and Installing Xcode

Xcode is free and runs on any recent Intel Mac. However, hobby developers and professionals have different hardware and software requirements. A system tuned for maximum productivity may be very different from one used for experimentation or hobby coding.

Selecting a Mac for Xcode

If you own an Intel Core 2 Duo Mac, you can run Xcode on it. But you will get more from your Mac if you understand the differences between a streamlined and productive working environment, and a slow and informal one.

Choosing a processor

Surprisingly, processors have less influence on productivity than other factors. A faster processor can speed up compilation times, but unless you're working on industrial projects with hundreds or thousands of source files, you'll find little obvious benefit to running Xcode on a high-speed multi-core Mac Pro.

Xcode compiles incrementally, which means that only updated files and their dependencies are recompiled after an edit. iPhone projects compile relatively quickly, even on a Mac mini. The initial build of an OS X project takes longer, but subsequent builds happen more quickly.

Smaller projects are practical on relatively old and slow hardware, and any of the Macs shown in Figure 2.1 will work for you. However, you need more powerful hardware if you are developing large, complex games.

In This Chapter

Selecting a Mac for Xcode

Getting started with development

Getting started with Xcode

Figure 2.1

You do not need the latest, fastest, and largest Mac to use Xcode. You can create professional iPhone apps on a MacBook or Mac mini.

CAUTION

Apple updates Xcode regularly, and releases a new version with each update of OS X or iOS. As a general rule, Macs that are more than two years old are unlikely to be supported for more than one or two update cycles. If you want to continue using Xcode, assume an upgrade cycle of two to three years.

Other Xcode features such as code completion and source control work faster on a speedier Mac. Xcode 5 checks code for errors as you type it, and it can display live help. The faster your Mac, and especially the faster your Mac's disk system, the more transparently these features work for you, and the less likely it is that your development environment will break your concentration with pauses and delays.

Selecting memory

Early versions of Xcode 4 had a small memory footprint and loaded features as they were needed. Later versions of Xcode 4 loaded as an all-in-one application. Xcode 5 follows this tradition, so 4GB of memory is a bare minimum for a Mac used exclusively for development.

However, most developers need to work with multiple open web pages, and some also work with a graphics suite when developing or editing app artwork. So 8GB is a practical minimum if you want to avoid disk thrashing and delays while working with multiple applications. You need 16GB or more to have a comfortable working environment that allows you to open all the tools you need at the same time.

Choosing a monitor

A monitor, or monitor bank, can be the biggest influence on overall productivity. The less time you spend rearranging screen content, the more quickly you can create code. Although you can develop projects successfully on a monitor with a resolution of 1024x768, a bare minimum resolution of 1680x1050 is much more productive. At this resolution, you can see the entire Xcode 5 workspace at once and use it as it was designed to be used.

Larger monitors are even easier to work with. Currently, 27" monitors hit the sweet spot of affordability and productivity. Larger monitors are better, but you can buy two or three cheaper 27" monitors for the cost of one good 30" model. A dual monitor system provides a significant speed boost because you can work on multiple projects or multiple files simultaneously.

After you've mastered the essentials of iOS, Xcode, and OS X, you'll spend significant time reviewing class references in the various frameworks and exploring message boards looking for code samples and developer tips. The most efficient way to view the references is to create a set of bookmarks with the most useful class references and view simultaneously in tabs in a web browser. You can then switch between them instantly as needed.

TIP

You can use Spaces to create a separate developer Space that's dedicated to Xcode and its supporting windows. Day-to-day apps such as Mail can be kept in a different Space, minimizing clutter.

Mission Control can be another timesaver. When you have many Xcode windows open at once, Mission Control is by far the easiest way to switch between them, although be careful to set up Mission Control to avoid time-consuming accidental switching. You can set up Mission Control and Spaces in the System Preferences.

The most luxurious and productive development environment has at least two monitors for code editing and testing and at least one further monitor for online browsing. The extra monitor may be on another machine—it can even be on a PC—but it's more efficient to use a three- or four-monitor Mac; it's often useful to copy and paste code directly into your project from the documentation or other online sources.

TIP

You do not need to use monitors with professional color accuracy. One monitor with reasonable color accuracy is a minimum for games. The other panels can be much cheaper; developers spend most of their time looking at text, not graphics or photographs.

Working with disk storage

Disk space and disk features can make a big difference to Xcode performance. Ideally, you should install Xcode on your main Mac hard drive, allowing at least 20GB for a full install of two separate versions (active and beta) with all documentation and your own project code.

A Mac with an SSD (Solid State Drive) for OS X and Xcode can be a significant timesaver. Xcode 5 takes a while to load. You can speed up the initial boot by running Xcode from a faster-than-average conventional disk, a RAID 0 system (Redundant Array of Independent Disks), or an SSD. SSDs are no longer the high-end luxury they were a few years ago, and this one extra can dramatically speed up launch times and productivity.

Choosing peripherals

Peripherals can make a significant difference to your productivity. It's good practice to choose extras that feel comfortable to work with and don't have quirks, design features, or extras that distract you.

Selecting a printer

A printer isn't essential and is discouraged for environmental reasons, but it may be useful for occasional debugging. It can be easier to trace execution through a paper listing than to view it in sections on a monitor. There are no special requirements for printing from Xcode. Any standard inkjet or laser printer works. Longer lines of code may need to be printed in landscape mode because they are too wide to fit onto a portrait page. A large-format printer is a useful—if expensive—option for code printing.

Choosing a pointing device

There's no lack of choice in the mouse market, and if you intend to develop professionally, getting a professional mouse with extra features can be well worth the extra money. You'll use it every day, and it's important that you're comfortable with it, that its shape doesn't leave you with RSI (Repetitive Strain Injury), and that it doesn't have extra or missing features that break your concentration. Extremely expensive mice with extra buttons may not be more productive than cheaper models. A good cordless mouse with a smooth scroll wheel can save significant time, particularly if it includes inertia for faster scrolling.

Opinions are mixed on Apple's own Magic Trackpad and mouse models. Some developers feel very comfortable with them, but others don't like them at all. Because pointing devices are a matter of taste, be sure to spend time trying out the various alternatives as thoroughly as you can. You can literally save hours or days over a year with a cheap upgrade to a pointing device that you feel comfortable with.

Choosing your Mac keyboard

Keyboard action is a matter of personal taste. Some developers love the Apple keyboards, but others find them impossible to work with. The absence of a numeric keypad on the Apple wireless keyboard remains an enduring mystery.

Be sure to visit a computer store to try some alternatives. Logitech PC keyboards offer a much wider range of actions and feels, and they can easily be customized to create Mac mappings. Logitech also offers a very small selection of Mac-ready keyboards.

Although some Apple enthusiasts may be horrified by the idea of using non-Apple peripherals, keyboard feel has a measurable influence on typing accuracy and comfort, so you must pick a feel that works for you.

TIP

Depending on your location, your Mac keyboard may have non-obvious character mappings. For example, in the UK, the critical # (hash) character is not included on Mac keyboards; it's available only with Left Alt+3. You can select different layouts in the Input Sources pane in the Keyboard preferences in System Preferences. Check the "Show Keyboard & Character Viewers in menu bar" option under the Keyboard pane to display a keyboard layout selector, with a selector for special characters, at the right of the menu bar.

Choosing supporting software

Although Xcode seems self-contained, in practice you're likely to use it with other software. For example, if you choose to view documentation online, your choice of web browser becomes a significant limiting factor. Safari and Google Chrome are reasonably well behaved. The stability of Firefox has improved significantly over the last couple of years, and it now provides a reasonable alternative.

Whichever browser you choose should include an ad blocker—not just to improve your browsing experience, but to avoid wasting memory by downloading unnecessary content. Note that all browsers use plenty of memory. If you have 8GB of memory or less, you should try to keep open tabs to a bare minimum. You can easily run out of memory with Xcode, a browser, and handful of class references, code examples, and forum discussions.

Xcode typically requires the most recent version of OS X. Members of the Mac Developer Program receive free previews and updates of OS X releases. Members of the iOS Developer Program do not. Minor updates are free. Major releases of OS X are available from the App Store—usually for a small fee, although OS X Mavericks broke with that tradition by being free.

Other tools can be added as needed. Unless you outsource graphic design, you need an editing suite to create start-up graphics, icons, buttons, and other images, as shown in Figure 2.2. This is an essential requirement for the iOS projects, where graphic design is extremely important, and a very useful extra for OS X development. Adobe's Creative Cloud is the de facto standard, but it's expensive. Free or cheap alternatives include Gimp for OS X (www.gimp.org/macintosh) and Pixelmator (www.pixelmator.com).

A small number of helper apps are available for developers. The Development Tools category on the App Store includes a small selection of ready-made starter apps and other add-ons that can help you be more productive with Xcode 5. For details, search the store for Xcode or browse the Development Tools category from the main listing page.

Figure 2.2

Although it isn't integrated directly into Xcode, Adobe Photoshop works well as an external editor for graphics.

CROSS-REFERENCE

For more information about selecting editors and helper applications for various file types, see Chapter 8.

Getting Started with Development

You do not need to sign up as a developer to use Xcode. Anyone can download and use the latest public version of Xcode from the App Store, as shown in Figure 2.3. Anyone who registers as a developer—a free process—can also access Apple's developer library to view documentation.

Figure 2.3

You can download Xcode 5 from the Mac App Store.

However, developers who also enroll in a development program get a number of important benefits, including these:

- The ability to distribute apps through the App Store
- The ability to test iOS apps on hardware
- Access to the latest pre-release beta versions of Xcode, iOS, and OS X
- Limited free technical support

Registering as a developer

To register as a developer, visit the Apple developer home page, which is currently at `https://developer.apple.com/`, shown in Figure 2.4. The design of this page changes regularly, but recent designs have included a selection of sign-up links for the various developer programs.

Figure 2.4

Begin the sign-up process at Apple's developer portal. This image shows the bottom of the page, with a list of programs. Selecting a link takes you to the sign-up page for each program.

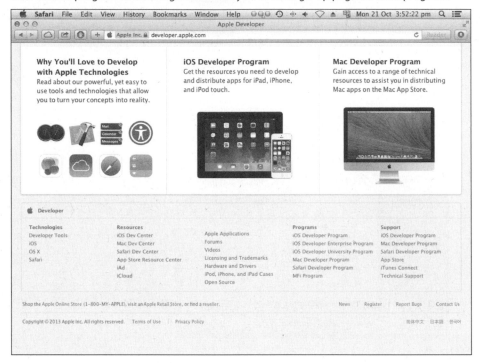

Choosing a program

Table 2.1 lists the current developer programs.

Layer	Cost	Comments
Mac Developer Program—Individual	$99/year	This program Includes the current production SDK and future seed releases of OS X for a solo developer. Registration typically takes 1 to 2 weeks. With this program, you can sell Mac apps through the Mac App Store. It does not give you access to the iPhone App Store.
Mac Developer Program—Company	$99/year	This program includes the current production SDK and future seed releases of OS X for one or more developers working as a team for a corporation or small business. Proof of incorporation must be faxed to Apple during sign-up. Registration may take a few weeks. With this program, you can sell Mac apps through the Mac App Store. It does not give you access to the iPhone App Store.

Table 2.1 Apple Developer Programs

Layer	Cost	Comments
iPhone Developer Program—Individual	$99/year	This program includes the current production SDK and future seed releases of the iPhone SDK for a solo developer. It includes access to the App Store. It allows local and remote beta testing on the Simulator and up to 100 devices. Registration typically takes 1 to 2 weeks. With this program, you can sell iOS apps through the iOS App Store. It does not include access to OS X seed builds (preview versions of OS X) or to the Mac App Store.
iPhone Developer Program—Company	$99/year	This program includes the features above, but is intended for small companies and corporations. It supports team management features that can allow or deny access to the program for individual developers. Proof of incorporation must be faxed to Apple during sign-up. Registration may take a few weeks. With this program, you can sell iOS apps through the iOS App Store. This program does not include access to OS X seed builds (preview versions of OS X) or to the Mac App Store.
iPhone Developer Enterprise Program	$299/year	This program is for corporations developing in-house apps for their employees. Apps must be distributed internally and cannot be sold through the App Store. It requires a Dun & Bradstreet number, which is an international business identification number that is made available only to larger businesses. It includes access to future versions of the SDK and iOS.
iPhone Developer University Program	Free	This program is for accredited degree-granting academic institutions. It allows testing on hardware devices and the Simulator, and it includes access to the current SDK, but not to forthcoming beta versions. It does not include access to the App Store, in-house distribution, or Apple's technical support.

Sign-up is straightforward. You must supply an e-mail address for the free program, and you must provide personal details, including an address and contact phone number for the paid programs. If you do not already have an Apple ID, you need to create one. If you already have an Apple ID for personal use, creating a separate company ID is useful if you are incorporated; this can simplify taxes and accounting.

N O T E
The MFi (Made For 'i') program is exclusively for makers of hardware accessories. Sign-up is free, but you are asked to provide contact details for legal counsel in addition to the other standard business requirements. You do not need to sign up if you create software apps.

The iOS developer programs

The chief benefits of the iOS developer program, whose portal is shown in Figure 2.5, are access to the App Store retail program and the ability to test apps on real hardware. Testing requires the generation and installation of *certificates* and *profiles*—files that allow you to develop and test apps, but prevent unauthorized copying and distribution—on a special area of the developer site. This process is described in Chapter 11.

Figure 2.5

Beginning enrollment in the iOS Developer Program can take up to three weeks for companies. Enrollment for individuals is sometimes processed within 24 hours, but it may take a couple of weeks.

CAUTION

Keep in mind that although the iOS program seems cheap, you need at least an iPod touch to test apps, and at least one recent iPhone model is strongly recommended. Adding an iPad to your hardware collection can push the total initial cost of app development during the first year to over $1,000—more if you also buy a Mac. Many developers do not earn this back from sales.

Business sign-up requires proof of incorporation. Documents must be faxed, not sent, to Apple's HQ in Cupertino. If you are a solo developer with an incorporated business, signing up as a company can take an extra week or so, but it simplifies foreign tax accounting for App Store sales. Without a company, a portion of foreign earnings can be withheld for tax reasons until local tax authorities receive paperwork that proves country of residence or tax domicile. With multiple territories (sales regions) in the App Store, this can create a small mountain of paperwork for individual developers and may also hold up payments.

NOTE
To find out more about U.S. tax requirements, search online for "ITIN" and "EIN." Applying for an ITIN is a complex, time-consuming process. Applying for an EIN is somewhat simpler and quicker. Successful developers may want to incorporate in the U.S. to simplify payments and accounting.

Enrolling for the iOS Developer Program also provides potential access to Apple's add-on services for iOS, including the iAD network, the GameCenter network, the in-app purchase scheme, and the push notification service. To use these services, you must enable them individually after enrollment. You also may need to authorize or sign further legal contracts.

The Mac developer programs

The Mac developer programs shown in Figure 2.6 give developers access to the App Store and the opportunity to install and develop for versions of OS X before they're made available to the public. OS X develops more slowly than iOS, but beta updates are made available regularly. These updates may not be completely stable, so it's a good idea—although an expensive one—to install them on a separate development machine.

Figure 2.6

The supplied tools and developer resources for those enrolling in the Mac Developer Program are almost identical to those available to iOS developers, except that Mac developers get access to beta versions of OS X.

Because it's possible to sell Mac applications independently from a website without using the App Store, and because anyone can buy and install Xcode for a nominal fee, the incentive to sign up as a full Mac developer may not be completely compelling. It can be worth downloading Xcode 5 first to experiment with it and then signing up as a full developer when you have developed a commercial app.

NOTE

Having a combined program for both OS X and iOS development would be useful. Unfortunately, Apple doesn't offer one. In practice, either program gives you access to a full version of Xcode with both iOS and OS X development tools and supporting documentation. The programs differ in access to beta versions for their respective platforms and to the two App Stores.

Accessing developer resources

Developer resources include the online reference libraries, a selection of developer videos, and the developer message boards.

Using the online documentation and references

The iOS and OS X reference libraries, which include documentation described in Chapter 6, are freely available and do not require registration. The URLs change regularly, but currently you can find the iOS library at `http://developer.apple.com/library/ios/navigation/` and the OS X library at `http://developer.apple.com/library/mac/navigation/`. If these URLs no longer work, search for "OS X Reference Library" and "iOS Reference Library."

Viewing developer videos

The developer videos, some of which are shown in Figure 2.7, include keynotes and background talks, typically taken from Apple's WWDC (World Wide Developer Conference) series. In the past, Apple made these videos available through iTunes. Currently, you can download them directly from the documentation web pages in SD and HD formats, with notes supplied as a separate PDF.

Some developers find that the hands-on examples in the videos offer a more successful introduction to key technologies and essential development techniques than the slightly chaotic explanations in the documentation.

The Mac and iOS Developer Programs allow access to different video collections. Only Mac developers are given access to the Mac Development Foundation Videos. Similarly, only iOS developers are allowed to download the iOS Development Videos.

Figure 2.7

The developer videos provide useful introductions and tutorials that supplement, and sometimes improve on, the written tutorials and guides.

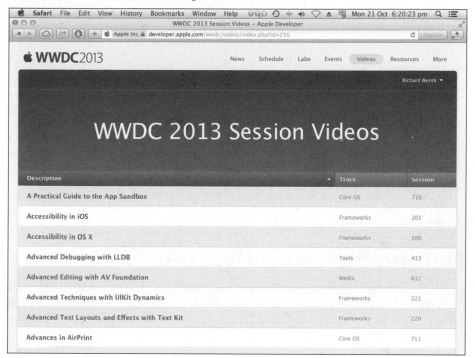

CAUTION

SD videos are around 300MB to 400MB. HD videos are around 600MB, although keynotes and extended presentations can be around 1.5GB.

Using the Apple developer discussion boards

The Apple Developer boards are perhaps the least useful developer resource. Alternative developer boards such as stackoverflow (www.stackoverflow.com) have built up a larger collection of questions and answers, discussed in more depth. They're also indexed by Google, which simplifies topic and keyword searches.

The chief advantage of the official developer boards is that Apple employees sometimes read and comment. Otherwise, you can typically get more detailed and more helpful comments from elsewhere, from developers who may have worked through a problem and posted the code for a full solution.

Asking for technical support

Both the iOS and OS X Developer Programs offer developers up to two code-level support incidents per year. You can use these to discuss your code with an Apple technical support engineer. The engineers won't be able to understand a huge project instantly, so technical support incidents are best used for mysterious but localized issues that resist conventional debugging and are beyond the insight of other developers.

Many of the internal features of iOS and OS X are undocumented, and code doesn't always work as you expect it to. For example, UI code may create extra ancillary views while managing transitions, or UI objects may have complex features that can't be accessed externally. Apple engineers are more likely to be aware of these quirks than external developers. But Apple doesn't guarantee that engineers will solve a problem, only that they will look at it. Developers who find the service useful can buy two extra incidents for $99 or five for $249.

CAUTION

Only public non-beta versions of iOS and OS X are supported. You won't be able to ask questions about bugs or features in beta releases.

Getting Started with Xcode

You can download and install Xcode in two ways. The "public" option gives you access to the most recent production version on the Mac App Store, which supports development for the current public versions of iOS and OS X. The developer version supports pre-release beta development for upcoming versions of iOS and OS X, which are restricted to developers.

The two versions of Xcode often have similar features, but specific OS support is included with a different SDK (Software Development Kit). The SDK includes headers, binary libraries, and documentation for each version of the OS.

NOTE

Xcode typically supports the current and previous SDKs, but it does not include earlier versions. If you want to develop legacy applications for an older version of iOS or OS X, you need to download one of the older versions of Xcode from the Developer Download area. For a link, see Appendix B.

Installing the Public Version

All Apple users with a compatible Mac can download this version. Currently, it downloads from the App Store as a 4GB file and installs itself in the /Applications folder automatically.

Note that this version may not have all the most recent features. For example, the current public version of Xcode may be 5.0.1, while the current pre-release version may be 5.1. Aside from OS support, the differences are usually minor and typically include bug fixes and small changes.

Installing the Developer Version

Registered developers can download and install the most recent pre-release beta versions of Xcode. After you enroll in a developer program and log in to one of the Dev Center pages, you can access a page like the one shown in Figure 2.8.

Figure 2.8

This example shows the current public and beta pre-release options for OS X.

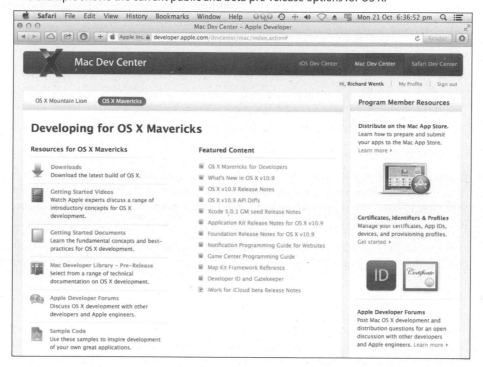

Typically, the page shows one or two tabs. The first tab links to the current public version of iOS or OS X, with an associated version of Xcode and access to the relevant documentation. The second tab links to an equivalent page with pre-release beta versions.

Apple makes updates accessible in two ways. You can either download a `.dmg` file directly. Or you can click a button to redeem a free code on the App Store, and download and install the update from there.

CAUTION

Depending on the update cycle, there are times when only the public version is available. Beta versions are usually available after WWDC and major product announcements. After a few months, the beta version becomes the public version. Further development continues in secret until the next update, when Apple releases the next beta to developers.

The public version of Xcode is relatively stable and may change once or twice over the course of a year. The developer version is updated every month or so while a new version of iOS or OS X approaches public release.

You do not have to download every update, although if you have fast broadband you should. Note that a complete update cycle includes new versions of the following:

- Xcode
- iOS, with different update files for each possible device *and/or*
- OS X
- Optional supporting OS X Apps, such as OS X Server
- iTunes (used to update iOS devices with new firmware)
- Documentation files

Xcode on its own is around 4GB. But a complete OS X update may require 10GB, while a complete iOS update for multiple devices can be 15GB or more. If you have slow broadband, you may have to allow the downloads to work overnight. There is no incremental install or upgrade option.

Note that the iOS and OS X update cycles are usually independent. If you are developing for both platforms, you need to keep on top of both. Otherwise, you typically need to update only one or the other.

TIP

If you have a spare older device, it can be useful to keep an older version of iOS on it and use it for compatibility testing. Conversely, if you have a single device such as an iPhone, you may be reluctant to upgrade it to beta firmware for testing. Older apps typically work on newer firmware. However, apps developed for new beta firmware don't work on devices with older versions of iOS, unless you deliberately make them compatible.

CAUTION

If you're limited to dial-up, Xcode may not be a practical solution for you. At best, you can try to find someone with faster broadband willing to download updates and burn them to a DVD or copy them to a memory stick. Unfortunately, the Xcode documentation is tightly integrated within the SDK, so this is only a partial solution.

Installing Xcode

If you download Xcode from the App Store, it installs itself in /Applications just like any other app.

If you download a developer version from the Developer Center, it arrives as a `.dmg` file. Double-click it to mount it, and select it in Finder to open it.

Earlier versions of Xcode used a standard Mac installer, which included some customization options. Xcode 5 uses the simpler installer shown in Figure 2.9. To install it, drag its icon onto the `/Applications` folder shortcut.

Figure 2.9

The Xcode `.dmg` package is completely conventional. You can mount it and install it in the usual way.

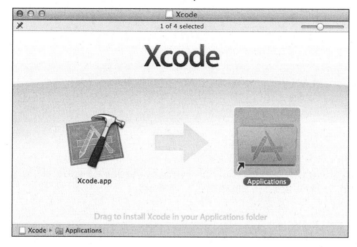

TIP
You can also drag the icon and drop it onto the `/Applications` folder in Finder. In fact, you can drop Xcode into any user folder and run it from there. There isn't usually a good reason to do this, but advanced developers may want to open and change the contents of the Xcode app package for special projects.

Creating and organizing project folders

After installing Xcode, you can create supporting folders for project development. Typically, you need individual folders for each project and extra folders for building trial apps for experimentation and testing.

There is no standard or recommended way to organize folders. You will probably create more experimental apps than you expect to, so it is a good idea to keep commercial and experimental apps in separate folders to prevent clutter. You may also want to work with version control, as described in Chapter 15.

It can be useful to put development downloads, including beta versions of Xcode, into a single folder so you can keep track of them, and delete them to save disk space when they are no longer current.

TIP
Prefixing project folders with a plus sign (+) lists them alphabetically in a separate order from the tool and support folders.

Working with multiple versions of Xcode

SDKs are updated regularly, and you often need to have more than one version installed and available simultaneously. For example, you may have:

- A production version of Xcode for production code
- A newer beta version, used to explore the features in a forthcoming OS update
- An optional alternative or preview SDK with broader changes

Earlier versions of Xcode were modular, with many options spread all over your disk. Currently, Xcode is a single self-contained file. This makes it easy to download and install multiple versions.

You can simply install them to /Applications and launch them as needed. You can even have different versions running at the same time or give each version a custom filename to make it easier to tell the versions apart in the Dock.

Uninstalling Xcode

Previous versions of Xcode required a complex manual uninstall script. Because Xcode is now a single file, you can uninstall it by dragging it to the trash.

Summary

Xcode 5 is easy to get hold of, and easy to install. If you're experimenting with development, the fact that it's free is a big attraction, but remember that setting up as a commercial developer costs extra, and the developer programs are all time-limited.

One of the biggest concerns is the volume of data you have to download to install and work with Xcode. Parallel beta and production versions and their associated documentation and hardware support files can push slower broadband connections to their limit, especially if your ISP imposes a data cap. Dial-up or cell/mobile downloads are completely impractical.

On the upside, the fact that Xcode 5 is a single file means that beta and production versions work together smoothly, and are easy to delete when they're no longer up to date.

Building Applications from Templates

Assembling an application from scratch isn't a trivial process in Xcode. It's faster and simpler to start from a ready-made template and extend it as needed. Xcode includes templates for different types of iOS and OS X applications. The template list includes some plug-in types and other special projects for OS X developers.

Getting started with a template is easy. All templates include a bare skeleton of essential code and are guaranteed to build and run successfully. You simply select a template when you create a new project, and Xcode automatically writes the files to a new folder.

Note that Xcode does not support custom templates, so you cannot add your own projects to the template list. Expert developers can hand-edit and extend the template files built into the Xcode package, but this takes some skill and experience. The process is neither simple nor convenient, and the templates have to be re-created every time you update Xcode.

However, workarounds are possible. The simplest is to manually duplicate a starting project folder in Finder. You need to make sure the project groups and files are set up correctly, and you must change a few of the settings to give your project a new name. But you can use this system to create a basic skeleton app with your own code and use it as a starting point for a series of projects.

Getting Started with Templates

You can access Xcode's template screen in two ways. Figure 3.1 shows the optional Welcome to Xcode window. In Xcode 4, this window appeared by default. In Xcode 5, you can display it by selecting Window ➪ Welcome to Xcode.

Figure 3.1

Xcode's optional launch window shows recent files, an Open Other option for not-so-recent files, and the Create a new Xcode project option for access to the templates.

TIP

Check the Show this window when Xcode launches box to make the window appear automatically on launch. You may want to do this for quick access to the Check out an existing project option, if you use a source control repository for your code. Inexplicably, this option only appears for a short period after you move your mouse.

The more straightforward option is shown in Figure 3.2. Select File ⇨ New ⇨ New Project to show the new project dialog.

Either option displays the drop-down panel shown in Figure 3.3. This is the unified list of templates for both iOS and OS X. The list of categories at the top left separates the two target operating systems and displays templates for each, collected into categories.

The Application category is the most useful, but many developers also use items from the Framework & Library collection. Application and System Plug-ins are more specialized, and the Other category includes a complete blank project for iOS and OS X and an External Build System template for OS X only that can work with an external makefile and command-line compiler.

Figure 3.2

The more usual way to access the templates is to select the New Project option from the Xcode menu tree.

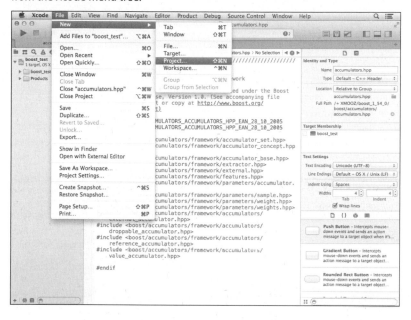

Figure 3.3

The list of standard templates is long, but typically you start with an Application template. The other templates are for more specialized projects.

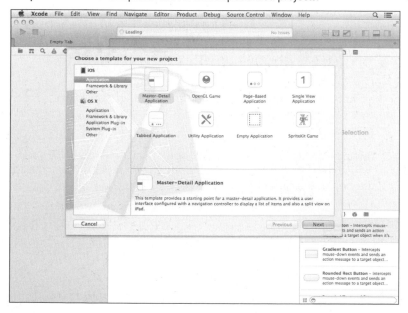

Table 3.1 summarizes the categories.

TIP
You can ignore the categories and show every template for an OS by clicking the iOS or Mac OS X headers.

CAUTION
Apple regularly changes, adds, and removes templates from Xcode. It's possible the list you see in your version of Xcode will not be the same as the list given here. The content of the basic project templates remains fairly constant, but sometimes the names change. The plug-in templates are less persistent. In the past, useful templates have disappeared from Xcode, so you cannot assume your favorite templates will always be available.

Table 3.1 Xcode Template Categories

Category	OS	Comments
Applications	iOS and OS X	Application skeletons. iOS offers a selection of standard application starting points. OS X offers a standard Cocoa application, a SpriteKit game, an AppleScript application with access to Cocoa, and a command-line tool.
Framework & Library	iOS and OS X	Custom frameworks. iOS supports static Cocoa Touch libraries only. OS X supports custom Cocoa frameworks and libraries, project bundles, XPC background services, and C and C++ libraries.
Application Plug-in	OS X only	Plug-ins for specific OS X applications, including Automator, Address Book, Installer, and Quartz Composer.
System Plug-in	OS X only	Low-level plug-ins that extend the features of OS X, such as Image Units, IOKit drivers for hardware support, custom screen savers, Quick Look and Spotlight plug-ins, and so on.
Other	iOS and OS X	In App Content, a blank template. OS X also offers an external build system template.

Building a project from an application template

Application templates are guaranteed to build successfully. For example, to build a simple iOS application for the iPhone or iPad, select the iOS application page in the templates pane, and then select the Single View Application template. Click Next, and select the Universal Devices option, as shown in Figure 3.4.

Type a name for the App into the Product Name box. You can include spaces. Xcode automatically adds dashes where needed. This box defines the name that appears under the app when it's installed in Springboard. You can change the name later using the build settings described in Chapters 12 and 13.

If you want Xcode to add a prefix string to all the classes you add to your project, type one into the Class Prefix box. If you reuse code, this option helps keep the class names clean and distinct.

Figure 3.4

Here you can set up the project options for an iOS app.

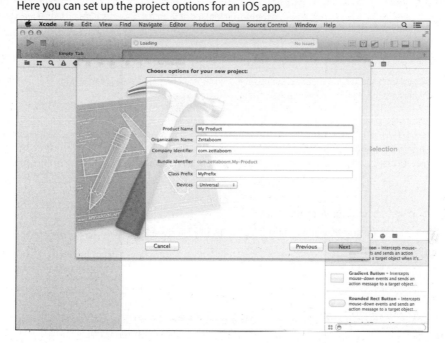

If you plan to upload your app to the App Store, type "com." followed by your company or developer name into the Company Identifier box. As you'll see in Chapters 13 and 14, Xcode glues the company identifier and product name together to create a unique Bundle Identifier, which uniquely identifies your app in the store.

CAUTION

The Universal option adds a UI resource file—technically, a storyboard—for both the iPad and the iPhone. The other options include a file for one or the other, but not both. Note that there is no simple single-file option for a universal app. Universal apps require separate resources for both platforms. Sometimes, they need different code too.

When you create an app from a template, a name and a copyright field that matches the company name are added to the top of every code file in the project. The easy but unexpected way to set the defaults for this content is to create a card with personal details in Address Book and choose Make This My Card from the Card menu. Xcode reads the information from Address Book when it creates a new project.

After you have created a project, you can change the default organization by clicking the project, opening the utility pane (described in the next chapter), and typing new values into the Organization and Class Prefix boxes of the Project Document sub-pane.

CAUTION

In earlier versions of Xcode 4, you could change these settings by editing `~/Library/Preferences/`
`com.apple.Xcode.plist` or by entering a command in Terminal. These options no longer work in Xcode 5.

TIP

Keep iOS app names short: Eight characters or less is ideal. Longer names are truncated with ellipses (. . .), which look
bad and don't help the user. The app name isn't fixed, so you can change it later.

Select Next again, and click Create, as shown in Figure 3.5. By default, Xcode automatically creates a new project folder, with the name you gave your app. Select the New Folder option at the bottom left only when you want to create a new enclosing folder for a number of related projects.

CROSS-REFERENCE

The Source Control option at the bottom of the dialog is described in Chapter 15. Ignore it for now.

Figure 3.5

You can create a new project folder. Xcode creates the folder automatically in the current folder. You can ignore the New Folder button, unless you want to create a new containing folder for multiple projects.

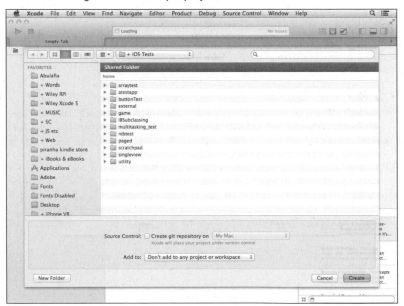

Figure 3.6 shows the initial new project page. There's a list of items that look like folders at the top left and various project options, including the supported versions of either iOS or OS X, at the right. The folders are called groups, and it's important to understand that they *do not exist on disk*. They're for Xcode's internal use, to help you keep project files organized efficiently.

N O T E

Many Xcode 5 templates automatically create a *test target* without asking you if you want one. You can use the test target for automated testing. Or you can ignore it. For details, see Chapter 18.

Figure 3.7 shows the files and directories that have been added and how they're arranged on disk. The folder structure is completely different.

The pane with the folder-like icons at the left of Xcode is known as the Project navigator. *It does not show a standard directory listing.*

In earlier versions of Xcode 3, the items listed in this pane were similar to web links; they looked like a directory and folder listing, but in fact they were loose symbolic links to items on disk. They were so loose that you could rename them without changing the files on disk.

This created almost limitless confusion, especially when the links became broken—which they often did. So in later versions of Xcode 3, the relationship was simplified. If you renamed an item in this pane, it was also renamed on disk. If you deleted an item, you could choose to move it to the trash or to remove it from the project but leave the file on disk.

Figure 3.6

For the new project in Xcode, the virtual folders—called groups—have been opened so you can see the files inside them.

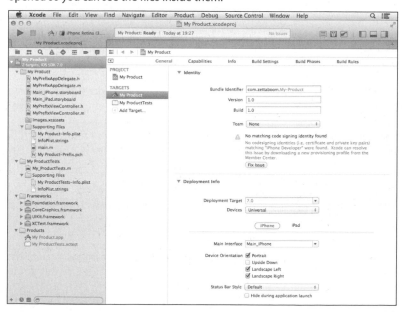

Figure 3.7

Here's how the new files appear on disk. Although the arrangement of files and folders is different, you don't usually need to access this folder directly; typically, you can use the more abstract view available in Xcode without worrying about the differences.

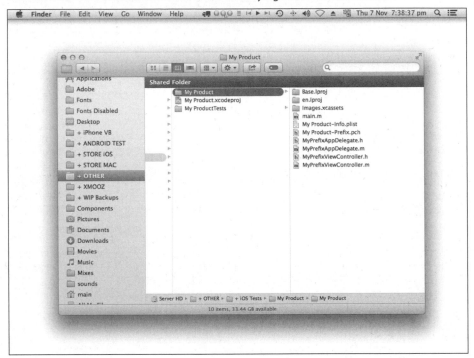

Xcode 4 simplified this system further, and Xcode 5 continues to use it. However, the folder-like icons remain entirely abstract. They're included to help you keep related files together in the Project navigator, *but they don't exist on disk.*

The symbolic link system may seem counterintuitive, but it makes it possible to add files to a project without copying them. For example, you can create a library or framework in a folder on disk and import it into various projects as a collection of symbolic links that access the original files in their original source folder. Similarly, you can keep image files or fonts in a single folder and import them via links into multiple projects without having to create multiple copies.

CROSS-REFERENCE
For more information about using the Project navigator and the other new navigators in Xcode 5, see Chapter 4.

The other key element to notice in Figure 3.6 is the Scheme/Destination menu near the top left. The Destination sets the platform—for example, a choice of devices in the Simulator, a hardware device for iOS, or a 64-bit environment for OS X.

Schemes manage the internal features of the build process. They're introduced in Chapters 12 and 13.

You can't test apps on a hardware device until you follow the provisioning steps described in Chapter 11. So for now, use this menu to select the Simulator. Click the area labeled "iPhone Retina (3. . ." in the figure, and select a simulated device.

NOTE

The Simulator is a separate application. Typically, you float the Simulator window on top of Xcode, so you can bring Xcode back to the foreground by clicking anywhere around the Simulator. You can also use the Dock to switch between Xcode and the Simulator. Note that each emulated device has independent app storage.

You can now click the Run button at the top left of Xcode to build and run your skeleton app. Xcode takes a while to precompile the project's headers, build the app, and load it into the Simulator. The first time you build an app or an application for a new target, the build and install process takes some time because Xcode must perform various one-time operations to complete the build.

Subsequent builds happen more quickly, because Xcode has much less work to do. Builds also take time to install, so the first time you run an app in the Simulator, you see a black screen. The screen usually persists for ten seconds or so, but the first time you build an app, it can take as long as a few minutes for the Simulator to finish launching on slower hardware with limited memory.

TIP

Using a Mac with an SSD drive can make a big difference to launch times.

CAUTION

You may be asked for your password before the Simulator launches so Xcode can load the debugger. This happens once per run. The first time it happens, you can ask Xcode to remember the password for future launches.

Eventually the app loads and runs, as shown in Figure 3.8. The empty white window isn't very exciting. It does nothing at all, but internally it is a complete skeleton app. You can now go back and begin editing the source files shown in Figure 3.6 to create the UI for the app.

To end the run, click the Stop button or select File ⇨ Quit in an OS X project. If you rebuild the same project, you can skip this step, after confirming with Xcode that you want it to quit and restart the simulation automatically.

If you build a different project, you must quit the run of your first project before Xcode allows you to run the second project. The Simulator isn't intelligent enough to switch between projects automatically.

Although this example creates an iOS application, the steps for an OS X application are almost identical, with the difference that an OS X application runs in a new window—not in the Simulator. The features of the different OS X and iOS templates are listed in more detail in the next section.

Figure 3.8

Run the template application in the Simulator. As a skeleton application, it does nothing except paint the window white.

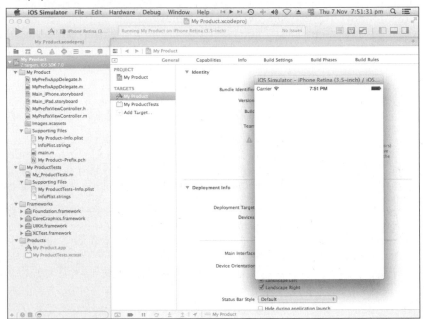

CROSS-REFERENCE

For more about editing, see Chapter 4. For an introduction to UI design, see Chapter 7.

Looking inside the Application templates

Most applications are built using Cocoa or Cocoa Touch. You can start with a minimal windowed application, or you can select a more complex template that includes one or more supporting views. The Cocoa and Cocoa Touch templates always include the following:

- *Class implementation* **files that define the basic elements of the application:** For Cocoa and Cocoa Touch applications, the elements always include an application delegate that receives and processes application management messages from the OS—for example, one message is sent when the application finishes loading, another when the application is about to quit, and so on. Depending on the template, the default classes may also include at least one UI view controller, which receives and processes user actions generated by the UI.

- *Class header* **files to support the implementation files:** The headers include `#import` directives for the essential UI framework on each platform. In templates with more than one class, the headers are imported correctly throughout.

● **One or more *nib files* or *storyboards*:** Nib files are OS X resource files that define the basic properties of a window, and optionally of a UI view. Storyboards are the iOS equivalent and can include optional *segues*—animations—for multi-view swapping. These files define the look and feel of the application UI. You can edit them to add UI objects such as images, buttons, sliders, and other controls. OS X applications include the menu tree in their nib files. But internally, nib files are treated as a general purpose inventory of objects loaded and initialized when the application runs.

● **An *Images.xcassets* file:** This file is a new option in Xcode 5. It holds image resources, including icons, in a single location. You can view the contents in Xcode and add files to the list of icons and launch images. You can't edit individual images.

TIP

An open secret of Cocoa development is that you can add any object or class to a nib file.

● ***Links* between the nib and storyboards, and the class files:** In Apple development, code can control and respond to UI objects only when these links are defined. They appear in two places: in the nib file, and in special directives within the class headers and the implementation code.

● **A *prefix header* file with `#import` directives for the essential application frameworks:** When you build an application, the headers added to this file are pre-compiled only once.

● **A *plist* (property list) file that includes a dictionary of application settings:** You can edit this dictionary to implement standard user preferences for the application. For details, see Appendix B.

● **An *infoPlist.strings* file that is used to *localize* the application so it supports other languages in addition to English:** The strings file includes pairs of strings. One string is used as a key in the application. The other string defines the text that appears when that string is used. Each language you support has its own strings file, with different output strings for each key. The default file is empty.

● **A *main.m* file:** This is a short block of boilerplate start-up code that loads the application and creates a memory pool for it. If you are developing for iOS or OS X you can ignore this file. If you are creating a command-line application in C or C++, this is where your code goes.

CROSS-REFERENCE

For more information about creating, editing, and using nib files and storyboards, see Chapters 7 and 8.

NOTE

OS X projects can also link code to the UI using bindings—indirect links between properties and UI elements. The standard OS X templates don't include any bindings; if you want to use them, you have to add your own. Bindings aren't available in iOS.

The templates also include some minor differences. For example, OS X templates include a *credits.rtf* file, which holds the text that appears when you click an app's About menu item.

CAUTION

Nib files have a `.xib` extension. They used to have a `.nib` extension, but now they contain XML.

Understanding Views in Apple Development

The word *view* has more than one meaning in Apple development. It can mean a complete UI design that defines all the elements in the UI: the buttons, images, and other features. But it also can mean individual UI elements within that configuration. For example, a button may include a *text view* that defines the text. A label may be called a *label view*. And so on. This seems inconsistent, but in general if an object is visible on the screen, it can be called a view. Individual UI items can also be called *controls*.

There's no doubt that the terminology could be simpler and clearer, especially for newcomers. It becomes easier to understand when you look at the classes used in Cocoa and Cocoa Touch. `UIView` and `NSView` are generic containers for on-screen content. Controls are usually subclasses of these top-level elements. The class relationships are easier to understand from the code level than from the top-down design level.

Apple is somewhat evangelical about a design pattern known as Model View Controller (MVC). This aims to split on-screen content from underlying data models, bridging the gap with *controller objects* that can abstract the underlying data from the UI. Done properly, MVC can create applications that are efficient and easy to maintain. The UI only needs to load and display a small subset of the underlying data, without having to make a separate working copy.

But confusion can occur because some classes that work as controllers also implement a complete view. For example, iOS has a class called `UIImagePickerController`, which not only accesses an iPhone's photo library and controls the camera, but it also displays its own complete UIs for both. Technically, this still fits the pattern—the controller abstracts the data and manages the UI—but it blurs developer expectations about what a controller class is likely to do.

It's best not to get hung up on these apparent inconsistencies. MVC is an influence, not a religion, and as long as you understand how to use the classes and what a view is in approximate terms, you have all the information you need to work with views successfully.

In iOS, navigation is managed by *view switching*. Typically, a top-level window object is associated with a navigation or view controller. When the user requests a new page, the controller loads the next view and displays it. Usually, it also deletes the previous view after it's no longer visible, to save memory—a process known as *lazy loading*. This makes it possible to display a book with a couple of views—current and next—without pre-creating views for every page.

In older versions of iOS, developers had to switch views manually. In more recent versions, segues help to automate the process. But there are many situations where developers still need to understand the view hierarchy, and work with it directly.

Practical UI design is a combination of object and control layout and view switching code. Usually, you create subclasses of views and view controllers to run your own UI-specific code, and you design the view layout in Interface Builder (IB). But you also can add and remove objects from a view under code control, and some developers prefer not to use IB at all.

OS X design can be simpler, because views are more static. However, view controllers are more sophisticated and may include optional data mapping and translation features that are not available in iOS. Generally though, the contents of a window are more likely to remain static, and page animation is less of an essential design technique and more of an optional extra.

Using the OS X Application templates

There are four OS X Application templates. Most include extra setup options.

Using the Cocoa Application template

The Cocoa Application template includes the ingredients listed earlier. The extra options are shown in Figure 3.9.

You can create a *Document-Based Application,* which is designed for multi-document apps. Each document loads and creates an instance of the same nib file in a separate window. If you specify this option, you can type the file extension into the Document Extension box.

The template uses Cocoa's `NSDocument` class to implement the document's features. It includes extra setup and tear-down features that aren't needed in an application that uses a single window, but it isn't a full implementation of a complete document-based application. You must add file save/load features, recent file support, and undo code.

Figure 3.9

Select a Cocoa Application template, and set the options. The grayed-out Spotlight Importer option isn't available, and you can ignore it.

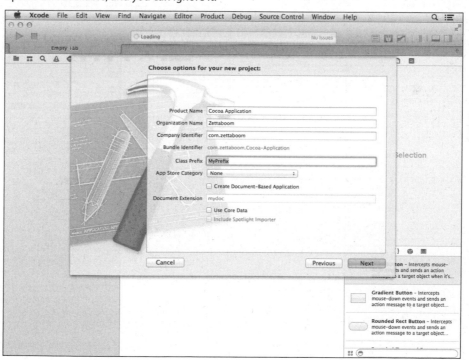

The Use Core Data option creates an application with support for *Core Data* storage. The code implements automatic archiving and loading of the data, but doesn't implement specific editing features. It also doesn't define a data model. Xcode includes a Core Data model editor. For a brief introduction to Core Data, see Appendix C.

N O T E

Core Data isn't a full relational database. Its features are more limited, but it can still be a useful way to manage data objects that can include multiple attributes.

You can also set the App Store Category, selecting one category from the menu. You can change this category later. Feel free to ignore this option if your project won't be sold in the App Store.

Using the SpriteKit Game template

The SpriteKit Game template is shown in Figure 3.10. It uses the SpriteKit framework, new in iOS 7 and OS X 10.9, to create a basic game template, with a *scene* class that sets up and runs the game. The class includes basic methods for initializing the scene with minimal placeholder content, managing `mouseDown` events, and updating the screen on a timer loop.

Figure 3.10

The SpriteKit game template builds a demo app with a basic background and a rotating spaceship.

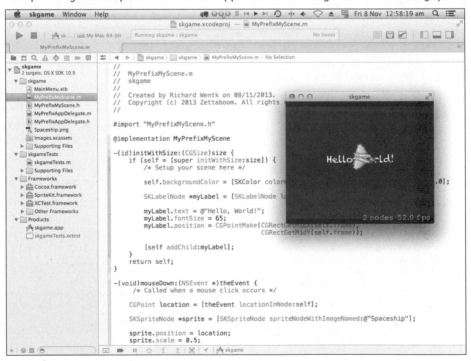

After the template builds, the scene loads a Hello World message. Clicking the mouse paints a rotating spaceship in the window. Like other templates, the code is not intended as a full tutorial, and you need to remove or rewrite most of it to create your own games.

NOTE

Unlike most of the OS X templates, the SpriteKit game includes an xctest target for automated unit testing.

Using the Cocoa-AppleScript Application template

The Cocoa-AppleScript Application template, shown in Figure 3.11, creates a minimal AppleScript application. It's effectively a drastically simplified version of the standard Cocoa Application template, rewritten in AppleScript instead of Objective-C. The application opens a blank window with a standard menu.

Only two methods appear here: `applicationWillFinishLaunching` and `application ShouldTerminate`. Real applications are likely to need more in the way of setup, so this template is a prime candidate for replacement with a more advanced project of your own design.

Figure 3.11

The Cocoa-AppleScript template creates a very simple AppleScript application, which launches and . . . does nothing.

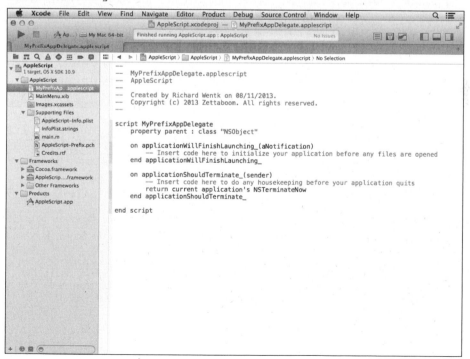

TIP

For a guide to developing AppleScript applications, see the companion *AppleScript* in Wiley's Developer Reference series.

Using the Command Line Tool template

In a Cocoa application, main.c loads and runs the application, and you can ignore it. In a command-line application, main.c *is* the application. As you might expect, the Command Line Tool template creates a C or C++ file designed to run from the command line. Parameters are passed in `argc` and `argv[]` in the usual way.

After building, the tool runs in the Console window, which is introduced in Chapter 4. You can also run the tool from Terminal. As shown in Figure 3.12, you can select one of six templates for the tool, although in fact the differences between most of the options are minimal and are mostly limited to the default linked framework headers.

The C and C++ templates include a bare minimum of standard language headers. Use them to build low-level command line tools that can work with any C or C++ library or feature and can potentially work on other UNIX variants.

Figure 3.12

The Command Line Tool template creates text-based applications without a GUI.

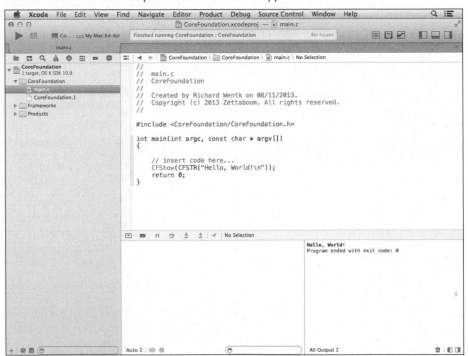

The other templates link against the named OS X libraries: Foundation links against Cocoa's Foundation base data classes; Core Foundation links against the older Carbon C-based libraries; Core Services is a generic services template. Only the CoreData template includes significant extra code.

Understanding the iOS Application templates

The default iOS templates include bare-bones examples of various possible iOS UI configurations. Understand that these outlines are a starting point, not a definitive guide to UI design. Real iOS applications rarely have much in common with the templates. As you become more experienced, the limitations of the templates become more obvious and more restrictive, and you'll almost certainly want to modify them or create new project starting files of your own.

TIP

You'll find it useful to build and run each of the templates in turn. Save each template project to a special templates folder so you can explore the projects later without having to re-create them.

Using the MasterDetail template

Formerly the Navigation-based template, the MasterDetail template, shown in Figure 3.13, includes a window that displays a single instance of the `UITableView` class. iOS doesn't support drop-down menus. Instead, you build menu-like navigation trees by combining a Navigation Controller object with one or more of these table views. Selecting a *cell*—an item in the table—is similar to selecting a menu item. Your code can respond by displaying the next table in a menu tree, or it can perform some other action at the end of each menu.

CAUTION

This is a complex template with more code than usual. Because master/detail view coding and table management are core skills in iOS development, it's worth taking the time to understand them fully, even if this takes you a while.

Navigation is managed by an instance of `UINavigationController`, which handles movement through the tree and displays a title and back/forward buttons. The template code automatically fills in cell contents and segues to a detail view when you tap on a non-empty cell.

iPad projects use the same template and the same code, but a different storyboard. When the iPad is in the portrait (vertical) orientation, the table slides in from the left and partially covers the detail view. In landscape (horizontal) orientation, the table is always visible.

TIP

You can change the rotation in the Simulator by selecting Hardware ⇨ Rotate Right or Rotate Left. You can also scale the iPad simulator by selecting Window ⇨ Scale 50%, 75% or 100%. The simulator mimics the native device resolution, so the 100% retina option needs a large retina monitor.

Figure 3.13

Run the MasterDetail template. The navigation controller creates the bar at the top of the UI, and the table view generates the table cell under it. Tapping the + (plus) fills in the current date and time, and creates a new detail view with the same contents in a larger area.

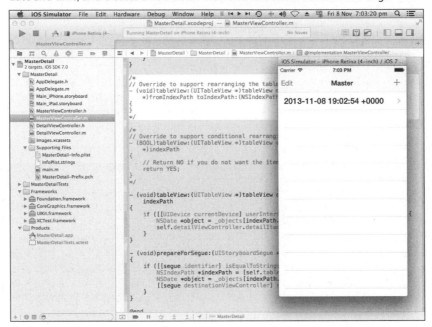

Using the OpenGL Game template

The OpenGL Game template, shown in Figure 3.14, includes setup and teardown for an application that uses the OpenGL graphics subsystem. The template animates a pair of shaded cubes.

OpenGL is used for games and for complex custom UIs. It's a specialized and challenging high-performance graphics environment. You can ignore it unless you need to create complex 3D animations. For 2D games, SpriteKit is much easier to work with.

The graphics are wrapped inside a class called `GLKViewController`, which uses an `EAGLContext` to define and render the graphics. The code uses *shaders*—small custom code blocks that manipulate geometric objects—to define the shapes, colors, and textures that appear in the scene. It also creates and runs an animation loop timer that calls the `update` method to calculate each screen frame.

Figure 3.14

The code of the OpenGL Game template animates a couple of shaded cubes. Significant setup and tear-down code is required to make this animation possible.

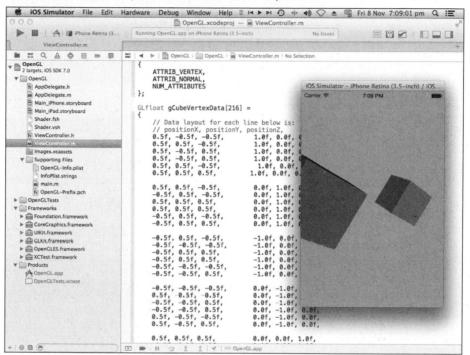

CAUTION

Mastering the Master/Detail Template will tell you most of what you need to know about practical table management. In comparison, the OpenGL Game Template is a tiny introduction to practical OpenGL. You can learn a little by pulling it apart, but to learn more, you need to do plenty of reading and experimenting. You also need a good grasp of 3D geometry and matrix arithmetic.

Using the Page-Based template

The Page-Based template illustrated in Figure 3.15 creates an app with "pages" the user can flip by dragging them. It illustrates Apple's Model-View-Controller design pattern. There are only ever two pages visible, and a model controller class keeps track of the content they display—in this case, a simple list of months. The iPad version is almost identical, but the pages appear inside a frame.

This is a useful template to explore, because it illustrates one possible way to manage view flipping. However, it is not a definitive guide to UI management, because UI design allows many options. The page curl effect is largely incidental and can easily be replaced with some other transition.

Figure 3.15

Flip pages with a Page-Based example app.

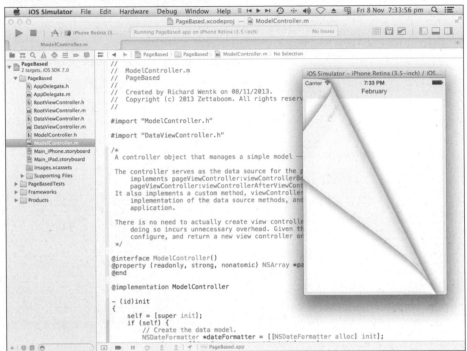

CAUTION

Confusingly, the icon for this template looks like a Page View Controller—a series of dots. But the template is entirely touch-driven and does not include a Page View Controller. Previous versions of Xcode included a template for this kind of controller, but in Xcode 5 Apple has kept the name while losing the feature.

Using the Single View Application template

This template, shown in Figure 3.16, is used by developers who want a minimum of setup code. It's also a good template for experimentation and learning, because it starts with no clutter or existing code, and if you want your app to do anything at all, you have to learn how to extend it as needed.

It includes a window, a view controller, and a view. The view controller is already subclassed, so you can start adding code to it immediately. Typically when you add UI objects, you link the code to this controller.

The view isn't subclassed, so although you can add objects and animations to it, you can't make them do anything until you create and assign a subclass—a moderately complex process, described in Chapters 5, 7, and 8. There are no predefined storyboard transitions; a single static white view is all you get, unless you add further controllers and views, and support for touch events and gestures.

Figure 3.16

The Single View Application template is a minimal starting point for app design.

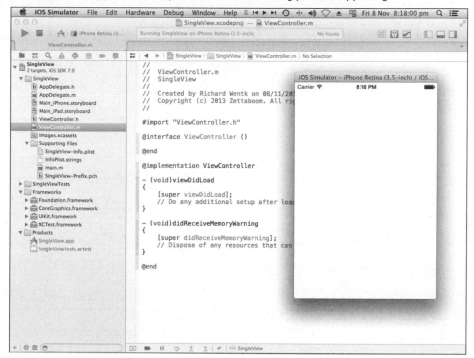

Using the Tabbed Application template

The Tabbed Application, shown in Figure 3.17, creates an app with a set of icons on a tab bar. The user can tap the icons to select different views. The view content is defined in the nib file in the storyboard, not generated by the code.

This is one of the more confusing templates, because the code doesn't appear to do anything. In fact, the Tab Bar Controller manages the switching for you automatically, as shown in the storyboard editor. You can use the editor to add further views—pages—by adding further view controllers and setting up segues to them.

There isn't space in this chapter to include a full step-by-step guide to this process, but after you've explored IB in the next few chapters, you can return to this template and experiment with it.

Figure 3.17

The Tab Bar Application template displays and switches views automatically, using the `UITabBarController` class to manage the switching and `UITabBar` class to display the buttons and respond to user taps.

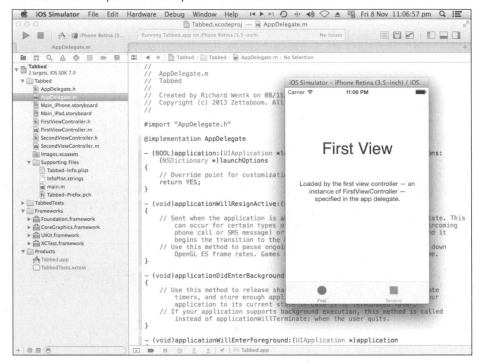

CAUTION

In previous versions of Xcode, you could set up further pages only by manually editing the Tab Bar Controller's properties. This process was almost totally opaque, and you were guaranteed to miss it if you didn't already know it was necessary. The storyboard equivalent makes the relationship between the elements much clearer. But it's still not obvious how to add pages, and there's no information in the code to explain what you need to do. It doesn't help that the page content mentions the app delegate, which is no longer relevant to the process.

Using the Utility Application template

The Utility Application template shown in Figure 3.18 creates an iPhone application with an info button at the bottom right. Tapping the button reveals a flip-side view with a navigation bar and a Done button. The two views have separate controllers. The flip view is typically used for preferences and other application features that don't need to be permanently visible. The iPad version of this template displays a *popover view*, with the utility content in a smaller window.

Although you can use this template as is, it has some nonessential features. The navigation bar on the flip-side wastes space. Note that it's simply a navigation bar—a holder for a button—and not a navigation controller. Often, you'll replace the bar and the button with a single return button at the bottom of the screen, perhaps with a custom graphic.

Figure 3.18

Think of the Utility Application template as a design example rather than a practical application starting point. Many apps use the main/flip view design idiom, but it's often implemented in simpler and more flexible ways.

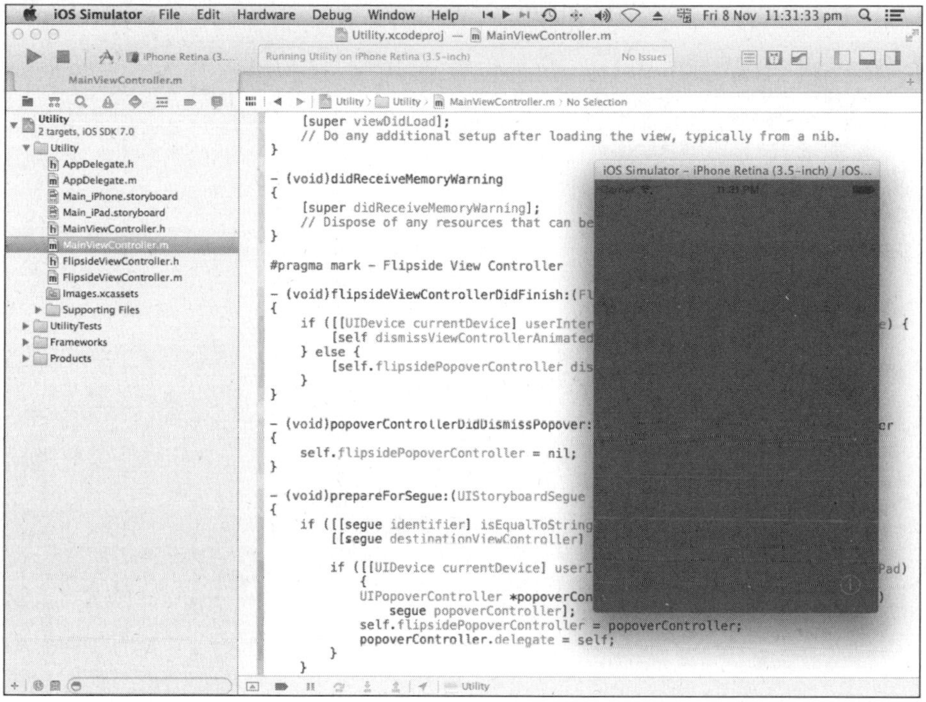

Also, the navigation bar fouls the status bar with the time, carrier name and signal strength, and battery life. This is harder to fix than you might think, because you have to work with *constraints* to force the bar into the correct location. You can't simply drag it and leave it.

So generally, use this template as a demonstration of certain options, rather than as a good solution.

T I P

For Cocoa experts, the flip code triggered by the Done button uses a protocol method call to the superview. Replacing this with a simpler call to `dismissViewController: animated: completion:` in the flip view works just as well. You can use `self` as the modal view parameter. The call automatically finds the superview, so you don't need to specify it.

Using the Empty Application template

The Empty application template, shown in Figure 3.19, is a minimal template. The running app looks like the Single View Application. But this template is even simpler. It doesn't include any storyboards or any view controllers. To create a finished app, you must add all of the above, with other UI objects, and manually link the elements to the code.

Figure 3.19

Turning the Empty Application template into a finished app requires extra time and effort.

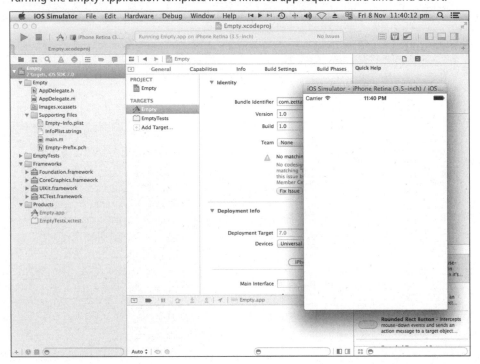

You can ignore this template for most projects. It's occasionally useful if you want to create a unique app with unusual UI requirements. But it doesn't help you learn about app development, and it doesn't create a useful starting point for most apps.

Using the SpriteKit Game template

The SpriteKit Game template, shown in Figure 3.20, is the iOS equivalent of the OS X SpriteKit Game template. It does the same things—creates an app skeleton for a game built with the SpriteKit framework—but it embeds it inside an iOS View Controller.

The scene code is very similar, and it demonstrates how easy it is to develop games for both platforms now. The key difference is the use of the `touchesBegan:` method to handle user touches, instead of the `mouseDown:` method used in OS X.

Figure 3.20

The SpriteKit Game Template looks and works very much like the OS X equivalent.

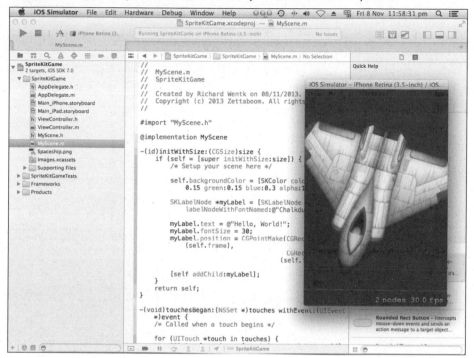

Introducing the Framework and Library templates

Figure 3.21 shows the Framework and Library templates for OS X. iOS supports only static libraries. You can't create or add a framework to an iOS project. OS X is less limited. You can create a Cocoa framework, a Cocoa library, a Cocoa bundle that includes code and resources, an XPC (system) service, a C/C++ library, or a Standard Template Library (STL) C++ library with debug symbols.

NOTE

A *library* is usually just a collection of code, with source files. A *framework* typically builds a single binary and supplies a list of headers for a #import directive. Frameworks can include media content, property lists, and other information as well as code. The framework's folder structure is fixed. In theory, frameworks include a complete class architecture, with implied usage patterns and relationships, while libraries are more likely to contain isolated discrete components. In practice, the distinction is sometimes less clear-cut.

NOTE

If you want to develop in C++, Xcode now supports C++11. Support is turned off by default. To enable it, turn on the C++11 compiler option in the Build Settings, which are described in Chapter 14.

Figure 3.21

You can use the Framework & Library option in the OS X templates to create a range of supporting frameworks and libraries for your projects—and potentially, for the projects of other developers.

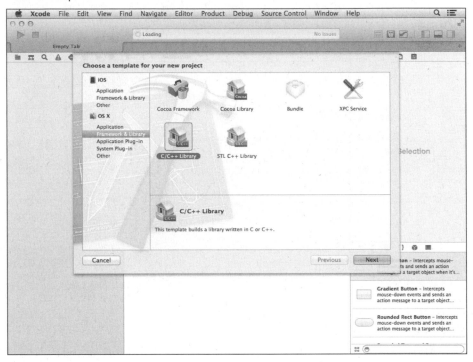

Introducing the Plug-In templates

In outline, the Application Plug-in templates are designed to add custom features to existing Apple applications, such as Address Book, Automator, and so on. These applications are designed with a standard interface, and the plug-in templates generate code and resource files that match their specific requirements. Experienced developers can use them to add new features to these applications. For example, you can use the Interface Builder plug-in to define your own collection of UI objects and add it to the standard list already built into IB.

The System Plug-in templates, shown in Figure 3.22, are more low level and can work with more than one application. For example, the Quick Look Plug-in can implement a preview of a custom data type used in your applications. The Preference Pane is useful if you want to add a pane to the standard System Preferences.

Some of the plug-in templates are minimally complex. The IOKit driver plug-in creates a complete empty C++ file and links it against the Kernel framework. If you're a newcomer to Apple development, you can ignore these more advanced options.

Figure 3.22

Although Xcode includes plug-in templates, developing working plug-ins typically requires research and persistent dedication.

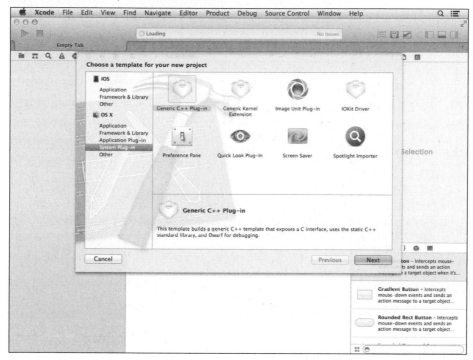

A full introduction to plug-in development is outside the scope of this book, but you can find basic help in the Apple documentation and more advanced examples on the relevant Apple mailing lists and other online forums.

NOTE

The plug-in templates support only Apple-standard APIs. If you want to develop a plug-in for some other application, such as an Adobe Photoshop 8BX plug-in or a VST (Virtual Studio Technology) music synthesizer or sound processor, you typically need to download a suitable SDK or framework and add it to Xcode by hand.

Introducing the Other templates

The most interesting Other template is for InApp content. In fact, this template simply creates an empty project with a single *plist*—an XML file used to store attributes and properties. You must fill in the other details by hand.

The remaining templates create an empty project—the project quite literally has no content or settings of any kind—and a slightly more complex template for an external build system. You can use the latter to add support for other languages to Xcode, assuming you have plenty of time and a command-line compiler.

Customizing Projects and Templates

It's important to understand that no template is complete. Templates include a bare minimum of features and are designed to eliminate repetitive setup chores and to provide very simple demo apps. They're not tutorials, and they're certainly not examples of best practice.

Many useful methods from these classes are missing from the templates, and you should review the class reference documentation, described in Chapter 6, to learn more about them. Typically, your applications will rely on methods and properties that don't appear in the standard templates.

The most productive templates are likely to be the ones you create yourself. Because Xcode makes it hard to modify the existing templates, the easiest way to create your own templates is to set up a project with code in a single folder and use Finder to duplicate it after you customize it to create a useful starting point for your own projects.

CAUTION

The disadvantage of this approach is that it duplicates file and project names. This is rarely a problem in practice. As long as you set up groups and folders correctly, Xcode allows you to move and duplicate entire project folders. The product name—the name of the final app—does not depend on the name of an Xcode project file. The folder name is also independent.

If you're feeling adventurous, you can find the project template files by selecting the Xcode.app file, right-clicking, and choosing Show Package Contents. For iOS projects, navigate to `Contents/Developer/Platforms/iPhoneOS.platform/Developer/Library/Xcode/Templates/Project Templates`.

The OS X templates are in `Contents/Developer/Library/Xcode/Templates/Project Templates/Mac`.

The templates are a mix of plists, resource files, json manifests, and other files. The template specifications aren't formally documented, but if you want to do some reverse engineering, you can experiment with editing these files and creating new ones to see what happens. Remember to save them in another location so you can overwrite the originals whenever you update Xcode.

Summary

Xcode templates are starting points. Even though they contain some sample code, they're not tutorials, and they're not fully loaded mini-apps. It's important to understand their limitations and not to expect too much from them.

If you want more detailed app examples, you can find them in the source code resources in the documentation, which is described in Chapter 6. But you still need to do lots of extra reading about Cocoa and Cocoa Touch programming to understand how to put together a working app. Fortunately, there's plenty of unofficial documentation online now to help you get started.

Navigating the Xcode Interface

X code 5 gathers together all its features into a single window that is split into working areas. You can choose to hide and reveal different features as you work. Understanding which features are available is one of the keys to maximizing productivity.

Understanding the Interface

Figure 4.1 shows one view of the Xcode interface. From left to right, the UI is split into navigation, editor, and utility areas. This mirrors Apple's official UI guidelines; all Apple applications follow a similar layout. However, it's a good idea not to take the area names too literally.

For example, the navigation area includes debugging features that are only very distantly related to code navigation. A more accurate description for the left area might be "finding and building." It not only lists files and objects but also reports build issues, supports searches, and simplifies error checking and debugging.

NOTE
Xcode includes a separate console and debugger, which is described in detail in Chapter 16.

The right area is most often used as a code and object library, but it includes extra features that reveal key information about selected items, including file paths and miscellaneous settings. This area also includes a built-in help feature.

In spite of the name, the editor area isn't exclusively dedicated to editing. You also use it to define critical project-wide build settings and to add frameworks to your project. For example, during iPhone development, you can use this area to select the app icons and launch images for an app.

The editor area is always visible, but you can hide and reveal the navigation, debug/console, and utility areas. Click the buttons near the top right of the Xcode 5 window, as shown in Figure 4.2. Each button toggles when you click it, hiding or revealing its corresponding area.

In This Chapter

Using the navigation area

Using the utility area

Working with the editor area

Getting started with code editing

Introducing build configurations

Figure 4.1

Look again at the Xcode interface and its three-way split.

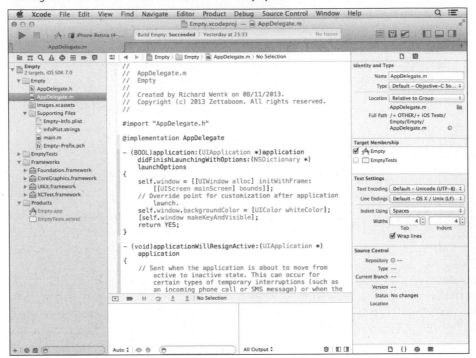

Figure 4.2

The show/hide buttons for the navigator include debug/console and utility areas.

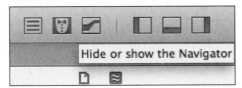

Using the Navigation Area

At the top left of the navigation area is a toolbar with eight icons, as shown in Figure 4.3. Selecting an icon changes the content that appears in the pane under the toolbar.

Figure 4.3

The selection icons for the navigation area

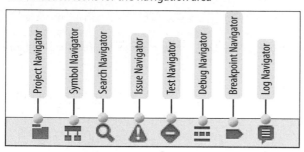

From left to right, the icons select these toolbars:

- Project Navigator
- Symbol Navigator
- Search Navigator
- Issue Navigator
- Test Navigator (new in Xcode 5)
- Debug Navigator
- Breakpoint Navigator
- Log Navigator

CAUTION

With a couple of exceptions, the images on these icons are perhaps best described as "abstract"; they're not a good guide to the features they select. The best way to learn what they do is to hover the mouse under them until a tooltip appears and then experiment with them.

The Project Navigator

When you select a file that Xcode can edit, its contents automatically load into the editor area. If Xcode can't edit it—for example, if it's an image file or a font—the editor area shows a preview.

Understanding groups

The file list in this navigator looks like a Finder directory listing. But this is misleading. The "folders" that appear here are called groups. When you create a project using a template, these folders don't exist on disk.

You can use groups to collect related items together. The default list of groups for a project varies according to the target OS and project type, but it typically includes a main group with the same name as the project that holds class files, other source code, nib files or storyboards, and a Supporting Files group that holds main.m and other more incidental files.

Projects that include test code include a Tests group. The two remaining items are a list of Apple frameworks used in the project and a Products group that shows the final compiled files. This includes at least an app file. If test code is included, it also has a separate xctest file target.

N O T E

Xcode shows files that exist in the project but not on disk—in other words, files it thinks it should be able to find but can't—in red. This is why the two files in the Products group are shown in red before you build them.

You can create new groups to help you organize the files in your project. For example, you could create a group called MyClasses for new classes. Because groups are arbitrary, you can create any structure that works for you.

To add a new group, right-click in the navigator area and select New Group from the menu that appears, as shown in Figure 4.4. You can rearrange the order of both groups and files by dragging them to a different position in the list.

Figure 4.4

When you create a new group, it is always added to the next highest level in the group tree.

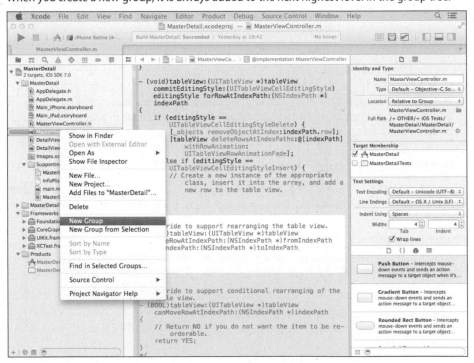

TIP

A new Group from Selection option in Xcode 5 creates a group to hold a collection of selected files. This saves some manual copying and moving.

In Xcode 5, if you rename a file in the navigator, Xcode also renames it on disk. This is a semi-reliable process: Xcode often gets slightly confused for a while after you do this. It's a good idea to save a project to disk, quit Xcode, and relaunch it after renaming files.

It's critically important to understand that the filenames that appear here are symbolic links to real files, and not file listings. The navigator displays a list of files in the project. It *doesn't* display the files and folders in the project directory. If you open the project directory with Finder, you see a different file structure.

This makes it possible for the navigator to display project files wherever they're located on disk. But as you see later in this chapter, Xcode can manage the relationship between groups and real file paths in various ways. If you don't understand how this process works, you can break the links by accident, forcing Xcode to lose the files from the project.

TIP

Although the template groups don't match real folders, you *can* set up folder references in Xcode. They appear in pale blue to distinguish them from standard Xcode groups. To create them when you add files, select the "Create folder references for any added folders" radio button. Folder references make it easy to share files between projects, but be careful about source control and editing. If you choose to refer to files without copying them, all edits are "live" and you may break other projects that use the same code.

Deleting files

To delete a file, you can either use the right-click menu shown in Figure 4.4, the Backspace key, or the Delete key. Deleting a file displays the dialog shown in Figure 4.5. You can choose to move the file to the trash, which deletes it from the project and from disk. Or you can remove the reference, which leaves the file on disk but removes it from the project.

TIP

If the *utility area* is visible when you select a file, you can view the file's disk path. Real projects may gather files from many different directories, so this can be a useful memory jogger. You also can use this feature to find framework header files. For more information about using the utility area, see the section later in this chapter.

CAUTION

The utility area also shows a file's type, which defines how Xcode handles the files when you build a project. The type may not match the file extension. The templates mostly set up file types correctly, but there are occasional issues; for example, in Xcode 5.0.2, C++ header files are treated as C headers and do not build correctly unless you set the type manually.

Figure 4.5

When deleting a file, you can leave it on disk or move it to the trash. Leaving a file on disk can be useful if you want to keep an older version or move it to another project.

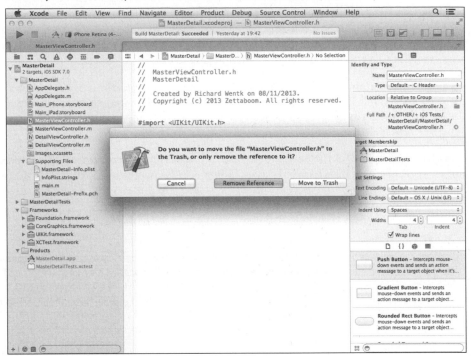

The Symbol Navigator

You can use the Symbol Navigator, shown at the left of Figure 4.6, to browse the symbols—classes, methods, and other code features—in your project. Selecting a symbol from the lists that appear in this navigator locates and loads the corresponding code into the editor. Effectively, the navigator is a quick index to the main features of your project.

The mini-toolbar has two buttons: Hierarchical and Flat. The Hierarchical view groups symbols showing subclasses and inheritance. The Flat view is a plain alphabetical list.

To find a specific method or code feature, click it in the list. Xcode automatically loads the matching code and makes it ready for editing. This view provides the same information as the navigator bar area above the editor window.

For simple projects, it's usually easier and quicker to select symbols and files from the navigator bar introduced in Chapter 1. The Symbol Navigator becomes quicker when the number of classes and features increases. It's especially useful when you have a big monitor that can display the complete list without scrolling.

Figure 4.6

Selecting a symbol in the Symbol Navigator displays it in the editor window and highlights it.

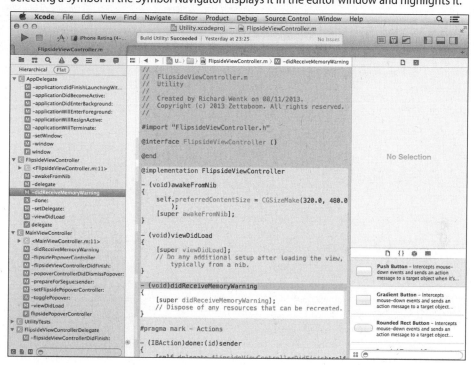

CAUTION

The System symbol view available in Xcode 4 is no longer included. To view information about system symbols, click a symbol with the utility pane open and the Quick Help sub-pane visible. You can now read a summary of the symbol. Often, you can click through to a . h file to view the header file where the symbol is defined.

The Search Navigator

The Search Navigator looks like a simple string search tool, but is unexpectedly powerful. To use it, type a full or partial search string into the search field, as shown in Figure 4.7. By default, the navigator searches for a string in the current file. But you can use the menu shown in Figure 4.7 to select other options, including find-and-replace.

The options are easy to understand and can save you lots of time. If you're a regular expression expert, you can use the Regular Expression option to perform pattern matching searches. The ability to search for References and Definitions is new in Xcode and makes it easy to narrow the results to the files and lines of code you are looking for.

Figure 4.7

Look at the search navigator options.

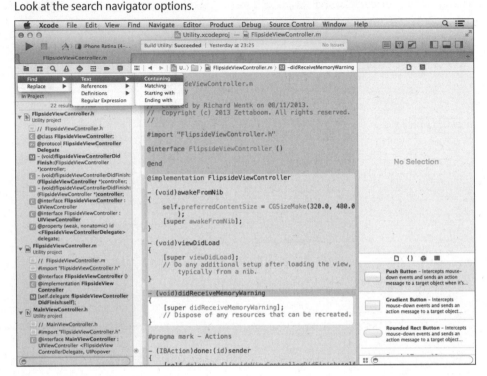

Figure 4.8 shows further new options. You can use the lower options to restrict the search to specific groups. With the upper option, you can define a *custom scope,* which limits the search by name, location, path, or type, within the project, its associated frameworks, or just the current folder. These advanced search tools make it much easier to perform intelligent, useful searches, especially in larger projects.

TIP

It's easy to write off the Search Navigator as a simple search tool. In fact, it's well worth taking the time to master its many features because it can be a real timesaver. For example, the regular expression search option can do a lot to improve the quality of search results.

The Find-and-Replace feature is dangerous. If you select the project as a scope, it replaces all the matching strings. You cannot undo this, although you can force quit Xcode without saving to avoid making a permanent change.

A more indirect alternative is the Find and Replace in Project. . . option in the main menu, shown in Figure 4.9. Enter your search string and replace string into the usual find-and-replace dialog at the top of the navigator. Press Enter to show the results, and click Preview to show the dialog in the figure.

Figure 4.8

Select more advanced search options.

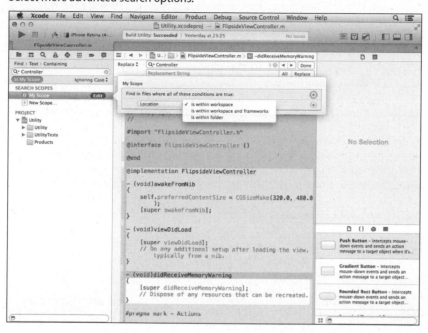

Figure 4.9

Use Find and Replace in Project. . ., with preview switching.

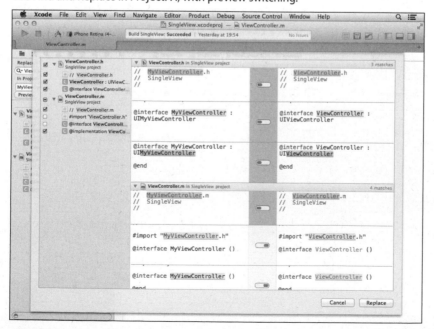

You can now see a list of possible before-and-after changes. The gutter between them includes a toggle switch for each change. You can set the switches individually to select or reject specific changes before clicking the Replace button at the bottom right to finalize the edit.

The Issue Navigator and the Log Navigator

The Issue Navigator, shown in Figure 4.10, lists fatal errors and warning messages after a build. Selecting an issue shows it in the editor window, with an adjacent red highlight and description. An icon also appears in the gutter to the left of the code editor. After a build, you can use this navigator to jump directly to problem code if it isn't already visible in the editor pane.

Note that Xcode tests code as you type it. This isn't always helpful: It often tells you that your code has errors before you have finished adding it, and on slow hardware, it takes a while for errors to disappear after you correct them. But it also means you can see issues without having to wait for a failed build to complete. So in practice, the Issue Navigator is most useful for linker errors and for displaying obscure issues that don't trip the in-line error checking.

Figure 4.10

Clicking any warning or error in the build results list displays related code in the editor window.

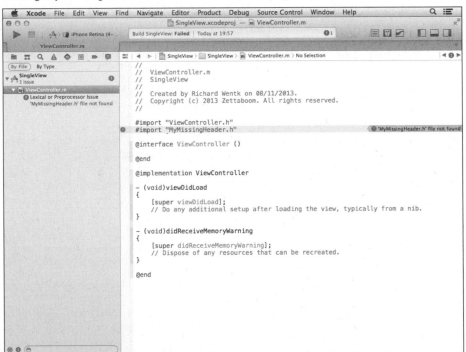

If you're new to development, it's important to understand that errors don't always appear on the correct line of code. For example, if you remove or comment out the closing curly bracket from a method definition, you create a cascade of errors in the rest of the file, but the missing bracket isn't flagged correctly. Some errors require experience and guesswork. Problems in code can often create multiple errors at the same location.

CAUTION

You can click a red dot in the editor to see more about any issue. Xcode includes a code hinting feature, and if the problem is easy to resolve, it sometimes suggests a fix. The fixes are often helpful, but sometimes they're misleading. If you're a beginner, don't assume the fixes are always correct.

Finally, there are many different possible warning messages, and you can select the ones you want to see. In the Project Navigator, select the project and then select Build Settings. Select All under it, and scroll down to show the Apple LLVM 5.0 Warnings panel, as shown in Figure 4.11. Many of these options assume intermediate or expert level experience, so it's best to leave them unchanged unless you know what they're for. As you gain experience, you can start to use this feature to choose the warnings you want to see.

Figure 4.11

You can enable or disable each warning message generated by the compiler. You also can disable all warnings, which is usually a bad thing to do.

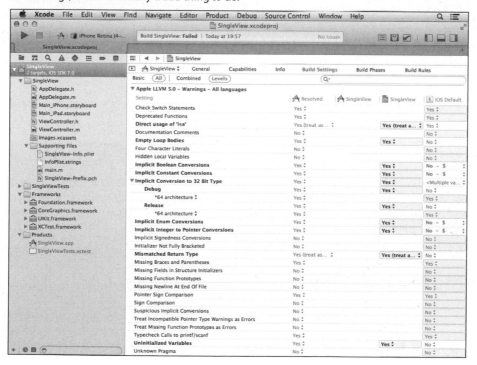

The Log Navigator, shown in Figure 4.12, is an alternate way to display build issues. You can refer to previous builds to compare errors. Double-clicking an issue in the editor window takes you to the code that caused it.

Figure 4.12

Where the Issues Navigator shows issues for the current build, the Log Navigator shows issues for previous builds too.

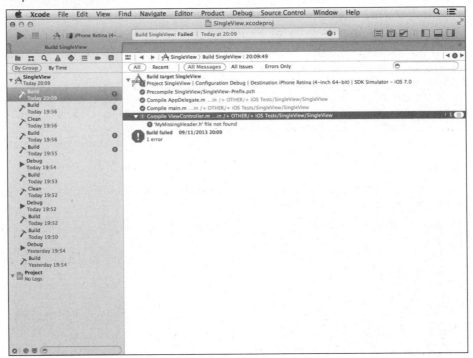

The issue listings here can give you more information than is available in the Issue Navigator. For a full untruncated view of each message, click the icon with a group of lines at the right of each message string. You also can select the message icon that appears next to the message/error count to view the raw compiler output, as shown in Figure 4.13. This isn't usually necessary, but it can be helpful when checking file paths and library locations on disk.

The Test Navigator

The Test Navigator, shown in Figure 4.14, displays a list of test targets and methods. You can enable and disable individual methods, and run the tests by right-clicking and selecting a test target. You can use the test code to run specific methods in your code so you can check that they're returning the results you expect. For details, see Chapter 18.

Figure 4.13

View raw compiler switches and output listings.

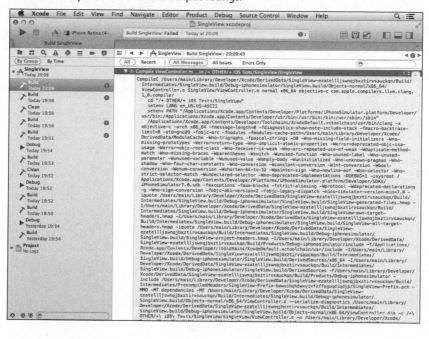

Figure 4.14

Introducing the Test Navigator.

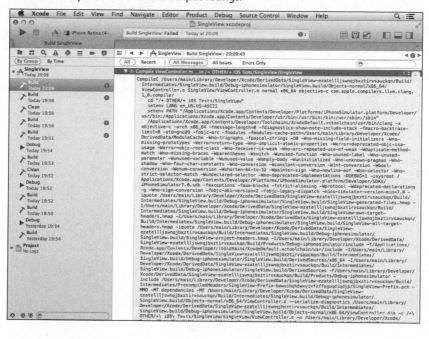

The Breakpoint Navigator and the Debug Navigator

You can add a debugging breakpoint—a feature that stops code execution at a certain line for testing and review—in the main code editor. Breakpoints remain in the code but are active only when *breakpoint mode* is enabled. Click in the breakpoint gutter to the left of any line of code. A blue arrow appears when the breakpoint is active. To disable a breakpoint, click its arrow again.

The Breakpoint Navigator, shown in Figure 4.15, lists all the breakpoints in a project. You can move to any breakpoint by clicking the list at the left. You also can set up conditional breakpoints that are triggered only after a certain number of repeats. Breakpoints are a powerful debugging aid, with many features and options. For details, see Chapter 16.

Figure 4.15

Set and list breakpoints.

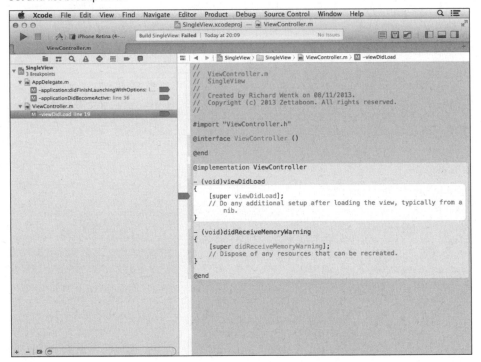

NOTE

Xcode 5 no longer has an explicit breakpoint mode. You can activate and deactivate breakpoints using the Debug ⇨ Deactivate Breakpoints menu item. Select the item again to reactivate breakpoints.

The Debug Navigator, shown in Figure 4.16, lists active threads after a breakpoint is triggered. A separate debug area at the bottom of the screen appears automatically and displays relevant values and objects. For a detailed example of debugging with breakpoints, see Chapter 16.

Loading the navigators from menus and keyboard shortcuts

You can access all the navigators from Xcode's menu tree or via keyboard shortcuts. The navigators are listed under View ⇨ Navigators. To select them from the keyboard, use ⌘+1-8. ⌘+0 shows/hides the navigator area.

Figure 4.16

View breakpoint and thread information in debug mode, with the Debug Navigator.

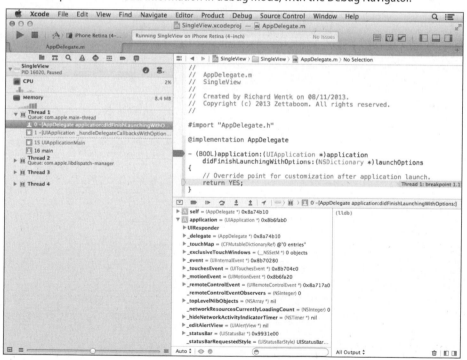

Using the Utility Area

The utility area at the right of the UI has two sub-panes. The top sub-pane displays file information and quick help. The lower sub-pane is a code and object library. You can hide the lower sub-pane by dragging its divider down until only the four icons on its top toolbar are visible.

Displaying file information

When displaying code files, the top sub-pane shows two icons. The icon on the left displays file information, as shown in Figure 4.17. To rename a file, type the new name into the File Name text field. To change the file type, select a new type from the File Type menu.

Figure 4.17

This option displays file path details and extra settings such as the text format.

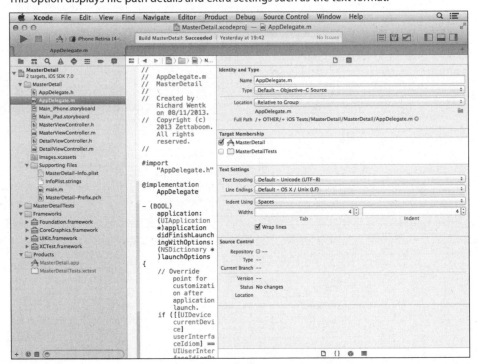

CAUTION

The file type isn't cosmetic; it defines how Xcode processes the file when it builds it. You can tell Xcode how to deal with each kind of file in the project build settings, introduced in Chapters 12, 13 and 14.

NOTE

Nib files and storyboard items are treated as a special case by the utility area. When you select a nib, the top sub-pane shows icons you can use to set the size, properties, and other key features of UI objects. For details, see Chapters 7 and 8.

The Location menu sets the root file path reference. The default Relative to Group option is the most useful. It creates a file path relative to the main project directory. You can copy the project directory to a different disk location without breaking this reference.

You also can change the file path to an absolute reference or to a path relative to some other disk folder, such as the /Developer directory. Use this option with care. If you copy or move a file with an absolute reference, Xcode can't find it again. If you do this by accident and lose a file from a project, you can use this pane to reset the path so the link works correctly. Click the tiny folder-window icon to the right of the area under the Location window to select a directory.

TIP

You can use the arrow icon next to the Full Path listing to reveal a file in Finder.

This sub-pane also displays supporting information about the file:

- **Target Membership** sets the build target for the file. Simple projects have a single build target, and you can ignore this option. For more complex projects, see Chapter 12.
- **Text Settings** defines the text encoding for the file. The default is UTF-8 (Unicode Text Format - 8 bit), which supports non-English characters. By default, Xcode creates indents with spaces. If you need code indented with tabs, select that option with the Indent Using menu. You also can set the number of spaces for each indent.
- **Source Control** is used for collaborative development, or development that uses a code repository. For information about repositories, see Chapter 15.

CAUTION

The Localization option that used to live in here in Xcode 4 has moved. Localization is now limited to storyboards and nib files. If you select one, you see the old Localizable Strings item. For more about localizing your app so it supports languages other than U.S. English, see Chapter 8.

Using Quick Help

The second icon at the top of the sub-pane displays a Quick Help window, shown in Figure 4.18. Clicking an OS X object or method displays a much longer list of information:

- **Name** is the item name.
- If the symbol is a method, **Declaration** shows the method signature.

- **Description** tells you what the symbol does.
- **Parameters** gives a list of the parameters used by a method.
- **Returns** lists the return options and values.
- **Availability** lists the OS X or iOS versions that first supported the symbol.
- **Declared in** links directly to the header file in which the symbol appears.
- **Reference** links directly to reference documentation; for more details, see Chapter 6.
- **Related** shows related methods and objects, where relevant.
- **Guides** show the related programming guides, where available.
- **Sample Code** lists a selection of sample projects that use the symbol or illustrate how it works.

CAUTION

Not all items are shown for every symbol. Note also that in Xcode 5, you can open the documentation browser from Quick Help or by selecting the Documentation and API Reference option under the Help menu.

Figure 4.18

The small Quick Help window contains a surprisingly large amount of useful information.

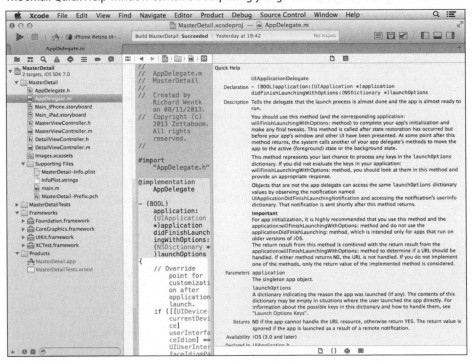

On a large monitor, you can leave this pane open so it finds and lists information as you type. This open pane can be sluggish on a slower Mac, but it is a useful tool on a faster one. But it also provides quick access to key help documentation. If your Mac is fast enough, it's worth leaving it enabled.

TIP

When the utility pane is hidden, you can option-click an item to open the pane and show quick help. System symbols appear underlined while you hold down the option key.

Adding custom comments

In Xcode 5, you can add your own content to Quick Help by adding comments in the correct format. In theory, Xcode 5 supports Header Doc and Doxygen formatting. In practice, as of Xcode 5.1, only some of the standard keywords seem to work. Figure 4.19 shows how you can comment a method using a standard comment block, as follows:

```
/**
@keywords and content go here, perhaps on multiple lines
*/
```

Figure 4.19

Add a method description to Quick Help with a formatted comment block.

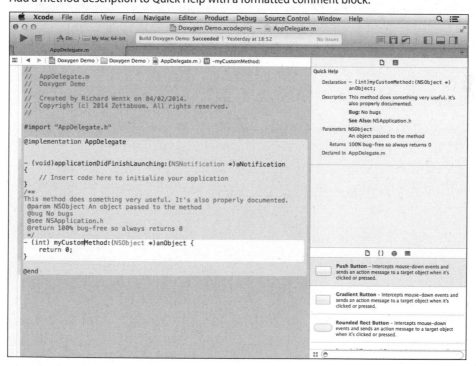

The figure shows a comment formatted with the @param, @bug, @see, and @return keywords, which define a parameter description, a highlighted bug description, a cross reference, and a return parameter description. You can see how Xcode renders the content in the Quick Help window.

Currently Xcode doesn't support extended formatting features, such as the use of @n to create a new line. This may change in future updates.

Figure 4.20 shows you can add a triple slash before a property declaration to create a Quick Help property description. You must use a triple slash, and the description must fit on a single line. Quick Help automatically adds the declaration, prints your description text, and adds a clickable cross reference.

CAUTION

If you use forward declarations, add the comment blocks to the forward declaration. If you add it later, Xcode ignores it.

Figure 4.20

...And you can create a property description with a triple slash line.

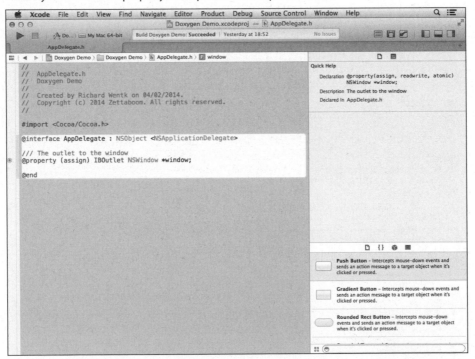

Using the library area

The library area, shown in Figure 4.21, displays four types of files and objects. You can select them with the icons that appear in the toolbar at the top of the sub-pane:

- The File Template Library is a list of file types that you can add to a project. There's some overlap with the file templates introduced in Chapter 3, but the list that appears here is longer and includes files that are used with Interface Builder (IB) and the Core Data editor. To add a file to your project, open the Project Navigator, drag a file from the list in this library, and drop it into a group.

- The Code Snippet Library was introduced in Chapter 1. You can use it to add boiler-plate code to your project. For details, see Chapter 9.

- The Object Library is used with Interface Builder. Use it to select a standard OS X or iOS UI or data object, and add it to your project. For details, see Chapter 7.

- The Media Library manages media files that you add to the project. For details, see Chapter 8.

Figure 4.21

Explore the File Templates in the library area to learn how to add files to your project by dragging them from this area and dropping them into the Project Navigator.

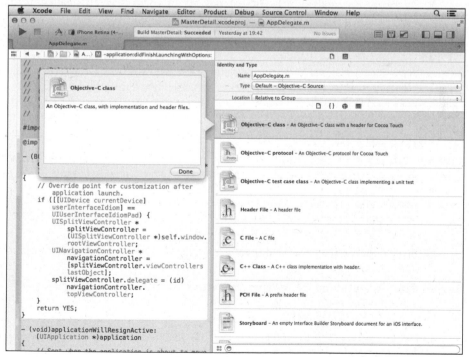

Most library use is drag and drop: You can drag objects from the library and drop them into the project's file list or in a suitable editor. iOS and OS X support different object and class libraries.

CAUTION
This library area allows you to drop OS X objects into an iOS project, and vice versa. This isn't usually a useful thing to do.

Working with the Editor Area

The key features of the editor area, including basic class and file navigation and the new Assistant feature, were outlined in Chapter 1. In this area, you can do the following:

- Edit code. In addition to simple typing, the code editor includes hidden features such as *code completion,* which automatically suggests code as you type.
- View two associated files in adjacent panes—typically an implementation file and its associated header, or a nib file and its related source code.
- Create a visual UI layout for your application.
- Design the schema of a Core Data database.
- Compare previous and current versions of a file side by side.
- Define *build settings*—the list of switches, options, files, and other elements that define how source files are converted into one or more binaries.

TIP
There are forward and back arrows at the top left of the editor. They're very easy to miss, but they're an essential timesaver. They work like the forward and back buttons on a browser. For example, if you are currently viewing code but you were previously viewing a UI layout in Interface Builder, the back button switches the editor back to IB for you automatically.

Getting started with code editing

Although code editing seems simple—start typing and stop when you're done—it can take time to get accustomed to the hidden features in Xcode, which include the following:

- **Code completion:** This is a fairly sophisticated feature that makes educated guesses about possible code as you type. You can insert the suggested code with the Tab key or select a different educated guess from a floating menu.
- **Error checking:** As you have already seen, Xcode checks code as you type and highlights errors.
- **Auto-indentation:** This indents the cursor position automatically, taking into account preceding code.
- **Bracket matching:** When you type a closing bracket or move the cursor over it with the right-arrow key, the matching open bracket flashes yellow. If there is no matching bracket, Xcode plays a short warning sound.
- **Bracket generation:** Type a new method signature and an opening curly bracket, and then press Return. Xcode adds a closing curly bracket and positions the cursor on the first blank line of the method.

- **Square bracket balancing:** For square brackets only, Xcode adds an opening square bracket when you type a closing square bracket. Although this feature can be useful, it lacks intelligence, and sometimes you need to remove the brackets it creates.

The easiest way to master these features is to experiment with them. They're often very helpful, but occasionally you may need to use them in a lateral way. For example, the simplest way to insert a new line of code is to click with the mouse at the end of the previous line and press Return. Xcode inserts a blank line and indents the cursor as needed. Placing the cursor before the insertion position doesn't indent the code when you begin typing.

Using code completion
The easiest way to illustrate code completion is with an example.

Create a new project using the iOS Single View Application template. Save it with any name; in this example, I use myCleverApp. Open the Project Navigator, and select the `AppDelegate.m` file so the code appears in the editor.

Click with the mouse at the end of a line of code in any method. In this example, I use the `application didFinishLaunchingWithOptions:` method. But code completion isn't limited to any one method or class; it works throughout a project.

Type **[UIA**, as shown in Figure 4.22. Code completion pops up the menu shown in the figure. `UIApplication` is highlighted to indicate that this is code completion's best guess. To accept the guess, press the Tab key or the Return key. Either inserts `UIApplication` in full. To select a different guess, you can scroll down the menu with the mouse or the cursor keys.

Figure 4.22

Xcode 5's Code Completion feature tries to guess what you're trying to type.

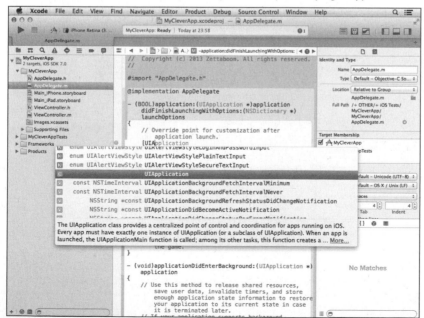

CAUTION

When you press Return, Xcode always inserts the most likely code completion. When you press Tab, Xcode inserts a partial completion, but leaves the selection menu open so you can choose the rest of the completion manually.

Code completion is a fast symbol listing tool. It has some very basic intelligence and context awareness, but it can't read your mind, and it can't tell whether you want to add a class, a function, or an enumerated constant, so it shows you all the options that fit your clue string.

TIP

In Xcode 5, code completion is somewhat aware of context. If you repeat the exercise in `ViewController.m`, you see that code completion recognizes `UIView`. It doesn't do so in the `AppDelegate.m` file because you wouldn't usually add a view to an app delegate.

To use code completion efficiently, type enough characters to allow it to find a match. The full extended list of pop-up guesses is less useful, although it can be a good memory jogger—for example, when you can't remember a list of constants.

If you add a method that takes parameters, code completion highlights the parameters for you and allows you to tab between them. In the example shown in Figure 4.23, you would tab to the `NSString` parameter and then type over it. When a method has multiple parameters, you can skip between them by tabbing.

Figure 4.23

Use the Tab key to skip to a parameter field. The current type-over area appears highlighted in blue.

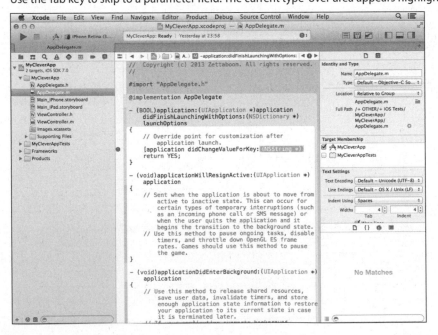

If you're getting started with Xcode, it's a good idea to spend enough time practicing with this feature to make it second nature. Although you can use the arrow keys to move between parameters, this tab-type-skip feature is a significant timesaver.

Using auto-indentation

Auto-indentation works as you'd expect, moving the cursor to the correct horizontal location in the code. It's smart enough to keep track of nest brackets and other features. If you auto-indent a line and the cursor doesn't appear where you expect it to, it's likely there's a missing bracket on a preceding line. This is a useful feature, not a bug. You can indent with spaces or tab characters and select the number of indentation spaces using the File Information area introduced earlier in this chapter.

Using the Structure pop-up menu

Select a few of lines of code inside a method, right-click, and select Structure from the menu that appears, as shown in Figure 4.24. This menu has some extremely useful features. You can move the code left or right as a single block manually, re-indent it automatically to its ideal indentation level, or convert it into a comment.

Figure 4.24

Use the Structure pop-up menu; it's a powerful timesaver.

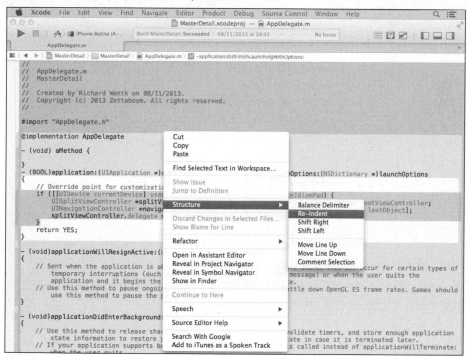

The Balance Delimiter feature highlights the code between matching brackets. Use it to confirm that your brackets are balanced correctly. Move Line Up and Move Line Down swap the code block with the line above it or below it.

This menu is another essential timesaver. Getting into the habit of using it without thinking about it can save significant development effort.

Introducing build management

Build management options are discussed in detail in Chapters 12, 13, and 14. The rest of this chapter includes a very simple introduction to the options, settings, and configurations, because they appear in the Editor window—as long as you know where to find them.

Build management options define the compiler and linker settings Xcode uses to build a project, and the sequence of steps it follows to convert your source code into one or more binaries.

Xcode includes a number of build management panes. You can edit compiler and linker options in one of the *build settings* panes. A major source of confusion is the fact that every project has two sets of settings, called *configurations.* Table 4.1 summarizes what they are, and how you use them. (You can add further custom configurations, but you rarely need to.)

Table 4.1 Default Build Configurations

Category	OS	Comments
Debug	iOS	Used for testing and development.
Release	iOS	Must be edited to create builds for the App Store and for Ad Hoc app release.
Debug	OS X	Used for testing and development.
Release	OS X	Can be used to create an application that can be used as-is or packaged with an installer. Can be edited to create a special build for the OS X App Store, or for public release signed with a developer identity certificate.

Understanding project and target build management

Xcode makes a further distinction between project and target build management. In Xcode, a target is a set of instructions for building a single binary. It includes the settings for both configurations, with further build instructions. A project is a file container that supplies build defaults and also holds the files that can be compiled into binaries. For example, a Mac OS X project might create an app and a framework as separate targets.

You can work with the project/target system in various ways. But typically, you set up project defaults for all binaries, then customize target settings only if you need to.

Figure 4.25 shows an example of project build settings. If you don't know how to find this page in the editor, it's easy to miss. To make it appear, click the project icon at the top of the Project Navigator. Click Build Settings from the header near the top of the editor. Then click the disclosure triangle near the top left of the editor to show the project and its targets.

Figure 4.25

Look again at project build settings. You can leave most of the compiler- and build-specific settings unchanged.

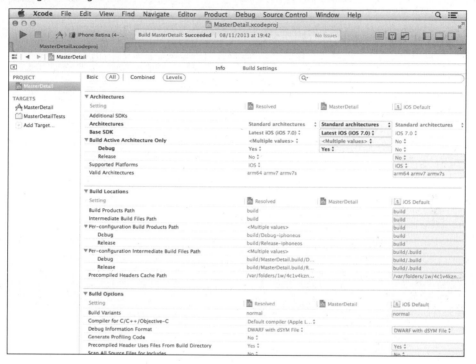

Next, click the Build Settings tab. You can now click the PROJECT icon in the gutter to edit the project build settings, or click one of the icons under TARGETS to edit the target settings.

Understanding project and target build settings

The settings are the heart of Xcode, and they're also one of its more complex features. A key point is that target settings can override the project defaults.

They're part of the general build management system, which defines extra runtime details for the target, including icon files, *plists* (property lists), and other specialized features used to create one particular binary. For example, under the Info tab you can see a list of optional settings, including supported document types, and URL types that allow applications to exchange data with each other. You can use them to define a *URL scheme* or a *Uniform Type Identifier*—an inter-application interface—that allows other apps to launch and run your app and to pass it data. Figure 4.26 shows some of the target settings.

Figure 4.26

Look at target build settings, which configure your app's special features.

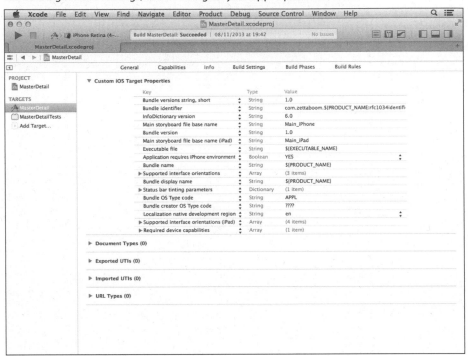

You can also set *Capabilities* for both iOS and OS X apps, which control the special Apple services that your app can access.

CAUTION

Although the Capabilities settings look like simple toggle switches, they need plenty of extra added code before your app can use them. Unfortunately, toggling the switch does not add the code.

As with the project build settings, you can leave most of the target build settings unchanged. A few are critical and are described below and in Chapters 12 and 13. Most can be left as defaults.

CAUTION

Although you can ignore most of the build system for simple app development, you must know how to make standard changes to the settings before you can sell apps through the App Stores. The full build system is complex and includes projects, targets, schemes, configurations, actions, phases, rules—and more. Don't worry if it doesn't make sense yet. Chapters 12, 13, and 14 introduce the details and explain how to manage builds as efficiently as possible.

Adding frameworks

Although you can ignore most of the detail you see here for now, one of the critical options in the Build section is the framework list. When you build an app that uses Apple's frameworks, you must tell Xcode to include the frameworks before you build. This is a two-stage process. You must include the framework headers. And you must add the frameworks to your target, so Xcode can link against them and include the binaries they use. For practical details, see the next chapter.

Summary

The three main Xcode 5 panes are the heart of Xcode. You can use them to write code and take advantage of code completion and live code checking. You can also use them to manage the files in your project, configure build settings, add code snippets and interface objects, and find help.

In general, these panes are straightforward and streamlined. They include a range of useful features, and you can save time and effort by taking the time to familiarize yourself with them, so using them becomes second nature.

Working with Files, Frameworks, and Classes

X code projects include a list of constituent files. When you build a project, Xcode processes each file in turn. Source code files are compiled into binaries and linked together. Resource files are copied to the project's output folder, also known as its *bundle*.

Each step in the process is known as a *build phase*. If your project has special requirements, you can customize the build phases or create custom build phases—for example, to compile source code in a specific sequence, allowing for dependencies. More typically, you can use the default build phases as they are.

You can define the files included in a project in two ways. The simple way is to use the file management features built into the Project navigator. For more advanced management, you can use the features introduced in Chapter 13 to customize Xcode's default build phases. For simple apps, you can usually ignore this option, because the build phases "just work."

CROSS-REFERENCE
For more information about custom builds and build phases, see Chapter 12.

In This Chapter

Adding new files to a project

Working with groups

Working with frameworks

Working with Files and Classes

The Project Navigator includes all the features you need for basic file and class management. The Navigator is easy to work with, but it's worth emphasizing again that there is an indirect relationship between the files and *folders* (or groups) that appear in the Navigator and the contents of the project folder on disk.

When you create a new Xcode project, the new files are added to a single folder. But this is a convenience, not a necessity.

You can create a working project where the "official" project folder is empty and every file is in a different physical folder. Project files don't have to be local; they can be anywhere on disk or on a network. This makes it easy to reuse source code and create libraries. The same library code can be referenced from multiple projects without copying.

This applies equally to C/C++ source code, Objective-C class definitions, and resources such as graphics files. If you use a library of custom icons or button graphics, you can keep the image files in a single folder and import them into multiple projects as needed.

There are advantages and disadvantages to keeping files in multiple locations. The advantage is that you can keep single copies and reuse them in multiple projects. The disadvantage is that it becomes harder to keep safety copies of the files in a project. It also becomes harder to use the source control management (SCM) features introduced in Chapter 15.

TIP

Typically, after you build a project, Xcode copies graphics files into the application bundle. It's not unusual to accumulate a small collection of test and comp images, only some of which appear in the project. With the new assets feature in Xcode 5, you can compile the images you want into a single file and avoid copying the others.

Adding new files to a project

Xcode includes a selection of *file templates* that add prewritten content. These typically include classes with headers and implementation files. Some include minimal but useful boilerplate setup and teardown code.

The templates are similar to the application templates introduced in Chapter 3. Instead of creating a complete application, they add a useful building block to an existing application. The templates for iOS and OS X are slightly different, but they overlap significantly—much more than for the equivalent application templates.

You can add new files to a project in two ways: using Xcode's New File menu option or by dragging and dropping the file from a template in Xcode's utility area.

Using the New File menu option

You can select the New File menu option from the main Xcode menu via File ➪ New ➪ New File. You can also right-click in or on a group and select New File from the contextual menu that appears when you right-click on a group, as shown in Figure 5.1.

Selecting New File displays the file template list, shown in Figure 5.2. You can select OS X or iOS templates from the list and then choose sub-types from the two panes at the left.

Figure 5.1

Add a file using the New File option.

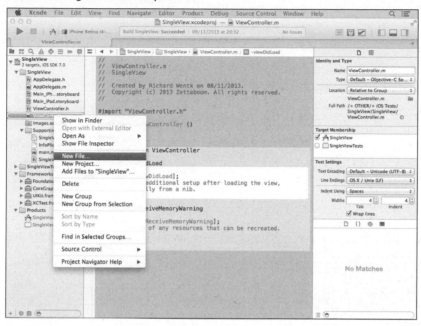

Figure 5.2

Select the file template from the iOS and OS X panes.

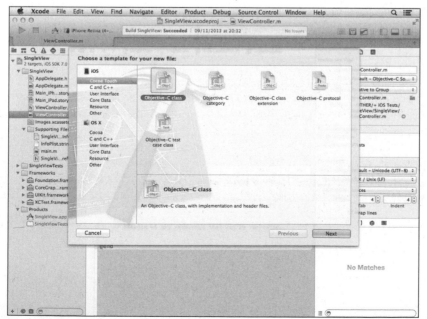

Use the dialog shown in Figure 5.3 to enter a name for your new class and to select the super-class it's going to be a subclass of. The Subclass of box has no intelligence or context awareness. It simply remembers the last selection you made.

Figure 5.3

Select the class name and superclass.

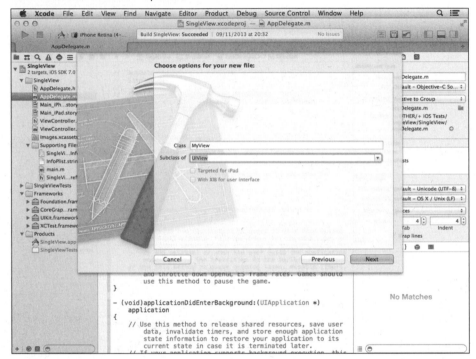

If you are creating a view controller subclass, you can choose to add an XIB (i.e., nib) file for UI resources and optionally to set it up for the iPad. Because iOS projects use storyboards, you can often—but not always—ignore these check boxes. For more information, see Chapters 12 and 13.

CAUTION

It can be easy to miss the fact that the Subclass of box includes a full list of Cocoa/Cocoa Touch classes, as well as any classes you added to the project. It looks like an automatic setting, but in fact it's a completely manual menu.

Select the on-disk file location and the project group with the dialog shown in Figure 5.4. By default, the file is added to the project folder and the default group. Optionally, you can choose to save it to a different location using the usual OS X file selection options and place it in a different group using the Group menu.

Figure 5.4

Select the file location, group, and target.

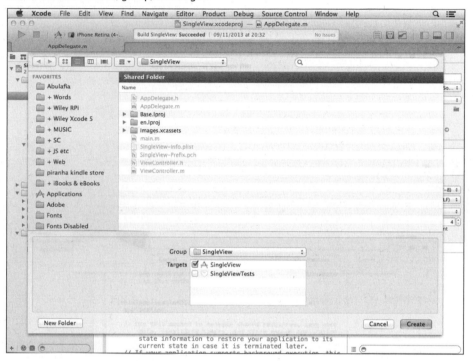

You can also choose to add the file to any of the optional targets in your project by clicking any of the extra Targets check boxes. The default option adds the file to the build list for the default target.

After this dialog disappears, the file is added to the Project Navigator inside the group that you right-clicked.

NOTE

To emphasize again, the file always appears in the Project Navigator, no matter where you save it on disk. For practical reasons, it's a good idea to save project files to the project folder. You don't have to do this, but if you don't, you may have to keep track of file locations by hand. If you move the project folder to a different location, Xcode may not be able to adjust its file references, and the project may not build.

Using drag-and-drop from the Utility area

To use the drag-and-drop feature, select the File Template Library icon if it isn't already selected, and drag the divider up from the bottom of the screen if the files aren't visible.

Xcode 4 included an option to filter the list to show either iOS or OS X files. Xcode 5 has lost the filter, so you not only see files for both operating systems, you also see what look like duplicates.

The iOS Cocoa Touch class and OS X Cocoa class files are subtly different, so leaving the distinction would have been helpful. As a general rule, the files above the OS X Cocoa class are compatible with iOS, and the rest are compatible with OS X. But some of the data types—GeoJSON, NSManagedObject, and GPX—are compatible with both.

With the drag-and-drop option, you can select a template and drop it directly into any group, as shown in Figure 5.5. The naming/saving step is identical to that shown in Figure 5.3.

Figure 5.5

Add a file with template drag-and-drop.

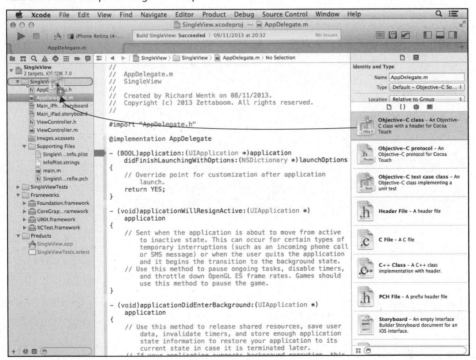

Comparing the New File and drag-and-drop options

The drag-and-drop option is quicker and simpler than using New File, because it skips the sub-class selection step and nib creation shown in Figure 5.3. If you create a class, it is set as a sub-class of NSObject, unless you edit the header manually.

However, you can add an optional tag to the file, as shown in Figure 5.6. This adds a colored dot next to the file in Finder. (Possibly not an essential extra.)

Figure 5.6

In Xcode 5, you can now tag files with a colored dot.

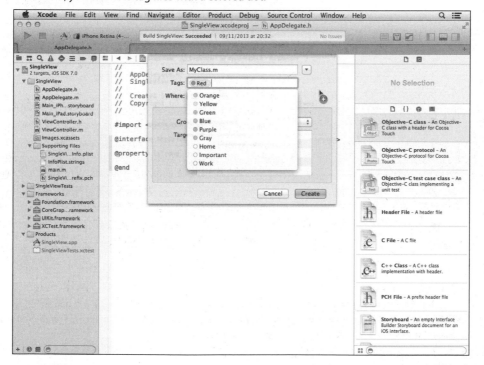

Naming new files

Xcode doesn't enforce a naming convention for new files. A few clases, such as view controllers and windows, get an automatic suffix such as viewcontroller or window, and you can add your own prefix. Others are left blank, so it's up to you to create a naming scheme that works for you. Terse and obscure names such as AClass or MyClass will confuse you later and are best avoided.

Adding a new class

When you add a new Objective-C class, Xcode automatically adds a header file to the project. Where needed, it also adds a matching implementation file to the project. There are six templates for iOS classes and five templates for OS X classes, with significant overlap, as shown in Table 5.1.

Table 5.1 Objective-C File Templates

Template	Availability	Comments
Objective-C class	iOS/OS X	This is a minimal Objective-C class with a header file. By default, this creates a subclass of `NSObject`. You can edit the header to create a subclass of any other Cocoa object.
`UIView Controller` subclass	iOS only	This creates a subclass of `UIViewController` with a header, an implementation with sample code. If you add this template with drag-and-drop, you can choose to create a default nib file and select iPhone or iPad screen sizes. The sample code includes code to load a nib file and an empty `viewDidLoad:` stub. There's no OS X equivalent that creates an `NSWindow` or `NSView` with an associated nib.
`NSManaged Object` subclass	iOS/OS X	This is a subclass of `NSManagedObject`, with a header, for use in Core Data applications. This template doesn't include sample code or method definitions.
Objective-C `NSObject` category	iOS/OS X	This creates a header and implementation file for an empty category on `NSObject`. You can edit the class name to create a category on some other Cocoa class, and you can add custom methods to extend that class with your own features.
Objective-C protocol	iOS/OS X	This creates a header file with a protocol declaration. Depending on the context, it's sometimes easier to ignore this option and add the protocol code directly to a class.
Objective-C test case class	iOS/OS X	This creates a header and implementation file for the XCTest test framework. This is used exclusively for automated testing. For more details, see Chapter 18.

CAUTION
You can add iOS templates to OS X projects, and vice versa. For example, Xcode 5 allows you to add an OS X menu to an iOS application. An iOS project with a menu nib file builds correctly, even though the menu isn't referenced by the code. It's included—as a waste of space—in the app bundle.

Adding new resources

Although it's often useful to add new windows and views to a project, the templates make this unnecessarily complex. It would be useful to add nibs and supporting source code in a single step, but the templates don't support this. Instead, you must add a suitable nib from a list of resource files and then add supporting classes manually.

The one exception to this is the `UIViewController` subclass template for iOS, which creates source code files and gives you the option to create an associated nib. (Although it's more likely you'll use a storyboard.) For other tasks, you must add and edit the nib files by hand, add supporting class files separately, and then reclass the nibs so they're linked to the source code. For more details, see Chapters 7 and 8. Table 5.2 lists the nib files that are available.

Table 5.2 Nib File Templates

Template	Availability	Comments
Application	iOS/OS X	The OS X nib includes a Font Manager, a Main Menu, a Window and View, and an Application object. Note that there's no App Delegate. The iOS version of this nib includes an App Delegate object and a `UIWindow`.
Storyboard	iOS Only	This is an empty storyboard for iOS. Add objects as needed.
Main Menu	OS X Only	A menu tree, with many default menu items. If you create an OS X application from a template, it already includes this item.
Window	iOS/OS X	The OS X nib includes an `NSWindow` with an associated `NSView`. The iOS nib includes a `UIWindow` only.
View	iOS/OS X	The OS X nib includes an `NSView`. The iOS nib includes a `UIView`.
Empty	iOS/OS X	On both platforms, this is a plain, empty nib. Only the File's Owner and First Responder placeholders are included.

TIP

It's worth repeating that in Cocoa and Cocoa Touch, nib files are *general object containers*. Although they're usually used for UI resources, you can use them for any application that needs to load objects from a file. They may not be the best solution for object loading, but they're always worth considering as a possibility.

Adding miscellaneous other files from the templates

The templates include a selection of other files. You can add them to a project in the usual ways.

- The C/C++ templates add a standard C or C++ pair of header and implementation files. The C++ files are minimal `ifndef`/`endif` pairs.

- The Shell Script and Assembly File templates support shell scripts and assembly code, respectively. You can run a shell script as part of a custom build. Assembly code is used for very specialized hardware-level coding.

- The Asset Catalog template creates an asset catalog file, with compressed support for images and other project assets.

- The Core Data templates include a Data Model file and a Mapping Model file. You can add these to projects that support Core Data. If your project doesn't use Core Data, you can ignore them.

- Use the Rich Text Format (RTF) and Strings File templates to add text-based data. The Strings file is used for *localization*—non-English language support. For details, see Chapter 12. The RTF file is a standard text file. You can use it to hold any string- or text-based data. For OS X applications, you can use an RTF file to define the information that appears in an application's About box.

- The Settings Bundle and Property Lists (plists) include an empty XML plist file for general property preferences and settings. Both iOS and OS X applications already include an `info.plist` file with basic application details. The iOS templates include a separate Settings Bundle, which uses an iOS-specific format to store an app's settings and preferences. Note that if you don't care about your app's preferences appearing on the iOS General Preferences page, you can invent your own system to store preferences.

- The SpriteKit Particle File defines a default particle emitter system—a graphics tool for creating animated sparks, fire, fog, snow, magic zaps, rocket exhausts, and other game effects. You can edit the system using the Node Editor in the utility pane, as shown in Figure 5.7.

Figure 5.7

Use this template to add and edit a particle emitter system.

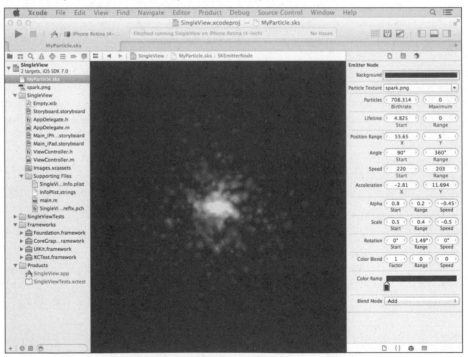

- Resource Rules are signed certificates that can be used to lock your application to specific hardware or software environments. Code-signing is a complex topic. For practical details, see Chapters 11 and 12.

● You can use a Configuration Settings File to create your own list of build settings for a project—for example, to create your own build setting defaults. For information about custom builds, see Chapters 12 and 13.

TIP

If you change the file extension of an Objective-C file to `.mm`, it builds as Objective-C++. As long as you keep the object trees separate, you can include both Cocoa and C++ objects, and use C++ code idioms.

CAUTION

However, if you create a C++ class from the Xcode file template, the `.cpp` file has the correct type, but the `.h` header file is set up as a C header. This can sometimes cause build problems. Be sure to set the `.h` file to the C++ header type in the utility pane when you create a class.

Deleting and renaming files

You can delete a file with the Delete key, or by right-clicking a file and selecting the Delete option from the contextual menu. When you delete a file, a dialog appears asking you if you want to remove it from the project and leave it on disk ("Remove Reference") or move it to the trash. If you leave it on disk, you can re-import it later if you change your mind about the deletion. This can be a good safety net for small projects, but on large projects, it's likely to clutter up the project folder with unnecessary files.

To rename a file, click once to select it in the Project Navigator and type in the new name. You also can enter the name in the file pane of the Utility area. Figure 5.8 is a composite that shows both options. Renaming a file changes its name in the project and also renames it on disk.

Figure 5.8

You can rename a file in two ways.

TIP

If you want to rename a class throughout a project, use the Refactor ⇨ Rename option. It renames files and class references in the code. Unfortunately, it works only for Objective-C code, and doesn't support C++.

CAUTION

File extensions are significant, but changing the extension isn't enough to change how Xcode processes the file during a build. If you need to change the type of a file and modify how it contributes to a build, select a new type from the list in the File Type drop-down menu in the File pane of the Utility area.

Renaming projects

As a rule—don't. It's important to understand that Xcode doesn't have a single project name. The project folder name, the Xcode project filename, the class prefixes used in the project, the target name, and the final app name as it appears on a device are all distinct and separate.

If you're not reusing code, the only name that really matters is the final app name. You can set this in the build settings. Otherwise, under the hood, Xcode only cares about file paths. As long as these are distinct, filenames are secondary. You can have two projects with the same name and the same filenames open in two editor windows, and Xcode won't get them confused.

If you are sharing code, it's useful to create different custom prefixes for each project or to define your own prefixes for a reusable library, depending on your needs.

Generally, the project name is for your convenience. It has no effect on the final application name, and duplicated project names don't cause problems.

Importing existing files

Because Xcode's file templates aren't exhaustive, you often need to import into project files created with other editors, such as graphics, sound files, HTML web pages, PDF documents, and so on. During a build, these non-standard file types are copied to the application folder without processing. Xcode includes preview features for a small selection of file types, most obviously for graphics. But you must edit and prepare these files using other tools.

To import a file or folder, right-click a group and select the Add Files to. . . menu option. You'll see the dialog in Figure 5.9. Navigate to the folder with the files, and then select the import options using the check box and radio button.

Optionally, you can copy files from the source folder into the project folder. If you leave the Destination box unchecked, files are left in their original location and accessed via a reference. Generally, it's good practice to copy files that are unique to the project, but to use references for files that are reused by many projects.

You can also create groups or folder references for added folders. Although I've emphasized that groups aren't necessarily mirrored in a project's folder structure, you can use this option and the group management features introduced in the next section to create folders on disk that match the groups in the Project Navigator. This step isn't essential, but it can make a project easier to navigate if you're reusing its classes and resources.

Figure 5.9

Add an image file to a project from the Pictures folder.

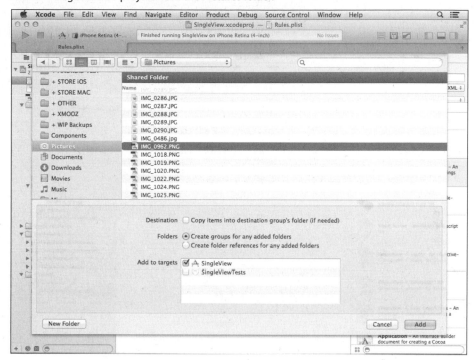

Reimporting missing files

As long as you leave a file's Location option set to Relative to Group in the File pane of the utility area, you can move a project folder to a different location on disk without breaking the file references.

However, Xcode does occasionally glitch and lose files from a project. If you move items that are referenced indirectly in a different folder, Xcode may not be able to find them. And if you import a project created by an older version of Xcode, the Location option may not have been set correctly.

Broken references appear in the Project Navigator in red. As long as you can find the original file on disk, you can fix a broken reference by hand. Click the folder-like icon next to the filename under the Location menu in the File pane, as shown in Figure 5.10. You'll see a standard file selector. Use it to navigate to the file and click Choose when done. Xcode repairs the reference.

Figure 5.10

Repairing a file path is easy.

TIP

You can use this option to swap in different versions of the same file. There are more powerful ways to manage source files in Xcode, but this option is a robust and simple way to compare the current version of a file with an older backup, as long as you create backup folders as you go.

Working with Groups

Groups are cosmetic, for your convenience. You can use any group structure, nested as deeply as you like. The default structure with separate class and resource folders is only one of many possible arrangements. You also may create a separate group for each class or (less usefully) a single group for every file in the project.

Moving groups and files

Files are compiled more or less in descending order through the Navigator. Circular class references are handled automatically, so there's no significant speed advantage to reordering the groups. But it's sometimes useful to modify the group order for clarity.

You can drag and drop groups in the Project Navigator, but dropping a group on another group nests it, which may not be what you want.

To move a group to the top of the list, drop it on the Project item at the top of the Navigator. To rearrange all groups into a new order, you need to do this repeatedly. This can be a tedious process, especially if you have many groups. As of Xcode 5.1, there doesn't appear to an easy way to drag a group and drop it so it appears between other groups.

Moving files is much easier. You can simply drag a file from one group and drop it in another. Any file can be moved to any group.

Creating a new group

To add a new group, right-click the Project item and select New Group from the menu, as shown in Figure 5.11. You also can select multiple items in the Navigator using any of the standard Mac multi-select options and collect them into a single new group by selecting New Group from Selection.

Figure 5.11

You can add a new group from the floating menu or use File ➪ New ➪ New Group in the main Xcode menu.

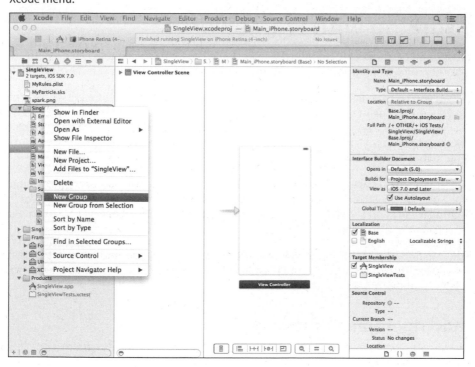

TIP
To create a new group inside an existing group, right-click the existing group instead of the Project item. You can nest groups almost indefinitely.

Organizing groups

Because groups are completely free-form, you can organize your project however you like. There's no need to use the default organization, with separate class and resource groups. For example:

● For an iOS project, collect each view controller and its associated nib into a separate group. This is usually easier to navigate than keeping classes and nibs separated.

● If your project uses many supporting graphics files, group them into a separate Graphics folder to keep them distinct from other resources. This simplifies graphic previews and makes it easier to find the project nib files.

● Similarly, you can keep other project resources such as plists and code-signing files in a separate group to keep them out of your way.

● Source code for frameworks and libraries should have its own separate groups, especially if the files are imported from a standard location on disk. It's a good idea to keep these items separated from project source code.

Working with Frameworks

Apple's frameworks are prewritten libraries that can be imported into any project to add specific features, such as support for video, sound, data management, or various hardware features.

When you build an OS X or iOS project, you may need to add one or more of Apple's frameworks to your project before you can use them. A selection of default frameworks is included in every application template; for example, OS X projects always include the Cocoa and AppKit frameworks, and iOS projects always include UIKit, CoreGraphics, and XCTest. All projects include the Foundation framework.

Other frameworks are optional, and you must add them manually. For example, you must add the SpriteKit framework to use the classes and methods built into SpriteKit. If you don't, the compiler can't find the symbols included in the framework, and your build fails, sometimes spectacularly, with hundreds of errors.

You can find a list of the frameworks included in your project near the lower left of the Project Navigator. This list is critical to a successful build. Adding frameworks to this list is not a completely intuitive process.

Adding Apple frameworks

Adding Apple frameworks is a two-stage process. You must include the framework headers in your project header files. And you must add the frameworks to your target, so Xcode can link against them and include the binaries they use. The framework list is hidden in the Link Binary with Libraries option under the Build Phases tab, as shown in Figure 5.12.

Figure 5.12

Framework management in Xcode 5 is not entirely intuitive.

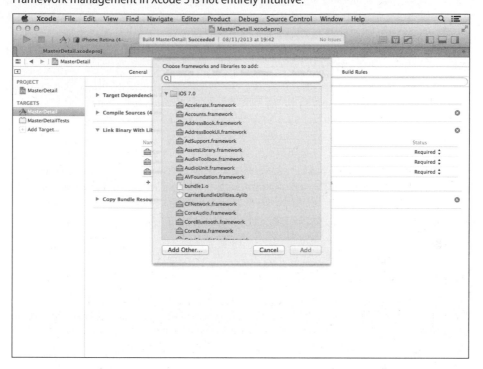

To add a framework, select your project in the Project Navigator, select the TARGETS icon in the gutter, and select Build Phases. Click the Link Binary with Libraries reveal triangle, and then select the plus (+) icon at the lower left.

You can now select a framework from the list that appears, as shown in the figure. Note that the framework is added to the project root, not to the Frameworks group. Although the location doesn't affect compilation, you may want to move it for clarity.

To delete a framework from the project, select it in the Link Binary with Libraries table and click the minus (-) icon.

TIP

Although you can't use the Add Files option to add system frameworks, you can *sometimes* use it to add third-party frameworks. When you add source code from a third-party framework to a project, in theory it's automatically added to the link list. In practice, third-party frameworks often have their own build tools, so it's more common to either build them from the command line and access them via headers, or—if you're lucky— the creators of the framework supply it as a complete Xcode project you can extend with your own code.

T I P

If you do get hundreds of errors while building, it usually means you've forgotten to import a framework. Typically, most of the errors disappear after you add the framework correctly. Don't forget that you also need to import the framework's header file into every file that references it in your project.

Using frameworks

Although you could add every framework to every project, this would slow build times to a crawl. Depending on the build options, including every framework might also create huge binaries. So it's standard practice to add only the frameworks that are referenced by your code.

T I P

You'll often use at least one of the standard graphics frameworks and perhaps also one of the animation frameworks. It's easy to forget to add frameworks, and adding the headers by hand is a chore. You can save time by creating a default project that already includes a more realistic and useful selection of frameworks than are included in the standard Apple templates.

Apple frameworks include a binary with associated header files, as shown in Figure 5.13. When you add a framework, Xcode adds both the header and the binary to its build list. The header is referenced during compilation, and references to the binary are added while linking.

Figure 5.13

The framework header files include useful comments that often add extra detail and insight that isn't available in the more formal class reference documentation.

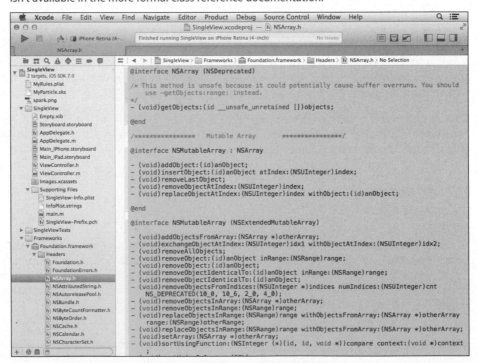

Adding other frameworks

You also can add third-party frameworks. Some frameworks are supplied as Xcode projects. The easiest way to work with these is to create a new *workspace*—a work area that can hold multiple projects—and set up your project so it builds the framework as a target first (known as a *dependency*, because your project depends on the framework) and then builds and links the rest of your project.

Some frameworks are supplied with full source code. You can usually add these by dragging the folders into your project. This does not always work, because Xcode imports headers by file path, not by relative references. So some experimentation may be necessary before you can get a framework to build from scratch.

More commonly, popular frameworks are supplied with their own build scripts. You must install the command-line tools, introduced in Appendix A, to build these frameworks using commands typed in Terminal. Typically, a single script runs a complex sequence of commands. You can then import the compiled binary as a library, using the same steps you would use for an Apple framework, but selecting the file location manually. Finally, you can import the headers with drag-and-drop and use them in your project.

The most popular and widely used frameworks are often supplied with instructions. They may also have mailing list and/or forum support if you have questions.

Less popular and more experimental frameworks are harder to work with. At worst, they may not build at all, for many possible reasons. At best, they build immediately. It's not unusual to spend hours or days trying to integrate a framework with your project.

TIP

You can sometimes save time by contacting the creator of a framework and asking for help. They're not obliged to help you, but many who can help do.

CROSS-REFERENCE

Chapter 14 includes an example of building a project around the code from a third-party framework.

Summary

The fact that the file and group management tools in the Project Navigator are symbolic links and not literal file listings confuses many Xcode newcomers. The symbolic link system is more flexible than literal file copying, and it simplifies code reuse. But it can take a while to understand the differences between a project folder listing and the Xcode 5 project.

Generally, there are some gotchas in file management, and it's important to understand them. The navigator and the utility pane file view hint at the deeper workings of Xcode, which only become clear after you understand the build process in more detail, as described in Chapters 12 and 13.

Using Documentation

The iOS and OS X development tools are supported by Reference Libraries, documentation that provides orientation information for new developers and describes specific features in detail.

Newcomers often assume it's trivially easy to use the documentation. In fact, the organization and content are complex, and using the files effectively is a key developer skill.

The contents are vast. In paper form, they would require many feet of shelf space. To simplify access and to guarantee that the details are always up to date, the documentation is now stored online. You can access it using a conventional web browser, as shown in Figure 6.1, which illustrates the main iOS Developer Library access page. You can also access it via the documentation tools built into Xcode 5, which are described in the rest of this chapter.

CAUTION

The URLs for Apple's online documentation can change. To access the documentation, log in to either the iOS or OS X developer page and click the iOS or OS X Developer Library link.

TIP

When you begin with iOS or OS X, you often return to the same documentation pages over and over. The Xcode documentation viewer includes a bookmark feature to help with this. But it also can be useful to load your favorite pages into a separate tabbed browser and keep them open while you work. You can use the OS X Spaces feature to give the browser its own desktop.

In earlier versions of Xcode, the documentation files were downloaded as a single `.docset` file for each library. Xcode 5 continues to use docset files, as shown in Figure 6.2. When you first install Xcode 5, none of the current docsets are available.

You must open the Downloads tab in Xcode ⇨ Preferences and click each down-arrow button to download them. Allow between 2GB and 5GB of disk space for a full download.

CAUTION

The Documentation tab in Xcode 4 has been replaced by a Downloads tab in Xcode 5. It links to docsets and other optional components, such as older versions of the iOS Simulator. If you have slow broadband, it can take a few hours to download everything. For reliability, download items one at a time.

In This Chapter

Understanding the Apple documentation

Understanding resource types

Using the Xcode documentation viewer

Using other documentation

Figure 6.1

You can access the Developer Library using any browser, as shown here, or from the documentation viewer built into Xcode.

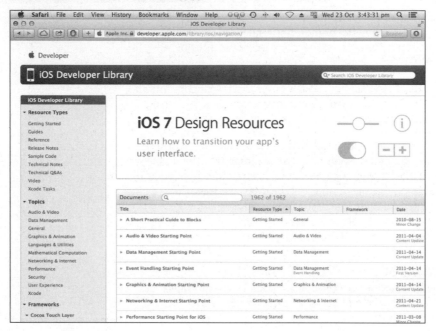

Figure 6.2

Because the docsets are large, allow plenty of time and bandwidth to download them.

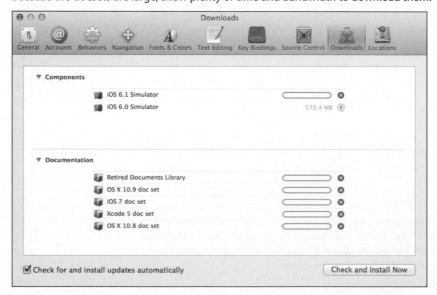

Understanding the Apple Documentation

Accessing the documentation from the web for the first time can feel overwhelming. The organization seems haphazard, and it's not clear which elements are essential, which are useful, and which are irrelevant. The contents are organized by OS and also by *resource types*—different kinds of information. Confusingly, there's significant overlap between the OS X and iOS documentation and between different versions of each OS.

Comparing iOS and OS X and their different versions

If you access the documentation from the web, the organization online doesn't distinguish between different versions of iOS and OS X. The iOS and OS X portals always show the most up-to-date content. This can be a beta version of the OS, which may not be what you want.

Xcode's own documentation viewer, shown in Figure 6.3, makes the differences between OS versions explicit. Each OS has a separate library header, so you can find the information you need without ambiguity. As shown in the figure, older versions may be absent, depending on where Apple is in its regular update cycle.

NOTE

You can access the viewer using Help ➪ Documentation and API Reference in the main menu or with the (option)+⌘+? keyboard shortcut.

Figure 6.3

Xcode's documentation can be accessed directly from the main menu or from the Quick Help option in the utility pane.

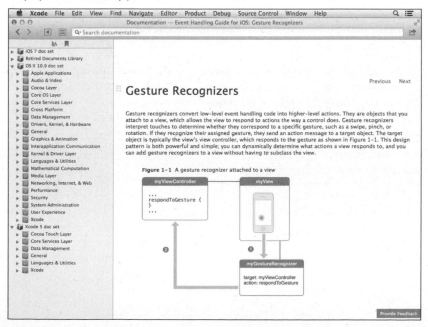

CAUTION

Xcode 5 no longer includes the documentation in the Organizer. You can access it only from the main menu or from Quick Help.

Some elements of Cocoa appear to be in both iOS and OS X. For example, iOS and OS X both include a class called NSArray. Most classes with identical names are genuinely identical on both platforms, but some have significant differences. You should always read the version for the correct OS.

In a beta version of an OS, the documentation may not be finished. You may find yourself reading about an OS X class even though you have followed a search trail looking for iOS classes. This doesn't often happen, but when it does, assume that the OS X details are also correct for iOS.

Understanding resource types

If you explore the web version of the documentation, you'll soon discover that topics are grouped in different ways and that there's significant redundancy and irrelevance in the libraries. Some elements in the documentation are more than 15 years old, and they describe features and techniques that are no longer in use.

To use the documentation effectively, you must understand these limitations and know how to find what you need without being distracted by irrelevant information. You also must understand the different resource types, which are listed at the top left of Figure 6.4. Whenever you view a collection of documents about a broad topic, you can sort them alphabetically or group them by resource type.

The resource types are less prominent when you view the documentation in Xcode. The content has been filtered so only the most relevant details appear. This makes the Xcode viewer easier to work with, especially when you're looking for specific information about a named class. But it does mean that some of the supporting details available on the web don't appear in the viewer.

Put simply, the web documentation and the Xcode documentation are not the same. Generally, the web version is set up to show all possible details, while the Xcode documentation is more focused by topic and sub-topic, with fewer distracting details.

NOTE

The Resource Types used to include Articles and Coding How-Tos. Both types have been pruned, with some content removed and other content folded into other types.

Figure 6.4

The resource types are listed at the top left of the Developer Library web pages. You're more likely to search for specific topics and references than for resource types.

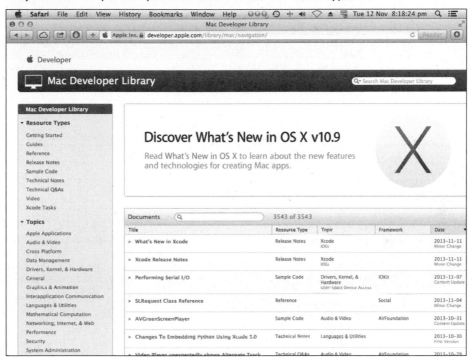

Getting Started

In spite of the name, the Getting Started guides aren't an ideal place to get started. Most guides are collections of links to detailed programming guides, surrounded by sparse extra information. These guides are factually accurate, but they gloss over many of the details and techniques used in actual programming practice. You can use them as orientation material that introduces key concepts and mentions useful classes, but you typically need to dig deeper and wider to fill in the gaps while coding. Figure 6.5 shows the Getting Started with Graphics and Animation document for OS X.

Figure 6.5

Don't think of the Getting Started guides as introductions to practical coding. But you can use them as outline orientations and as very brief and abstract introductions to key OS features.

Guides

The Guides include more detailed information about development and coding topics. These are the key orientation documents. Some guides, especially the human interface guidelines for iOS, iPad, and OS X, are essential reading. Part of the iPad Human Interface Guidelines document is shown in Figure 6.6.

However, the guide contents are often terse, and important practical points may be glossed over or missing. In practice, you sometimes need to look for successful working code in independent developer forums or in the code samples included with the documentation.

Figure 6.6

You should certainly read the Human Interface Guidelines for your target platforms before you begin developing. But you'll find it equally useful to look at the interfaces of popular and successful applications for a more practical view of application design.

References

The references—see Figure 6.7 for an example—are the most useful documents, and you'll spend most of your time reading them. The key references are listed below, and there's more detail about the structure of the references later in this chapter:

- Class references detail the properties, methods, and constants used in a class. This is key information: You won't be able to code without it.

- Protocol references are similar to class references, but list useful methods that you can build into your own subclasses using the Objective-C protocol mechanism. (For detailed information about protocols, see the companion *Cocoa* Developer Reference.)

● Framework references list the classes, functions, and protocols used in each framework. You should view the framework reference page for every framework you use in a project before you begin coding. Figure 6.7 shows the Foundation Framework, which is one of the most critical frameworks for Apple development. If you don't review the frameworks, you may miss useful functions, data types, and constants that aren't listed elsewhere. *Don't consider this optional.* You'll save hours of time if you review the features of each framework before you use it.

● Services references list extra OS interfaces that typically use C rather than Objective-C, and they work at a lower level than the main Cocoa libraries. These references are useful for specialized audio and graphics programming, but beginners can usually ignore them.

Figure 6.7

Because the frameworks aren't prioritized, it's not obvious that some frameworks are more important than others. The Foundation framework, AppKit on the Mac, and UIKit on iOS are key, and you should review their reference documentation before you start working with them.

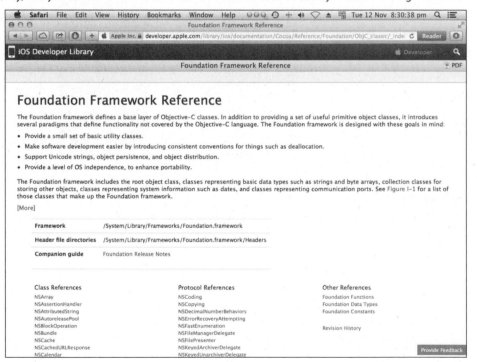

Release notes and API diffs

Release notes are short summaries of the new features and changes in an OS update. This type includes API diffs, which are a more formal list of changes detailing new classes added, old classes removed, and changed features within each class. API diffs are more useful, but it's worth reviewing both before you begin working with an OS update. Figure 6.8 shows part of a typical API diff file.

Figure 6.8

This API diff file lists the differences between iOS 6.1 and 7.0.

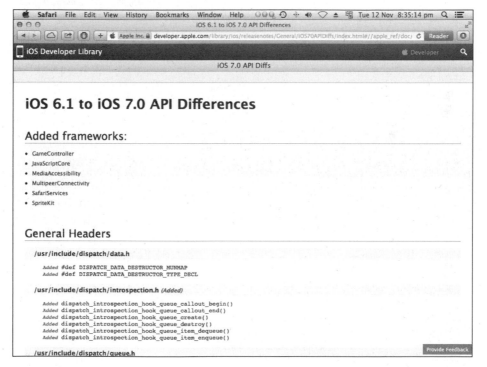

T I P

Note that each entry in the API diff file is a clickable link that takes you to the reference file for the class or method that has changed.

Sample code

The sample code section of the documentation is a library of sample projects that demonstrate key features and techniques. Many code samples are fairly complex and can be difficult to follow. Some are overly complex; they use advanced techniques and solutions when simpler code would work almost as effectively. Try reviewing the sample code for specific solutions and reverse-engineering it or using it with minor modifications. You can also find alternative solutions from other sources online, and they often illustrate useful techniques in a simpler and more accessible way.

If you view the sample code in a browser, you can list each file in a browser window. You can also click a Download Sample Code button at the top left of the window to download a complete zipped project file. For example, Figure 6.9 shows a project called CryptoExercise that implements a selection of cryptographic features.

Figure 6.9

With sample code, you can view the files individually or download the complete project, unzip it, and build it.

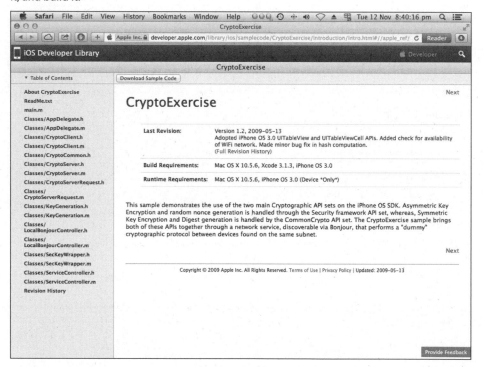

If you view the sample code in Xcode itself, you can click an Open Project button that loads the sample project with all the source code.

CAUTION

Sample projects almost always build successfully, but if you load a project for an older version of OS X or iOS, some elements of the code may occasionally be deprecated or no longer available. If you find this, try to find a more recent version. You can also work through the errors by hand. (This is likely to be educational, but time-consuming.)

Technical notes and Technical Q&As

Technical notes expand on topics that aren't typically based on specific frameworks or code features. Technical Q&As deal with specific reported issues and common error messages; they also answer frequently asked questions. Both may include small samples of useful code and discuss solutions to common problems.

In practice, notes and Q&As are a grab bag of assorted unrelated programming and development topics. They could be included elsewhere in the documentation, but for somewhat arbitrary reasons, each has been given a unique reference number.

For example, Figure 6.10 shows Technical Q&A QA1806, which explains why you should always use the most recent version of Xcode with the most up-to-date SDK.

Figure 6.10

This is a technical Q&A document, from a collection of at least 1,806.

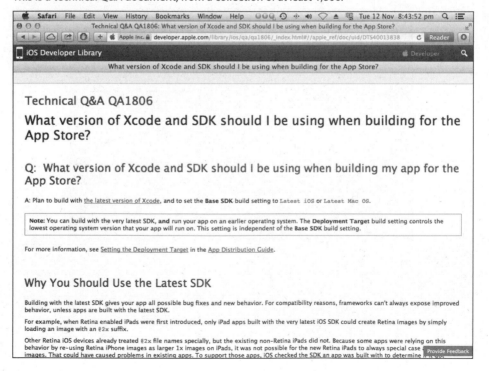

The notes and Q&As are far from comprehensive. You'll find a wider selection of useful—even essential—examples, FAQs, and background information on independent developer message boards.

Videos

Videos are now included in the documentation. Figure 6.11 shows an example. Many were recorded at Apple's WWDC (World Wide Developer Conference) and can be helpful resources. Even though video is a slow and lightweight medium compared to text, take time to view the walk-through videos that demonstrate key techniques and skills; they're more practically focused than the abstract text documentation.

Figure 6.11

This is one of the small selection of videos that are included in the current documentation. Future updates of the documentation will include more video content.

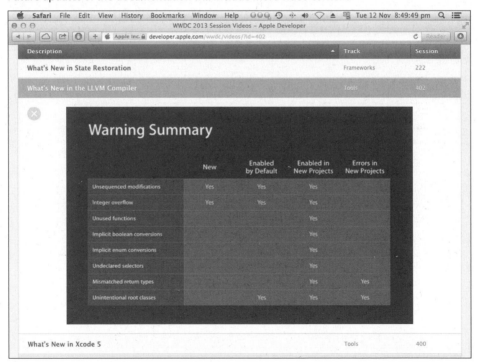

TIP

Videos are now available on both developer libraries. You no longer need to download them separately using iTunes. Don't miss the download options under each video, which give you the choice of HD or SD resolutions for download to your disk, and an optional PDF file of lecture notes.

Xcode Help

Over the last couple of years, Apple added and then expanded a new Xcode Help resource type, shown in Figure 6.12. As you'd expect, the content includes a series of help files for key Xcode features.

Figure 6.12

Look at one of the Xcode Help resources.

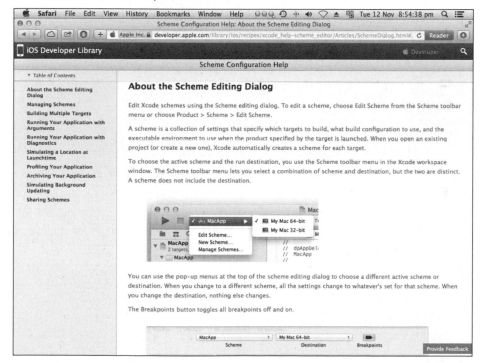

While these files are worth reviewing as an orientation, they typically lag behind new Xcode updates. At the time of this writing, many of the examples refer to Xcode 4, which was subtly different from Xcode 5. This resource type is still very useful: It's one of the more detailed and comprehensive of all the resources. But don't be confused if what you see in your browser isn't the same as what you see on your screen.

Using Topics

The Topics heading organizes the documentation by subject. From one point of view, the topics are self-explanatory. As you'd expect, the Audio & Video topic lists resources relevant to audio and video applications.

What's less obvious is that each of the headers in the Documents list can rearrange the data to emphasize different elements. For example, clicking Title lists all elements alphabetically. The result is an arbitrary jumble of different resource types, as shown in Figure 6.13.

Figure 6.13

Sorting a topic alphabetically by title creates a jumbled list of content that doesn't prioritize the documents in any way.

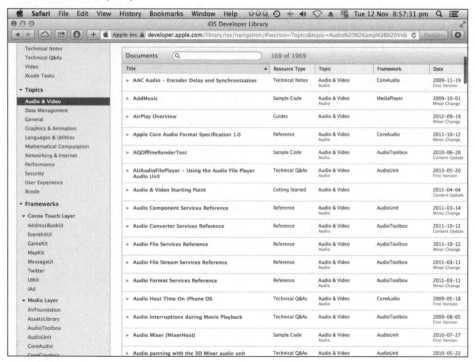

Because titles are somewhat arbitrary, it's often more useful to sort by resource types. Clicking the Resource Type header creates the list shown in Figure 6.14. This helps prioritize the documents and organize them in a more useful way. Note that each resource type list is alphabetized separately.

You also can sort by Framework, which is described below, and by Date. Sorting by date is a useful way to eliminate out-of-date information. Some of the help documents are historical and no longer relevant. Sorting by date can tell you which documents are out of date.

Figure 6.14

Sorting by resource types gives you a more useful view of the content, grouping orientation information, class references, and technical notes into separate lists.

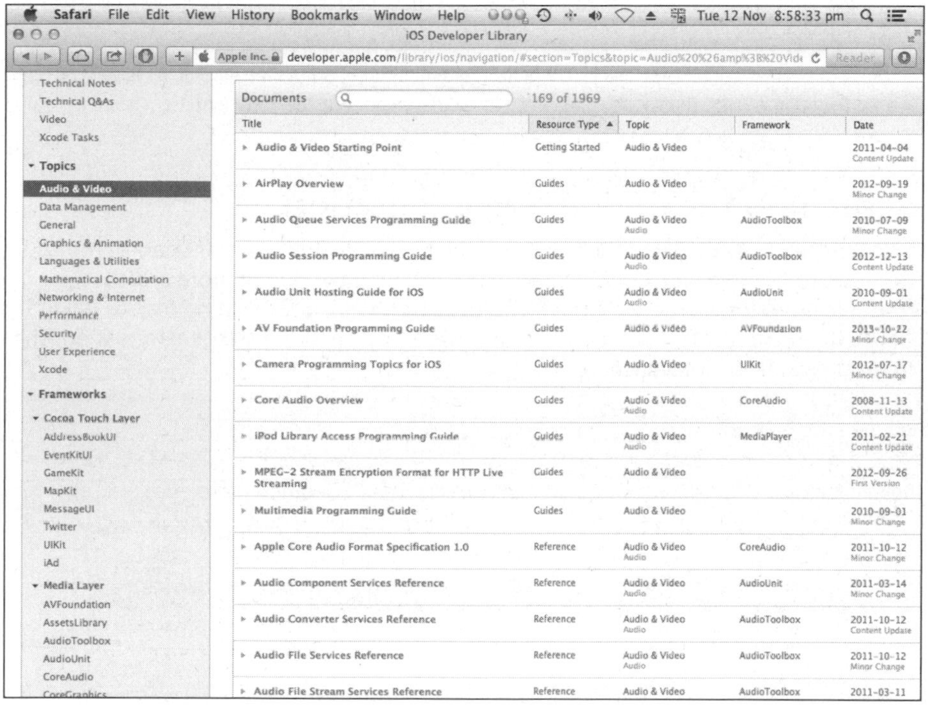

Using frameworks and layers

Although iOS and OS X have different frameworks and layers, the principle is similar for both. A *framework* is a code library with an API that implements one or more useful features. A *layer* is a broad group of frameworks collected together.

The layer groupings are rather arbitrary and do not always include critical information you need. For example, in OS X, the Foundation framework includes functions such as NSMakePoint and NSEqualPoints that are critical for graphics programming. But the Foundation framework is a grab bag of utility features and appears in the Core Services Layer; these critical functions aren't listed in the Media layer, even though it appears to be a complete reference to OS X graphics.

Here as elsewhere, the documentation doesn't distinguish between critical, optional, and barely relevant information. To save confusion, ignore the full list of frameworks and concentrate on the three frameworks used in the default application templates: AppKit, Foundation for OS X; UIKit, Foundation, and CoreGraphics for iOS. In addition, you often need to use the Quartz frameworks and CoreAnimation framework on both platforms, and you may need to use Core Data.

Other frameworks add optional features. You can ignore them unless you want to add specific features to a project.

N O T E

The Cocoa framework that appears in OS X projects is a simple header file that imports the AppKit and Foundation and Core Data frameworks. There is no stand-alone Cocoa framework, and the documentation describes Cocoa as a layer.

Searching the online documentation

A search field is available at the top left of the main Developer Library pages. You can use this to run a limited simple word-match search. The results show one or more matches, grouped by resource type. For example, Figure 6.15 shows the results of searching for CGGeometry—the Core Graphics geometry library. The word-match search isn't intelligent, and it doesn't attempt to group results by relevance.

Figure 6.15

Search for a specific resource by name—in this case, the CGGeometry reference.

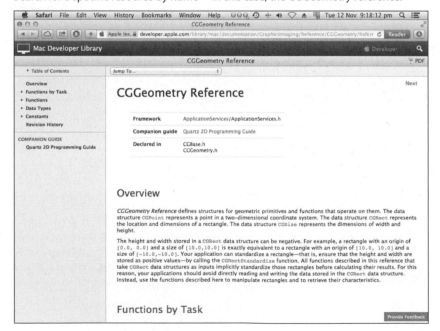

Previously, search could find specific functions and constants; for example, you could search for definitions of `NSRect` or `CGPointMake`, both of which are key elements in the geometry libraries.

More recently, Apple has removed this option. Word-search now appears to search for resource titles only, and no longer tries to look inside them. This makes the online search tool much less useful. It also means that you're more likely to get useful results by drilling down through the various framework references than by looking for specific functions by name.

TIP

You can make searches more specific by clicking the items in the column at the left. Clicking the Mac or iOS Developer Library header at the top broadens the search to include the entire library. Clicking any of the items narrows the search to just that item. Note that you can load any of the topic types from the main developer login page by clicking them, instead of clicking the main Mac or iOS Developer Library link.

Using the Xcode Documentation Viewer

The documentation browser is built into the Xcode Organizer. You can access it in three ways:

- Select Help ⇨ Developer Documentation.
- Use the Quick Help feature to highlight and search for a symbol in a code listing.
- Use option/alt clicks on symbols to load it directly from your code.

CAUTION

The Search feature in the Help menu *doesn't* search the documentation. In fact, it provides help only for Xcode features. You can't use it to search the rest of the developer library.

Previously, the Xcode browser was a web view that linked to the online documentation. More recently, the online and built-in documentation sets have diverged. Some of the content is similar, but the organization is different. Some links remain, especially in legacy documentation. But more of the content is included in the docsets, so you do not have to wait while each item downloads into the viewer.

The key difference is that items have three resource types:

- **Sample Code:** This is identical to the online sample code, but you can build projects without having to download them first by clicking an Open Project link.
- **Guides:** In spite of the name, this type includes any combination of online resource types. In practice, it includes a small selection of actual guides and many technical notes.
- **References:** This type duplicates the online class references and is perhaps the most useful feature.

As shown in Figure 6.16, the docsets are grouped into headings. Each—more or less—includes information matching the heading name. However, there is still some overlap between the OS X and iOS content.

Figure 6.16

Drill down through the resources to view an item in the window. This example shows the classes included in the AV Foundation framework.

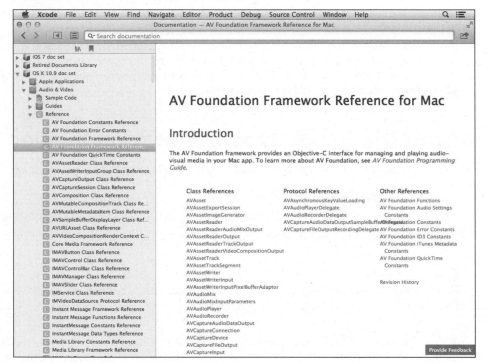

Exploring documentation options

The browser includes a selection of icons for controlling the window layout and working with the content. You can do these things:

- **Explore:** Use this to browse the document hierarchy.
- **Search:** Perform a word-match search by typing words into the search bar.
- **Share:** Click the share icon at the top right to view share options, as shown in Figure 6.17.

Figure 6.17

View the new share options. Note that you can bookmark an item here.

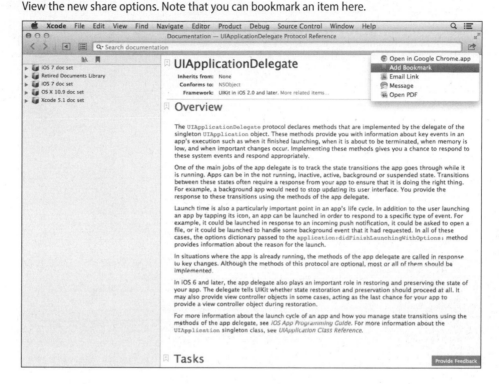

- **View/Hide Contents:** Click the icon to the left of the search bar to open a contents gutter. (This is often empty.)
- **View/Hide the Browse List:** Click the arrow to the left again to view or hide the browser list.
- **Add Bookmarks:** Create your own list of bookmarks. Click the bookmark (ribbon) + (plus) icon on a page to add it to your bookmark list.

Browsing the documentation

Figure 6.18 shows a typical main topic list. To view the documents for each topic, click the disclosure triangles at the left. Topics may include subtopics; for example, the Audio & Video topic lists common classes and other features, and includes further separate Audio and Video subtopics with documentation that's unique to each.

Figure 6.18

View source code from the Audio topic for iOS 7.

CAUTION

The Open Project button has now become an Open Project link. It does the same thing, but it's now less prominent, so it's easy to miss it.

Generally, topic browsing is most useful if you already have a basic understanding of a topic and need quick access to reference material about specific features. The topics include the same introductory guides that are available online, with the same limitations: They can be useful reminders, but they're heavy going if you're looking for a good, practical hands-on introduction to entry-level coding techniques. Otherwise, the organization is slightly haphazard. You can use browsing to discover and explore OS features that may be lost online, but you need to explore the code samples, code snippets, and independent developer discussions to develop a good working knowledge in practice.

Searching the documentation

To perform a word search, click the search icon and type the target word. The viewer lists all documents and resource types featuring that word. Class references typically appear at the top of the list.

The word search is very literal and doesn't attempt to find matches based on content or context. It also reads a period as a delimiter, so you can't look for a specific source code header file, because the search returns a somewhat random selection of files that include ".h" or "h" in some combination.

However, it can find document titles, as shown in Figure 6.19. If you know the name of a project or class, the search displays preview links. If the item you are looking for is not in the preview content, you can broaden the search by clicking Show All Results.

Figure 6.19

Showing the search results for avtouch—a sample code project that is mentioned elsewhere in the documentation.

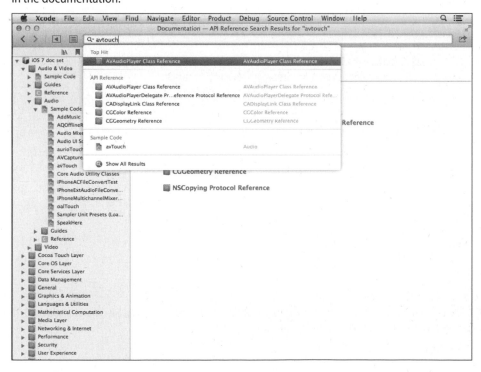

CAUTION

In Xcode 4, the documentation showed code symbols, tagged with a symbol—C for class, F for function, K for constant, G for a global constant, T for a `typedef`, and E for an `enum`. In the Xcode 5 documentation, only classes remain in the topics at the left, but the other items can appear in searches.

NOTE

If you click the triangle next to the search bar's magnifying glass, you can narrow to search to either iOS or OS X. Note also that the search and preview options aren't completely intuitive. The preview appears as you type, but pressing Return doesn't necessarily run the search as you might expect.

Using class references

The Reference section takes up the bulk of the documentation. Most are code references, with formal lists of properties/variables and code interfaces. This group includes Objective-C object references and C function and struct references for all layers of OS X and iOS. Code references are grouped into the layers introduced earlier. The class references follow a fixed format, part of which is shown in Figure 6.20. A small number of class references include an extra Class at a Glance overview summary:

- The Overview is a short text article that sketches the function of the class and how it should be used.
- The Tasks section provides a plain list of methods grouped by function. Each method is a link; you can click it to display more information.
- The optional Properties section lists the class properties and briefly sketches their features. Not all classes include a Properties section.
- The Class Methods section lists class methods in more detail, with a sketch of their features and function.
- The Instance Methods section lists the instance methods, using the same format.
- A final optional section lists other information that may include constants, further optional methods, or information about exceptions or other messages generated by the class.

Items in blue are clickable links. For example, the `sendEvent:` method in `UIApplication` includes a link to the `UIEvent` class. To view the reference for `UIEvent`, click the link.

CAUTION

In previous versions of Xcode, the forward and back link features didn't always work correctly. In Xcode 5, they still don't work as you'd expect them to.

TIP

When you have a class reference open, you can click the Table of Contents button to the left of the search bar to see a table of contents for the class. This can save you scrolling through the whole of the content.

Figure 6.20

The Class References are long documents; use internal links to drill down through the references.

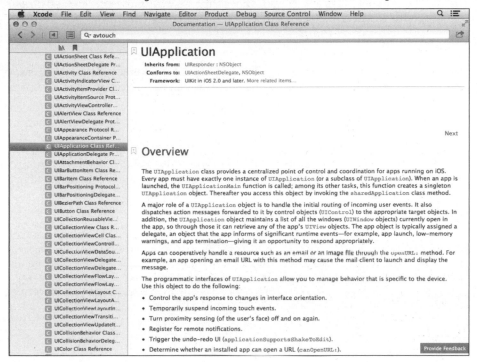

Accessing documentation from code

The documentation browser is useful for general background searches and for browsing support documents. While coding, you typically want to find the documentation for classes, methods, and other symbols as quickly as possible.

The search feature in the browser is an inefficient way to do this. Xcode includes three faster options:

- Quick Help
- Command-click
- Option-click

Using Quick Help

When the Utilities pane is open at the right, you can display a Quick Help tip for any symbol by clicking it. When the symbol is part of the OS, the tip includes live links to the documentation. For example, if you select a class and click to the right of the Reference item, Xcode opens the documentation browser—if it isn't already open—and displays the class reference.

This feature is Xcode's version of contextual help. In addition to reference and definition links, it also lists related APIs, related documents, and useful sample code. You can use it for a bottom-up, in-depth exploration of any symbol. This is almost always more efficient and productive than top-down browsing. It's also a quick way to check method parameters.

TIP

Quick Help works as you type. As soon as Xcode recognizes a class, the Quick Help window displays the relevant links. This feature is more obvious and more useful on faster Macs, because the help content appears almost instantly.

Using command-click

If you Command-click a symbol, Xcode jumps directly to the symbol definition. If the symbol is defined in a framework, Xcode displays the corresponding item in the framework header file. This feature is identical to the Jump to Definition feature described in Chapter 9—but quicker and more intuitive.

Using option-click

If you Option-click a symbol, Xcode displays a pop-up that duplicates the quick-help information, as shown in Figure 6.21. This can be a slightly quicker way to access the same information. It's always available, even when the Utilities pane is hidden. Two links at the bottom of the pop-up can take you to the header the symbol is defined in and a class reference (if there is one).

Figure 6.21

Use Option-click to view Quick Help. This pop-up appears even when the Utilities pane is hidden.

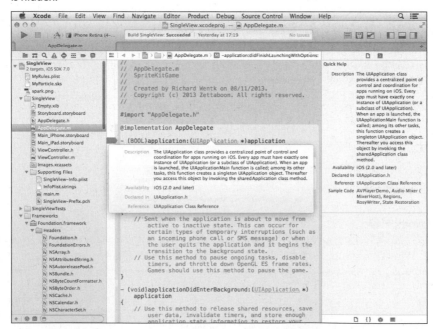

Using Other Documentation

The Internet is a vast resource, and you can find useful tips and code samples by searching for specific classes. But some of the classes use names that are used in other contexts. For example, searching for UIView returns hits that aren't relevant to iOS. You can narrow searches by adding extra keywords such as "iOS," "OS X," and "iPhone." Figure 6.22 shows the results of a combined search. All the hits are relevant, and the results include a good selection of tutorials, discussions, and examples.

Figure 6.22

The web is invaluable for general searches that fill in the gaps in the official documentation. A simple web search returns a jumble of potentially relevant information, but you can often find something of value.

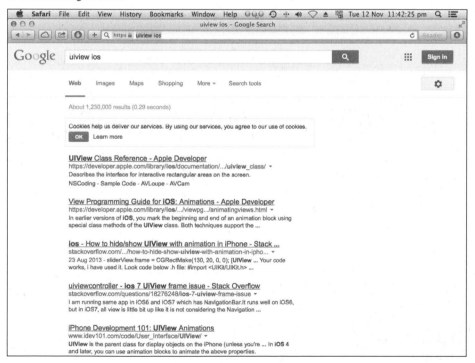

Developer forums offer a tighter focus with more obviously relevant examples. Apple's own developer forums are at `http://devforums.apple.com`. The conversations are grouped by topic and are often lively. By default, topics are listed chronologically, but you can search for keywords.

The most popular forum is `http://stackoverflow.com/`. Other forums exist, but they aren't as widely known. Stackoverflow is a vast community of developers and regular discussions at all levels of expertise. Figure 6.23 shows an example topic search.

Figure 6.23

The equivalent search on `stackoverflow.com` returns a good selection of useful beginner-level hits, mixed with more advanced discussions.

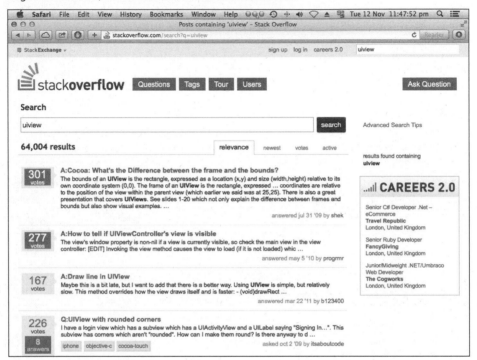

TIP

You can get lots of useful content by adding "tutorial" to a web search. For example, try 'ios storyboard tutorial" for some good examples. Content comes and goes, and iOS and OS X features change regularly, so it's difficult to build up a permanent set of bookmarks. But searches for recent content can find many useful tips, tricks, and solutions.

Summary

The official documentation is harder to use than it looks. This is partly because the sheer volume of information makes it difficult to organize and maintain. But it's also partly because introductory tutorials are often terse and aimed at experienced developers. Beginners may need to get up to speed on basic concepts by looking elsewhere on the web for help and relying on the official documentation for reference material.

However, the relatively recent trend toward video tutorials is helping replace some of the dense introductions with more accessible material. And source code listings are another very useful resource.

Getting Started with Interface Builder

A lthough Interface Builder (IB) can be used as a UI editor, you must understand that it's a more general object management tool.

Understanding IB

Figure 7.1 shows a first look at IB. In Xcode, IB has five functions:

- You can use IB to design your application's UI. The UI design includes one or more windows and views, with associated controls—objects such as buttons, sliders, text boxes, and so on. The design process presets the properties of these objects. For example, you can set the default position of an OS X window and control whether it has a drop shadow. Similarly, when you add a button to a UI, you use IB to set its position in the window or view, set its color, and so on. Optionally, you can define custom graphics and other more specialized features.

- You can use IB to pre-instantiate objects in your application. Any object you add to a nib file is created in memory when the file is loaded. This option is completely general: Objects do not have to be visible on screen or be part of a UI. The standard application templates for both iOS and OS X rely on this feature to load the core application classes.

- You can use IB to create your own kit of UI objects. Very advanced developers can create a complete external library of custom UI objects, with associated code. This is a major project and outside the scope of this book. But simple customization is relatively easy. For example, the layout of a standard table cell can be designed in IB as a stand-alone object, and then loaded and repeated as needed in one or more tables. In this mode, you use IB to create useful nib files with collections of objects that can be loaded as needed. These objects can be fragments of a UI, or they can be data collections.

- You can use IB to link code features to UI objects. User actions and events are sent to your code using *actions*—methods that are triggered in the code when the user interacts with a view or a control. UI object properties such as size, position, color, state, text, and so on are set with *outlets*. Outlets link Objective-C properties to corresponding properties in UI objects.

● You must *subclass* objects before you can add code to them. You must then tell IB to use your subclassed objects instead of the standard default objects. Otherwise, your code is ignored!

● In OS X only, IB objects can include *bindings.* Bindings link objects and properties indirectly, with semi-automated format translation. In outline, when your code sets a bound property, the UI is updated automatically. Similarly, user interactions are copied to a bound property automatically. Bindings are an alternative to outlets, with extra features that make them ideal for use with data collection objects such as arrays. Bindings are not available in iOS.

Figure 7.1

Unlike the text editor used for code, the IB editor works graphically.

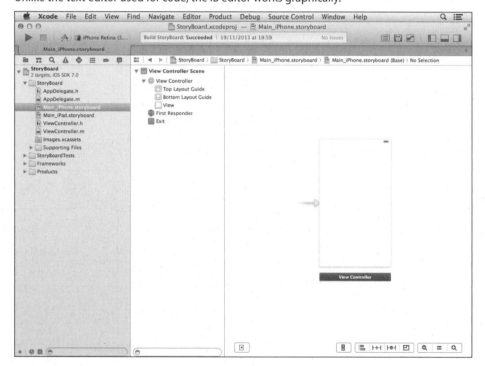

TIP
IB now follows OS X conventions and saves changes automatically. You no longer need to remember to save edits before building.

Understanding nib files and storyboards

IB has two jobs. You can use it to design an application's UI. You can also use it as a general object loader for all kinds of content, including UI content you may want to load on demand.

On OS X, the main UI uses *nib files*. The files have a `.xib` extension—short for XML nib file, because the content is serialized XML. (You can open the files in any text editor and change them by hand, although this isn't recommended.)

On iOS, nib files are built into *storyboards*. Storyboards, such as the iPad storyboard shown in Figure 7.2, are similar to nib files, with three critical differences:

- A nib file typically holds the UI content for a single view controller (on iOS) or window controller (on OS X). A storyboard can contain multiple view controllers, each with its own content.

- Storyboards create a map of the UI, showing how a user can navigate between the views. View transitions can be enhanced with *segues,* which define how exactly the views move as they swap on the screen.

- There is no single universal UI container in iOS, so Xcode creates separate iPhone and iPad storyboard files. The files hold independent content, but you can link them to the same view controller to minimize code duplication. You can also add extra UI features to just one storyboard and add extra methods to the view controller to manage those features on one platform.

Figure 7.2

iOS automatically loads either an iPhone or iPad storyboard, depending on the platform an app is running on.

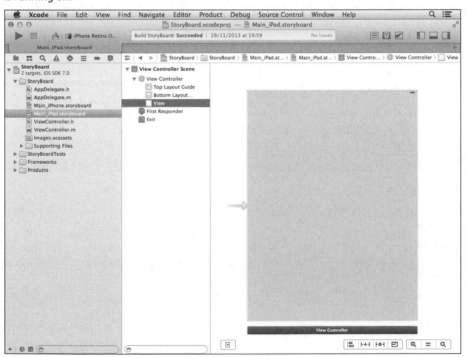

NOTE
You can, of course, create separate view controller files for each platform. There isn't usually a good reason to do this, but the possibility is there if you need it.

CAUTION
It's more accurate to say that storyboards create a *partial* map of the UI. The segue system works in surprising ways; features you might expect to exist either aren't available or don't work how you expect. Typically, you need to supplement the visual map you see in IB with extra code to manage view transitions.

Understanding controllers and views

Both nibs and storyboards hold view controller objects, which manage and draw views. It's important to understand that controllers are *invisible*. They don't appear on-screen. As the name suggests, they contain the views that appear on-screen and draw them in a set order. They can also respond to user events. Your code can swap the views that a controller draws, and storyboards are a semi-automated way to make this happen. But keep in mind that only views are visible. Controllers are objects that only exist in logic.

Getting Started with IB

To begin exploring IB, we'll look at sample OS X and iOS projects, created using standard templates introduced in Chapter 3.

Introducing IB for iOS

Create a new Single View Application, select Universal from the Devices menu, and save the application as "IB." Open the IB group, and select Main-iPhone.storyboard, as shown in Figure 7.3. IB launches within Xcode, and displays the file as a graphic preview of the empty UI.

CAUTION
In Xcode 3, IB was a separate application. Even though IB is built into Xcode 4 and 5, it still takes a while to load the first time you launch it.

TIP
Depending on your screen resolution, the UI preview may be too big or too small. Use the + (plus) and − (minus) zoom buttons in the group on the right of the toolbar at the bottom of the IB window to change the preview zoom.

NOTE
The figures are shot at low resolution, and the Project Navigator and utility pane are hidden to show as much detail as possible. On a bigger monitor, you'd typically have all three panes visible at the same time.

Figure 7.3

Here's another look at IB, showing an iPhone storyboard.

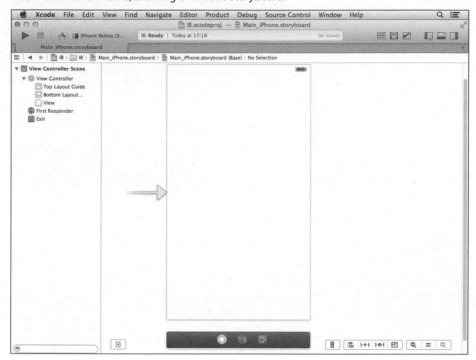

Looking at key features

Note these key features available in iOS projects:

- The area at the left lists the contents of the selected storyboard.
- A disclosure triangle at the bottom of the main area hides or reveals the contents list.
- The area at the right displays the editor view, with a map of the view controllers in the storyboard, each filled with a preview of its contents.
- When you zoom in, the "View Controller" label under each view controller is replaced by a cryptic collection of colored icons.
- A fixed *dock* at the bottom of the editor has icons for object alignment and preview zoom.
- For iPhone storyboards only, you can click the icon at the left of the toolbar to preview either the 3.5" or 4" screen form factor.
- There is no equivalent option for previewing for the iPad Mini for the iPad storyboard.
- You can move a view controller by clicking and dragging it. This is purely cosmetic; it changes the layout in the editor but has no effect on a device.

If you've hidden the Project Navigator, unhide it and click the `Main-iPad.storyboard` file in the project to view it, as shown in Figure 7.4. You'll see some differences. The UI structure is very similar: It's a single empty view controller. Look out for the following:

- The iPad preview is bigger and has the iPad's form factor.
- There is no icon for changing the form factor.
- There is no option to select an iPad Mini preview, or a non-Retina preview.

Figure 7.4

The iPad storyboard preview is very similar to the iPhone storyboard, with minor differences.

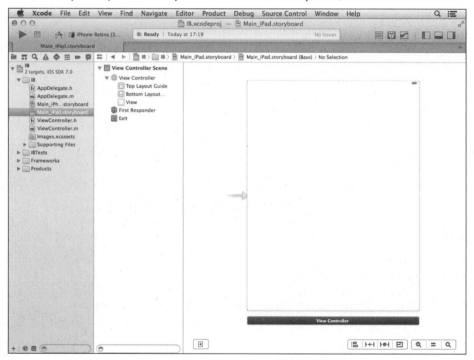

NOTE

Apple is rumored to be working on a larger 12- or 13-inch iPad model. If the rumors are true, it's possible this model will have a separate preview mode in future versions of Xcode.

CAUTION

If you can see colored icons in a black toolbar under a view controller, you can move it only by clicking the toolbar. If you can't see the toolbar, you can move it by clicking in the frame. The toolbar only appears above a certain zoom level.

Introducing IB for OS X

OS X uses nib files instead of storyboards. Create a new OS X Cocoa project, save it as IBMac, and click the `MainMenu.xib` file to load the project's nib file into IB, as shown in Figure 7.5.

Figure 7.5

The contents of the OS X nib file are related to those of an iOS storyboard, with different objects, similar placeholders, but no segues.

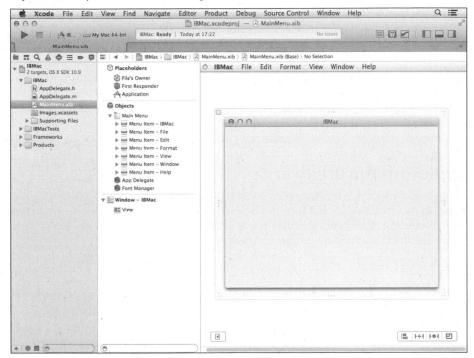

The contents of the nib file are clearly different than the contents of a storyboard. The key differences are:

- The nib file includes a collection of *placeholders*. These are similar to the mysterious icons that appear under the view controller in the iOS storyboard.

- The nib file also includes a list of *objects*. The main menu object is the app's menu tree. This is pre-populated with useful defaults. The defaults are pre-linked to useful app actions, so the Quit item quits the app. You do not need to do anything further to use these links; they just work.

- The two other objects are the *App Delegate* and the *Font Manager*. The App Delegate is the main body of the app. The Font Manager is an optional element. You can delete it if your app doesn't need to offer font selection features.

- The *Window* is the equivalent of an iOS view controller. It manages UI events. By default, it loads and displays a *view*. Neither is subclassed, so you must add subclasses before you can add UI management code.

- The disclosure triangle and editor toolbar work as they do in the iOS storyboard.

- There are no segues, but there is a "transparent" area around the window. As in the iOS preview, you can move the window around the screen. This is cosmetic; it doesn't affect the window's launch position.

N O T E

It's possible that Apple may move to supporting segues for OS X UI design in a future release.

N O T E

You should understand that only views are visible on the screen. Put simply, views draw content. View controllers draw views in order. View controllers exist in code only. They don't appear on-screen. This becomes important later, when dealing with other kinds of controllers, such as segue controllers.

Exploring the utility area

When the IB editor is in use, the utility area displays extra icons. Use these icons to select sub-panes in this area. You use the sub-panes to set up defaults for the objects in your UI, control their positions in the UI, set how they move when the UI rotates or the window resizes, and tell IB to load an object subclass so your code works.

There are six icons in an iOS storyboard file and eight in an OS X nib, as listed here:

- The File and Quick Help panes are identical to those for the code editor. For details, see Chapter 3.

- The main use of the Identity Inspector, shown in Figure 7.6, is to set the object's custom class. When you subclass an object—for example, when you create a customized copy of a `UIViewController` or an `NSWindow`—you must select the new class name in the drop-down menu. Otherwise, IB won't know that you want to use a subclassed version with custom code.

- The Identity Inspector also includes optional key-value pairs that you can add to any object for initialization or tagging, a document feature for selecting text layouts, fonts, and accessibility information.

- The Attributes Inspector, shown in Figure 7.7, is a list of default properties. This Inspector has different contents for every object in IB. For example, the UIView shown in the figure includes background color, drawing mode, and interaction properties, which can enable multi-touch control.

Figure 7.6

In IB, the utility area lists a selected object's properties and options, and displays them for editing. Use the icons at the top of the area to access different sets of properties.

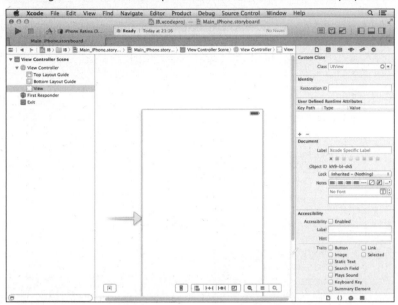

Figure 7.7

The Attributes Inspector sets an object's default properties.

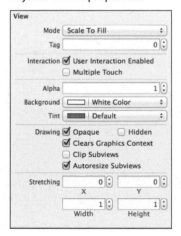

TIP

Almost every property that appears in either of these inspectors can also be set in code. But it's easier to preview the results in IB.

● The Size Inspector, shown in Figure 7.8, sets the dimensions and alignment of an object. It also sets the *positioning constraints*—the system Apple uses to align objects with each other and keep them aligned across different screen sizes, resolutions, and screen rotations.

● The Connections Inspector, shown in Figure 7.9, lists an object's outlets and actions. When properties and methods are linked to code, you can review and change them here.

Figure 7.8

The Size Inspector defines an object's position, size, and alignment options.

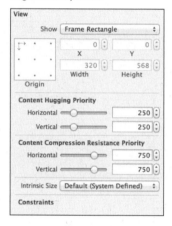

Figure 7.9

The Connections Inspector defines the links between an object's outlets and actions and supporting code. You also can define a delegate object, where relevant.

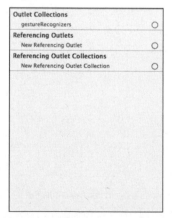

Two more icons appear in OS X projects, as shown in Figures 7.10 and 7.11.

Figure 7.10

View the Bindings Inspector in an OS X project. Bindings are optional and are best left for intermediate and advanced projects.

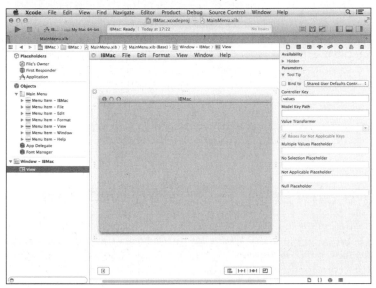

Figure 7.11

Explore the View Effects Inspector in an OS X project. To view a list of filters, click the Add (+) icon under the Content Filters tab and select the Filter menu.

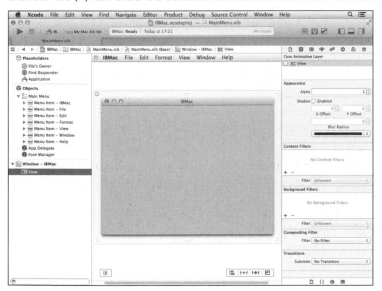

- The Bindings Inspector displays an object's bindings—properties that can be linked using the Key Value Observing (KVO) system built into OS X, and which support optional translation and pre-processing of various Cocoa data container objects.

- Some objects, including the menu items and the main app window, have special binding options. By default, most are set up to read font and other basic settings from the applications preferences, so you can define some of the look and feel of your app in one location and have all visible objects follow the default setting.

- The View Effects Inspector defines the filters and transitions that are applied to a visible object. You can use this inspector to add blur and sharpen effects, color adjustments, tilings, and so on. This is an easy way to apply one or more standard filters to a view, similar to those available in Adobe Photoshop or GIMP. Filter effects can be animated with custom code.

Both of these icons add optional features that aren't critical to basic app design. For a detailed explanation, see the companion *Cocoa* in Wiley's Developer Reference series.

Creating a Simple iOS Project with IB

This section demonstrates how to use IB to create a very simple app, with a text label and a button. Tapping the button triggers code that reads the text from the label and changes it. The code uses one action, which is triggered by the button, and one outlet, which connects the label in the UI to a corresponding instance of `UILabel` in the code.

NOTE

Because this isn't a primer on Cocoa Touch, the code in this example is very simple. For more information about app design, see the companion *Cocoa Touch* in Wiley's Developer Reference series.

Understanding UI design

These are the basic rules for UI design:

- Start by dragging objects from the Object library and dropping them into a view (iOS) or a window (OS X).

- If you want to read or change the properties of an object, you must create an *outlet* by click-dragging from the object to the corresponding view controller header file.

- The outlet creates an access point for the object in your code—through an Objective-C pointer. In spite of the name, outlets can be used to read or write property values.

- If you want the object to respond to mouse clicks (OS X) or user touches (iOS), you must define an *action* for each event. An action is a special method added to the code to handle user events. Create it by click-dragging from an object to the controller's header or implementation files.

- Actions respond to a selection of "pre-packaged" touch types, including an initial touch down, a subsequent touch up, a change in value, and so on. These events are members of a special set of constants called `UIControlEvents`. They are generated by control objects. IB lists them for you as you're creating an action.
- Not all objects generate all possible events. But on iOS, the "event library" is the same for all controls.
- UI objects can support outlets and actions at the same time.
- You can create "dumb" objects that support neither outlets nor actions. Use dumb objects to decorate the UI—for example, to add a fixed graphic as a background to a view. A dumb object doesn't respond to the user, and it can't be changed from your code.

NOTE

Technically, actions rely on the Target-Action model in Cocoa and Cocoa Touch. You can define actions in IB, but you can also define them in code, and for advanced effects, you can redefine them dynamically. A full discussion of Target-Action is outside the scope of this book. For details, see the *Cocoa* companion title in Wiley's Developer Reference series.

To summarize: Outlets give your app read/write access to the properties of visible objects, and actions trigger methods in your code when a user interacts with your UI.

Understanding IB and touch events

It's critically important to understand that IB controls *only* generate pre-packaged `UIControlEvents`. All other touch events, including taps that don't interact with a control somewhere within a view, must be managed elsewhere in your code—specifically by adding standard gesture recognizers or by adding `touchesBegan:` and `touchesEnded:` methods.

IB has nothing to say about these touch types. They're not mentioned anywhere in IB, so remember that IB is only part of the story. If you don't include extra custom touch method code, these other touches are ignored.

Adding objects to a view

The Object library appears in the area at the bottom right of the utility pane, as shown in Figure 7.12. By default, it's partially hidden, but you can drag a divider above the icon bar upward to show more of it. The larger your monitor, the more of the library you can see without scrolling.

CAUTION

If you have a small monitor, this feature can be difficult to work with because you continually have to scroll through it and move the divider to show object properties so you can edit them. You can save time by creating one tab in which the Object library fills the area on the right and another in which only the properties are visible.

The Object library shares this lower area with other libraries. To select the Object library, click the cube icon, which is third from the left. Objects in the library are pre-filtered by the project OS; you can't add iOS objects to a Mac project, and vice versa.

In Xcode 5, the process of adding outlets and actions is semi-automated. The automation eliminates many common errors.

Using the IB project from earlier in this chapter, arrange the Xcode interface as shown in
Figure 7.12. Select the `Main_iPhone.storyboard` object for editing, and click the Assistant
editor to split the window, as shown in the figure. The Assistant should show the
`ViewController.m` file. If it doesn't, select it manually from the selection menu bar above
the editor area on the right.

In the bottom right of the Utility area, click the cube icon. If the icons are at the bottom of the
area, drag the divider up to show the contents of the library.

In the object list at the left, click the View object.

NOTE

If your monitor is wide enough to show the Project Navigator at the left without hiding the other areas, you can leave
it in place. It's not critical for this project.

Figure 7.12

When setting up IB for basic UI editing, you can use the assistant editor to select the relevant
view controller file. The Utility area at the right is essential.

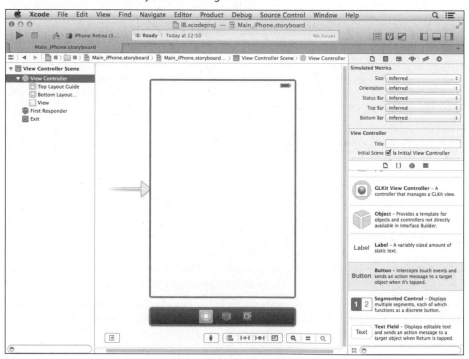

Drag and drop a Button object from the Object library onto the view, as shown in Figure 7.13.

NOTE
Figure 7.13 temporarily hides the code in the assistant editor for clarity.

Xcode does three things as you do this:

- When you click any item in the library, a large tool tip appears to the left with a description of the object. You can dismiss the tool tip by clicking the Done button, or by clicking elsewhere in the editor area.

- When you drag an item onto a view, guidelines appear, as shown in Figure 7.13. You can use the lines to center an object in the view or to align it with other objects. In the figure, the button is centered in the view.

- When you drop the item, it appears *under* the view in the object list at the left. It is indented. In IB, this means the view *contains* the item, much like a folder contains a file.

CAUTION
You can drop items under the view manually, by dropping them onto the object list at the left. IB makes it easy to replace an object by dropping another onto it. If you drop a button onto the view instead of under it, IB deletes the view and replaces it with the button. This is not what you want!

Figure 7.13
Add a button using IB's automatic guidelines to center it in the view.

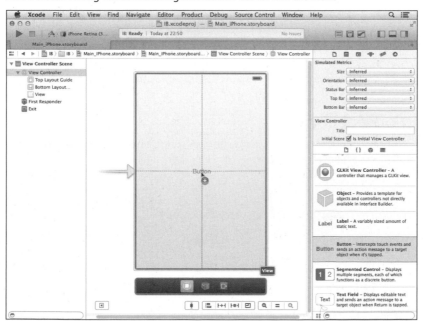

Add a Label object in the same way, as shown in Figure 7.14. The guidelines indicate when the label is centered. If you move the label around the view before releasing it, you see that you can also left- and right-justify the label with respect to the button. Similarly, if you drag to one side of the button, you can align it with the top, bottom, or vertical center of the button.

Figure 7.14

Add a label. As you move the label, guidelines appear to show various center lines and horizontal and vertical alignment lines with other objects in the view.

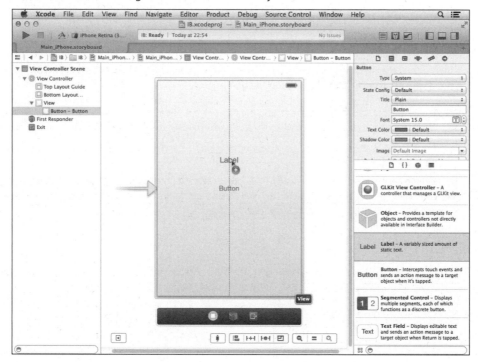

Setting object contents

Setting the contents of UI objects remains a chore. Although both labels and buttons are simple, you typically need to follow these steps:

1. Set the text label.

2. Optionally, change the font, text size, and color.

3. Change the text justification and line breaks.

4. Optionally, add a drop shadow.

5. Resize the object to make sure the text displays correctly.

6. Realign the object after your changes.

Similar steps are needed to set the contents of other objects, such as image views. See the example later in this chapter.

To change the label text, double-click it. The label edge and interior are highlighted. Type **This is off**, as shown in Figure 7.15. When you press Return, you see that the label is no longer centered.

Figure 7.15

When setting text in a label, the label doesn't remain centered after editing.

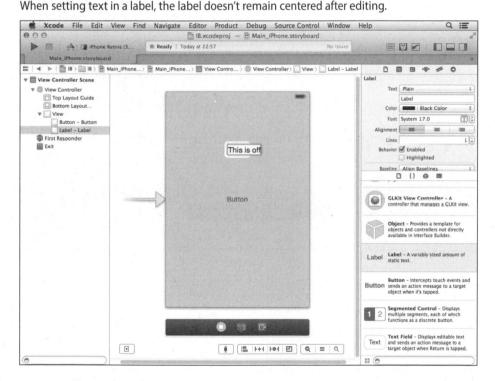

Setting font attributes

Select the Attributes Inspector if it isn't already selected, and click the Font icon—the T in a box—at the right of the Font menu selector.

Set the font size to 24 and the Font Family to Custom, as shown in Figure 7.16. Click Done to confirm the selection. Click the center Alignment selector below the font box to set center justification.

CAUTION

You may need to reselect the Label object in the object list at the left of the window if it deselects itself.

Figure 7.16

Basic font features appear in a pop-up dialog.

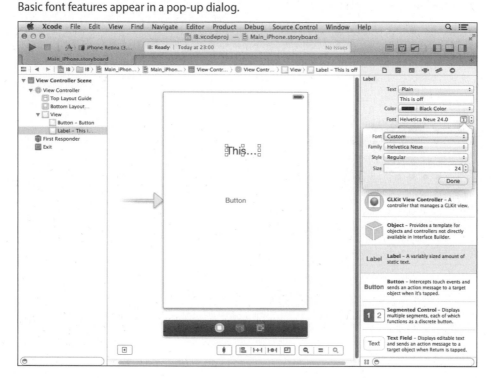

Setting fonts

You can change an object's font in IB. iOS 7 includes a good selection of fonts; the list is much more comprehensive than in earlier versions of iOS. Click the Family box to see a list, as shown in Figure 7.17.

You can use non-standard fonts in an iOS project, but you must import them into the project bundle and load them with special code. Non-standard font support isn't an IB feature, and the code can become complex, so it's outside the scope of this book. (As of Xcode 5.1, there are hints Xcode will be able to work directly with custom fonts. But this feature hasn't been implemented yet.)

TIP

You can see the full list of available fonts, with variants, in the tech note at `http://support.apple.com/ kb/HT5878`.

TIP

Unfortunately, there's no font preview feature, either in IB or in the tech note. If you want to preview the fonts, use Apple's Font Book app in `/Applications`.

Figure 7.17

View the list of supported font families.

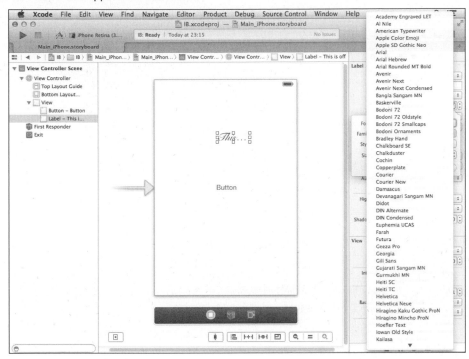

Adding drop shadows and other text effects

The drop shadow effect in iOS is . . . understated. The drop shadow isn't blurred, so the effect isn't good at creating actual drop shadows. But the iOS 7 look is flatter than previous versions of iOS, so drop shadows are no longer recommended.

You can still use the Shadow feature to add a deboss (chiseled) effect. Click the View object in the object list at the left. Click the Attributes inspector icon if it is not already selected. Click the Background attribute menu, and select the Light Gray Color.

Click the label or button in the UI, and then click the Shadow color picker and select white. Experiment with the Shadow Offset settings. Variations on 1 and -1 in either or both boxes create a subtle effect. Larger values create less successful exaggerated results. One possible example is shown in Figure 7.18.

T I P

In Xcode 5, you can click to the right of a color menu to select from a list of predefined colors or click the color box at the left to immediately open the standard Color Picker.

Figure 7.18

Create a deboss effect.

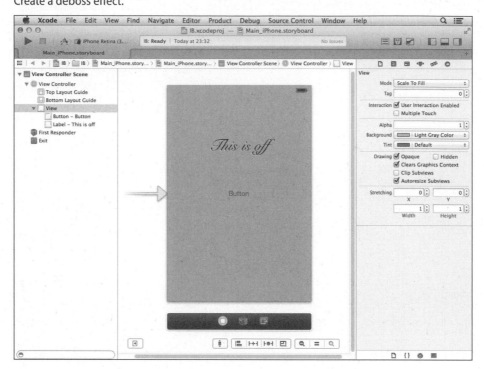

Resizing objects with the mouse

To resize an object, select it. Drag handles (small black squares) appear at each corner and at the centers of each edge. Drag a handle to resize the object, as shown in Figure 7.19. While you're changing the size, you see a pop-up window with the object's dimensions. Guidelines also appear, as shown in the figure.

Labels, buttons, and editable text fields can be set to shrink text so it fits into the available area. Xcode 5 includes a new feature to manage this, labeled Autoshrink, which improves legibility by specifying minimum acceptable font sizes.

You have three menu options:

- **Fixed Font Size:** This simply fixes the letter size. Text that doesn't fit into a control is truncated with ellipses (. . .).

- **Minimum Font Scale:** This sets the smallest allowed font size fraction. The font size is scaled to this minimum, and text is truncated if it is still too large. For example, if the font size is set to 36pt and the minimum scale is set to 0.5, the font shrinks to a minimum size of 18pt—but no smaller.

- **Minimum Font Size:** Select this if you want to set the smallest allowable font size manually.

Figure 7.19

Set object dimensions by dragging with the mouse.

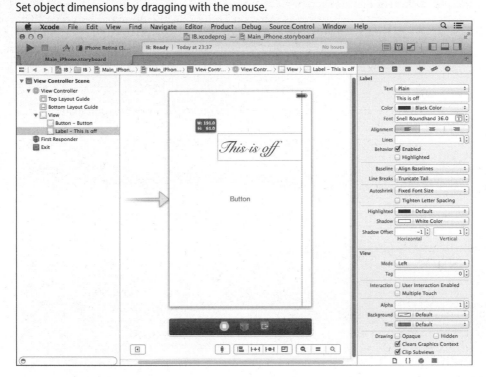

For a simple UI, you often drag the left edge of a text area object until a left guideline appears and drag the right edge to the right guideline. This sets the width to the maximum available.

For a more complex UI, you have to trade off the dimensions and positions of the various items for maximum clarity, keeping in mind that the UI may need to rotate to a different orientation. In extreme cases, you may need to design separate UIs for different orientations or use constraints or custom code to move objects when the orientation changes.

NOTE

The left, right, top, and bottom guidelines indicate the edge of the usable area in the UI, as defined in Apple's Human Interface Guideline documents. Although Apple likes to emphasize these documents, in practice, they're suggestions to help create a neater UI, not absolutes. But note that there are separate final "end-of-the-world" guidelines around the edges. Keep items within these second guidelines.

Resizing and aligning objects numerically

The top sub-pane of the Size Inspector includes an Origin box and four number fields. You can use these to set the size and position of an object with pixel precision.

The Origin box selects the reference point used to determine the object's position. The dots in the box correspond to the drag handles around the object. If the origin reference point is set to the top left of the grid in the box, as shown in Figure 7.20, the number fields refer to the object's top-left corner. If the origin is at the center, the numbers refer to the object's center, and so on. If you click the dots in the box, the X and Y coordinates are updated to show the new reference.

Figure 7.20

Set a top-left origin reference for the label. The X and Y numbers show the coordinates of the top-left point.

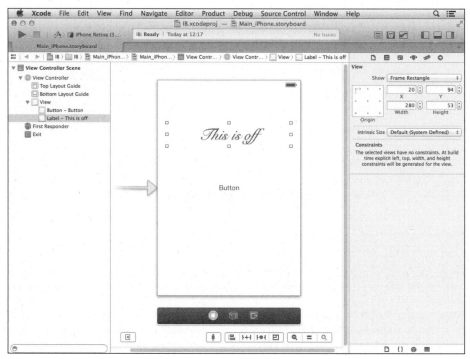

The Width and Height boxes set the width and height, as you'd expect. You can use the up/down arrows next to each box to increment and decrement each field. As you do this, the object moves and its dimensions change. You also can type numbers into each box to set it directly.

TIP

When this Inspector is visible, the numbers update automatically when you move or resize an object with the mouse. You can use this feature to create very precise edits. The 0,0 point is at the top left. Numbers can be negative when an object is outside the top or left of the object that contains it. (For more information about containers, see the section about the IB Object Hierarchy later in this chapter.)

TIP
You can move selected objects by single pixels with the arrow keys.

Introducing constraints and alignment

Earlier versions of Xcode 4 had explicit centering and alignment options for managing object relationships. Because iOS now supports a wider range of resolutions, Xcode 5 uses a more complex system of *constraints* to manage object positioning.

You must create constraints for each object before you can use them, so by default this option is almost invisible; it appears in some menus, but not in the inspectors. Constraints are complex and are introduced in the next chapter. For this exercise, center objects horizontally by placing them on guidelines. But ignore the constraint option for now.

Some controls, such as buttons, include a much simpler *alignment* option. This simply aligns the text along the center or edges of the bounding box, as shown in Figure 7.21. You can also preselect and/or highlight some items to indicate a default.

Figure 7.21 also shows the finished UI. Experiment with font selection, text sizes, and colors to create your own design. At this point, the layout is complete, but it isn't yet linked to active code.

Figure 7.21

Here's the finished UI, before it's linked to active code.

Note that although the design process can seem complex when you encounter it for the first time, it soon becomes more straightforward. With practice, you'll find that it becomes automatic. After you master the features of the different Inspector panes in the utility area, you've made a good start with IB.

NOTE

The IB inspectors have many, many options. The easiest way to find out what they do is to experiment with them and take notes. Unfortunately, Apple has yet to produce a definitive and comprehensive guide to every feature. Fortunately, you can ignore most of the options when you're starting out.

Linking objects to code

Creating actions and outlets is a relatively simple process. When you create an action, Xcode 5 automatically inserts a method stub. When you create an outlet, Xcode adds an Objective-C class property.

It's up to you to fill in the details, adding code that makes the stub do something useful and reads and/or writes property data. But Xcode adds the essentials for you.

CAUTION

Apple keeps changing this part of Xcode. Currently, properties are public, and Xcode automatically adds an invisible @synthesize directive for properties, so you can set and read properties without having to write your own getter and setter code to access them. To use this feature, you must add an underscore in front of your property names. If you don't want to add underscores everywhere, you can also add @synthesize manually and use the default property names.

Future versions may work differently again.

Understanding actions

In an iOS app, you should add actions to a view controller. You *can* add them to some other class—they work in a view, or the app delegate, or even in a subclass of some other UI object. But it's considered good practice to keep all UI code in a view controller class, unless there's a compelling and unusual reason not to. (On OS X, UIWindow does the same job.)

Selecting a source event

To add an action, you drag a link by selecting a source event and releasing it on a destination, which is usually a code window, and *not* a named class from the list at the left of IB. You can select a source as follows:

- Right-click a control and select one of the possible events from a floating dialog, as shown in Figure 7.22.

- Click a control with the Connections Inspector open, and select from a similar list of possible events in the Inspector.

- Control-click a control to create a draggable link. This option generates a dialog when you release it, which includes a menu that you can use to select the event type.

Figure 7.22

Right-clicking brings up the floating dialog with a list of the events that can be generated by a UI control.

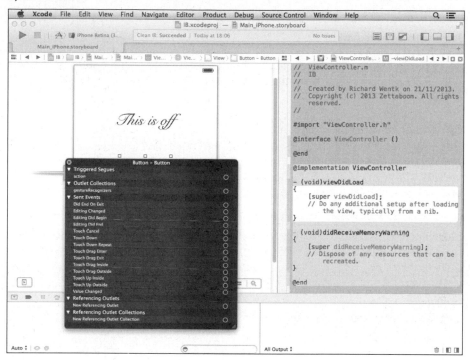

TIP

If the floating dialog is floating over your code, you can drag it to a different location.

CAUTION

It's not always easy to select a source control. If nothing seems to be happening, click the control again until it's highlighted or outlined.

Choosing events

Not all controls implement all events. A button isn't editable, so it makes no sense for it to send an Editing Did Begin message. Options that make sense for a button include Touch Down and Touch Up Inside.

The former sends an event as soon as the user touches a button. The latter sends an event when the user lifts their finger. The former feels more responsive and immediate, but the latter gives users the option to drag a finger beyond the edges of the control to cancel the touch. Officially, Apple prefers the latter. But either works.

Selecting a destination

You can drop the other end of a link on either the view controller header file or the implementation file. The former creates a public declaration, which means other classes can call the method if they need to. The latter creates a private declaration: The action is a secret kept between IB and the view controller.

Typically, you can keep actions secret. iOS and OS X allow runtime action-swapping. For example, the same button can trigger different methods depending on the state of a game. But for this introduction, you'll use the simplest possible option and add the action directly to the view controller implementation.

Naming and initializing the action

To complete the link, drag it from your source onto the `ViewController.m` file and release it somewhere between the words `@implementation` and `@end`, *not* within any existing curly brackets. Xcode draws a blue line between the source and destination and includes a floating tooltip at the latter, as shown in Figure 7.23.

When you release the mouse, the pop-up dialog shown in Figure 7.24 appears. To finish adding the action, you must give it a name. Optionally, you can define the parameters that are passed to the method.

Figure 7.23

Create a link from a source to a destination.

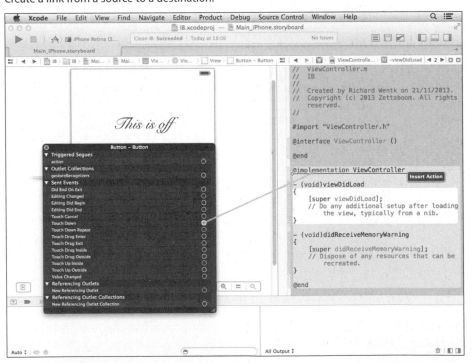

Figure 7.24

When adding an action, add a name and ignore the rest, unless your code demands the extra features.

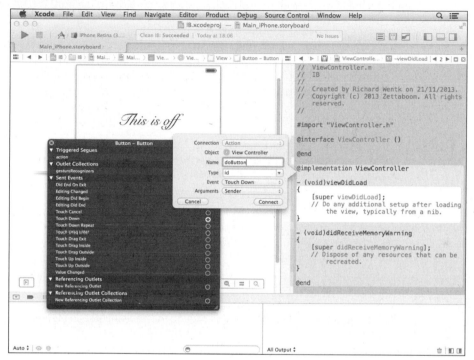

The *Name* field sets the name. It's best to give each method a clear and descriptive title. Otherwise, the name is arbitrary, but it must be unique to the class it appears in. This example uses doButton.

NOTE

Class and property names use camel code. The first letter is lowercase. For clarity, subsequent words begin with a capital letter. It's good practice to add an adjective to actions—for example doButtonPressed—and this is especially useful when a single control can trigger multiple actions. (I've left out the adjective in this example for simplicity.)

The *Type* option selects id, or the class of the object sending the message—UIButton, in this example. Use id when you use the same method to handle messages from multiple different objects. You can then add extra code that determines the class of the object that sent the message. You also can use id if you don't need to read the object's properties. Use a specific class when you need to read information from the button or change one of its properties.

In this example, you need to know that the button was tapped, but you don't need to know its color, position, or anything else about it; the default id setting is fine.

NOTE

In Objective-C, id is a catch-all class label. It means "this object is some class, but we either don't know or don't care which one."

The *Event* option duplicates the standard list of possible events. If you're dragging a link from one of the event dialogs, this option defaults to the source you selected.

If you're dragging a link directly from the control, Xcode selects a useful default. You can select a different option using this menu.

The *Arguments* option selects one of the following: None, Sender, or Sender and Event. Choose None when you don't need to know anything about the sender object. Choose Sender when you want to read the sender object's properties. Choose Sender and Event when you also want to read information from an optional `UIEvent` object that arrives with the message—for example, if you want to find the event timestamp.

TIP
To save time, you can leave the default options in this dialog as they are. You get an action method that includes an `(id) sender` parameter. Your code can ignore this parameter if your code doesn't use it.

To finish creating the action, select Connect. Figure 7.25 shows the result. Xcode adds an action stub to the implementation file. If you build and run the app now, the action method is triggered if you click or tap the button. It doesn't do anything because there's no code inside the stub, but you have added a button handler to your app.

Figure 7.25

To help you complete the action, Xcode adds suitable code to the implementation file and optionally to the interface.

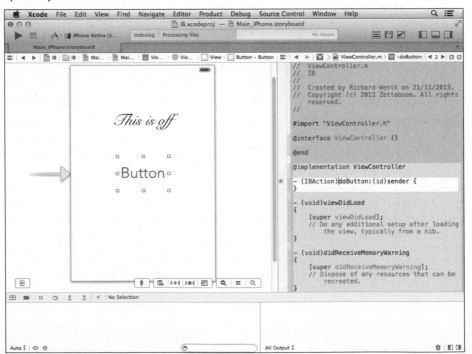

TIP

If you drop the action to the view controller header file, Xcode adds the stub to the implementation and adds a declaration in the header to make the action public. For convenience, you can achieve the same result by dropping the action between the `@interface` and `@end` words at the top of the implementation. These are a convenient extension of the interface included in the top of the file so you can choose either option without having to open the header.

Adding an outlet

Now that you have an action, you need an outlet, so you can change the label text when the user taps the button. To create an outlet, repeat the control-click and drag process to create a link between a UI object and the code, as shown in Figure 7.26.

Figure 7.26

Add an outlet to the convenient interface extension in the implementation file.

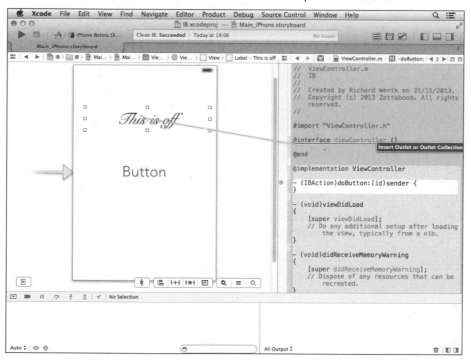

You can use the same source options. If you use the floating dialog or the Connections inspector, click the circle next to New Referencing Outlet to begin your link.

This time, the destination must be in the `@interface` area. Release the link between `@interface` and `@end`—Xcode doesn't let you create an outlet anywhere else. As before, you can use the extension of the interface area in the implementation file for convenience, to avoid switching back and forth between the implementation file with your code and the header.

When you release the mouse button, you see the dialog in Figure 7.27. In this example, we've added the outlet name: `theLabel`.

Figure 7.27

Name and define an outlet.

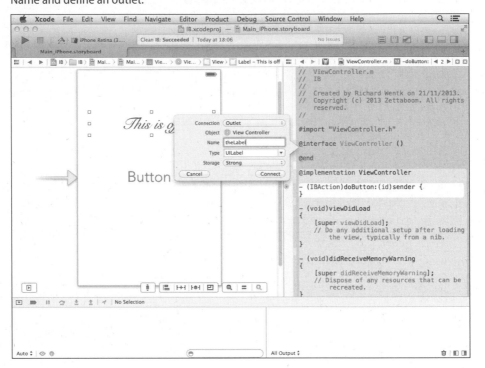

Naming and initializing the outlet

In a simple app, you can leave the other options set to their defaults. But here's a list of what they do:

- **Connection:** You can change your outlet into an action by selecting the other item in this menu. You won't usually need to—or want to.
- **Type:** If you have subclassed a control, you can select your subclass here.
- **Storage:** strong is used by the iOS ARC (Advanced Reference Counting) memory management system. Typically, a view controller has sole ownership over UI objects, so leave this set to strong.

When you click Done, Xcode adds the outlet code, as shown in Figure 7.28. Specifically, it adds a property declaration, creating a pointer to a control object—in this case, of the UILabel class.

Synthesizing the outlet

To use the outlet in your code, add an underscore when you use it. This autosynthesizes setters and getters. You can also use @synthesize after @implementation followed by the outlet name, and avoid the underscores.

Figure 7.28

Here's the interface with the new outlet.

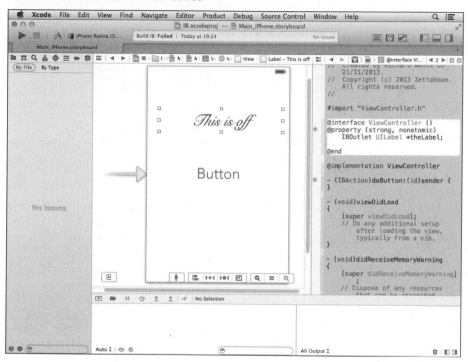

NOTE

If you're new to object-oriented programming, `@synthesize` highlights one of the standard quirks—properties are inaccessible without explicit setter and getter code to write and read their values. You can add your own code by hand, but `@synthesize` and autosynthesize with underscores save you from this chore.

Filling out an action stub

The app is nearly finished. The missing feature is custom code in the action stub that updates the label when the button is tapped.

In the implementation file, add this code between the curly brackets in the `IBAction` stub, as shown in Figure 7.29:

```
if ([theLabel.text isEqualToString: "@This is off"])
     theLabel.text = @"This is on";
else
     theLabel.text = @"This is off";
```

This code reads the current label text and updates the text to an alternate message when the button is tapped. The key point is that the outlet allows the label text to be read and written.

Figure 7.29

The completed app has a working message handler.

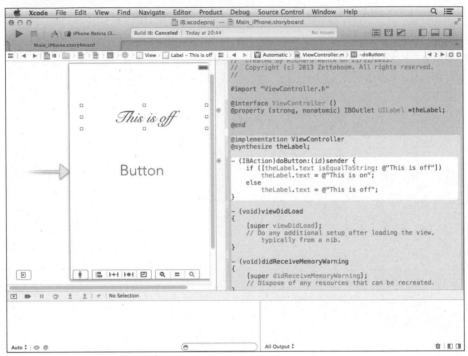

You can read and write any property. For example, you could change the label's position or the size or color of the text. This example makes a trivial change to the label text, but more complex objects work in the same way. For example, you can read a block of text entered by a user from a more complex text field object. You also can read or write image data to an image view.

NOTE

Another quirk of Objective-C is that you can't use `==` to compare strings, because it compares pointer addresses, not string content. You must use the `isEqualToString:` method to compare string content. Note also that you always set control objects via their properties. You might think you could just set the label to a string, but you can't—you must read and write its `text` property instead.

Testing the app

Select the iPhone Simulator, and click the arrow at the top left of the Xcode toolbar. The app should build and run in the Simulator window. Clicking the button in the UI toggles the label text between "This is off" and "This is on," as shown in Figure 7.30.

NOTE

For more advanced projects, you can create an *outlet collection*—a group of outlets held in a standard `NSArray`. Use this option when you want to collect a single object—often a controller—to multiple UI elements. To create a collection, drag a link from the New Referencing Outlet Collection item to your controller. Collections are optional, but they can be useful when you need to update multiple objects. For example, you can use NSArray's `makeObjects PerformSelector:` method to update every object in a collection with a single line of code.

Figure 7.30

The finished app is running in the Simulator.

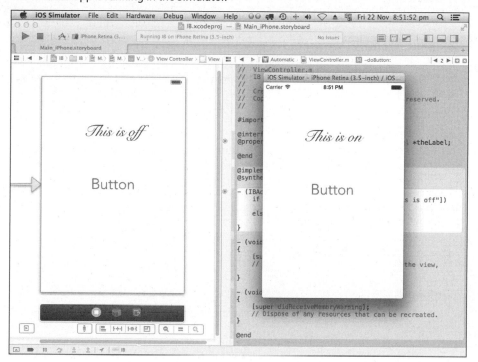

TIP

Did your app crash? Open the Connections inspector and check you didn't leave any spare unwanted properties or methods created by accident while you were experimenting. If you define an action or property in IB but don't link it to code, your app will crash.

Creating a universal app

To create a universal app, click the `Main_iPad.storyboard` file to load it into IB in place of the iPhone storyboard. Use the Assistant Editor to open the `ViewController.m` in the adjacent pane.

You now have two choices. You can create a separate set of UI objects, with different actions and outlets. Both can live in the same view controller file, but they work independently. You effectively have two completely separate storyboards with unique objects and code, although the code is in one shared file.

Copying objects

A more efficient approach is to copy and reuse the objects and code you created. You can add further objects to an iPad project if you need to, but reproducing the iPhone UI is often a good beginning.

To duplicate objects, use the Assistant Editor to place both storyboards side by side. Click a control in the iPhone storyboard, select File ⇨ Copy from the main Xcode menu, click anywhere in the view controller area of the iPad storyboard, and select File ⇨ Paste. This creates a copy of the control, keeping its styling and properties—except for the position, which you must fix manually.

TIP

You don't have to copy objects one at a time. You can drag a rubber-band box around a group and copy/paste the entire group in one go.

Duplicating links

Copying objects doesn't copy their links. To duplicate a link, select any object and either right-click it to show the floating event dialog or open the Connections inspector.

You can now drag a link from a control/event to an *existing* method, as shown in Figure 7.31. When you release the mouse, IB highlights the target method with a "Connect Action" label, so you can tell that you're connecting the event to an existing action instead of creating a new one. You can duplicate outlets in a similar way. Because only one storyboard is loaded at a time, depending on the platform the app is running on, there's no danger of confusion.

Figure 7.31

Duplicate iPhone UI elements in the iPad storyboard. You can create your UI in the opposite order.

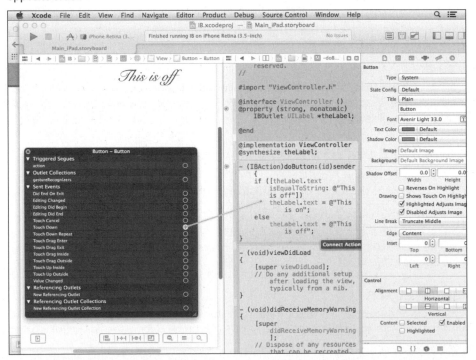

TIP
You can use this option to make multiple events trigger a single action in a single storyboard.

Understanding the IB Object Hierarchy

It's important to understand that objects in IB are drawn in a fixed order. In fact, they're organized in a hierarchy, which is drawn top-down. If you open the object list in IB, objects lower down the list cover objects higher up, because they're drawn last.

Some objects, such as `UIViews`, can contain other objects. In the example, the label and the button are both inside the main `UIView`. The structure is rather like a folder in Finder. You can use reveal triangles to open and close objects, showing and hiding the objects inside them. An object inside another appears indented in the list. When you change the physical position of an object in the hierarchy, all the objects inside it move with it.

You could, in theory, add a separate `UIView` to the UI, resizing both to create a split UI with two panes. Some commercial apps use this split format to create designs with multiple active areas that respond to the user in different ways. For example, a game might have a control panel with fixed buttons and a display area with animated scrolling graphics.

In complex apps, the hierarchy can become deep, with many objects. OS X apps tend to be more complex, because the menu tree includes many levels. If you look back to Figure 7.5, you can swap the File and Edit menus simply by swapping their top-level objects. This isn't a useful thing to do, but it demonstrates how the hierarchy is organized and how you can modify it to create your own menu and UI designs.

After you gain more experience with Xcode and Cocoa, you can manipulate this hierarchy in code, creating, adding, removing, and deleting your own views and controls as needed.

Designing without IB

IB is ideal for simpler interfaces that use Apple's standard kit of UI objects. Beginners typically create simple interfaces that use these objects as is, using IB as a layout and preview tool that controls the aesthetic elements of the interface—object justification and alignment, centering, and so on.

More advanced developers can create a complete UI without using IB at all, by calling the standard `alloc` and `init` methods on Cocoa objects to create the UI elements they want to use.

You can use this technique to create and destroy objects dynamically, assign useful defaults, define target objects and actions for user events, and make them appear on screen by linking them into your app's view hierarchy. This option is worth considering for universal UIs that have to work across all platforms and resolutions. IB includes smart positioning features that can make UIs somewhat platform-independent—but these features are not outstandingly intuitive. Experienced designers may prefer to make everything happen in code, for total control and for ease of customization.

But even if that's your aim, it's still useful to start with a practical introduction to IB to discover how UI design and object/code linking work in practice.

Summary

IB can seem intimidatingly complex when you first begin using it. There are many steps to remember, and even a simple UI can seem like lots of work. However, although the process has been simplified from earlier versions of Xcode, it could still be automated further. Don't underestimate the amount of time it takes to make a successful UI.

But like any other skill, UI creation gets easier with practice. If you're completely new to app development, you'll be trying to learn Cocoa and Objective-C at the same time as you learn Xcode and IB. It's a good idea not to try to master everything at once. Try to create a few very simple apps with IB, perhaps working with a few controls and perhaps some touch methods. After you've mastered the basics, you can move on to more complex projects, such as table views, which are significantly more complex and built largely with view-specific code outside of IB.

Creating More Advanced Effects with Interface Builder

C reating outlets and actions is a key step in application design with Interface Builder (IB). More complex applications require more advanced skills, which are discussed in this chapter.

Working with Constraints

If you change the form factor of the iPhone version of the IB project created in Chapter 7, by switching between the 3.5" and 4" Simulator views or by rotating the display, you'll see that the button is no longer centered vertically. When you place objects using IB's guidelines, the positions are static. They're not *responsive*—they don't keep track of the form factor and screen rotation and rearrange themselves automatically.

Figure 8.1 shows what happens when you rotate the layout in the Simulator when starting with a simplified version of the IB project UI from Chapter 7. Both objects keep their relative alignments but lose their overall alignment to the center line.

The main view works like a window into the UI. If you rotate the UI, the objects don't move inside it. If you change the widths of either object, you'll see they don't keep their horizontal alignment either.

NOTE
To rotate the Simulator, make sure the Simulator menu is visible, and then select Hardware ➪ Rotate Right or Hardware ➪ Rotate Left.

Introducing constraints and auto-layout

In previous versions of Xcode, objects were aligned dynamically using a springs-and-struts system. As the name suggests, struts had a fixed positions, and springs added a "force" that pushed items from a reference point—usually the edge of the view or some other object.

Figure 8.1

When you rotate a UI without constraints, bad things can happen.

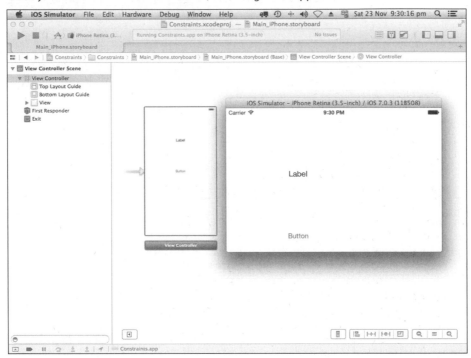

The constraints in Xcode are an extension of this idea. Constraints are undoubtedly more powerful and flexible. But they're also less intuitive and harder to work with. This is partly because the constraint system is more complex—you often need a large number of constraints to create a relatively simple result—but also because adding and managing constraints requires unexpected "hidden" effort.

Constraints are disabled by default, so you must add them manually. There are also occasional bugs, which means that previews do not reliably reflect what happens after you build and run an app.

TIP

As of Xcode 5.1, you can still use the old spring/strut system. Click any object in IB and select the File Inspector. Uncheck the Use Auto Layout box. The Size Inspector now shows the old Origin/Autosizing options. Use the Origin box to select a reference point for any object. You can select any corner, side, or center. Use the outer lines in the Autosizing box to lock the position of an object relative to any or all of the four sides of the containing view, and the inner lines to automatically adjust its size and/or position.

Understanding constraints

Constraints define a collection of size and positioning requirements. Unlike the springs-and-struts system, objects can change size as well as position. This makes it possible to fine-tune a UI so the layout looks good in all possible orientations and form factors, at the cost of some extra work.

Objects can:

- **Align their edges with the edges of any surrounding objects, plus or minus an offset.** The objects do not need to be adjacent. In addition to bounding edges, you can also align the *baseline* of an object—the bottom edge of its contents.

- **Swap *leading* and *trailing* edges.** Leading and trailing mean "left" and "right" in Western languages, but are swapped if your UI is localized to work in a right-to-left text locale.

- **Match the height, width, and/or position of any object.**

- **Support *compression*, which allows them to change size and shape as the form factor changes.**

- **Support a priority order.** Constraints with a higher priority are more likely to be satisfied exactly.

- **Support approximate solutions.** The constraints engine does the best it can, given your requirements, but objects may not be placed exactly.

- **Support justified alignment with *hidden views.*** Constraints do not perform justification automatically. If you want to justify an object—for example, to keep it centered between two other edges—you must add hidden views on either side of the object and set up their constraints so their heights match and the justified object is locked between them.

- **Not compile.** If you do not add enough constraints or your requests make no sense to IB, it reports errors and does not build your UI.

TIP

As you'll see, the constraints system includes a priority slider. A useful rule is to set up basic constraints first and experiment with priority later. It's difficult to work out exactly what priority does, but according to the official documentation, it simply sets the dynamic calculation order. It doesn't change the positioning influence of a constraint. So increasing priority won't change how much an item moves. But it may change whether or not it moves.

Getting started with constraints

You can reuse the IB project from the previous chapter or create a new project with a button and a label. Use guidelines to center the button vertically and horizontally and to center the label horizontally only, roughly halfway up the view.

As a first step, we add a constraint to keep the button centered. Click the button to select it, and click the Align button in the dock, as shown in Figure 8.2, to show a pop-over.

Click the two lower check boxes to constrain the position of the button. Note that you can't click any of the other check boxes. They're available only if you select *at least two objects*. This can be confusing the first time you encounter it because the other options aren't grayed out, so they look as if they should be active.

Most of IB's settings do not have a confirm option. Constraints are different. They take effect only when you click the Add Constraints button at the bottom of the pop-over. You *must* click this button, as shown in Figure 8.3; otherwise, IB ignores your changes.

Figure 8.2

Add an alignment constraint.

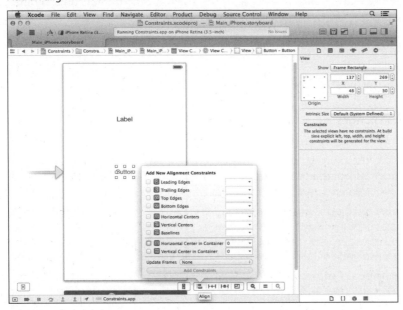

Figure 8.3

Confirm the constraints.

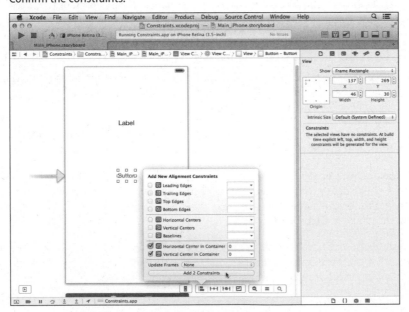

Figure 8.4 shows how IB adds a list of constraints to the Size Inspector with a description for each one and also adds solid guidelines to show constraints are active. To delete a constraint, click the gear icon and select Delete. You can also click Select and Edit . . . to display the constraint's editable settings.

Figure 8.4

View an object's constraints in the Size Inspector.

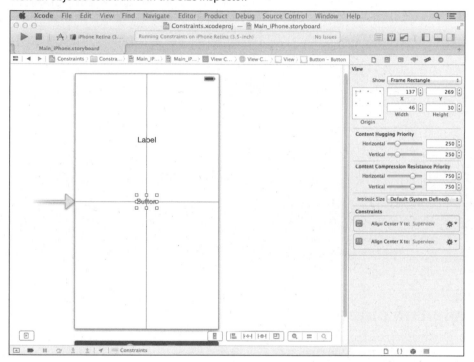

Figure 8.5 shows how the button stays centered when you rotate the view in the Simulator. The label still has no constraints, so it keeps its old relative position. If you change the device form factor, you see the button is still centered.

CAUTION

If you keep rotating the view, you see it doesn't rotate to the upside-down orientation. The orientation check boxes in the General tab of the build settings don't change this. On iOS 6 and later, you need to add some code to your view controller:

```
- (NSUInteger)supportedInterfaceOrientations
{
    return UIInterfaceOrientationMaskAll;
}
```

Figure 8.5

Check the constraint in the Simulator.

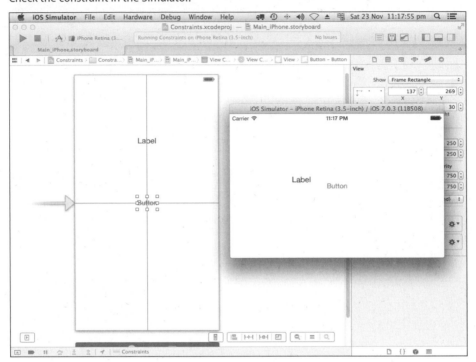

Aligning object edges

UI design is as much an art as a science, and the constraint system gives you many creative options. Where should the label appear? It needs to be horizontally centered. This can be handled with a simple horizontal centering constraint, similar to the one we just created for the button. But how should it be positioned vertically?

The simplest option is to lock it with a fixed offset to either the top view edge or the top of the button. Locking it to the button keeps the layout fixed when the view rotates. Locking to the edge changes the layout. Either option is acceptable, and it's up to you to decide which works best in your app's UI.

To lock edges, select an object and click the Pin icon in the dock, to display the pop-over shown in Figure 8.6. This is one of the key constraint dialogs, and it's more intuitive than perhaps it looks.

The top area shows the current distances to the next nearest edges. You can click the disclosure triangle in each quadrant to measure the distance to any other object in the UI. Because this is a simple UI, you get three choices: the button, and the main containing view, and the (invisible) containing view inner layout guideline, as shown in Figure 8.7.

Figure 8.6

Show the constraint pinning pop-over.

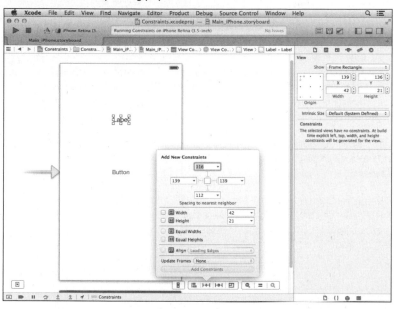

Figure 8.7

Set up and confirm a constraint. Note the red line on the main preview, which indicates that a constraint exists.

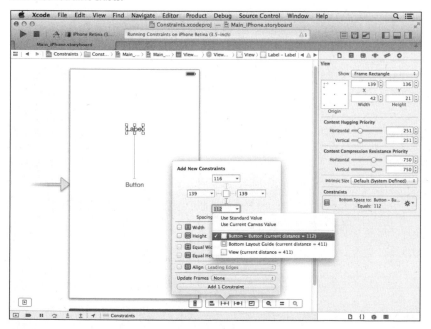

To fix a distance, click one or more of the red bars. In the figure, we fixed the distance to the top of the button. The bar becomes solid to indicate the distance is pinned, and a corresponding line appears on the main preview.

This dialog has a couple of quirks. The first is that *you must remember to click the Add Constraints button at the bottom of the pop-over.* If you don't, your changes are ignored.

The second is that if you display the pop-over again, the solid red bar is no longer visible. Most users might assume this means the constraint isn't active. But it is—it's just not shown in the pop-over. Counterintuitively, the red bars in the pop-over don't indicate existing constraints. They only change state while you're adding a new constraint.

After you add an alignment constraint, add another constraint to center the label horizontally. You can repeat the steps from the previous section, but this time check only the Horizontal Center in Container box.

Build and run the project, and rotate the view in the Simulator to landscape mode. Figure 8.8 shows the result. The label's position is now fixed, but it's too high. We could fix this by lowering the label so it's closer to the button in both orientations. But this would make the UI look squashed in portrait mode.

Figure 8.8

Rotate the UI with a fixed offset.

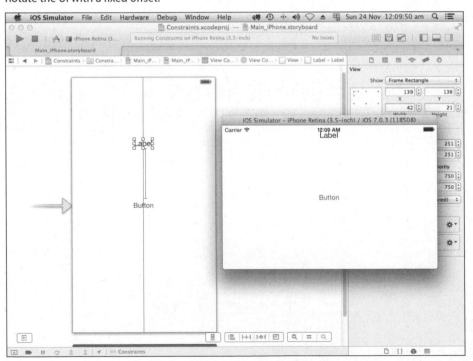

Is there a better solution? There is, but it's not straightforward. The ideal would be a simple "place this button halfway between these two edges" constraint. In fact, the Tab Bar class has a very similar feature. You can auto-align objects on the tab bar by including spacers, which automatically shrink and stretch as the UI rotates.

Unfortunately, the constraint system doesn't include this. But we can create the same effect manually at the cost of some time and effort, by adding a couple of *invisible spacer views.*

Justifying objects with spacer views

Begin by clearing all existing constraints. Click the Resolve Auto Layout Issue icon to the right of the Pin icon in the dock, and select Clear All Constraints in View Controller.

You won't find invisible spacer views in the IB Object Library. To create one, add a standard view and make it invisible by setting its color to Transparent Color. This leaves its positioning influence but makes it disappear.

Open the Utility pane, click the cube to select the Object Library, and drag a view from the library so it covers the label and the button. Use the center guidelines to center the view, and drag the top and bottom edge center drag handles until the top of the view aligns with the guideline under the label and the bottom aligns with the guidelines over the button. Figure 8.9 shows the result.

Figure 8.9

Add a spacer view.

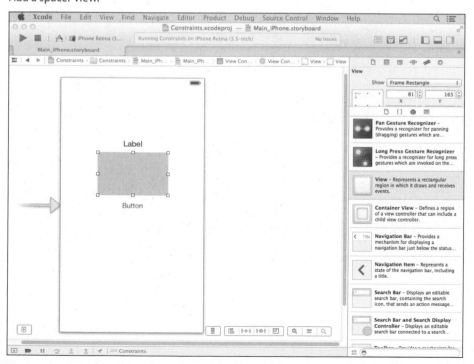

T I P

The default view background color is white. You can see the spacer view while it's selected, but it disappears against the main white background when you deselect it. You may find it useful to change the spacer's background color in the Attributes Inspector to something more visible while you're working. You can change the color to Transparent Color after the constraints are in place.

Copy and paste the spacer to create another. Drag the copy above the label. Resize it so the top edge aligns with the top guideline, and the bottom edge aligns with the label, as shown in Figure 8.10. Unless you have a very good eye, the two spacers will be different heights. This doesn't matter; after constraints are added, auto layout fixes that automatically.

Now we can begin adding constraints. The first requirement is horizontal centering. Drag a rubber-band box around all the objects, click the Align icon, check the Horizontal Center in Container check boxes, and—of course—click the Add 4 Constraints button at the bottom of the pop-over.

For the button only, repeat the process to center it vertically. You can now use the button as an anchor for the rest of the layout.

Figure 8.10

Add and position a duplicate spacer.

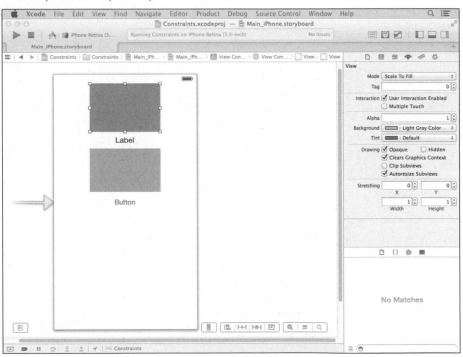

The rest of the process is long-winded. The goal is a chain of constraints anchored by the button at the bottom and the top guideline at the top of the view, as follows:

- The bottom edge of the lower spacer needs to be locked to an offset from the top of the button.
- The top edge of the upper view should be locked to the guideline at the top of the view.
- The top of the label should be locked to the bottom of the upper spacer.
- The bottom of the label should be locked to the top of the lower spacer.
- The two spacers should have an equal width and height. This constraint keeps the label equally spaced between them, which creates the justification effect we want.

Figure 8.11 shows one step in the process—adding the top and bottom constraints to the label, so it's locked to the top and bottom edges of the spacers.

Figure 8.11

This is what the button looks like midway through adding the full list of constraints.

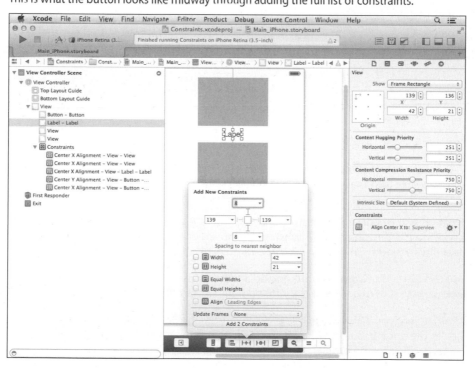

Figure 8.12 shows the (almost) final list of constraints. If you look at the top right of the object list, you see a small red dot with an arrow. This understated indicator tells you that the constraints system doesn't have enough information to define the layout unambiguously. In fact, layout lines are orange when the object's layout isn't fully defined, and blue when it is.

Figure 8.12

And here's our first attempt at a finished list of constraints.

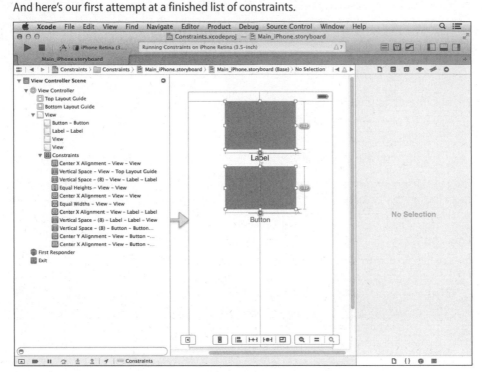

TIP

To match widths or heights, select any two or more items, click the Pin icon in the dock, and check Equal Widths and/or Equal Heights. Don't forget to click the Add Constraints button at the bottom of the pop-over.

What's missing? Click the button to find out. Figure 8.13 shows that the spacer views don't have a width set. Unfortunately, the constraints system isn't intelligent enough to work with the default view width, so you have to set a width explicitly.

You can fix this in two ways. You can add another constraint manually; for example, you could lock the edges of one view to the left and right edges of the container view.

Alternatively, you can try to fix the problem automatically. Click the Resolve Auto Layout Issues icon in the dock and select Add Missing Constraints in View Controller. IB tries to guess what it needs to do to fix the problem.

In this example, the guess is good. It adds extra view width constraints that generate enough information to create an unambiguous layout.

NOTE
If the guess isn't good—which can happen with complex layouts—select Undo, and try adding further constraints manually until a good guess becomes possible.

Figure 8.13

Fix constraint issues automatically.

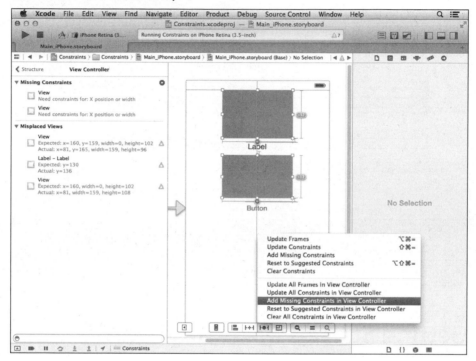

Figure 8.14 shows the finished layout. The spacer views have been left gray so you can see how they're automatically compressed by the rotation while still matching sizes, so the label stays an equal distance between them.

Constraint programming can take up a significant amount of the time spent on UI design. It becomes more straightforward as you gain experience, but the lack of simple automation for common problems means that it's rarely an easy system to work with.

TIP
You can also manage constraints in code, through a mini-language. See the Auto Layout Guide for details and examples. Code can make it easier to manage complex UIs with many aligned elements.

Figure 8.14

The finished view shows automatic vertical justification.

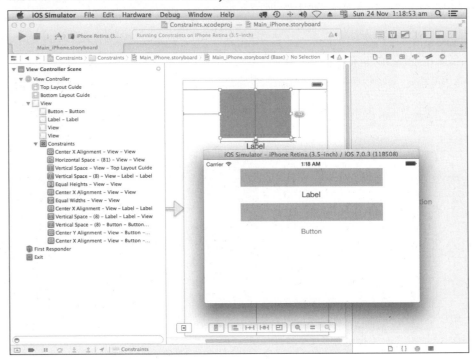

Getting Started with Storyboards

In previous versions of Xcode, apps with multiple views required manual *view swapping*. Often, this meant leaving a view controller in memory, while loading and releasing further view controllers, often linking the views defined in their nib files into the "master" controller. This created unintuitive app logic, where a master controller managed the screen appearance, while other controllers managed the events in each set of views.

Storyboards make view swapping simpler, more explicit, and more intuitive. However, storyboards in IB are not a complete view management solution. You must add your own custom controller subclasses with extra code, even for basic effects.

Because so much of view and segue management is code-based, the following example introduces some basic concepts, but it is not a complete primer on segue and transition design. Fortunately, you can find plenty of detailed examples, with reusable sample code, online. But you need to understand how segues and subclassing work before you can add them to your own apps.

CAUTION

Don't forget that if you want a universal app, you must duplicate storyboard content across both iPhone and iPad storyboards. Note that as of iOS 7 and OS X 10.9, storyboards are for iOS only, but this may change in a future version of OS X.

Understanding segue types

A *modal* segue displays a temporary view that can be dismissed by the user. By default, the view slides up from the bottom of the screen and slides down again when dismissed. You can choose from a small selection of alternative transitions.

A *push* segue slides the next view in from the left and slides it back to the right when the user goes back one level.

With a *custom* segue, you can create your own segue subclass and fill it with exciting view transition code. Use this option when you want to create visual transitions that aren't built into iOS.

Modal segues are intended as one-offs. The user stops what he or she is doing, looks at a new view for a short period, perhaps changes a setting or two, and then returns to the original task. A typical example would be a single app preferences view.

The other segues are designed for more complex app navigation. The user works with them to move through the app, revealing features that are grouped together for a good reason. The user then typically moves back through the views one by one.

NOTE

With some tricky coding, it's possible in iOS to return to the start of the view sequence with a single operation. Sometimes, this can be a good thing to do—but only if the operation is clearly labeled and doesn't confuse users.

You can add a modal segue between any two views. The other segues work only if the app includes a *root view navigation controller*. To use a root view navigation controller, you must *embed* the view at the start of the chain into the controller. The controller then keeps track of forward and back movement for you.

A modal view can be dismissed only with code in the corresponding view controller. For the other views, the root controller manages movement without code. You can add code for custom effects and to manage object passing. But it's not essential for basic navigation.

Creating a modal segue

For this example, create a blank Single View application from the template. Save it as Segue. Select the view in the storyboard, add a button to the view in the view controller, and change the button text to "Modal Segue." Figure 8.15 shows the result. The Modal Segue button loads the next view with a modal transition when the user taps it.

Figure 8.15

Add a forward button to a view.

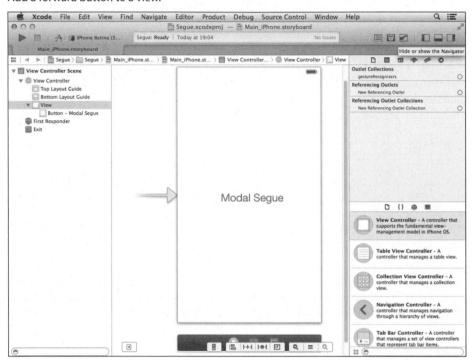

N O T E

You can add constraints to the layout. We'll skip that step for this storyboard example. The constraints system and the segue system are independent.

From the Object Library, drag and drop another View Controller. You can drop it anywhere—remember, the view controller layout is cosmetic—but it makes sense to drop it to the right of the source controller.

Ctrl-click the button and drag a link to the second controller. When you release it, you see the menu shown in Figure 8.16. Click the modal option.

Xcode adds a graphic link between the two views to show you there's a segue between them. It also adds a modal segue to the Triggered Segues list in the Connections Inspector, as shown in Figure 8.17.

You can delete the segue by clicking the tiny cross to the left of "modal" in the Connections Inspector or by clicking the new segue graphic between the views and pressing the Delete key.

Figure 8.16

Select the segue type after control-clicking a link.

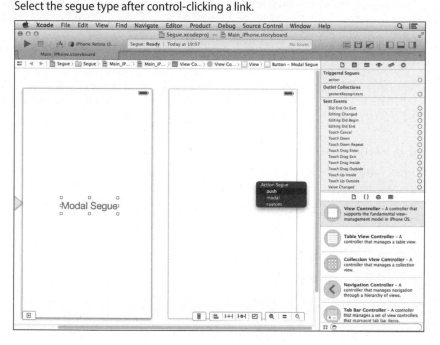

Figure 8.17

Review the segue.

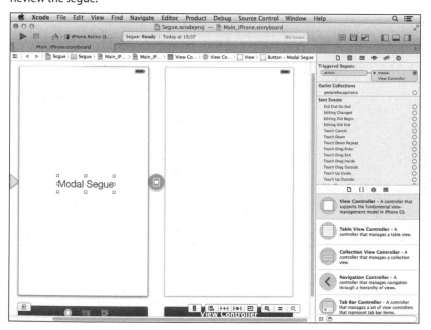

Optionally, you can select the view you added and change its background color in the Attributes Inspector, to make it more obvious how the segue works. This step is optional, but it's difficult to see the movement with a plain white view on top of another plain white view.

If you build and run the app and tap the Modal Segue button, you see the new view slides up from the bottom. There's no back option yet, so it stays there forever, trapping the user in a dead end.

To fix this, we need to add some code to the new view controller. But where does the code go? When you add a new view controller to a storyboard, Xcode doesn't create corresponding code files for you. So you have to add them by hand and then tell IB to use them.

Adding a view controller subclass

With the Project Navigator open, click the Segue folder to highlight it, right-click it, select New File. . . Select Objective-C class, and click Next. Type **UIViewController** into the "Subclass of" menu box. Leave the check boxes unchecked. Type **MyModalViewController** into the Class box, as shown in Figure 8.18, click Next, and then click Create.

Figure 8.18

Add code files for the new view controller.

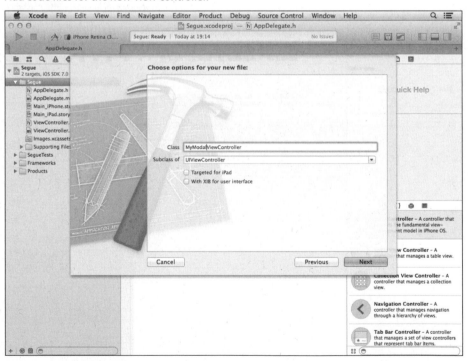

Xcode adds the new files to the project. But IB doesn't know about them yet. Click your story-board file again. Click the view controller you added in the previous sub-section, and click the Identity Inspector.

TIP

The easy way to select files in IB is to keep the Object List open and click the files in the list. Clicking in the preview window can be hit and miss. (It's often more miss than hit.) Be careful to select the view controller, not the view inside it.

Click the Class menu in the Custom Class sub-pane, and select MyModalViewController, as shown in Figure 8.19. This subclassing process is a key skill in IB. It tells IB that the object on-screen, and visible in the preview, contains the code in the file you just added.

CAUTION

If you forget this step, IB assumes your new on-screen view controller is a plain vanilla instance of UIViewController, with no custom code. This is rarely, if ever, what you want.

NOTE

If you can't see your view controller in the list, you've probably selected a view object instead of the view controller. The other items in the list are existing Cocoa Touch subclasses of UIViewController.

You can now add a back button and connect it to an action that returns the user to the original view. (This is called *dismissing* the modal view.)

Drag a button from the Object library, and drop it on the view. Edit its text to "Return." Add an `IBAction` called `returnFromModal:` to `MyModalViewController`, using the steps in the preceding chapter.

Figure 8.19

Select your new subclass in IB.

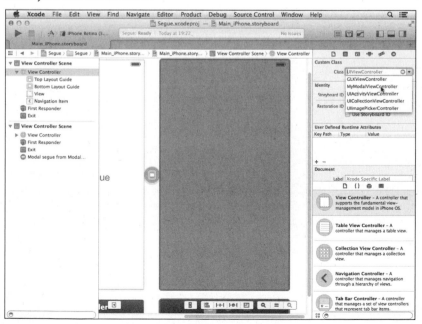

Add the following code to the action:

```
-(IBAction)returnFromModal:(id)sender {
    [self dismissViewControllerAnimated: YES completion: nil];
}
```

Build and run the app. As shown in Figure 8.20, the Return button dismisses the modal view, returning the user to the original view.

Figure 8.20

This app has a modal segue.

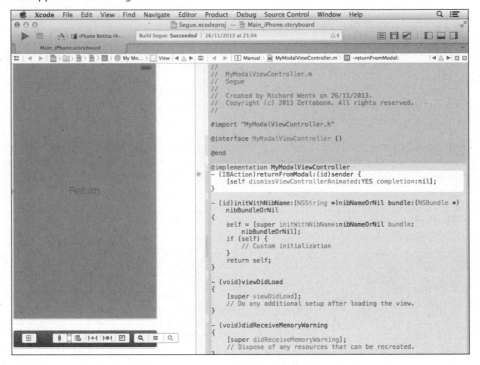

TIP

If you want to see the other standard transition types, click the segue icon between the views, open the Utility pane if it isn't open already, and select the Attributes Inspector. Click Storyboard Segue if there are no details under it. The transitions appear in the Transitions menu. You can also select a different segue type here. But if your main controller isn't embedded into a `UINavigationController`, the other options will crash your app.

Adding a navigation controller

The push and modal segue options work only with a navigation controller. Unhelpfully, there's no template that includes a controller and makes it accessible in a simple way. (The Master/Detail template includes a controller, but it also adds custom code that you don't need for a simple app.)

You can add a navigation controller in two ways. The complicated option is to drag a Navigation Controller from the Object Library and drop it into the preview window, as shown in Figure 8.21. You'll see it comes with a free Table View, which you probably don't want. Click the Table View to select it, and type Delete. Optionally, you can move the new controller to the left of the others, for neatness.

Figure 8.21

Add a new Navigation Controller object.

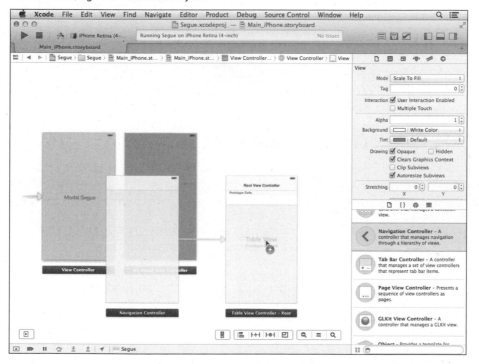

Optionally, use the zoom out button—it looks like a magnifier with a – (minus) sign—so you can see both controllers in the window at the same time. You can now control drag from the navigation controller to the view controller, and click the Root View option in the pop-up, as shown in Figure 8.22.

The simpler option is to select the view controller, and click Editor ⇨ Embed In ⇨ Navigation Controller from the main menu. IB adds an arrow pointing from the navigation controller to the view controller. This option doesn't create an unwanted table view—although often you'll create segues using a table view, so you may find the first option more useful.

We can now add yet another view controller, and make it appear with a push segue. Drag another view controller from the Object Library, and drop it on the canvas. Optionally, you can rearrange the existing controllers to make the layout neater.

Figure 8.22

Embed the original controller in the new controller.

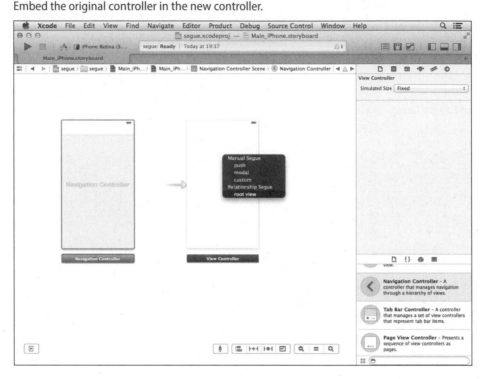

Move the original Modal Segue button up, and add another button to the view controller. Change the label to read "Push Segue." Optionally, you can change the color of the view in the new view controller to make it distinct from the other views. The result so far looks like Figure 8.23.

To create the segue, simply drag a link from the button, release it on the new view controller, and select the Push segue from the floating menu. IB adds a segue link on the canvas. If you build and run the app, you get the result shown in Figure 8.24. You don't need to add further code or a Back button. iOS adds a Back button inside a navigation bar automatically—and it just works.

CAUTION

Of course, in a real app you would populate the second view controller with further controls, so you would still need to subclass it to manage them. However, basic forward/back navigation works without further code.

Figure 8.23

Get ready for a push segue.

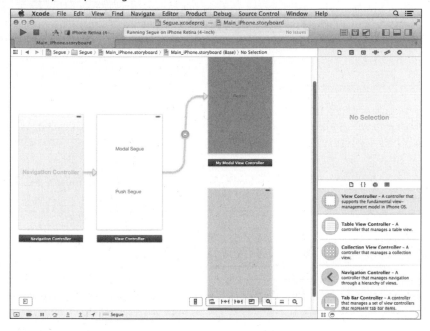

Figure 8.24

Here's the view after a push segue.

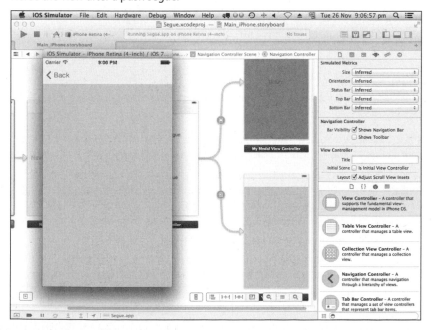

CAUTION

Did your app crash? Xcode isn't good at keeping track of changes to storyboards. Try the following, in order. Select Product ⇨ Clean in the main menu; then build and run again. Close the project, and reload it. Close Xcode, and restart it. This is also a problem if you use the Exit button under the view controllers, which is an alternative way to add a Back button. Xcode often ignores return actions unless you restart it. Finally, you can also try deleting the app in the Simulator or device.

Using table views

You might think that with a navigation controller and a table view with a few custom cells, you can create a menu with simple forward/back navigation. Unfortunately, this isn't possible. IB shows "prototype content" for table views in IB, which means the content isn't available to your app.

Table view design turns out to be far more complex and code-based. You must use a data source method to supply the table view with the cell contents you want. The full details are beyond the scope of this book, but you can find worked examples in many places online.

Understanding Placeholders

View controllers in iOS and the object list in OS X include extra items that don't correspond to specific objects. The two items are called *File's Owner* and *First Responder*. They are similar to "'real" objects, with some differences.

Using File's Owner

In OS X, File's Owner is a placeholder for the object that loaded the nib. Because any object can load any nib, IB doesn't always know the identity of the loader ahead of time. In practice, you can usually treat File's Owner as a placeholder for the current view controller (iOS) or window (OS X.) In fact, iOS Storyboards make this relationship explicit.

Using First Responder

All iOS and OS X applications include a *responder chain*—an implied hierarchy of objects that handles user events. Here's what to expect:

- Windows, views, and certain other objects are subclasses of an abstract event management class (`UIResponder` in iOS and `NSResponder` in OS X).
- This class includes a prewritten selection of methods that can handle standard user events such as copy, paste, undo, and so on. You can make controls send messages that trigger these methods just by linking them in IB. But nothing happens unless you add code to implement the method.
- You can add your own custom events to this list.
- Unlike a standard action, these messages are passed from object to object until a matching event handler method is found. A common test sequence is view ⇨ view controller ⇨ window ⇨ application, but this may vary, because it depends on the design of the application.

- The First Responder icon is the connection point for this chain. It lists *all* the valid handler methods, in all objects that are part of the responder chain. It's the central event handler for an application, and it provides a convenient single access point for responder methods that may be scattered across multiple objects.

- Events without a handler are ignored.

In practice, you link objects that generate messages to the responder chain in the usual way. Figure 8.25 shows the standard messages available in iOS.

Figure 8.25

View the First Responder actions in an iOS application.

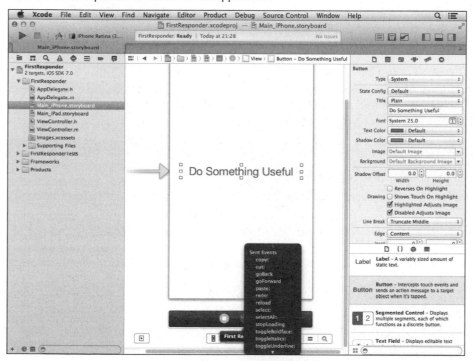

Unlike a standard action, linking a button to these default actions *doesn't generate code for you.* IB doesn't know which object you want to put the handler code in, so it doesn't try to guess. Instead, you must add the code by hand to whichever object in the chain works best for your app.

Typically, this means copying a method signature from the `UIResponder` or `NSResponder` class—for example, for the `copy:` method—and creating your own full implementation.

Note that the methods you need to implement aren't mentioned in the UIResponder Class Reference. They're defined in the UIResponderStandardEditActions Protocol Reference, which is part of the UIKit Framework Reference. You won't find them unless you know this document exists.

It's worth repeating again that you should review all the references used in a framework; otherwise, you may miss critical features. To add custom methods to the responder chain, define them as an `IBAction` and add them to a nib object. They appear in the responder list automatically, and you can link to them in the usual way.

For comparison, Figure 8.26 shows the First Responder list created by the standard OS X application template. iOS includes a handful of standard responder methods. OS X supports around 200.

In the application template, many are pre-linked to menu items. Some of the useful methods are implemented. You can easily add code to your own subclasses to make any of the rest "live."

NOTE

An OS X application includes an extra placeholder object called Application, which stands in for the main application object. It includes a selection of predefined actions, most of which aren't implemented. For information about handling these and other related application events, see the companion *Cocoa* Developer Reference title.

CAUTION

Some very important events don't appear in IB. For example, iOS and OS X touch messages—`touchesBegan:`, among others—aren't listed anywhere in IB. They're hardwired into the responder chain, and you can't redirect them in IB. You can only respond to them with code.

Figure 8.26

OS X supports many more First Responder actions than iOS.

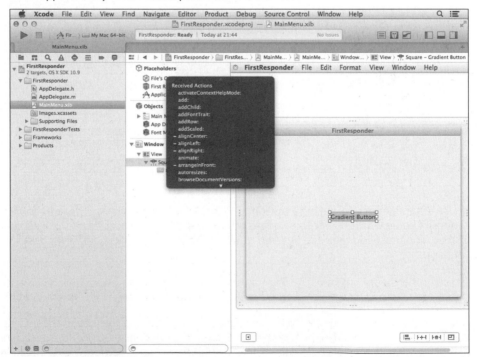

Using Exit

Storyboards have a separate placeholder called Exit. In theory, this should provide an exit point for the segue, similar to the Back button generated by a navigation controller. In practice, in Xcode 5.0.x this feature seems to be buggy and unreliable, and it often ignores exit methods. It's better to use an alternative scheme for exiting a view in a storyboard, such as the ones introduced earlier in this chapter.

Subclassing and Customizing Views

You can subclass any object in IB, including controls and views. Sometimes, you need to customize controls with your own code; for example, you may want to capture touch events and process them without losing them. You can do this by adding a touch event handler and then copying and sending the events to a different object in your app.

More often, you need to customize the main view managed by a view controller—for example, to create custom animations or even to create completely customized UI elements.

Creating simple subclasses

To subclass any object, follow the steps you used to customize the view controller:

1. Add a new subclass to the project in the main Xcode editor, and add custom code to implement new features.

2. Assign the subclass to an existing object in IB.

After you have completed Step 2, you can continue to develop and debug your custom code and the new code will be active in your UI.

CAUTION

Customizing Apple's own subclasses of `UIView` and `NSView`—map views, web views, image views, and so on—can be a frustrating experience. The more complex subclasses include undocumented features and properties, and it's often impossible to add new features without tricks and work-arounds. For example, in some situations, animated view swaps are handled by "invisible" views that aren't part of the officially documented view system. Always check unofficial online developer forums to see if other developers have experienced problems—and if they have already solved them.

Working with more advanced subclassing techniques

The following techniques are more specialized. You may not need to use them at all, but it's useful to know they're available.

Adding User Defined Attributes to a subclass

If you subclass an object in the IB library, it automatically inherits that object's attributes. For example, a subclass of `UIViewController` includes options to set a default orientation and a status bar, a top bar, and a bottom bar. You can't change these attributes, and you can't add further attributes of your own.

But not all Cocoa and Cocoa Touch objects have IB attributes; in fact, most objects don't. How can you set initial values for these objects?

One option is to use code. But IB includes a User Defined Runtime Attributes feature, illustrated in Figure 8.27. Objects without "official" attributes include a general purpose keypath, value, and type editor in the Identity Inspector. You can add initial values/types here, and they're loaded and set when the nib loads.

Each item is equivalent to running the `setValue: forKeyPath:` method on an object. In the figure, the example has the same effect as adding

```
[self setValue: @"This is my string" forKeyPath: @"thisIsMyKey"];
```

to an `init` method in the application delegate. Supported types include strings, localized strings, Booleans, numbers, and `nil`.

Figure 8.27

Add custom attributes to an object.

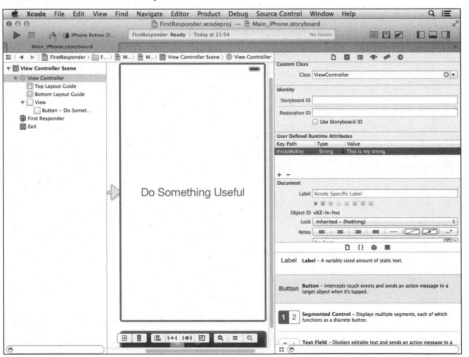

CAUTION

This option doesn't always work. Check it before you use it.

Subclassing File's Owner

Note that you can follow the steps given previously to subclass File's Owner. Typically, you don't need to do this unless you want to add features to the NSApplication/UIApplication classes, or you have a complex nib hierarchy and you need to add code to an element buried in the view hierarchy. For simpler apps, you can leave the default File's Owner class assignments unchanged. But it's useful to remember that even though File's Owner is a placeholder, you can still set its class using the Identity Inspector.

Creating static image backgrounds

To create a static background in an iOS project, use a `UIImageView` object. Drag and drop it on the UI, as shown in Figure 8.28. Then drag its position in the object list so it's behind the other objects and higher up the list and is drawn first, so it appears behind them. By default, the image view doesn't fill the UI. Resize it manually by dragging the edges and corners.

Figure 8.28

Add an image view to a UI to create static wallpaper.

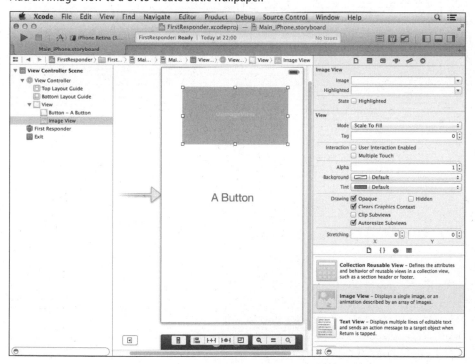

Creating a colored background

The image view doesn't have to contain an image; you can use it to create a static colored background. To select a preset color, click the blue up and down arrows at the right of the Background menu. You see the list shown in Figure 8.29, which displays standard system colors.

While black, white, and gray appear as you'd expect, some of the background colors are more or less obviously textured. For example, the Group Table View Background Color includes vertical stripes, and the Simulator may not always display this accurately.

CAUTION

Some of the textures look good, but textures may be OS dependent, and they may not appear correctly in the Simulator. If you build an app that supports an older version of iOS, users may not see what you expect them to. To test this, keep one or more hardware test units running older versions of iOS. Differences aren't usually critical, but it's useful to be aware of this issue.

To set a custom color, click in the area to the left of the menu's up and down arrows to reveal a standard OS X Color Picker. Use the controls to select a color for the image view in the usual way. You can change the opacity for special effects.

Figure 8.29

Set a static background color.

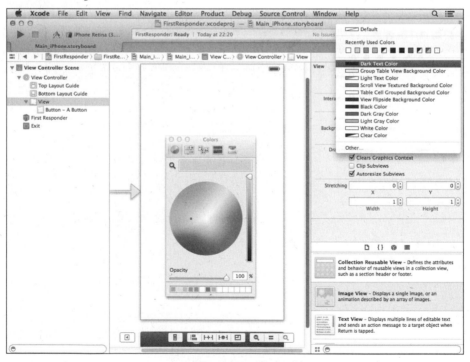

TIP

To make the image view transparent, select the Clear Color from the default list or set the Opacity to 0 in the Color Picker. Occasionally, you may want to include a dummy view that collects and processes events before passing them on to other objects—rather like a constraint spacer, but with touch code. To do this, use a subclassed transparent view.

TIP
You can select a background color for any view. You don't need to add an image view.

Importing an image file

For more complex static effects, you can import an image file. This example demonstrates how to import a file for a full-sized background view that creates a wallpaper effect. The procedure for customizing button graphics is very similar.

You also can extend the procedure to create custom objects such as radio buttons or game tokens. Active features require extra code.

To add a media file, right-click the Resources group in the Project Navigator and select Add Files to <Project Name>... When a dialog appears, navigate to a suitable file.

TIP
You can also drag and drop media files from Finder into the Project Navigator.

You can add the contents of one or more complete folders from this dialog and optionally create a group for each folder. You also can choose to copy the file into the project or to create an indirect reference. For this project, select the Copy option, as shown in Figure 8.30.

Figure 8.30

Use this procedure to import any media file, including graphics, sounds, HTML content, text, and so on.

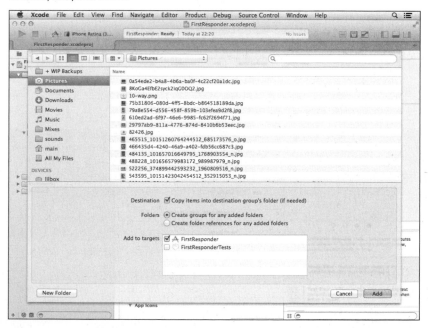

After import, you see the file in two places, as shown in Figure 8.31. It's added to the Supporting Files group in the Project Navigator. It also appears in the Media library, which is selected by the icon at the top right of the library area. If you add further files, they appear in both locations.

Figure 8.31

After import, the new file appears as a Supporting File and is also added to the Media library.

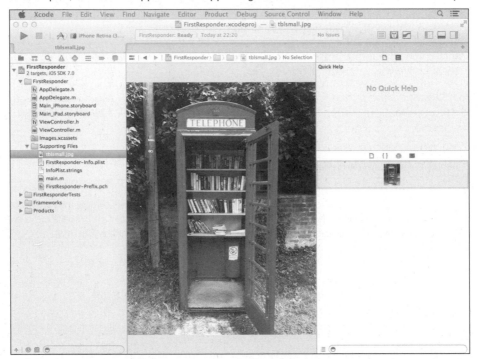

In a complex project with many media files, it can be useful to create new groups to collect related media files into one location. You also can create a group for each class and include any associated media files, perhaps in a sub-group to simplify navigation.

You can right-click any file and select Open with External Editor to load an editor that isn't built into Xcode. If you save the file afterward, Xcode reloads the new content automatically.

As of iOS 7, it's considered good practice to pack images into the `Images.xcassets` file. In Xcode 5.1, you can add only .png files. No other file format is supported.

To use the assets file, click it to select it in the Editor pane. By default, it includes AppIcon and LaunchImage sets, which are described in Chapter 13. To add a new image, click the + (plus) icon at the bottom of the pane with the list of assets and select New Image Set.

The pane now shows two image slots with 1x and 2x resolutions. Drag two .png files with the correct resolutions to the two slots. You can now assign them, as discussed in the next section.

Assigning an image file

Figure 8.32 shows how to assign the image file to the image view. In the Attributes Inspector, select the image from the Image drop-down menu. All compatible images loaded into the project appear in the menu.

Figure 8.32

Assign an image file to the image view.

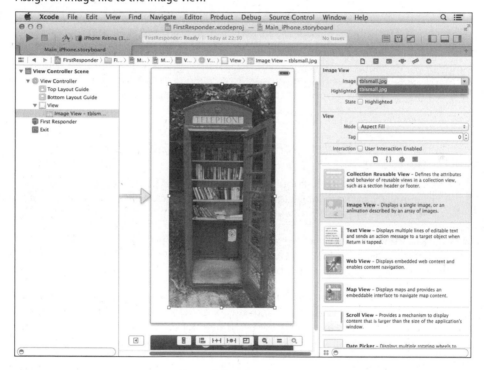

Once assigned, the image view loads the file automatically when the app runs. No further code is needed. You also can preview the image in place in the UI, although certain features such as PNG transparency may not work reliably.

TIP

To assign a custom image to a button, set the button type to Custom in the Attributes Inspector and assign the image file to the Background property—*not* the Image property. This is enough to implement basic highlighting, and the button darkens when tapped. Buttons have four potential states, but you can ignore the other states unless you're creating complex effects. The Background property defines the button's default look. You can layer the Image property on top of the button for more complex effects.

NOTE

Although OS X supports an `NSImageView` class that is similar to `UIImageView` in iOS, OS X applications are less likely to use background wallpaper. Images are usually used as decorative icons. The iOS Media Library is empty by default. The OS X Media Library includes a selection of standard icons and sounds that you can drag into your application without having to import them. Use the Image Well object with no border to duplicate the effect of an iOS image view.

Supporting Non-English Languages

Translating labels and messages into languages other than English is known as *localizing* an application. Localization improves an application's sales prospects, but it can be time-consuming and should be done selectively. Dialects of French and Spanish cover much of the non-English world and should be considered essential. China is becoming an important market. Germany, Japan, and Korea have enthusiastic technology markets and are worth considering. Other languages can be supported as needed for specific applications and locations.

In Xcode 5, IB supports localization in two ways:

- For OS X projects, each supported language can have a separate nib file, with custom labeling.

- For iOS projects, each language can have a separate storyboard. Or it can read from a .strings file for each language, which includes a dictionary of translations of the strings in the "base localization," which is usually English.

To begin localizing a project, click the project icon in the Project Navigator, select Project—localization is not available for individual targets—and find the Localizations sub-pane. Click the + (plus) icon to add a language, as shown in Figure 8.33.

You can then select the strings used in the base (reference) localization, as shown in Figure 8.34. The default is to create a localizable strings file for each language. The more intuitive but time-consuming option is to create a separate storyboard for each language. Neither option tries to translate any content. It simply creates files that you can then update.

The advantage of the localized strings file is that you can hand it to a translator without handing over the rest of your app. The translator can replace the strings in the file with language-specific strings. This approach can also handle error strings more easily. The disadvantage is that some code may be necessary in some controllers.

The storyboard approach is better suited for projects where graphics and the overall look and feel are important. You can preview the look of the translated storyboards and check for truncated or misaligned strings.

Both options can be time-consuming and potentially expensive. Common sense suggests you should only add localization if there's a reasonable chance of making a return on the time and money spent.

Figure 8.33

Add support for another language.

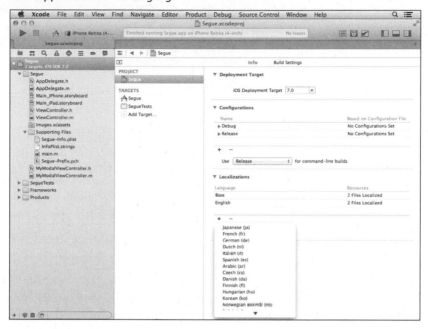

Figure 8.34

Select the starting files for localization.

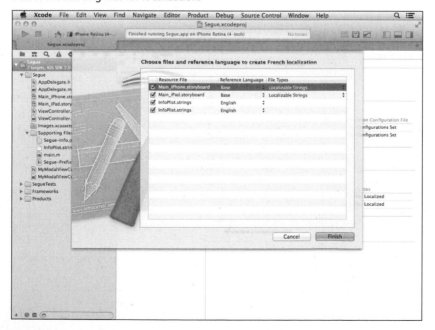

CAUTION

Don't forget that you must include non-English fonts for non-Western languages. You may need to use a non-Western keyboard to enter the correct characters. You can also attempt to work with the standard Character Viewer utility.

Working with Advanced IB Techniques

IB is a deep application with many hidden features. There isn't room in this book to explore them all—in fact, hardly anyone uses IB to its fullest possible extent. But it's worth becoming familiar with some of the more accessible advanced techniques.

Using tags

Many IB objects include a Tag field, as shown in Figure 8.35. You can use this field to search a nib—or more usually, a view in a nib—to find a matching object. For example, to find the button in the figure, you might add the following code to the view controller:

```
UIButton* theButtonImLookingFor
= (UIButton *)[self.view viewWithTag: 101010];
```

Figure 8.35

Define a tag for a UI button.

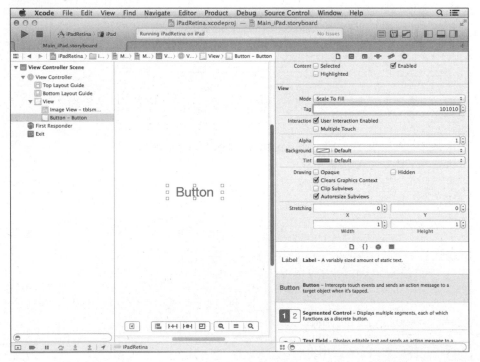

Typically, you *wouldn't* do this for simple object updates—outlets are a better option. But tags can be very useful when you work with table views. You can create cells dynamically and use tags to define how they're displayed—for example, to create cells with alternating colors. Tags can also be a good way to manage UI elements when you generate them in code without using IB at all.

Converting iPhone projects to the iPad

As a rule—don't. In Xcode, you can update a project's build settings from iPhone (or iPad) to Universal. But this feature isn't implemented properly, so you can't rely on it.

It's always better to start with a Universal project, even if you are aiming for only one platform. You can leave the storyboard for the other platform empty and delete it before you upload your app to the App Store.

To convert an existing single-platform project to a universal app, simply add another storyboard for the new platform from the File Library. You can then add controls and link them to the view controller in the usual way.

To force the app to load the new storyboard, open the Project Navigator, click the project icon at the top of the navigator, click the app icon under Targets in the gutter, click General, and scroll down to the Deployment Info sub-pane.

Click the iPhone and iPad buttons to select each platform. Use the Main Interface menu to select the correct storyboard for each platform, as shown in Figure 8.36.

Figure 8.36

Select the storyboard to load on launch for each platform.

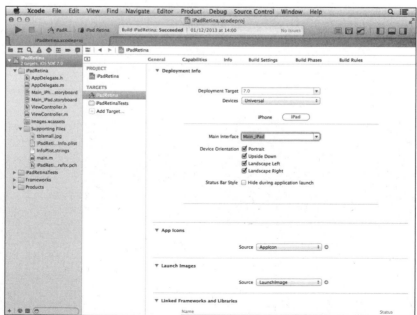

Handling resolution issues

UIKit on the iPad and iPhone is resolution-independent. UI controls scale automatically for Retina devices. The equivalent elements on OS X work the same way. You do not need to create different versions of the UI for different resolutions.

Imported images are a partial exception. If you select Aspect Fill mode for a view that has an imported image, it scales automatically. However, you should start with a high-resolution source, so the operating system can shrink the image into a smaller area without losing resolution.

Designing iPhone UIs that work equally well on 3.5" and 4" devices—and possibly on larger screens, should Apple release any in the future—can be more of a challenge. You can use constraints to squash the UI into the smaller area, or you can add a scroll view that automatically cuts off the lower area on a smaller device, but allows users to scroll it into view.

Constraints are a better option from the user's point of view, because users may not notice scrolling elements. But creating a UI that works equally well and looks equally good on both form factors can take some time.

Summary

Constraints, storyboards, and placeholders add extra complexity to UI design. They also make your app more flexible and responsive, so it's worth taking the time to master them. If you're starting out, learn about placeholders first, then work with storyboards, and leave constraints and localization until later.

It's more important and useful to get the basics working before you try to create more advanced effects. And it's a good idea not to underestimate the amount of learning and experimentation you need to do to master each of these tools. None of these options is trivially straightforward.

Going Deeper

Saving Time in Xcode

Many editing operations are repetitive, while others can help you organize your code more effectively to simplify development and maintenance. Some basic timesaving features are built into Xcode. For example, Xcode 5 creates paired curly brackets automatically. It also adds a matching square bracket at the start of an Objective-C statement if you type the final closing square bracket.

Other features are more complex. Xcode 5 includes these tools:

- Code folding
- Structure editing
- Refactoring
- Code snippets
- Jumping to a definition

Using Code Folding

Code folding is a simple feature that can hide code while it isn't being edited. It's a display-only feature that makes it easier for you to concentrate on one section of code without being distracted by surrounding elements.

CAUTION

It's easy to activate code folding by accident. If you're not familiar with this feature, you'll wonder why most of your code has disappeared and whether you deleted it by accident. It's important to understand how code folding works, even if you never use it. The code folding gutter described below is very thin, with small gray blocks that indicate delimited code areas. It's adjacent to the gutter used for debugging. It's easy to select one when you're trying to select the other.

To fold a section of code, hover the mouse cursor in the gutter at the left of the editor, as shown in Figure 9.1. The selected code is highlighted with a white background, and the surrounding code is grayed out, as shown.

Click the disclosure triangle in the gutter. Xcode hides the selected code and replaces it with a placeholder {. . .} graphic, as shown in Figure 9.2. To unhide the code, double-click the placeholder or click the disclosure triangle once.

In This Chapter

Using code folding

Editing structure

Refactoring code

Using code snippets

Jumping to a definition

Revealing symbols

Figure 9.1

You can select a block of code to hide. Code within the nearest matching curly brackets is highlighted and selected automatically.

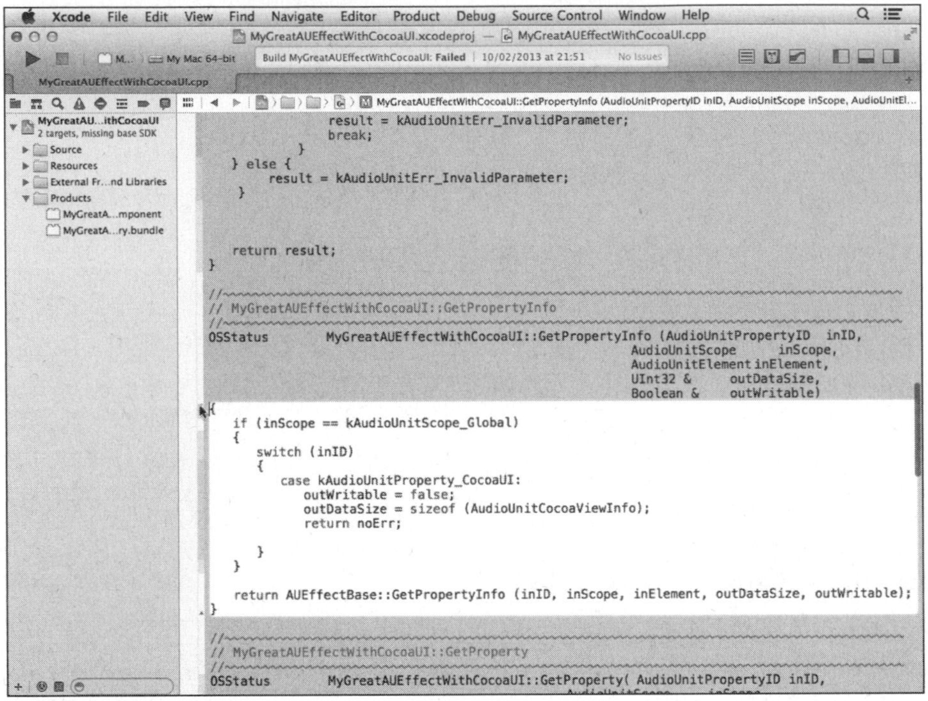

Code hiding selects paired curly brackets, so you can hide entire methods or specific code segments. If you hide a complete method, the signature remains. If you hide a smaller segment, such as the contents of an `if` statement, the first line of the statement remains as a guide and the contents are hidden. Before you fold, Xcode displays scoped sections in various shades of gray, so you can estimate how much code will be hidden.

For convenience, you can also fold all the code in a file. Select Editor ⇨ Code Folding, and choose one of these options:

- **All:** Folds/unfolds everything between two matching delimeters.
- **Methods & Functions:** Folds/unfolds methods and functions only.
- **Comment Blocks:** Folds/unfolds comment blocks only.

You can use this feature to hide the large comment block that Apple always includes at the start of sample code. But note that this option recognizes `/* ... */` comment blocks only. Multiple lines of `//` comment blocks remain unfolded.

Figure 9.2

You can unhide code by clicking in the gutter or double-clicking the placeholder graphic.

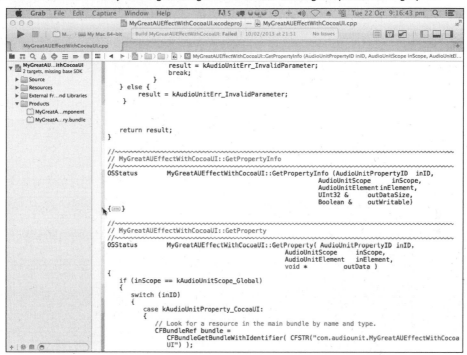

CAUTION

Xcode's code folding is simple and limited compared to the equivalent feature on other platforms. It's delimiter-based and has no syntactic intelligence. It cannot hide long property lists or class headers.

Editing Structure

It's often useful to comment or uncomment blocks of code, clean up indentation, check delimiters, move lines up or down within a method, and so on. Xcode's editor includes a contextual right-click menu that implements these features, as shown in Figure 9.3.

TIP

Newcomers to Xcode sometimes miss this menu or ignore it because there's so much else to learn. But it's one of the keys to improving productivity in Xcode, and it's the best way to avoid wasting time on manual code tidying chores. Note also that you can use key commands for most of the options. Cmd / is a particularly convenient way to put code inside a comment block.

Figure 9.3

You can view the Structure editing menu, an unglamorous but very useful timesaver.

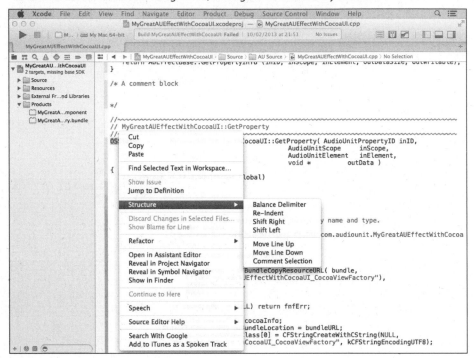

TIP

Xcode includes a selection of extra editing commands that can be accessed only through keystrokes. These commands are unassigned by default, so you must define your own keystroke combinations to use them. Select Xcode ⇨ Preferences ⇨ Key Bindings to see the list. Select any item and double-click in the Key column to define a shortcut. The Case Change options near the end of the list are particularly useful.

To display the menu, right-click anywhere in the editor area. Some options in this menu require you to select a block of code. These features are available:

- **Balance Delimiter:** This is a display-only feature that helps you fix delimiter mismatches. When you select it, Xcode highlights the matching delimiters nearest to the edit point. Select it again, and it highlights the next matching pair. And so on. You also can double-click any delimiter to find its partner and highlight the code between them.

- **Reindent:** This corrects the indentation within a selected block of code. Code features within matching delimiters are indented by the same number of spaces. This is a good way to clean up a messy edit.

- **Shift Right/Left:** These options move a selected block of code by the number of spaces used for an indentation step. You can use this feature to correct indentation after a major change to a method, but it's often easier and quicker to use the Reindent option after editing.

● **Move Line Up/Down:** In spite of the name, these options can move a single line or a selected block up and down. The line above or below the selection changes position.

● **Comment Selection:** If the selection is uncommented, this option inserts two slashes before each line. If it's commented with two slashes on each line, the slashes are removed. This feature isn't intelligent enough to recognize / * . . . * / comment blocks and doesn't uncomment them correctly, so it doesn't match the comment folding feature described in the previous sub-section.

TIP

To make code structures easier to follow, you can change the fonts and colors used by Xcode. Although the changes are cosmetic, they can have a significant impact on productivity, because a good color scheme can make structures stand out clearly. Select Xcode ➪ Preferences, and choose the Fonts & Colors tab. You can change the font globally by selecting every item that appears in the list and choosing a new font or font size in the Font box.

Refactoring Code

The Structure menu is used for relatively simple edits, but the Refactor menu, shown in Figure 9.4, can create more complex changes. Some changes affect every file in a project.

Figure 9.4

The contents of the Refactor menu are context-dependent. Some options are grayed out in some contexts.

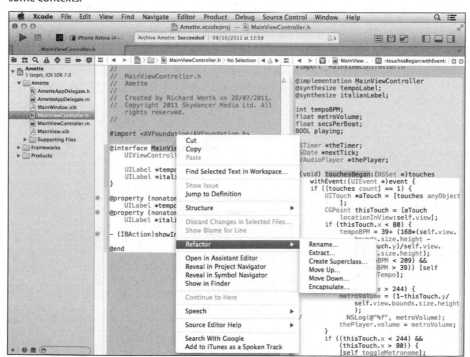

Refactoring is a powerful but sometimes tricky feature that changes or renames structural features in your project. The aim of refactoring is to create clearer organized code that is easier to extend and maintain. Edits shouldn't change basic behavior or introduce bugs. You can refactor code with the options shown in the Refactor menu. You also can use a feature called *Edit All In Scope* to rename symbols within a file.

Using the Refactor menu

In Xcode, you can use the Refactor menu to do the following:

- Rename classes, methods, and other symbols within a class
- Rename classes, methods, and symbols across a project
- Create new superclasses
- Move code into a superclass
- Move code into a subclass
- Create new setters and getters for a symbol

Refactoring can seem mysterious because the options that appear in the Refactor menu are context- and selection-dependent. Xcode displays only the options that make sense; for example, you can't create a superclass for a property.

NOTE

Xcode's refactoring features are based on ideas introduced by developer Martin Fowler. For more information, see http://martinfowler.com. Refactoring has been hotly debated, but you don't need to be familiar with the debate to use the Refactor menu to work with your code.

CAUTION

Refactoring can make drastic, wide-ranging changes to a project. It's a good idea to back up a project using one of the options introduced in Chapter 15 before you use this feature. Note that some refactoring options, such as rename, can be very slow.

Refactoring typically works in two stages. First, you select an operation and type a parameter, such as a new name, into a dialog. Next, Xcode displays the preview and confirmation dialog shown in Figure 9.5. The preview shows a list of proposed changes in various files at the left, and before/after views of the code at the right.

Clicking Save actions the changes. You can also deselect one or more of the check boxes at the left to leave those items unchanged. For some operations, the proposed changes can be complex and may be spread across multiple sections in multiple files.

These options are available:

- **Rename:** This works on classes, properties, and methods. Select a feature and the Rename option from the menu. Type a new name into the dialog. Xcode searches every file in the project—which can take a while—and shows the preview/confirmation dialog.

● **Extract:** This works on methods or code sections. You can move a section of code into a separate method or function. Xcode automatically creates a new signature for you. You can edit this before you confirm the change.

● **Create Superclass:** This works on class names. It creates a new superclass. The definition code can be written to a new file, which is the most useful option, or it can be added to the current file, which can be confusing and isn't usually useful. You typically need to fix included/imported headers manually in the superclass definition.

● **Move Up/Down:** This works on methods and properties. Move Up moves the item to the superclass; in other words, it removes the code from the current file and moves it to the superclass definition file. Move Down moves it from the superclass to a subclass.

● **Encapsulate:** This works on properties. It creates code for a getter and/or a setter. You don't need to use this feature if you're already using @synthesize for your properties.

NOTE

Some of the refactoring options modify project nib files. You can confirm or cancel edits using the same split before/ after view used to display code files, but the panes show the XML (eXtended Markup Language) data inside a nib. This may appear unfamiliar if you've never looked inside a nib with a text editor. There's no way to view the changes graphically; typically, it wouldn't make sense to show them in this way.

Figure 9.5

You can use the preview/confirmation dialog while renaming a class. Xcode searches every file in the project and lists the possible edits here.

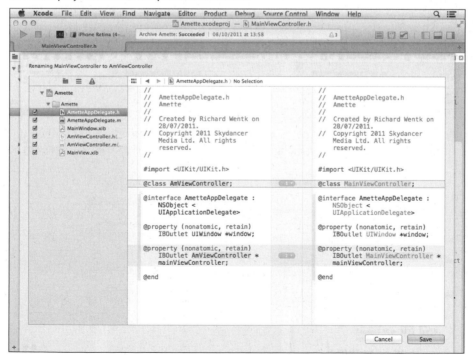

TIP
The rename option is the quickest way to rename a class across a project. It can save lots of manual editing.
Unfortunately, you can use this option only with Objective-C code. C++ isn't supported.

Using the Edit All in Scope feature

It's sometimes useful to rename symbols used in a file. You can use the global find/replace feature in the main menu to rename a symbol in a project, but sometimes you need to limit the changes to a single class, method, or function.

With the Edit All in Scope feature, you can rename one instance of a symbol, and your edit is copied to all matching symbols within the selected scope. Typically, you use this within a method or function, but you can also use it to change local variables in a class.

It can be easy to miss Edit All in Scope. To use it, select any object and hover over it with the mouse cursor. Xcode displays a floating selection triangle to the right of the property. It can take a couple of attempts before the triangle appears.

Click the triangle, and Xcode displays a right-click contextual menu with the Edit All in Scope entry (and nothing else), as shown in Figure 9.6.

Figure 9.6

Using Edit All in Scope is an easy way to rename a group of objects, but it's easy to miss this feature!

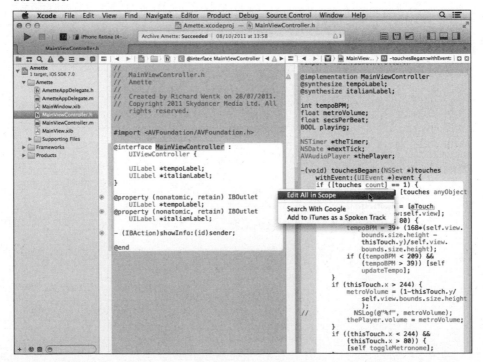

Select this entry, and Xcode highlights all instances of that object in the file. You can now type a new name, and all instances of the name are changed at the same time. Press Return to make the change permanent or Escape to cancel.

CAUTION

Don't use Edit All in Scope to change properties/ivars. If a symbol is accessed from outside a class, use one of the refactor options to rename it.

Using Code Snippets

With earlier versions of Xcode, many developers realized that it was useful to create a dummy file with boilerplate code that could be copied into an active project. Xcode 5 includes a *code snippets* feature. Code snippets add complete sections of code to a project. Xcode includes a small selection of default snippets, but you can expand the library with your own code.

A code snippet can be a line or two of code such as an alert generator or timer initializer, a more complex section of code that implements a standard feature such as animation, or a complete method. Potentially, you can create snippets that implement an entire class with complex default code.

TIP

Code snippets are built into Code Sense, making a very powerful feature. When you create a new snippet, you can define a custom auto-completion string. When you type that string in the editor and press Return, Code Sense copies the snippet code from the library and inserts it. You can add your own placeholder tokens.

TIP

Snippets persist across Xcode updates, so you do not need to add them again when you install a new Xcode version.

Inserting a snippet

To insert a snippet, select the Code Snippet ({}) icon in the Library area of the utility pane. Select a snippet from the list, and drag and drop it into the code editor. The code is copied and added, as shown at the top of Figure 9.7.

Placeholder variables appear in gray. To complete the edit, select and rename them. You can skip between them with the Tab key. A preview window with the code appears to the left of the snippets. You can use this window to edit snippets in the library.

CAUTION

In Xcode 4, you could filter the list to show iOS, OS X, or User snippets. In Xcode 5, the list is always unfiltered, so you can add OS X snippets to an iOS project, and vice versa. The snippets won't work, but Xcode allows you to add them anyway. In fact, many useful iOS and OS X snippets have been removed, leaving a core collection of basic C/C++/ Objective-C snippets.

Figure 9.7

In this example, an `if` statement with placeholders is being previewed. The floating preview window displays the snippet so you can review it before you add it.

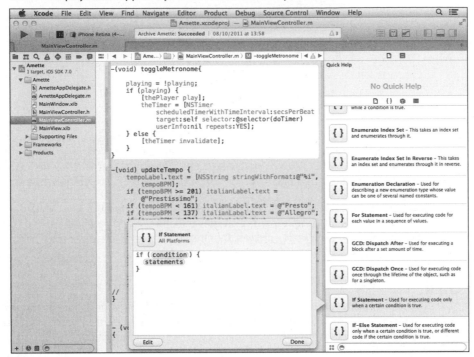

Creating a new snippet

Creating a new snippet is easy after you understand how to do it, but until you do, the process is unintuitive.

Creating a snippet with drag and drop

It's unexpectedly easy to miss this feature, and it has some hidden subtleties. To create a snippet, drag-highlight the code you want to include, click the highlighted area, and *hold down the mouse button until the cursor changes to a pointer*. If you don't hold down the mouse button, Xcode assumes you're attempting to highlight a different section of code.

Drag the snippet to the Code Snippet library and release it anywhere. The snippet is added as the last item in the User library with a default name—My Code Snippet.

After you have created a snippet, you can edit the name and add optional symbol placeholders, as described in the next section.

Editing a snippet

To edit a snippet, click anywhere on it in the Library to view the code, and click the Edit button at the lower right. You'll see the dialog shown in Figure 9.8.

Figure 9.8

You can edit a snippet.

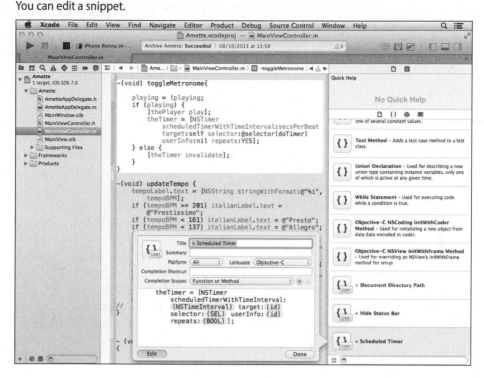

NOTE

Currently, you can only edit User snippets. To create your own version of one of the existing snippets, copy and paste the code into a User snippet and save it with a new name.

You can now edit these settings:

- **Title:** This defines the name that appears in the Library list.
- **Summary:** This defines the short description that appears in the Library list.
- **Platform:** Select iOS, OS X, or All. Currently, this feature does nothing—all snippets are user snippets—but it may be more useful in future versions of Xcode.
- **Language:** This defaults to Objective-C. You can select a different language manually.
- **Completion shortcut:** You can leave this empty or fill it with any unique string to provide a quick-access keyboard shortcut for Code Completion.
- **Completion scope:** You can control how widely Xcode searches when looking for completion matches. The default is Function or Method.

Snippets often need placeholder tokens, which can be filled in later when you use the snippet. For example, when creating an alert, you can use a placeholder for the message text.

To create placeholder tokens, type the following:

```
<#placeholderName#>
```

The `placeHolder` name string is arbitrary and doesn't have to be unique, so you can use the same placeholder strings in different snippets. Placeholders are highlighted with light gray. You can tab between them and edit them in the usual Code Completion way.

In Figure 9.8, the snippet includes five placeholders: `<#NSTimeInterval#>`, `<#id#>`, and so on. The choice of the number and placing of the placeholders is up to you. Optionally, you can create different versions of the same snippet with different placeholders; for example, you can create one for an alert that uses standard text and another in which the labels are place-holders and can be filled in as needed.

N O T E

The snippet feature in Xcode doesn't support open development; there's no way to share snippets across a team or make them available online. Many sites now offer snippet sharing. They're often optimized for scripted language such as PHP or Python, but usually work with C-family languages. For details, search online for "snippet sharing."

T I P

To delete a snippet, click it to select it, press Delete, and click or select OK to confirm the deletion. Undo is not available.

Jumping to a Definition

It's often useful to jump to a method signature or symbol definition. You can find definitions by searching for them, but it's much quicker to use the Jump to Definition feature.

To use it, highlight a symbol, right-click to show the contextual menu, and select the Jump to Definition option. You can also cmd-click any symbol.

If there's a single definition, Xcode displays it in the main code window. Note that the definition may be in one of the Cocoa or Cocoa Touch header files, and not in your code—in which case you'll see a method signature, and perhaps some supporting comments from Apple.

T I P

This is a good way to remind yourself how to use the options in iOS and OS X. For example, if you want to use `NSTimer` but can't remember how, this approach is often quicker than looking up the details in the documentation.

If you have multiple definitions—for example, when there are multiple classes with `dealloc` methods—Xcode displays a new menu with a list of definitions. You can select one to view it.

Note that definitions *don't* appear in the Assistant window when it's open; they take you away from your original editing location into a different file or to a different part of the same file. To move back to the original location, use the back arrow at the top left of the edit window.

Revealing Symbols

As an alternative to jumping to a definition, you can use a selection of options to find the file that holds the definition. Right-click the symbol, and select one of the following:

- **Open in Assistant Editor:** This opens the Assistant Editor window if it is not already open and loads the file that defines the symbol. This option is useful in larger, complex projects. For smaller projects where the symbol scope is limited, it often opens another copy of the same file.

- **Reveal in Project Navigator:** This opens the Project Navigator and highlights the relevant file.

- **Reveal in Symbol Navigator:** This opens the Symbol Navigator and highlights the symbol. This is a quick way to see a list of the other symbols in the same file and optionally to navigate to them with a single click.

- **Show in Finder:** This opens a Finder window and highlights the file that contains the symbol. You can use this option to find source files if you are not sure where they are.

Summary

Xcode's timesaving features can seem obscure, but you can dramatically improve your productivity by practicing with them. Code-folding makes it easier to concentrate on larger code structures and overall program flow. The other structure options automate repetitive chores to minimize unnecessary typing.

It may take you longer to master the refactoring options, but they can save you even more time when you want to make big changes. Xcode refactoring is fairly robust, so even though global edits can feel uncertain, they usually aren't.

Similarly, snippets can help you take some of the drudgery out of coding by making it easy to add boilerplate. Snippets do not have to be limited to a few lines of code. You can create and re-use much longer sections, which can save hours or days on larger projects.

Using the Organizer

The Xcode Organizer, shown in Figure 10.1, appears in a separate window and contains an "and the rest . . ." collection of miscellaneous features. The Organizer is used for project and device management.

CAUTION

In Xcode 4, the Organizer included the documentation browser. In Xcode 5, you can no longer access the browser directly. Use Quick Help or key/mouse access, as described in Chapter 6. Similarly, Apple has removed the direct link to the Organizer from the main toolbar.

To display the Organizer, select Window ➪ Organizer in the main menu, or type Shift+Command+1.

You can use the Organizer's features to manage these things:

- Development devices
- Code repositories
- Active projects

The window uses the standard OS X layout. To select the main features, click the icons at the top. Sub-features appear in groups at the left. The active area fills the rest of the screen. Some features include a separate toolbar at the bottom of the screen, with icons for specific options. Because the Organizer is a grab bag of miscellaneous unrelated options, the UI of each page is different.

CROSS-REFERENCE

This chapter introduces the basic features of the Organizer. For a detailed walk-through of the complexities of the provisioning process, including the steps you need to follow before you can test apps on your own hardware and upload finished archives to the App Store, see Chapter 11.

CAUTION

In Xcode 5, provisioning and certificates are managed in the Accounts pane in Preferences. For details, see later in this chapter.

In This Chapter

Working with devices

Using device logs

Managing individual devices

Working with projects and archives

Working with the Library

You can—and usually should—test iOS apps on a number of devices. You don't often need to set up devices manually. When you plug in a new device, Xcode downloads the relevant details and makes it available for testing. This can take a few seconds but isn't a complex process.

Figure 10.1

The Xcode Organizer.

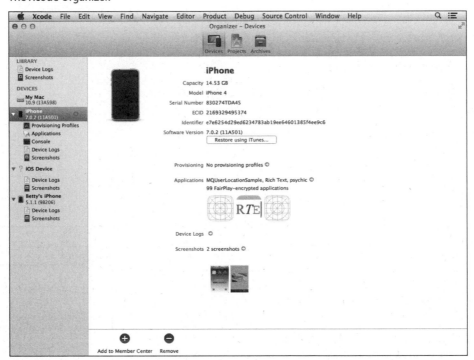

The Device Manager, shown in Figure 10.2, includes useful but optional features that make device testing more productive. The Library sub-pane at the top left is a menu of general device-related features. The Devices sub-pane is a list of devices. Each displays a similar list of options.

CAUTION

Some options are available only when a device is connected. For example, you can always see stored screenshots and device logs. But the Console, Provisioning Profiles, and Applications options are visible only for the currently attached device, if there is one.

Figure 10.2

The Device Manager shows the list of devices at the left, device management options at the top left, and an active display and management area in the rest of the screen.

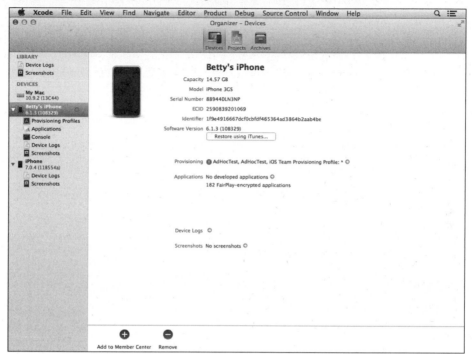

You can use the Manager to perform these tasks:

- Set up a Mac for development. This option tells Xcode to remember your system password, so you don't need to re-enter it every time you launch Xcode and use the debugging tools or Instruments.
- Set up iOS devices so you can use them for development and run your apps on them.
- Review and manage OS updates. You can check the current installed OS on each device, and update or restore to other versions.
- View device logs. Logs include stack dumps collected during crashes and listings that can help diagnose memory errors.
- Create and manage app screenshots. Screenshots can be saved for reference or collected for use in a new App Store listing.

Enabling developer mode

If you select your Mac in the Devices list and click the Enable Developer Mode button, shown in Figure 10.3, Xcode stops asking you for your password when you launch the debugger. This is a useful thing to do.

If you want to use your Mac for OS X development with code signing, click the Add to Member Center button. This uploads the details to the Member Center. It also downloads a generic development profile, but Xcode hides this under the Account Preferences, so there's no visual indication that the profile is correctly installed.

Figure 10.3

Use the Enable Developer Mode button to avoid unnecessary confirmations.

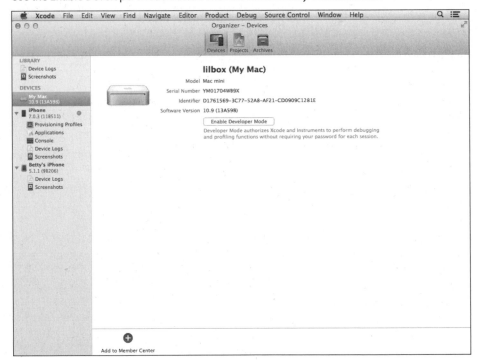

Reviewing and managing profiles

In Xcode 4, you could review and manage profiles and certificates in Xcode. In Xcode 5, this feature has been moved to the Account Preferences pane, shown in Figure 10.4. I've included a first look at this pane here, even though it's described in detail in the next chapter. Select Xcode ⇨ Preferences ⇨ Accounts, and log in with your developer ID and password to see the details.

Figure 10.4

The certificate and profiles manager has been moved from the Organizer to the Accounts Preferences.

TIP

If you need a more powerful provisioning tool, you can download Apple's free iPhone Configuration Utility. It restores the Software Profiles option in Xcode and includes other useful device management features.

Finding and installing iOS updates

Xcode 4's Organizer included a Software Images section you could use to manage the `.ipsw` files Apple uses to distribute iOS firmware. Xcode 5 is missing this section.

Public updates can be installed via iTunes or over the air in the usual way. But beta updates are reserved for developers, and you must download and install the files manually. You typically update device firmware whenever you download a new beta release of the SDK.

When update files are available, they're listed on the iOS Dev Center page. You must select the correct file for each type of device, as shown in Figure 10.5.

To install a firmware file, connect your device and launch iTunes if it isn't already open. Open the Device page, and back up your device. Option-click the Restore button currently near the top right of the window to select and load an `.ipsw` file. You can then restore the device again to reload your data.

Figure 10.5

The list of supported devices for each iOS update continues to grow.

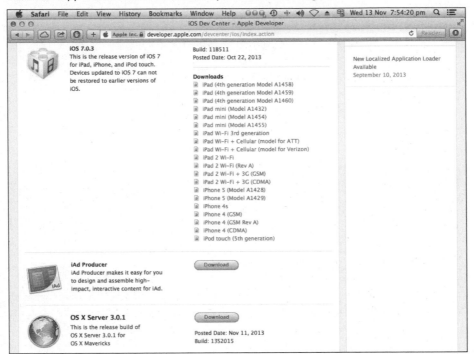

TIP

Firmware files are big—from 300MB to 500MB. It's a good idea to save them all to a single folder and remove them when you no longer need them.

CAUTION

For security reasons, you cannot update firmware if you are using the Find My iPhone service. Turn it off before you update your device.

Using device logs

Device logs provide crash reports and other OS interventions. The list includes watch-dog time-out events, where the OS kills an unresponsive app. The most recent logs are copied to Xcode whenever a device is connected.

Reading crash reports

A crash report (also known as a backtrace) is a context summary and a stack dump. The context includes information about the hardware and OS, and the stack dump is very similar to the real-time dumps available in Xcode's debugger.

Crash reports make it possible to collect crash information from apps that are being run and tested live. Reports are recorded for every crash, anywhere. The device doesn't have to be connected to a Mac running the Xcode debugger.

CROSS-REFERENCE

Debugging is introduced in Chapter 16.

Figure 10.6 shows a typical example. The panel at the left is a list of crashes on the selected device. The panel at the right shows the details of each crash. In this example, Skype couldn't find a string it was looking for and took too long to launch.

This isn't useful information—unless you're the author of the Skype app—but if your apps crash or are killed by the OS, they get the same treatment, and you can see what your app was trying to do before it died.

Figure 10.6

To make sense of a crash report stack dump, you should understand that events appear in reverse chronological order. The most recent event caused the crash, but earlier events may have set it up.

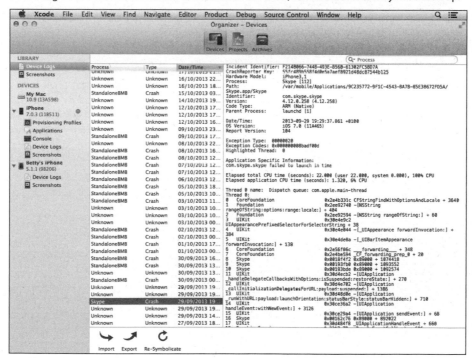

CAUTION

Crash dumps often list internal runtime system calls and undocumented internal Cocoa/Cocoa Touch methods. For example, you may know that `objc_msgSend` is part of the Objective-C runtime. But you will find listings for undocumented internal Cocoa methods. This doesn't often matter, because the backtrace usually shows in your code the method that created a problem. But occasionally with beta code, the dump tells you that you've run into an internal bug, and you'll have to find a work-around until it's fixed.

Understanding other reports

Figure 10.7 shows a Type Unknown report. Instead of a stack dump, the panel at the right shows processes and various statistics. These reports are occasionally interesting, but they're usually caused by iOS bugs rather than your apps, so they're less likely to be directly useful. However, they can sometimes suggest your device is having hardware issues—especially if the thermal data section suggests it's overheating.

Figure 10.7

Making sense of a Type Unknown report, which is effectively just a process list.

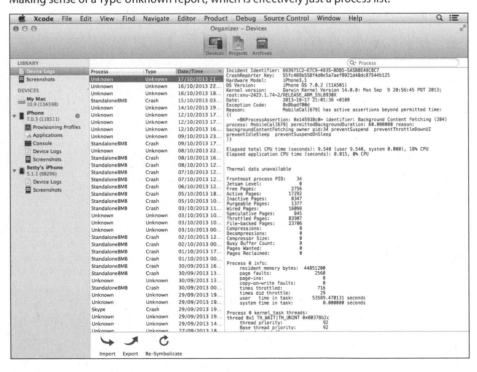

Note that the dump shows only RAM—internal working memory, which is separate from the main flash memory. The available RAM for each device is shown in Table 10.1.

NOTE

iOS supports limited paging. Read-only executables can be paged, but there's no swap file. The available RAM is the system maximum. In practice, as little as 20MB or so may be available to an app. To test memory effectively, use an older device with limited RAM.

Table 10.1 iOS Device Available RAM

Device	Available RAM
iPhone first generation	128MB
iPhone 3G	128MB
iPhone 3GS	256MB
iPhone 4/4S	512MB
iPhone 5/5S/5C	1024MB
iPod touch first/second generation	128MB
iPod touch third/fourth generation	256MB
iPod touch fifth generation	512MB
iPad first generation	256MB
iPad second generation	512MB
iPad third/fourth generation	1024MB
iPad Air	1024MB
iPad Mini	512MB
iPad Mini second generation	1024MB

Importing and exporting device logs

The import and export arrows at the bottom of the window make it possible to pass debugging information back to developers. This isn't a useful feature for solo developers. But team developers can export a crash event from Xcode to a file and share it by e-mail, upload it to a server, and so on. Importing a crash report from a file adds it to the list of current device logs.

Re-Symbolicating logs

Use the colorfully named Re-Symbolicate option when a crash report shows raw hex instead of symbols. The process can take a while; it converts a string of numbers into a crash log with function and method names. Xcode does this best if it has a copy of the original build, with debug information, but it can sometimes do a good job of guessing the symbols in third-party apps.

Working with screenshots

The Screenshots feature is a convenient way to create, review, and export screenshots of active apps. It bypasses the image download features in iPhoto and iTunes and displays screenshots directly. It offers alternative functionality that overlaps with the standard iOS screenshot options. There's no "killer app" advantage; it does some of the same things in a slightly different way. Typically, you'll use both.

The Organizer's Screenshots feature appears in two locations, with a subtle difference. The main Screenshots option, shown in Figure 10.8, displays saved screenshots for all devices. But it doesn't allow you to take a new screenshot for the currently connected device.

Each device has a separate Screenshots option, which includes a green New Screenshot button at the lower right of the page. Click this button to take a screenshot and add it to the display list. This feature is independent of the device's photo library; it doesn't display screenshots created with the standard iOS two-button click operation.

Figure 10.8

Use the Screenshots option to view the screenshot collection.

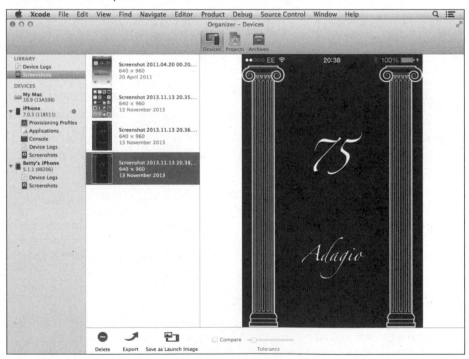

N O T E

If you're new to iOS, note that you can capture a screenshot manually by pressing and holding down a device's power button and then clicking the Home Button. When you trigger this feature, the screen flashes white and the speaker plays a photo shutter sound. Screenshots are added to the current photo roll, and they can be exported and viewed in iPhoto or in the iTunes image loader. They do *not* appear in Xcode.

You can do these things in Screenshots using the icons along the bottom of the page:

- **Delete a screenshot from the list:** This deletes it from the display list and from disk.
- **Export a screenshot:** This saves it to a file location of your choice as an uncompressed PNG file.
- **Nominate the screenshot as an app's launch image:** The launch image appears after the application begins to load but before it runs. This is a simplified and less useful version of the equivalent feature in the Target Build Settings, which are discussed in more detail in Chapter 12.
- **Compare two screenshots to reveal differences:** The comparison applies a difference filter, with a variable tolerance. Color information is ignored, and differences appear white or gray. To select two shots for comparison, hold down the Option (⌥) key and select them with the mouse. Click the Compare check box to see a single combined view.
- **Make a new screenshot, as described above.** Remember that this option works only in the Screenshots option for each device. It's not available in the Library screenshot option.

You can access further features using a contextual right-click context menu, including these features (refer to Figure 10.8):

- **Save as Default Image:** This is identical to the Save as Launch Image feature.
- **Open Image with Finder:** This shows the image in Preview. If you have the PNG file type assigned to an editor, it runs the editor and loads the image.
- **Reveal Image in Finder:** This opens the Finder and displays the folder containing the image.

N O T E

A feature that's missing from the Screenshots page is the ability to upload images to iTunes Connect. (It would also be useful to view screenshots taken with the device itself, but you can't.) To use Screenshots in iTunes Connect, export them to a folder. It can be convenient to keep all PR material for iTunes Connect and supporting web pages in a single location.

Managing individual devices

Whenever you connect an iOS device, the Organizer automatically adds it to the device list shown in Figure 10.9. It also downloads the most recent logs from the device. Connected devices support a wide selection of options, including these:

- A device summary page
- A list of installed provisioning profiles
- A list of installed applications
- A Console dump
- A list of device logs for that device only
- A list of screenshots for the device

Figure 10.9

Use the Organizer to view key information about a connected device. You can view a simplified version of this page for disconnected devices, but most of the details in the full view aren't shown.

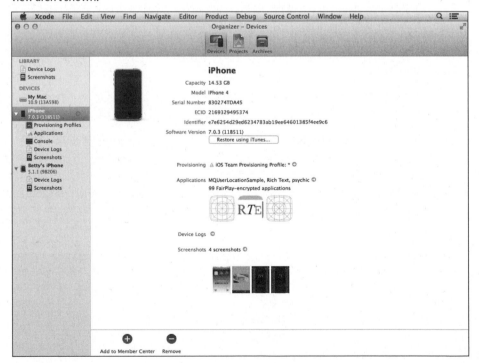

Using the device summary

The device summary displays a selection of useful information about a connected device, including the following:

- **Device name:** This displays a name you specify when setting up the device for development.
- **Capacity:** This is the actual memory size in GB. This is the formatted memory size and is not the same as the rounded-up "marketing" memory size.
- **Device model:** This displays the model number.
- **Serial Number:** This displays a unique serial number.
- **ECID (Exclusive Chip Identification Number):** This is another unique serial number embedded in each device. Apple added ECIDs to iOS devices from the iPhone 3GS onward. The ECID is passed back to Apple's servers when you attempt a firmware restore or update. (The technology was supposed to prevent jailbreaking, but it was circumvented almost immediately.)
- **Identifier:** This is a long hex string and is another unique device identifier. This identifier is embedded in provisioning profiles and in apps downloaded from the App Store and is used in the App Store DRM (Digital Rights Management) technology.
- **Software version:** The menu shows the version of iOS installed on the device. Click the Restore using iTunes . . . button to launch iTunes.
- **Provisioning:** This displays a summary of the installed provisioning profiles. A small red cross appears when profiles are out of date. Select the small gray arrow to view the separate Provisioning Profiles page, described later.
- **Applications:** This item lists your test apps in full. Use the small gray arrow to select the separate Applications page. The app icons appear under the list. The "FairPlay-encrypted applications" text tells you how many apps are installed in total, including test apps and other apps.

NOTE

FairPlay is the name of the DRM technology used to lock apps to a specific device. In theory, it prevents copying. In practice, it's easy to strip it, but apps will then run only on a device with an unlocked DRM and a customized open OS.

- **Device Logs:** This item displays a count of the available logs. To view them in the Device Logs, select the small gray arrow.
- **Screenshots:** This displays a count of the screenshots, with a small preview of each. To view the main device Screenshots page, select the small gray arrow.

Using the Add to Member Center feature

The two toolbar buttons on this page—Add to Member Center and Remove—add and remove a device from the list stored in your account on the Provisioning Portal in iTunes Connect.

Clicking Add to Member Center uploads the device identifier to your Member Center device list. Confusingly, you might think you can then click Provisioning to install a provisioning profile on the device, but in fact you need to use the profile manager under Xcode ⇨ Preferences ⇨ Accounts to do this.

NOTE

Ad Hoc—beta test—provisioning is usually done remotely, so you still need to know how to get a device identifier remotely and how to add it to the online device list by hand. For details, see Chapter 11.

Checking provisioning profiles

The device Provisioning Profiles page, shown in Figure 10.10, displays the profiles installed on the device. This page lists the profiles that allow you to run test apps *on that one device.* All other profiles used by Xcode appear under Accounts Preferences. So you may only see one profile here, even though there's a much longer list of profiles in the Preferences.

TIP

Profiles aren't large files, but it's useful to delete expired profiles to avoid list clutter on the provisioning pages.

Figure 10.10

Check the profiles installed on a device. You can remove expired profiles and install new profiles manually here, although Accounts Preferences has now largely automated the process.

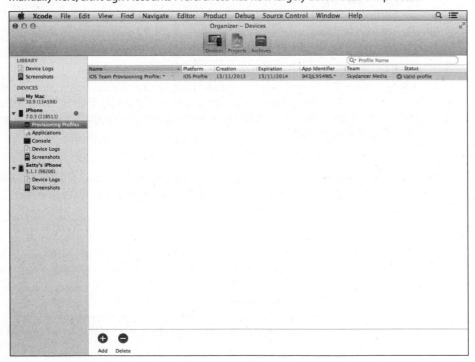

CROSS-REFERENCE

Provisioning is a very complex topic and is described in full in Chapter 11.

Managing applications

The Applications page, shown in Figure 10.11, displays the apps installed on the device. This list includes your own test apps and Apple/third-party apps. Each entry includes these items:

- The name
- The Bundle ID
- The version number
- The icon (if there is one)

Figure 10.11

This is where you manage installed applications. This page isn't quite a key feature of Xcode—you can develop apps without it—but it does include useful options.

CAUTION

Xcode 4 displayed the minimum OS version here. Apple removed this feature in Xcode 5.

For your test apps, you set these details in the build settings, which are described in Chapters 12 and 13. You can use this page to check that you have set them correctly.

You have four options for app management:

- **Download:** This copies the files in an app's sandbox directories—`/Documents`, `/Library`, and `/tmp`—to a location on your Mac's disk. You can use this option for debugging to check that files are being created and removed correctly and to retrieve useful data created by the app.
- **Upload:** Use this option to copy files to your app's sandbox folders. Xcode 5 includes a handy sandbox folder viewer.
- **Add:** This copies and installs a precompiled app. Xcode can install an app automatically after a build, so you don't need to use this option while testing. But you can use it to install app files created by other developers for testing, as long as they are supplied with a compatible provisioning profile. You also can use this option to reinstall prebuilt apps after a deletion without rebuilding them.
- **Delete:** This deletes the app from the device.

Viewing the Device Console

The Console page, shown in Figure 10.12, is a simplified iOS version of the OS X Console application. It collects and displays general system logs. You can save the log to a file, for review, analysis, or sharing.

CAUTION

This console is *not* the same as the debugging console described in Chapter 15. The debugging console shows messages from one app. The Device Console shows messages from all apps and from iOS.

There isn't usually much of interest in the console log. Most of the device chatter is hardware-related and includes information about WiFi, battery, USB, and sleep events. You may find the details useful if you are developing hardware accessories or if you are testing an app with NSLog calls outside the debugger. But aside from the curiosity value, there's little that helps with app debugging and isn't covered in more detail in the Device Logs.

Figure 10.12

Viewing the Device Console, which is just a copy of the main iOS log file.

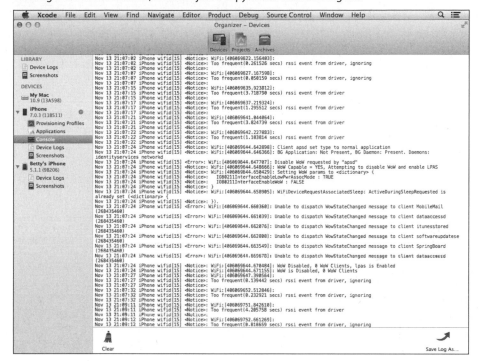

Using Device Logs and Screenshots

These features are identical to the Device Logs and Screenshots in the main Library window, with the minor differences that were described earlier in this chapter.

Working with Projects and Archives

The Organizer's Projects and Archives features include project management and archiving features that aren't available elsewhere in Xcode.

Managing Projects

The Projects window, shown in Figure 10.13, is a long list of projects with a number of extra features that include snapshot management and cleanup. This feature is a useful extra and can save you time and disk space. It's not a critical part of Xcode, but it can save time and make you more productive.

Figure 10.13

In the Project page, the list at the left is similar to but longer than the recent files list in Xcode's File menu.

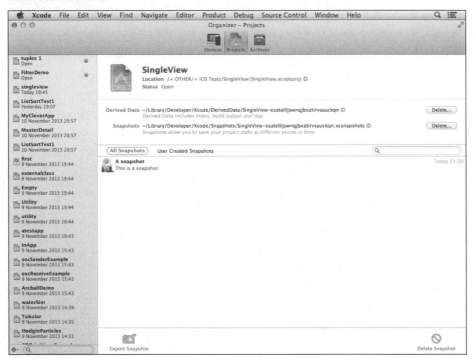

For example, it's often useful to open an older project in Xcode. The main recent files list includes 20 entries. The list on the Projects page grows indefinitely, which makes it a useful shortcut when you want to access older files without looking for them in Finder, although the down side is that it can take a while to load. Currently open projects appear at the top of the list and are marked with a pale blue dot.

Each entry includes these features:

- **Double-click to open:** Double-clicking any project in the list loads it into Xcode.
- **Derived Data review:** When you build a project, Xcode creates a collection of temporary files, which are called Derived Data and can take up significant disk space. The gray arrow to the right of Derived Data field for each project opens Xcode's temporary files folder and highlights the project.

TIP
You don't usually need to look inside the build folders. You do need to know where to find the built application, but you can reveal it by clicking the file in the Products group in the Symbol Navigator and using the Show in Finder . . . option.

- **Derived Data cleanup:** Temporary build files take up unnecessary space. When you complete a project, you can use the Delete option to remove them. This is *not* equivalent to the Product ⇨ Clean option in the main Xcode menu. Clean removes build-related files. Delete removes all other supporting files created by Xcode, including logs and indexes.

- **Snapshot management:** Project snapshots, if any, are listed in the lower part of the main area. You can use the Export Snapshot button at the lower left of the main area, which exports the snapshot to a complete project. You also can delete unneeded snapshots to save disk space. You cannot create or restore snapshots here; use the snapshot options near the bottom of the main File menu instead.

NOTE

Xcode 5 creates derived data—the files created during a build—in an independent folder. Before you delete a project from disk, use the Delete option in the Organizer to delete this data; otherwise, it's never removed. Note that you can click the arrow next to the Derived Data path to open the relevant folder in Finder.

CROSS-REFERENCE

For information about creating and comparing snapshots, see Chapter 15.

Creating Archives

In spite of the name, the Archives feature, shown in Figure 10.14, has nothing to do with archiving or backups in the sense of keeping old copies of source code. In Xcode, an archive is a packaged, provisioned, and code-signed application build that can be sent to beta testers or uploaded to the App Store.

To create an archive, use the Product ⇨ Archive option in the main Xcode menu. Creating an archive adds the app to the list that appears at the left of this page. You can build an archive as often as you want. Each build adds a new entry to the list in the bottom half of the main area.

The buttons at the top left implement two archive-related features:

- **Validate:** This runs basic checks on an archive to confirm that it's suitable for the App Store, and it verifies that the contents have been code-signed correctly.

- **Distribute:** This uploads the app to the App Store. You need to prepare a marketing description with supporting images and text before the App Store accepts an upload.

CROSS-REFERENCE

For more information about these features, see Chapters 12 and 13.

Figure 10.14

The Archive page has nothing to do with backups.

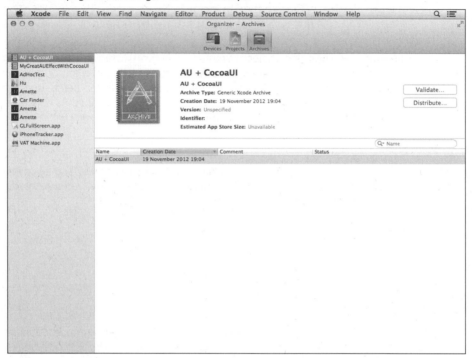

Summary

Because the Organizer isn't as structured or as focused as the rest of Xcode, it can be a slightly confusing place. The key point to remember is that it's there to help you keep track of devices, projects, and archives. And it has a very long memory. It remembers its content across multiple updates, and if you've forgotten what you did with a project you worked on a couple of years ago, the Organizer will help you find it and re-open it.

The device-specific options can be equally useful. You don't usually need to worry about snapshots, but the crash reports can help you find problems that happen in live use, when your device isn't physically connected to Xcode.

Managing Certificates, Identifiers, and Provisioning Profiles

P arts of the development process require secure access to Apple services, so Xcode includes built-in features that manage these. Security management is known as *provisioning*. Provisioning is simpler in Xcode 5 than it was in previous versions of Xcode, but the learning curve remains non-trivial.

Understanding Provisioning

For commercial and technical reasons, Apple needs to control what developers and users can do. The provisioning and account management system controls access to three main privileges:

- Developing iOS apps and testing them on hardware (This option includes distributing apps to beta testers.)
- Distributing Mac and iOS apps through the App Store
- *Signing* Mac Apps so users can install them easily even if they are not distributed through the App Store

iOS and OS X development privileges are managed separately. You can sign up for either program or for both. If you sign up for one program only, you are locked out of the other. For example, OS X program members can build iOS apps in the Simulator but cannot test them on devices. iOS program members can build Mac apps but cannot sign them for distribution.

In This Chapter

Understanding provisioning

Getting started with provisioning

Creating certificates and identities

NOTE
As of OS X Mavericks, users can still install unsigned apps, but they need to manually override a warning. It's not obvious how to override the warning, so assume that if you don't bundle your app with good instructions, many users can't do it. It's possible that Apple will stop supporting unsigned apps altogether in a future version of OS X.

NOTE
Code-signing technology can seem complicated, but in practice it simply means telling Xcode to include a few special files with a test or distribution build. The files include a *certificate* that identifies you as a legitimate Apple developer or app distributor. The certificate includes the public part of a secure public/private key pair.

Understanding accounts and team roles

Many apps are developed by teams. Developers in teams can have three separate roles, which are currently described in the Managing Your Team section of the App Distribution Guide, as shown in Figure 11.1. The details are likely to change in the future, but as of iOS 7, these are the roles:

- **Agent:** This role is the main management role, with full privileges. Agents can assign other roles to team members. They can also control access to various developer privileges for each member. They can develop and test apps. And they can submit apps to the App Store.
- **Admin:** Admins can give the developers under them access to development, testing, and distribution privileges. They can also develop, test, and manage device lists. An admin can't submit an app to the App Store.
- **Developers:** Developers can only develop. If they want to test apps on hardware or distribute apps through an App Store, they must *request* this option from an agent or admin. The agent or admin can accept or deny the request. If the request is accepted, the developer can then refresh the privileges associated with his or her account.

Figure 11.1

Apple's own description of iOS team roles may change in the future. OS X team roles are similar.

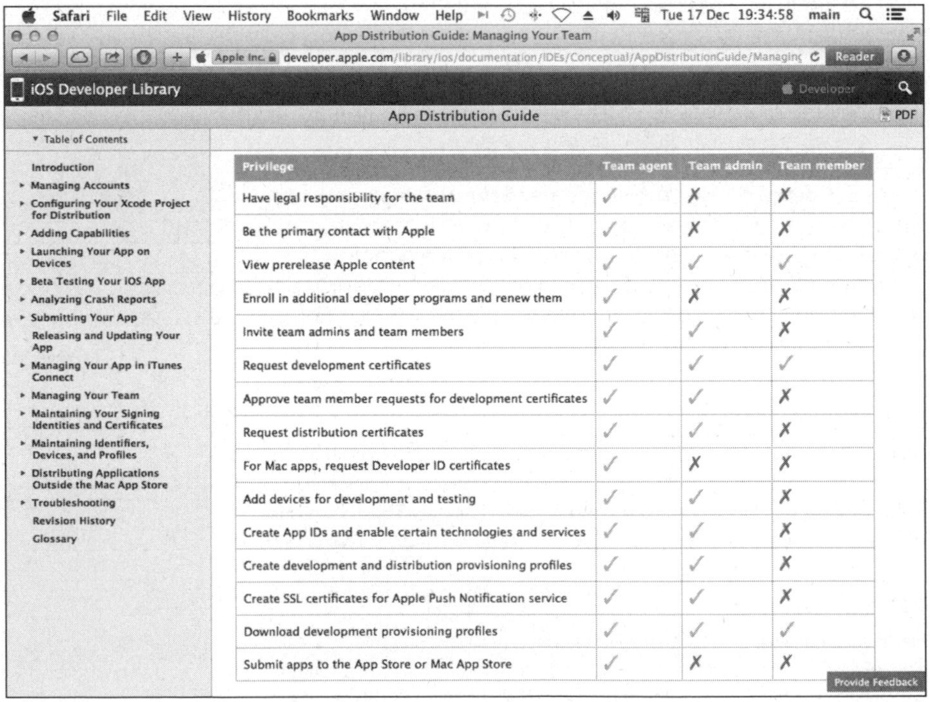

Privilege	Team agent	Team admin	Team member
Have legal responsibility for the team	✓	✗	✗
Be the primary contact with Apple	✓	✗	✗
View prerelease Apple content	✓	✓	✓
Enroll in additional developer programs and renew them	✓	✗	✗
Invite team admins and team members	✓	✓	✗
Request development certificates	✓	✓	✓
Approve team member requests for development certificates	✓	✓	✗
Request distribution certificates	✓	✓	✗
For Mac apps, request Developer ID certificates	✓	✗	✗
Add devices for development and testing	✓	✓	✗
Create App IDs and enable certain technologies and services	✓	✓	✗
Create development and distribution provisioning profiles	✓	✓	✗
Create SSL certificates for Apple Push Notification service	✓	✓	✗
Download development provisioning profiles	✓	✓	✓
Submit apps to the App Store or Mac App Store	✓	✗	✗

Solo developers are always agents. In the past, they had to make requests to themselves and grant them manually by refreshing a page on the developer resources site. In Xcode 5, this process seems to have been streamlined, and the permissions process for basic development—but not for app distribution—"just works." Solo developers can still create a team by inviting other developers to work on a project. They then take on the full agent role and can control admin/ developer privileges for the other team members.

N O T E

Agents can also set up the all-important Contracts, Tax, and Banking page on iTunes Connect. This page makes sure the team as a whole gets paid for app sales and nominates a bank account for income. Contracts change regularly, and agents should check the contracts page at least once a month and update it as necessary.

Understanding entitlements, devices, and profiles

Apps have their own set of privileges, called *capabilities* or *entitlements*. These privileges control access to Apple services such as iCloud, Game Center, Push Notifications, and Maps. You can set these entitlements in Xcode, as shown in Figure 11.2.

Entitlements are not self-contained. They are built into an *app ID:* an identifier used by the App Store to identify an app or a group of related apps. The App ID in turn is built into a *provisioning profile,* which allows apps to be tested on real iOS devices, and is also bundled with an app when it is distributed through the App Store or sent out to beta testers.

The first kind of profile is called a *development profile.* The second kind of profile is called a *distribution or production* profile. For iOS, you can specify two kinds of distribution profiles: one that works for the App Store and one that works for beta test distribution outside the App Store. The second kind is called an *Ad Hoc Distribution Profile* for obscure reasons that involve engineers and Latin.

To test an app on a device, developers must install a suitable provisioning profile on a test device. The profile includes an app ID that specifies which app, or group of apps, is allowed to run. It also defines *entitlements,* which allow an app to use Apple support features, such as maps and access to the Game Center. Ad Hoc profiles also include a list of test devices on which they can run. Devices not on the list cannot run the app.

Developers must *register* a device before they can test on it. To allow testing on a device, the provisioning profile file must match the app ID of the app being tested *and* include the device the app is being tested on *and* include a valid developer identity.

The first time you try to test an app on a device, Xcode automatically copies a matching profile to the device. You can save time by asking Xcode to create a generic *development profile* with a wild-card ID ('*') that supports all apps. This feature works for basic app development. Occasionally, you may need to create a customized profile to access further options. You can do this only in the online Member Center.

Figure 11.2

Look at entitlements and capabilities in Xcode.

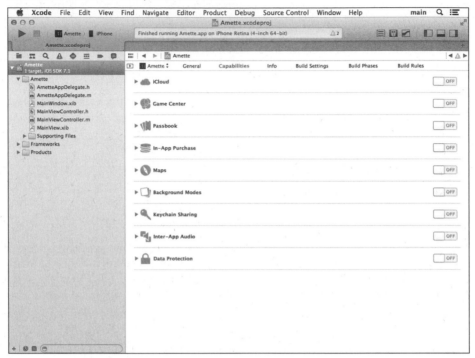

CAUTION

iOS development certificates expire after a set period. This means you can't build an app for yourself and run it on your own devices indefinitely. Currently, certificates expire a year after creation. Apps you installed on your devices stop working unless you re-subscribe or "buy" the app and install from the App Store. (The latter option is free, if you use an iTunes Connect promo code. But it assumes your app can pass Apple's approval process.)

Getting Started with Provisioning

In earlier versions of Xcode, you identified yourself to the permissions system by generating your own signing keys and uploading them to the developer center. In Xcode 5, roles and accounts are linked to Apple IDs, and the identification certificates you need for device testing and App Store distribution are generated automatically in Xcode. Development profiles can also be generated by Xcode.

Distribution profiles may begin to be generated by Xcode within the life of this book. But at the time of this writing, you have to use the Member Center website to create distribution profiles for App Store and Ad Hoc distribution, and then use Xcode to download them.

To view account information, select Xcode ⇨ Preferences ⇨ Accounts, as shown in Figure 11.3. Click the + (plus) button in the lower left to display the dialog shown in the figure. Enter the Apple ID and password you used when you signed up for a developer program, and click Add.

Figure 11.3

This is how you set up a developer account.

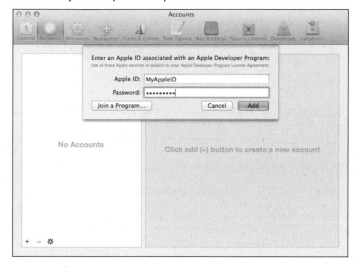

NOTE

If you haven't already signed up for a program, click Join a Program and work through the steps. For details, see Chapter 2.

After signup, Xcode adds your Apple ID to the list at the left. In the lower-right area, you see one or more teams associated with the ID and a list of roles for each team, as shown in Figure 11.4. If you're a solo developer, you appear as an agent for your team. If you're a team developer, you may need to ask an agent or admin to set up a role for you first.

TIP

This dialog also shows a list of repositories and servers associated with your Apple ID. Initially, there aren't any, but as you add them, they appear here. This feature replaces the Repositories page that appeared in the Organizer in Xcode 4. Repositories are introduced in Chapter 15. Servers are described in Chapter 18.

Figure 11.4

Review teams and roles for an Apple ID.

Collecting developer resources

To summarize, the development process works with four kinds of resources:

- **Certificates:** These are linked to an Apple ID. Access to certificates is controlled by team agents and team admins. A *development certificate* allows an ID to test apps on iOS hardware. A *distribution or production certificate* allows an ID to distribute apps through the App Store. Mac apps can also have an optional *Developer ID certificate* and an *Installer ID certificate*. These allow apps to be installed and run on OS X without forcing the user to manually override security.

- **Identifiers:** These include App IDs, which give apps a unique App Store ID and also define which Apple services they can access. On iOS, you can also generate optional *Pass IDs,* which are necessary if you create apps that work with Passbook, and *Website Push IDs,* which work with Apple's push notifications.

- **A device list:** For iOS development, devices must be *registered*—added to the list—before they can be used for testing.

- **Provisioning profiles:** These files link all of the above into a single key file that is copied to a device. iOS tests the provisioning profile for various permissions to see if an app is allowed to run on a specific device. The profile also defines which Apple services the app is allowed to use.

Developer resources are managed in two places. You can do lots of the setup work in Xcode. Xcode can communicate with the Apple and ask it to register devices, create and download certificates, and set up a default provisioning profile for testing.

This semi-automated process manages basic app development requirements. But some parts need manual access, using the features of your Member Center, shown in Figure 11.5.

TIP

It's easy to miss the link to the Member Center. Currently, it's near the top right on the main Dev Center page, visible after you log in with your Apple ID.

There are two key elements in the Member Center. To manage teams and roles, click the People button in the tab near the top of the window. The People page, shown in Figure 11.6, lists the members of your team. You can also use it to invite other developers by e-mail. If a developer accepts your invitation, the Member Center adds her to the All People list. You can then use iOS and/or Mac Developer lists to assign a role.

Figure 11.5

Here's a first look at the Member Center.

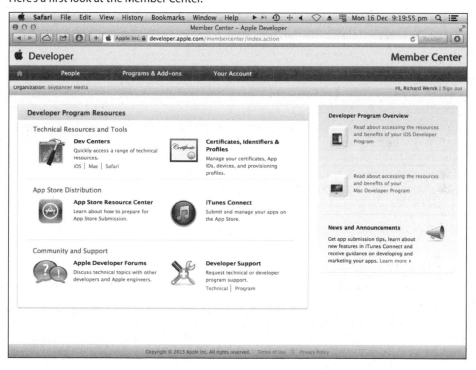

Figure 11.6

Manage the People page in the Member Center.

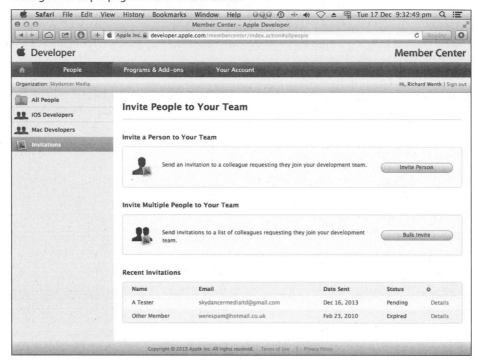

To manage other developer resources, click the Certificates, Identifiers & Profiles link, which appears near the top/middle of Figure 11.4. Clicking the link takes you to a page that lists the resources for each of your developer programs, as shown in Figure 11.7.

In outline, the development process follows these steps:

1. If you are managing a team, use the People tab to set up team roles.

2. For basic development, use Xcode to set up certificates, identifiers, and profiles.

3. For projects with special requirements, use the Certificates, Identifiers & Profiles page to manage developer resources for your team and your projects.

4. Use iTunes Connect to set up Contracts, Tax, and Banking for your team.

5. When a new app is ready, create a distribution profile.

6. Fill in some (virtual) paperwork in the Manage Your Apps section in iTunes Connect.

7. Make some changes to the app build to make sure the app is *code signed* correctly to match the distribution profile and your team developer ID.

8. Build the app as an archive, and upload it to the App Store from Xcode's Organizer.

Figure 11.7

Looking at Certificates, Identifiers & Profiles.

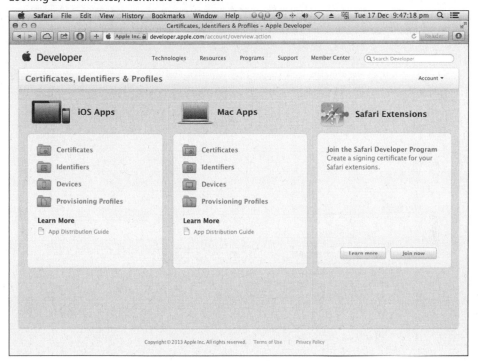

TIP

This page includes the useful App Distribution Guides for both platforms. Take the time to read through them. They explain the app packaging and submission process in detail.

CROSS-REFERENCE

This chapter works through the first three steps. Steps 4 to 8 are described in Chapters 12, 13, and 14.

Creating Certificates and Identities

Xcode 5 automates much of the work needed to create basic development (device testing, for example) and production (distribution, for example) identities. Select Xcode ⇨ Preferences ⇨ Accounts, log in with your Apple ID if you haven't already, and click View Details at the bottom right. Initially, the Signing Identities area is empty.

To generate/download an identity, click the + (plus) icon and select an identity from the menu, as shown in Figure 11.8. Xcode communicates with your developer account and downloads and installs the identity, assuming your team role includes permission.

Figure 11.8

Generate signing identities.

If you are working with devices, Xcode generates Mac and/or iOS team provisioning profiles for you. If you already have some app IDs defined, they appear automatically in the Provisioning Profiles window at the bottom of the dialog.

For basic development, this is all you need to do. You can update signing identities and provisioning profiles at any time by clicking the refresh button at the lower left.

Working on more than one Mac

If you're working in the Simulator only or developing for OS X, working on two Macs is trivial. Hardware testing and App Store distribution are more complex. The simple rule of thumb is that you can develop and test on two Macs if you copy all your certificates and keychain information. But it's a good idea to reserve one Mac for distribution.

You'll often want to keep a current production version of OS X for maintenance and testing, and a beta version of the next OS X release for future development. You can continue to build and test on both systems without duplicating certificates.

Of course, you may want to move certificates to a different Mac if you upgrade your development machine. Click the gear icon at the bottom left of the Accounts Preferences dialog to show an import/export menu. Figure 11.9 shows how you can specify a file location for the certificates while exporting them and secure them with a password.

You can use the corresponding import dialog on the other Mac to import the certificates into a new copy of Xcode.

Figure 11.9

Export a developer profile to another Mac.

Managing devices

For local development, you can use the Devices page in the Organizer to manage devices for testing, as described in Chapter 10. However, you may also want to supply your app to beta testers. Beta testers can be located anywhere, so you often need to register their devices manually. This is a two-stage process.

Begin by asking your beta tester to connect his device to iTunes, open the device page, and click the Serial Number listed to the right of the device. The serial number is replaced by an identifier code called a UDID.

The tester can then click Edit ⇨ Copy Identifier, as shown in Figure 11.10, and paste the UDID into an e-mail to you.

Figure 11.10

Copy a device UDID.

To register the device, open the Certificates, Identifiers & Profiles page in the Member Center. Click Devices to see a list of registered devices. Click the + (plus) icon near the top right. Give the device a name. Copy the UDID from the tester's e-mail, and paste it into the UDID field, as shown in Figure 11.11. Click Continue to add the device.

Development teams sometimes automate the process of collecting and entering device IDs with a custom script that scans e-mails sent to a special address, extracts the UDIDs from them, and copies them to a file. The Devices page includes an option to register up to 100 devices loaded from a file. Designing and implementing a harvesting script is outside the scope of this book, but it's worth considering for large-scale testing programs.

TIP
You can simplify the provisioning, testing, and beta data collection by using third-party services such as **TestFlight** https://www.testflightapp.com/) or **HockeyApp** (http://hockeyapp.net/features/).

Figure 11.11

Register the device in the Member Center.

Creating Certificates Manually

Xcode and the Member Center create a basic set of certificates and profiles automatically. However, some applications require a manually generated certificate, including these:

- **Apple Push Notification Sandbox:** This gives you access to a special limited test server you can use to test push notification features.
- **App Store Distribution:** As mentioned already, the most reliable way to create a profile for App Store distribution is using the Member Center website.
- **Ad Hoc Testing:** This is Apple jargon for apps distributed directly to beta testers, without passing through the App Store.
- **Pass ID:** This is a certificate needed to manage Passbook.
- **Website Push ID:** This is a certificate needed to access push notification features.

Before you can generate these certificates, you must create a Certificate Signing Request (CSR) on your Mac. You'll be asked to upload the CSR to the Member Center as part of the certification process.

NOTE

A CSR is a public/private key pair that identifies you to the Member Center and to the Apple app and device management infrastructure. The private key remains in your Mac's keychain. The public key is distributed with your apps or uploaded to a website you are developing, depending on the application.

CAUTION

This system isn't as secure as it seems. If your Mac is stolen and your main system password is easy to guess, the stored keys and web passwords may include enough information for a skilled third party to impersonate you online. Although the key system is supposed to prevent app piracy, it's relatively easy to strip out the keys from an app and distribute it illegally to users who *jailbreak*—bypass the security—in their iOS devices.

Creating a CSR

To create a CSR, use your Mac's Keychain Access application. You can find it in `/Application/Utilities`. Select Keychain Access ⇨ Certificate Assistance ⇨ Request a Certificate From a Certificate Authority.

Enter the e-mail address you used when you registered as a developer. In the Common Name field, add your name and a note about the application. Leave the CA (Certificate Authority) Email Address field blank. Select the option labeled Saved to disk, as shown in Figure 11.12.

Figure 11.12

To create a CSR, enter your name and e-mail address and select the CSR options.

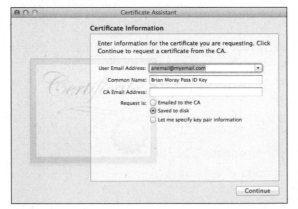

TIP

Before you start, create a folder or sub-folder for files used in the provisioning process, so you know where they are. The default save location for the CSR file is the desktop, which may not be ideal.

CAUTION
You must keep a record of the details you enter here; they're essential if you move to another Mac.

Select the filename and save path on the next sheet, so the file is saved to your new `Provisioning` folder. When Keychain Access creates the certificate, it gives you the option of viewing its location in Finder. By default, the filename is `CertificateSigningRequest.certSigningRequest`. You need to know the location of this file for the next part of the process, where you upload the CSR to the Member Center.

In the Member Center, select the certificate you want, and click through until you see the Choose File button. Click it, and upload the CSR file you created. Click Generate.

You can use the Download button, shown in Figure 11.13, to download the new certificate. Double-clicking it installs it in your keychain. It should then be available in Xcode. If it isn't, restart Xcode to load it.

Figure 11.13

Download a manually generated certificate.

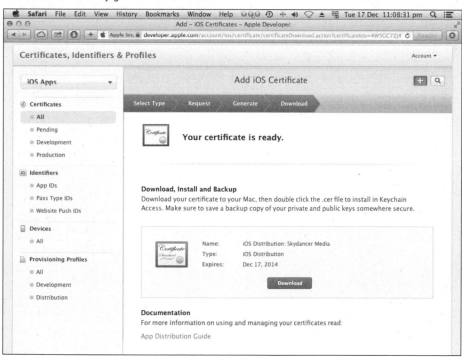

Now that you know how to create certificates, you can start building them into your Xcode projects, as described in Chapters 13 and 14.

Summary

Apple has simplified the provisioning and certification process with Xcode 5. Testing an app on a device is now much easier than it was. It's not quite click-and-go, but you probably won't waste lots of time on it.

Creating and using distribution profiles can still be a challenge. Chapters 13 and 14 include full details. Because Xcode makes development seem easy, it's tempting to follow the shortcuts it seems to include for distribution.

Unfortunately, these shortcuts don't work reliably, and if you try to use them, it's somewhere between not impossible and quite likely that you'll produce a distribution build you can't distribute. So expect to spend more time setting up distribution than development.

In fact, the process isn't impossibly complicated. But it includes many elements that you must get right and assemble in the right way, both on the Developer Center website and in Xcode.

Working with Builds, Schemes, and Workspaces

S o far in this book, builds have been treated as one-click processes, and projects have been treated as stand-alone collections of files.

But it's a key feature of Xcode that the build process is almost infinitely customizable. Instead of treating the build process as a black box that takes source files and converts them into an app, you can break the build process into steps, change the settings and outputs from each step, or even add completely new steps—for example, to create hybrid projects with code written in other languages.

You also can combine projects and files in various ways to create hybrid builds that share related code; for example, you can develop a framework and a project that tests it or uses it at the same time.

This chapter outlines the key features of the Xcode 5 build system and introduces the editors and options that control the build process.

Chapter 13 introduces some practical examples of build customization and explores more advanced build control options.

In This Chapter

Getting started with the Xcode build system

Understanding settings and options

Working with schemes and build configurations

Managing schemes, build actions, and targets

Getting Started with the Xcode Build System

Although you can use the build system in a simple one-click way, the underlying technology is powerful, but complex. The default one-click option deliberately hides the complexity, but you must be familiar with its key elements before you can begin customizing builds.

Figure 12.1 is a first look at how Xcode builds are organized.

Figure 12.1

These are components of the Xcode build system.

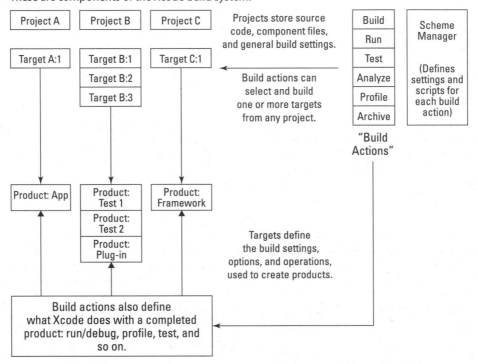

These are the key elements:

- **Projects:** A *project* is a collection of source files that you can select and change using the editing tools introduced earlier in this book.

- **Workspaces:** A *workspace* is a container for one or more projects. It's not unusual to use combinations of files from the same code base in multiple related projects. Workspaces make it easy to do this. All projects in a workspace share the same build space, and you can use Xcode's build features to define how the sources are combined. Potentially, you can also build multiple projects with a single build operation.

- **Targets:** A *target* is a recipe for building the files in a project, and it defines its product—for example, an app or a framework. In Xcode 5, many projects include a default target and an optional target for unit testing, which you can ignore until you have read Chapter 18. You can add further targets, as needed. Note that a target doesn't have to be a finished app. You can also create targets that process code in other ways—for example, to run a selection of optional test macros to check that important features work correctly.

- **Products:** A *product* is the collection of files created by a target: an app, framework, test build, and so on.
- **Build actions:** There are six standard actions, as shown in the figure. *Build actions* select one or more targets, build them, and then run them through further Xcode features. For example, the Run action loads the code into a runtime environment and launches a debugger, and the Analyze action runs the code through an analyzer to check for basic errors.
- **Scheme manager/editor:** A workspace can have one or more schemes, which are defined in the *scheme manager/editor*. You can use schemes to customize build actions; for example, the Run action in one scheme builds one target, but in another scheme, it builds every target in the workspace.
- **Scripts:** You can set up build actions to run pre-action and post-action *scripts,* which can play sounds, send e-mail messages, open alert boxes, copy files, and so on.
- **Settings and configurations:** Although not shown in the figure, *settings and configurations* define low-level options for compilation, linking, and packaging. They're introduced in more detail later in this chapter.

The relationship between the different elements involved in a build isn't self-evident. You may need to read this chapter more than once before the relationships become clear.

NOTE
You don't need to understand the process in detail to create a simple App Store build, but some elements interact in unexpected ways. You'll find it easier to use productively if you have a good understanding of the build system.

Creating and organizing a workspace

When you create a new project, you automatically create a workspace to hold it. For simple app projects, you can ignore workspaces and simply save each new project as a stand-alone unit. For more complex applications that hold multiple projects, you can use a workspace to group related projects together.

The easiest way to use a workspace is to create an empty workspace and then add projects to it. To create a blank workspace, select File ➪ New ➪ New Workspace from the main Xcode menu. You can then add projects by right-clicking in the blank area at the bottom of the Project navigator, and selecting New Project. . . .

You also can add existing projects. Select Add Files . . . , navigate to an existing project's .xcodeproj file, and select it.

CAUTION
This is useful for simple shared development, but this option doesn't support source control, so use it with care. For more advanced source control options, see Chapter 14.

CAUTION
You can drag an Xcode project file from Finder and drop it into a workspace, but this doesn't add the project files.

The workspace acts as an implied master group in the Project navigator. When you save your new project for the first time, you can use the Group pop-up at the bottom of the dialog to control the group to which it's added. The default is the new workspace, as shown in Figure 12.2.

You also can use this dialog to define the project's save path in the usual way. Projects in a workspace can be saved to any path; they don't have to be saved to the same folder.

NOTE
You can nest projects and put a project inside another project's group. This isn't usually a useful thing to do; projects are easier to work with when each has its own group.

Figure 12.2
When selecting a project's group in a workspace, the default selection is usually correct.

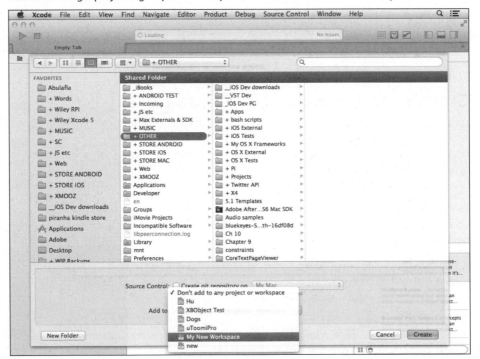

CAUTION
A workspace doesn't automatically build all the projects inside it. Typically, only the first project you add is built. If you want to build the other projects, you must tell Xcode to treat them as *dependencies.* For details, see Chapter 14.

Working with projects and targets

A workspace is a container and has no build settings or options. It's effectively a master group that holds other items. Projects and targets do have build options—hundreds of them. Xcode includes a separate build editor to manage them, shown in Figure 12.3. To open this editor, select the project name at the top left of the Project navigator. A list of options appears at the right, as shown in the figure.

TIP
It may not be intuitively obvious that you need to click the project name to display the build editor. It's worth taking a few moments to fix this step in your mind to help you remember it later.

Figure 12.3

Navigate to the build editor. The project settings are shown by default.

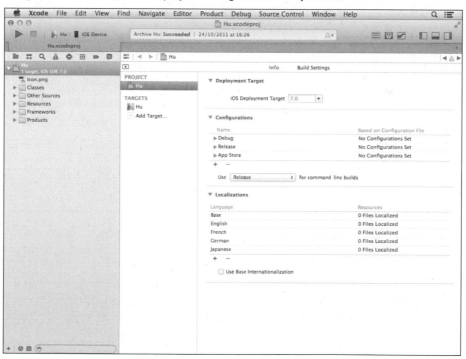

The build editor is complex. There are two items in the gutter area to the left of the options: the PROJECT and TARGETS headings. As you might expect, the project icon displays the options for the project as a whole, while each target icon displays options for each target. Select a target, and you see a longer list of tab options at the top of the window, as shown in Figure 12.4.

By default, most new iOS and OS X projects have a main target and a test target. Older projects like the one in the figure have a single target. If you need to process a project's files in further ways, you can define extra targets for a single project. Usually, you don't.

Figure 12.4

Navigate to the target build settings. The tabs at the top include extra items that aren't included in project settings.

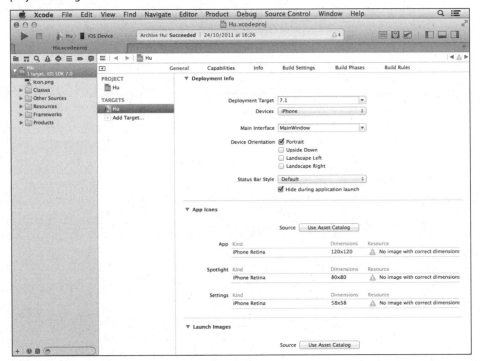

Understanding settings and options

There are five critical points to remember about projects and targets:

- Projects and targets can have separate build options.
- Build options are not the same as build *settings*.
- Build options include information needed to make a target, including selected artwork files, supported orientations, version numbers, property lists, and so on. They also include build settings.
- Build settings are a list of low-level compiler, linker, and packager switches.
- Target options override project options.

Xcode uses a priority hierarchy to calculate which settings and options to use when building a target. There's more information about this later in this chapter.

Understanding the project options

If you select the project icon, you see two tabs:

- **Info:** This includes a minimum supported OS version, a list of configurations (selected build setting presets), and a summary of the files localized for specific languages. In practice, the Localizations option is essential for foreign language support, the Configurations option is useful to App Store build customization, and the SDK/Deployment/OS option is usually overridden by the target.

- **Build Settings:** This is a long list with hundreds of compiler, linker, and deployment options that apply to the project as a whole. They can be overridden by the equivalent settings for each target.

Understanding the target options

If you select the target icon, or select one target if your project has many, you see five tabs with different options. Note that target options are independent. If your project has multiple targets, each has different options. These are the tabs you see:

- **General:** This includes basic build information, including an app version number, minimum OS, default nib/storyboard, and so on. You must customize these settings to make a valid App Store build as described in Chapters 13 and 14.

- **Capabilities:** This is a list of switches that gives your app access to special Apple features, such as Game Center, iCloud, Maps, and so on. These features are explained in more detail in Chapters 13 and 14.

- **Info:** This is a textlike list of options that control app launch. Again, you must customize these settings for an App Store build. Note that this list is a *plist*—an XML property list.

- **Build Settings:** At first sight, this list looks identical to the project build settings: It's another list of compiler, linker, and deployment options. The two lists are very similar, but there are some minor differences. Remember that these target build settings override the project build settings.

- **Build Phases:** The contents of this tab control the files that are processed and the order in which they're processed. Each phase defines the files and frameworks included in the build sequence. Here, you also can set dependencies to force a rebuild of a target when some related files are modified. For simple apps, you can ignore most of the features on this page, except for one: the option to include standard frameworks in your project.

- **Build Rules:** The rules define how files of each type are processed. Specifically, you can define or create custom scripts for each existing file type in the list, and you can add new file types of your own, with custom processing options. These advanced options aren't needed for simple apps; they become useful in more complex projects.

CROSS-REFERENCE
Build settings are introduced in this chapter. Build phases and rules are described in more detail in Chapter 13.

Introducing build settings

As mentioned earlier in this chapter, the build settings include every compiler, linker, and packager option. When you build a project, Xcode converts these settings into command-line switches and includes them in the compiler scripts. The full list of settings is very long and can seem intimidating. In practice, you can leave most settings unchanged in a typical project.

To work with the build settings, select the Build Settings tab in the build options window. The settings appear in an editor, with four buttons that control the layout of the UI. The first two buttons control which settings are visible, and the second two control how they're displayed. The settings appear in a list or table, with group headings. These are the settings:

- **Basic:** This layout lists a small sub-set of the build settings, as shown in Figure 12.5. It's not the most useful sub-set, but it does include some important settings. The list of settings is fixed, so you can't create your own selection.

- **All:** This layout lists every setting, as shown in Figure 12.6.

Figure 12.5
Within the basic build settings, the two most useful options are the Compiler Version and the Targeted Device Family.

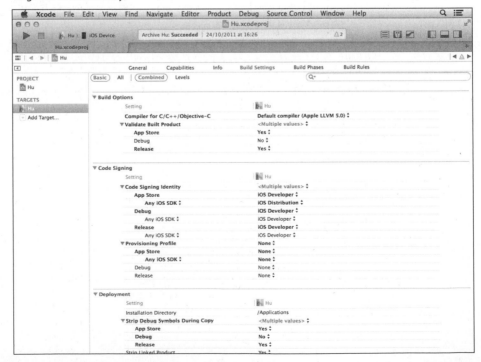

FIGURE 12.6

The complete list of settings is shown by the All button.

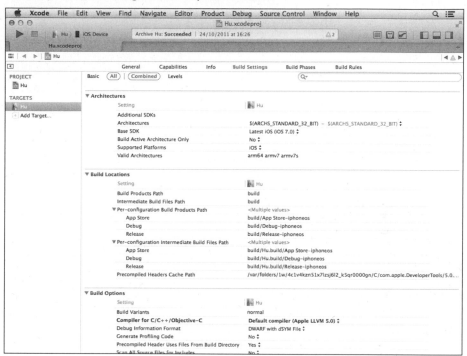

- **Combined:** Switches with multiple values appear as embedded menus. You can click a setting to select a different value.
- **Levels:** This is a complex view that illustrates how the settings cascade through various levels of defaults, as shown in Figure 12.7. This feature is explained later.

TIP

You can use the disclosure triangles in the group headings to hide the less-useful settings and simplify the display.

TIP

If you open the Quick Help in the utility pane and select a build setting, you see a short but helpful description of the setting and the equivalent command-line switch. For more advanced customization, the settings are described in slightly (but not much) more detail in the official documentation, which has extra information about how some settings interact with others. Search for Build Setting Reference in the documentation in the Organizer.

Figure 12.7

The new Levels view shows multiple build settings in a single window.

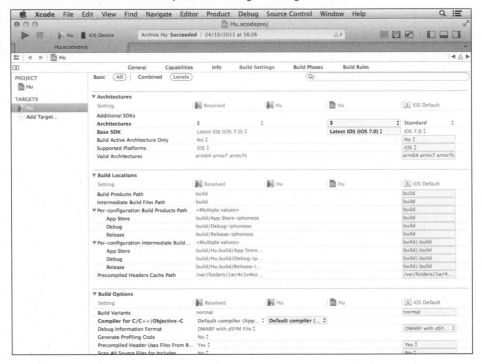

Understanding the Levels view

The Levels view has four columns when viewing target settings and three columns when viewing project settings. It's not immediately obvious how this view works, but the design becomes clearer after you understand how it's organized.

There are two key points. The first is that Xcode build settings cascade through multiple levels of defaults. Each level overrides the previous level. When Xcode creates a build, it uses this table to find the settings with the highest priority and applies those to the build.

The order of priority flows from right to left. These columns are present:

- **OS default:** These are the standard default switches that apply when the other rows are empty.
- **Project settings:** This list shows the Project build settings. It's identical to the list you can view by selecting the PROJECT icon and All/Combined buttons under the Build Settings tab. These settings override the OS defaults. If a project has multiple targets, the settings apply to all of them.

- **Target settings:** This list shows the Target build settings for the current selected target. It's identical to the list you can view by selecting the All/Combined buttons. These settings override the project settings and the OS defaults. If your project has multiple targets, the settings in this column apply to the currently selected target. Other targets can have different settings.
- **Resolved:** These are the final calculated settings applied to the build. Because they're calculated from the other columns, you can't edit them.

Figure 12.8 illustrates how each level overrides the next. Levels with higher priority override those lower down the list.

Figure 12.8

Build settings are arranged in levels. The diagram shows how levels with higher priority override lower levels.

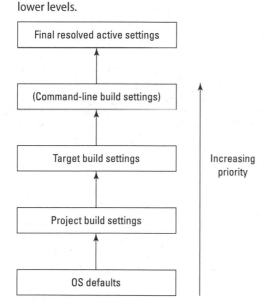

The second key point is that *Xcode only stores the highest level setting needed to create an unambiguous resolution.*

If you scroll through the table, you see that many settings are left to their system defaults. There's no entry for either the project or the target. Because they're left empty, the resolved value is the same as the default.

This may seem like a trivial point, but in fact it's crucial. When you edit a target or project setting, you're not only modifying its value, *you're also adding a new entry to the settings table.*

Why does this matter? Consider the following sequence of actions:

1. You edit a project setting.

2. The setting has the highest priority, so it applies to all targets. You can change it repeatedly, and it's always applied.

3. Later on, you decide to edit that setting for one target.

4. The new target setting is applied as you'd expect.

5. You change the project setting again.

6. Because a target setting exists now, the new project setting *isn't applied to the target.* The target setting continues to override it.

As soon as you change a setting at the target level, you lock out all future project-level changes to that setting.

This is almost intuitive—but not quite. If you work exclusively in the Combined view, it can be difficult to understand what's happening, because sometimes changes you make are applied as you'd expect, and sometimes they aren't.

The Combined view doesn't illustrate the difference in priority between target and project settings. It also doesn't make it clear that if no target setting has been defined, a project setting can—confusingly—appear to override a target setting.

NOTE
Advanced developers who use the command-line tools can override all settings by hand. This is a specialized and advanced technique, included in the figure for completeness. It's not supported from Xcode directly.

The Levels view has some quirks:

- The central columns aren't clearly labeled. If you view the project settings, you'll see the project name and an icon. If you view the target settings, you'll see the target name, the project name, and an icon for each. But there's no label that says "Project" or "Target."

- You can't edit the OS defaults or the Resolved column.

- There are some minor differences between the settings shown for a project and for a target.

- Both the target and project build settings include a Levels view. However, the version in the project settings doesn't include the target settings column.

As a simple working rule, if you're developing an app with a single target, it's easier to ignore the project settings and work exclusively at the target level. Use the Target Levels view to edit and confirm the settings you want to change. Ignore the project column entirely. This guarantees that changes will do what you expect, and there are no hidden surprises.

If your project has multiple targets, it's standard practice to make project-level settings. But beware of the target-level lockout described earlier. Note also that the empty rows in the project and target columns aren't really empty. If you select them, you see that you can edit them.

TIP

You can delete target-level settings, but it's not obvious how to do this. The secret is to highlight an item and use the Delete key. You can't delete items with the mouse.

CROSS-REFERENCE

Chapter 13 features a more advanced guide to build settings.

Working with Schemes and Build Configurations

Developers often need to customize builds for different purposes; for example, a test build for debugging is likely to have different build settings than a final App Store build. Xcode handles this in two ways.

Build configurations allow you to change a sub-set of build settings for a specific aim: debugging, release, and so on. Potentially, every build setting can hold a different value for each configuration. By default, most settings take a single value; only a small number are initialized with multiple values.

Schemes give you wider control. The key feature of schemes is that they define build actions that allow you to build your project for different purposes: testing and debugging, code analysis, archiving, and so on. Schemes include build configurations, but add other build and test options.

Getting started with build configurations

Switching configurations is a quick way to change a group of build settings in a single operation, as shown in Figure 12.9. When you select a configuration, Xcode automatically selects the corresponding values and applies them to the build. Single-valued settings remain constant.

Figure 12.9

Most build settings have a single value. Settings included in a configuration file can take and display multiple values. The resolved value depends on which configuration is active.

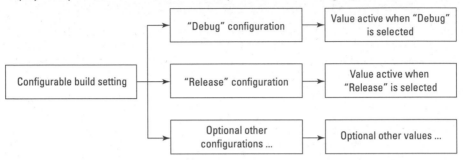

In practice, this means that you can quickly customize a configuration to create a build for a specific aim—debugging, local testing, App Store release, Ad Hoc release, and so on—without having to create a separate independent list of build settings.

Conveniently, configurations include the settings needed to create useful debug and distribution builds. Less conveniently, these settings are scattered randomly throughout the full list of all build settings.

NOTE

Why not duplicate every build setting for a configuration? The practical reason is that the settings editor can display multiple values for different configurations. But duplicating every setting for all possible configurations would make the editor unwieldy and difficult to work with. In practice, most settings don't need to be modified, so most of the duplication would be unnecessary.

By default, each new project is created with two configurations: Debug and Release. You can create your own configurations by duplicating either or both of these and giving your new configuration a different name. You can then modify its settings and save it with your project.

To create a setting with multiple values, select it and click the reveal triangle at the far left. The setting opens to show a list of configurations. You can now set different values for each configuration.

The settings editor gives multiple values special treatment. It displays them with a `<Multiple Values>` tag, and the configuration settings appear in rows under it. Figure 12.10 illustrates this with an example of a key configuration setting for iOS projects: the Code Signing Identity.

Figure 12.10

View multiple configuration values for the Code Signing Identity setting.

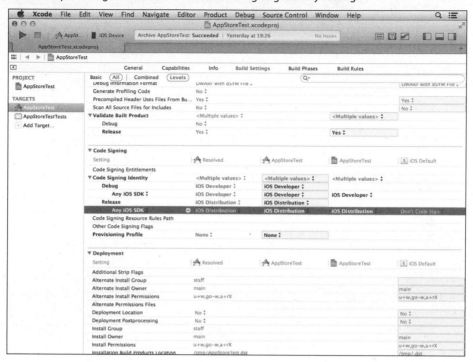

NOTE

Configurations are project-specific. Configuration names and settings are part of a project. For more advanced configuration customization, see Chapter 13.

Table 12.1 lists every setting that defaults to multiple values. In practice, you can ignore most of them, because the essential differences can be summarized as follows:

- **Debug:** This configuration includes debug symbols—an appended list of strings and memory addresses used to display human-readable information in the debugger. On iOS, this configuration signs code with the Developer Identity so it can be tested on live hardware.

- **Release:** You can use this configuration as the basis of a build suitable for distribution—for example, Ad Hoc beta testing or App Store upload. But it typically must be modified to achieve this. This configuration doesn't include debug symbols. On OS X, this configuration creates an app that can be run by double-clicking, but it doesn't include App Store distribution information and isn't wrapped in an installer package. On iOS, this configuration is useless without further customization. It doesn't create a build that you can upload to the App Store or e-mail to beta testers.

Table 12.1 Settings Included in a Configuration

Setting	Included in OS	Should be edited?	Notes
Build Active Architecture Only	Both	Not usually	This specifies builds for 32-bit only, 64-bit only, or both architectures. For debug builds, this setting should match the hardware for debug builds on your test Mac. For distribution builds, it can enable or disable support for a specific architecture.
Code Signing Identity	iOS, optional for OS X	Yes	For a distribution build, select the iPhone distribution identity created and downloaded in Chapter 11. For live hardware debug builds, the iPhone Developer identity is selected by default.
Per-Configuration Build Products Path	Both	No	This defines the file path to the intermediate build products.
Debug Information Format	OS X	No	This controls whether symbols are included with the build.
Search Paths	Both	Not usually	You can add optional search paths when working with external libraries and their headers.
Validate Built Product	iOS	No	This enables an extra build validation pass. It should be enabled for final App Store distribution builds, but not for debugging.
C/C++ Language Dialects	Both	Optional	This includes two switches you can use to select a specific compiler variant.
Strip Debug Symbols During Copy	Both	No	By default, this removes symbols from a distribution build.
Path to Link Map File	Both	No	This defines the file path to intermediate files generated by the linker.
Generate Position-Dependent Code	OS X	No	By default, code is position-independent.
Optimization Level	Both	Not usually	You can experiment with this setting to trade off code size against performance.
Other C Flags	iOS	Not usually	Use this option to add custom compiler flags for C code.
Other C++ Flags	iOS	Not usually	Use this option to add custom compiler flags for C++ code.
Preprocessor Macros	Both	No	This enables the optional DEBUG preprocessor macro for debug builds.

Understanding schemes and build actions

Schemes take the various build options and configuration settings and wrap extra features around them.

By default, when you build a project, Xcode creates a test build that includes debugging symbols. It launches the debugger and attaches it to the active runtime automatically.

In Xcode, this sequence is one of six standard build actions—options that build and process targets in various ways. The complete set of build action settings defines a scheme.

These are the standard actions:

- **Build:** Builds one or more targets—in other words, creates their products, but doesn't launch, process, or use them in any other way. This action is the master action. It's an essential first step and is performed automatically by all other actions. You also can run it manually with the Project ⇨ Build option in the main Xcode menu.
- **Run:** Builds and runs the app in the debugger. This is the default action, triggered when you click the big Run button in the main Xcode toolbar.
- **Test:** Builds and runs the unit testing features described in Chapter 17. If the project doesn't include a unit testing target, this action does nothing.
- **Profile:** Builds, launches the Instruments profiling and testing application described in Chapter 16, and loads the app into it.
- **Analyze:** Builds and runs the code analyzer described in Chapter 15. Although a full build may not be necessary for code analysis, Xcode runs the Build action anyway.
- **Archive:** Builds and packages an app ready for distribution, adding it to the Archive list in the Organizer (introduced in Chapter 10). This option is accessible only through the Product menu and isn't included in the toolbar pop-up.

The easy way to get started with schemes is to click **and hold** the master Build button at the top left of the Xcode toolbar. You see four of the actions in the pop-up list, as shown in Figure 12.11. You can select from the full list of actions under the Product header in the main Xcode menu.

TIP

It's easy to miss the click-and-hold feature, especially if you don't know it's there. Practice it a few times to learn it. You can use these build actions without changing them, but you also can customize them. At the very least, you should be familiar with the action options, because they interact with Xcode's main menu, build configurations, and build settings in ways that aren't obvious.

NOTE

You can't easily create your own custom build actions. The standard actions are hardwired into Xcode, and you can't extend or modify the list directly. Expert developers can create their own customized build scripts and run them from the command line, but this takes them out of the Xcode environment.

Figure 12.11

Select a build action from the toolbar.

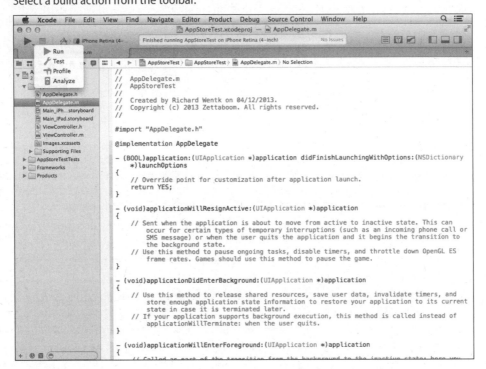

Editing schemes

Schemes define how each build action is customized, to define what happens before, during, and after each action. You also can set up each action to build a selection of targets.

Schemes are managed using Xcode's scheme editor/manager, which has separate dialogs for editing schemes and for managing them. You can use the editor/manager to create a new scheme, edit an existing scheme, or manage a collection of schemes. Simple projects typically need a single scheme, so the edit option is the most useful.

You can access the editor/manager in two ways:

- The main Xcode Product menu header includes three scheme options at the bottom of the list.
- The same options appear at the bottom of the destination (platform) drop-down menu in the main Xcode toolbar, as shown in Figure 12.12.

Figure 12.12

This is the simple way to display the Scheme editor.

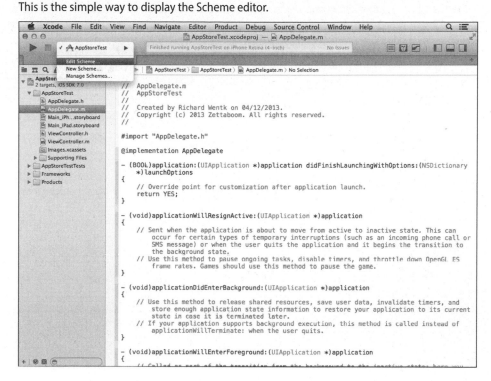

The editor is shown in Figure 12.13. It's a deceptively simple dialog that hides some very powerful features. The five standard build actions are shown in a list at the left, with a special Build catch-all option that controls which actions are supported by the project. (The Build option is described in more detail later in this chapter.)

You can do the following in the editor:

- Click the disclosure triangle to reveal a list of pre-action scripts, action options, and post-action scripts.

- Change the build action options under the Info tab in the pane on the right.

- For selected actions, you can set further customization options, including optional command-line arguments.

- For the Run action only, you also can enable extra low-level diagnostics and logging features.

- For the Build action only, you can include other possible targets and select the targets that are built by the other standard actions.

- Click the Manage Schemes button to open the Scheme Manager dialog.

Figure 12.13

Using the Scheme editor allows you to change many build actions and schemes.

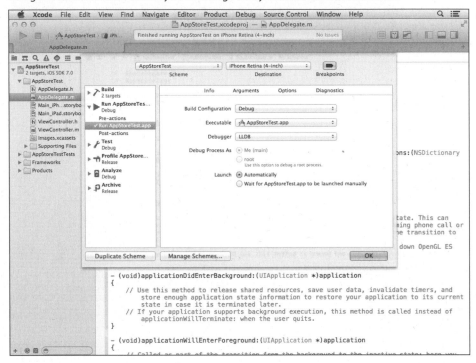

Each action has different options you can modify, although there's some overlap between them. The options control what happens after a build, what happens before and during the build run, and what happens after the run. By default, nothing happens before or after an action, but you can change this by adding custom scripts for each build action. The options also control other settings, including the build configuration used by the action.

Selecting a build configuration

This option is available for every action. Use the drop-down menu to select one of your project's build configurations. If you create a custom build configuration, it appears in the menu automatically.

Adding pre-action and post-action scripts

Each build action has six stages. The first three stages run the default build action. The last three define what Xcode does with the output from the build.

1. **Xcode runs one or more pre-action scripts for the build, if defined.**

2. **The project runs the default build action: It compiles, links, copies, and otherwise processes the files to create one or more targets.**

3. **Xcode runs one or more post-action scripts for the build, if defined.**

4. **The main action runs one or more optional pre-action scripts.**

5. **The main action performs its task—built files are loaded into the debugger, analyzed, profiled, tested, and so on.**

6. **The main action runs one or more optional post-action scripts.**

You can use pre-action and post-action scripts for setup and teardown, messaging, and to trigger other arbitrary events. Scripts can be shell scripts or AppleScript code. You also can select a pre-written script that sends an e-mail message.

These are some possible applications of scripts:

- Playing a sound at the end of an automated test or debugging run
- Copying files generated during testing or debugging to another Mac, uploading them to a server, or e-mailing them
- Launching another application that uses the results of a test run
- Using the speech synthesizer to report test results from a run
- Bringing some other window to the front of the desktop

If you can write AppleScript, scripting is an immensely powerful feature for automated testing and test reporting.

NOTE
For information about AppleScript development, see the companion *AppleScript* Developer Reference title.

CAUTION
Note that although you can import build settings, it's better not to use scripting for basic build control without a very good reason. If you need to set build switches, control which files are included in a project, or define how they're processed, use the Build Phases feature described in Chapter 13. Scripting is ideal for controlling what happens before and after a build, not what happens during a build.

To add a pre-action or post-action script, select an action, click its disclosure triangle to show the three optional stages, and select either the Pre-actions or Post-actions option. By default, you see a message telling you that no actions are defined. Click the + (plus) icon at the bottom left of the pane, and select either the New Run Script Action or New Send Email Action option, as shown in Figure 12.14.

Figure 12.14

Add a couple of pre-action scripts.

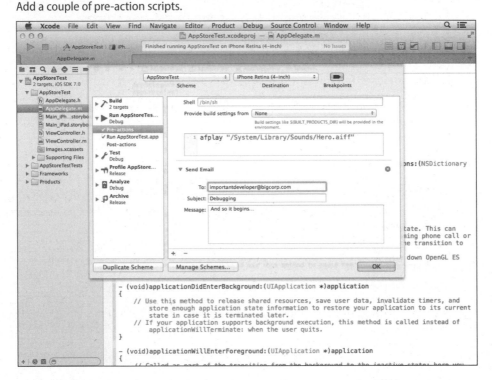

For a scripted action, you can either type a script or drag and drop an existing script into the script pane. The example code in the figure plays one of the system sounds. You can add multiple independent scripts.

For an e-mail action, fill in the e-mail fields. The e-mail message is sent automatically when the script runs.

To remove an action, click the close box at the top left of the script's sub-pane, or select the action by clicking its title bar. Click the - (minus) icon at the bottom left of the pane to delete it.

NOTE
To clarify the terminology, scripted actions are optional and can be run before and after one of the five standard build actions, which are fixed.

Setting arguments and environment variables

The Run, Test, and Profile actions include an Arguments dialog. You can use it to specify arguments and environment variables that are passed to your application when it launches, via the standard C language `argc/argv` placeholders. It's up to you to define what your application does with these variables. Click the + (plus) and - (minus) icons in the panes of the Arguments dialog to add and remove items.

C A U T I O N

These are not build flags or switches. They're passed to your application, not to the compiler/linker.

Selecting a debugger

In later versions of Xcode 4, you could choose either LLDB or GDB. In Xcode 5, LLDB is the only option.

Setting Run action options

The Run action has some unique features. You can use the Executable menu to select which file is run. By default, this menu selects the app created by the build, but for more complex projects, such as testing a plug-in in a wrapper/master application, you can nominate some other file.

In the Arguments dialog, you can add an optional list of modules with further debug symbols. This is a specialized feature used to include symbols from modules that may not be built into your project.

The Diagnostics dialog enables specialized low-level diagnostic options. You can control memory management, enable logging for various events and exceptions, and allow your application to send messages to the debugger. Table 12.2 lists the options.

Table 12.2 Run Process Diagnostics Options

Setting	Notes
Memory management options	
Enable Scribble	Fill memory with `0xAA` on allocation and `0x55` on release.
Enable Guard Edges	Add guard pages before and after large allocations to prevent corruption from small overruns.
Enable Guard Malloc	Use the `libgmalloc` library to monitor and report common memory errors.
Enable Zombie Objects	Enable Zombie—dangling pointer—tracking. (This option is less useful with ARC than it was in previous memory management schemes.)

continued

Table 12.2 Continued

Logging options	
Distributed Objects	Enable logging for `NSConnection`, `NSInvocation`, `NSDistantObject`, and `NSConcretePortCoder` objects.
Garbage Collection Activity	Log collection events, new region allocations, and weak reference manipulations.
Malloc Stack	Log the state of the stack during allocations and deallocations.
Log Exceptions	Log Objective-C runtime exceptions.
Log DYLD API Usage	Log API calls to the dynamic-linker.
Log Library Loads	Log library loads by the dynamic-linker.
Debugger	
Legacy Stop on Debugger() and DebugStr()	Allow your code to call these routines to start the debugger with a message and send a SIGINT signal to the current process.

Setting Profile action options

The Profile action options are very similar to the Run process options. In fact, for the Arguments list, you can check the Use the Run action's options box to copy the arguments and environment variables from the Run action's settings.

The significant feature here is the Instrument option. You can use this to launch a default instrument automatically. This saves you having to select an instrument by hand.

CROSS-REFERENCE

For more about instruments and profiling, see Chapter 17.

Setting Archive process options

App Store and Ad Hoc distribution builds are described in detail in the next chapter. But as a preview, you typically either edit the standard Release configuration or make a copy. A key fact to remember is that if you create a copy for a distribution build, you must select the copy for the Archive action. Otherwise, the Archive action defaults to the standard Release configuration, which is likely to have incorrect settings.

Working with the Build action

The Build action has been left until last because it has some unusual features and a unique edit page.

Selecting common scripts

You can add pre-action and post-action scripts in the usual way. Because Build is the master action and is included automatically in the other actions, any scripts you add here are run by every action.

Selecting targets for each action

The editor also defines which targets are built by the other standard actions. The design of this editor isn't outstandingly intuitive, so it's worth taking the time to understand how to use it effectively.

As shown in Figure 12.15, targets are listed vertically at the left and the standard build actions are listed across the top. When you check a box under an action, it tells Xcode to build that target when you run that action. Put simply, you work with the check boxes under each build action to control which targets it builds.

Figure 12.15

Select the targets built by each action.

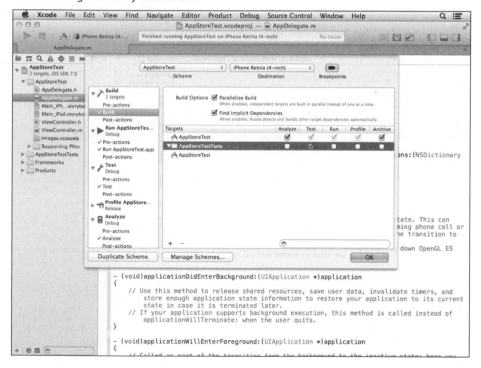

For example, with the default settings in the figure, most build actions build the AppStoreTest target. Running Test also builds the AppStoreTestTests target—the target used for unit testing.

CAUTION

In Xcode 5, some of the check boxes are preset, and you can't edit them. The main build actions always build the main target. Test always builds the main target and a test target.

When you check the Parallelize Build box, Xcode builds independent targets in parallel. This isn't usually a timesaver on a single machine. But if you have more than one Mac, you can split the build process across a network, which is a timesaver, especially for complex projects.

The Find Implicit Dependencies option tells Xcode to find and build dependent targets automatically.

Adding targets

Before you can select a target, you must add it. Unfortunately, when you create a new target in Xcode, it doesn't appear on this page automatically. You must add it manually before you can force a build action to build it.

To add a target, use the main build options pages shown earlier in this chapter. You can then add the target to this page by clicking the + (plus) icon near the bottom left and selecting the new target from the list, as shown in Figure 12.16.

Figure 12.16

Add a target.

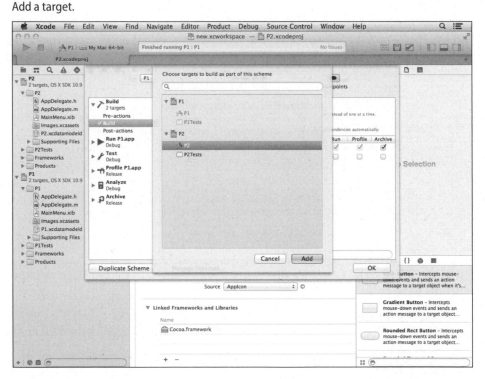

Note that if your workspace has multiple projects, you can select a target from any project in the workspace. This is the easiest way to create complex multi-target builds.

CAUTION

You can't create new targets for a project here; you can only add targets that were already created elsewhere in Xcode.

Understanding hidden effects

When there's a single target, enabling and disabling the actions has some erratic effects elsewhere in Xcode. With a single target, you can't disable the Run and Profile actions at all. If you disable Test and Archive, the corresponding options in the main Xcode menu become grayed out, so you can't select them. If you disable Analyze, the corresponding menu option isn't grayed out.

You can still select the actions with the pop-up menu shown earlier (refer to Figure 12.11), but if you do, you get an error message telling you that the action has been disabled.

Because none of these effects makes a great of deal of sense, it's easier to ignore this page when your project has a single target. The default settings leave every action enabled.

Managing schemes, build actions, and targets

By default, each project has a single scheme. But whenever you create a new target, Xcode 5 autocreates a new scheme for it.

There's almost limitless potential for confusion in this arrangement, because the UI doesn't make the distinction between schemes and targets clear. In fact, the new scheme and the new target have the same name.

To clarify the relationship, remember the following:

- The scheme menu selects schemes, not targets.
- In Xcode 5, you never build a target directly. Instead, you run a standard build action.
- The action defines which targets are built.
- A scheme can define separate multiple targets for each action.
- Before a scheme can build multiple targets, you must add each target to the scheme by hand.

Figure 12.17 clarifies the anatomy of a scheme. The Build action is central because it's run by every other action and it selects which targets are built by each action.

Figure 12.17

The anatomy of a scheme: The Build action is effectively a sub-routine for the other actions, and it can be run independently.

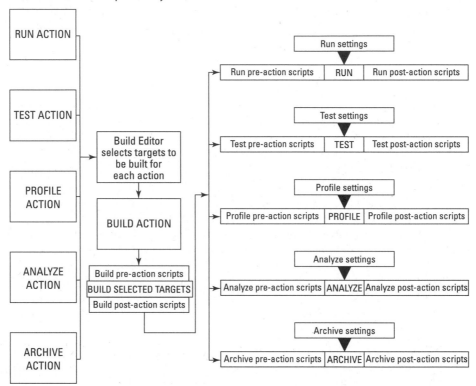

When you create a new target and Xcode autocreates a scheme for it, all the build actions for it are enabled. This may or may not match your needs, depending on how your project is organized. For example, if you're creating a framework and building a test project around it, you're more likely to build both at the same time.

Often, to avoid possible confusion, it's useful to turn off autocreation and manage schemes manually. You can create them by hand as needed, or if you have multiple targets and need a scheme for each, you can click the Autocreate Schemes Now button.

It's also helpful to create and rename schemes for specific build and test events—for example, "Build All." Naming your schemes after your targets is likely to distract you, except for those relatively rare occasions when you have a project with multiple independent targets that you want to build separately.

The key point isn't that there's a right way and a wrong way to use schemes, but that you must understand the relationship among targets, schemes, and autocreation to work with multiple targets effectively.

Figure 12.18 shows the Manage Schemes dialog. To disable autocreation, make sure the Autocreate schemes box at the top left is unchecked. To create a new scheme manually, select the + (plus) icon near the bottom left. You can choose to create a new scheme or duplicate an existing scheme. The - (minus) icon deletes a scheme. You can use the gear (action) icon to import and export schemes for reuse across other projects.

Figure 12.18

Managing multiple schemes is easy with the Manage Schemes dialog.

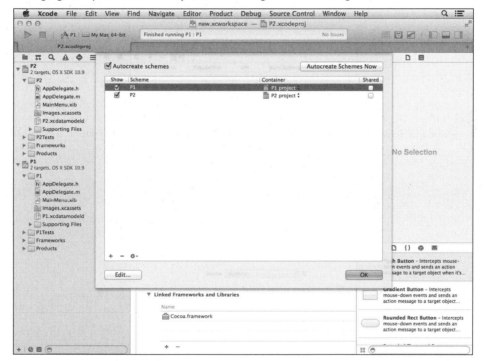

The final option is the container column, which defines whether the scheme is stored in a project or workspace. The advantage of storing a scheme in a project is that when you select the Shared option to the right of the Container column, everyone who is using that project can use the scheme also.

 C A U T I O N
Sharing a scheme means that others can delete it or modify it without your permission.

NOTE

Note that the scheme menu displays multiple destinations for each scheme. A *destination* is a platform—or more technically, an SDK. For example, an iOS scheme can select an iOS device or one of the various simulated devices available in the Simulator. Destinations aren't stored or selected in a scheme, and you'll see that every scheme gives you the same platform choices. Typically, you select a scheme, then you select an SDK, and finally you select a build action, to create a build for that SDK.

Summary

With Xcode 5, you can mostly ignore the build system unless you have a good reason to customize it. It's set up to "just work" for basic development. However, you need to make a few adjustments to create a successful App Store build, so it's important to take the time to understand it in outline even if you don't plan to improve your builds with custom scripts and e-mail warnings.

Like many other parts of Xcode, it appears simple but has unexpectedly complex details. Don't be surprised if you need to spend some time reviewing its features and clicking through the various dialogs and options before you really understand it.

Customizing Builds for Development and Distribution

C hapter 12 introduced the Xcode build system. This chapter introduces some useful examples of simple customization, explains how to create and distribute App Store and Ad Hoc builds, and introduces more advanced build customization techniques that work with build phases and build rules—the steps in the build sequence that define how individual files are processed.

NOTE
If you haven't read Chapter 12 yet, start there. The contents are a prerequisite for this chapter.

Introducing Common Basic Customizations

Basic build customizations are very common. As you develop apps, you'll find that you typically need to perform the same customizations over and over. This section includes a selection of useful customizations. It isn't a definitive list, but it includes tasks that developers need to perform regularly that aren't highlighted in the official documentation. As you gain more experience, it's likely you'll extend this list with standard customizations of your own.

All required changes to the build options and build settings for projects and/or targets were introduced in Chapter 12. They don't modify the build rules, which are introduced later in this chapter.

The customization process for iOS and OS X projects is recognizably similar. OS X and iOS projects have slightly different low-level compiler settings and noticeably different app-specific options under their respective Info tabs, but the settings are organized in the same way and appear in the same editor. Most of the customizations in this section are relevant to both platforms.

CAUTION
Be aware that some of the build settings and options interact with each other, while others may not do what you expect them to. These gotchas are listed in this section, with suggested work-arounds.

Creating a build for testing and debugging

The debug/test build is the default in Xcode. So for iOS Simulator testing and OS X testing, you don't need to do any customization. Optionally, you can select the runtime platform using the pop-up menu at the top left of the main Xcode toolbar and customize other build settings as needed. But the defaults should create a build that can be debugged, and launch it.

Selecting the Base SDK

The Base SDK is the version of the libraries and headers used to generate apps for a specific version of either iOS or OS X. Whenever a new version of either OS is released, Apple generates a new version of Xcode for developers with an updated SDK.

In Xcode 5, the project build settings include Latest iOS and Latest Mac OS X placeholders, as shown in Figure 13.1. If you save your projects with this setting and reload them into a later release of Xcode, they should select the most recent SDK automatically, even if it's different from the SDK used for the original project.

Figure 13.1

Select the Latest OS option to ensure that projects always load with a current SDK.

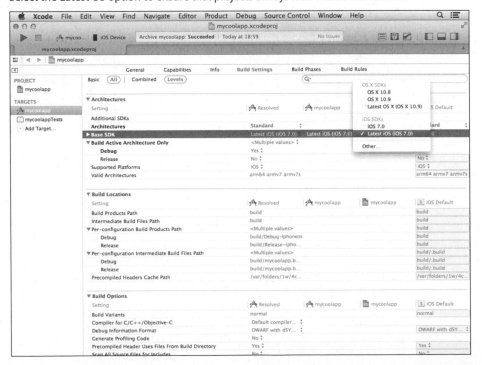

Projects saved with older versions of Xcode may show an unhelpful "SDK missing" error message. (This is a common error when you try to load a sample project downloaded from a developer's blog.) To fix the problem, select the Latest iOS or Latest Mac SDK manually in the build settings after loading the project.

Note that you can build against a single, fixed SDK instead of the "Latest SDK" placeholder. This is occasionally useful if you specifically want to support an older SDK. (iOS users typically upgrade regularly. Mac users may not, so it's not unusual to build against an older version of OS X for maximum compatibility.)

Note also that Xcode allows you to select an iOS SDK for an OS X project, and vice versa. This is never a wise thing to do. Occasionally, you can load an older Mac project and Xcode assumes it's an iOS project—and vice versa. So you may need to correct this by hand.

Finally, you can set different SDKs for Release, Debug, and custom configurations. Very occasionally, you may discover a practical need for this, but it's not a widely used feature.

N O T E

You may want to change this setting for final distribution builds, as described later.

C A U T I O N

Selecting the latest SDK may mean your project no longer builds, because the old code is no longer compatible with the newest OS. There is no quick fix for this. Xcode will list objects and methods that are no longer supported. You can sometimes use the OS diff files described in Chapter 6 to find replacements. Often, you'll need to find out more about the changes in class documentation.

Setting the minimum supported OS version

With each new version of iOS and OS X, new functions, classes, and methods are added, and older elements are removed. Not all users upgrade to the most recent version of each OS, especially not those running OS X, who have to pay for upgrades. iOS users of older devices are typically limited to an older version of the OS.

Creating products that are compatible with an older version of the OS is often useful, but that also can run on newer versions. The minimum supported OS version is known as the *Deployment Target*. If a user tries to run the product on an older version, the loader displays an error message.

Understanding the SDK and the deployment target

Newcomers to Xcode are often confused by the relationship between the base SDK, the deployment target, and the OS version shown in the Simulator. The key point to understand is that the SDK defines the symbols and libraries that appear in the product. The deployment target is simply a number used by the loader to check OS compatibility.

CAUTION

Don't confuse the deployment target with the targets used in a project. The deployment target is an OS version. The build targets are processes and file specifications that create a product. For clarity, the deployment target could have been labeled the deployment OS, but unfortunately it wasn't.

The SDK supplied with any version of Xcode includes support for older versions of the OS, up to some arbitrary limit. For example, the iOS 4.3 SDK can build projects that run under iPhone OS 3.0 and later, but not iPhone OS 2.x and 1.x.

An often-repeated rule for selecting an SDK and deployment target is that you should always select the Latest OS SDK (as described earlier) and the most ancient supported deployment target. In practice, beta development complicates the requirements. Here's a more comprehensive guide:

- Select the Latest OS SDK for all development builds. With a beta SDK, you can use this option to experiment with new features.

- If you have a beta SDK installed, select the current public release of the OS—the version before the current beta—as the Base SDK for App Store distribution builds.

- Not all beta SDKs include this previous version. If you've installed a beta SDK and find the current public OS SDK is missing, you must use or reinstall a separate older copy of Xcode for distribution builds.

- Don't try to create a final production build with a beta version of the OS until the beta SDK is upgraded to a final GM (Gold Master) seed and Apple confirms this seed is suitable for production code. This usually happens just before public release.

- You can use a beta SDK for Ad Hoc test builds only if your testers have access to the equivalent beta versions of the OS for their devices. If they don't, which is often the case, select the previous public SDK as the active SDK. You can give them access, but some assembly is required. For details, see the "Working with iOS Ad Hoc builds" section later in this chapter.

- The Simulator supports various older versions of the OS. You can use this option to partially test code for backward-compatibility.

- You also can test compatibility on real devices, if you have them. If you need to, you can use Xcode's Organizer to downgrade newer devices to older versions of the OS for testing. (Don't do this on devices you use personally; you're likely to lose data.)

- Set the deployment target as low as possible, for maximum backward-compatibility. This gives users the best chance of being able to buy and use your app.

A key point is that when you set the deployment target to an older version of the target OS, your code must test for OS-dependent features. Figure 13.2 illustrates this graphically.

In the figure, your app can run on any device with iOS 4.0 or later. The latest features from the iOS 4.3 SDK aren't available on devices with older versions of iOS, so your code must check that they exist before it tries to use them. Your code will of course *compile* with the iOS 4.3 SDK, but when the deployment target is set to support older version of iOS, it won't *run* reliably on a range of supported OS versions unless you include versions-specific tests and code features.

Figure 13.2

This is the most general view of SDK and deployment selection. Code must include tests to check for OS-dependent features that may not be available on a user's device. Missing features must be implemented with workarounds and fallbacks.

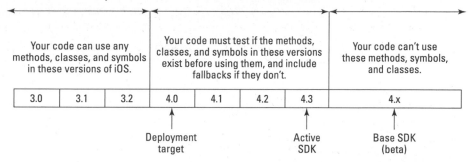

Supporting multiple versions of an OS is non-trivial. It's also difficult to test in full. The only true test is to run the code on multiple devices, each of which has a different version of the OS—or on a single device multiple times, updating the installed OS each until every version has been tested.

N O T E

This can be lots of work. It's not unusual to test code on the oldest and newest supported OS, check by inspection that the code is likely to work on intermediate versions, and hope there are no surprises.

N O T E

The version numbers in the figure are for example purposes only. At the time of this writing, the public version of iOS is 7.0, and 7.1 is available in beta. The numbers will continue to increase. But the principle remains true: You can always build your app to support versions from the deployment target up to the base SDK. But you must include tests and fallbacks if you want your code to run on older versions without crashing.

Common practical techniques for multi-OS support include the following:

- Use variations on the `respondsToSelector:` method to check whether methods are available.
- Use `NSClassFromString` to check whether a class is supported.
- Read the supported system version from `UIDevice`.
- Include conditional compilation elements to manually select OS-dependent code. (This option is typically used to check for a platform—for example, OS X, the iOS Simulator, or an iOS device—during compilation. Don't use it to manage OS versions.)

T I P

For practical examples of multiple OS support with code, search for "Using SDK-Based Development" in the documentation. There's more about conditional compilation later in this chapter.

Setting the deployment target

You can set the deployment target in three ways:

- Select the deployment OS with the Deployment Target menu in the Project ⇨ Info tab, as shown in Figure 13.3.
- Select the deployment OS with the Deployment Target menu in the Target ⇨ General tab.
- Select the Deployment Target item in the Deployment list of items in the Build Settings table for either the project or the target.

These options appear interchangeable, but they're subtly different. The first option creates a project build setting. The second creates a target build setting. The final option can create either a project or a target setting.

CROSS-REFERENCE

The differences between project and target settings and the interactions between them were introduced in Chapter 12. If you're not yet familiar with them, read that chapter before continuing—the differences are crucial.

Figure 13.3

Select the Deployment Target. This feature appears in three places, but for single-target apps, it's easiest to set it here.

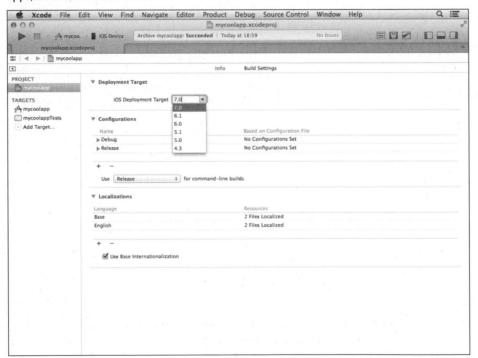

For single-target iOS and OS X apps, use the target summary setting for simplicity and clarity. For more complex projects with multiple targets, it's up to you to select the option that works best in the context of the project.

Including a framework or library in a build

This topic was introduced in Chapter 5, but it's expanded here. To add a framework or library, follow these steps:

1. **Navigate to the Build Phases tab.**

2. **Open the Link Binary With Libraries item.**

3. **Click the + (plus) button at the bottom left of the item.**

4. **Select the framework or library from the menu, as shown in Figure 13.4.**

5. **Xcode adds the framework to the Frameworks group in the Project navigator. You can now import headers from the framework in your project files.**

Figure 13.4

Add a framework to a target. You can rearrange the compile order by dragging frameworks up and down the list, although this isn't usually necessary.

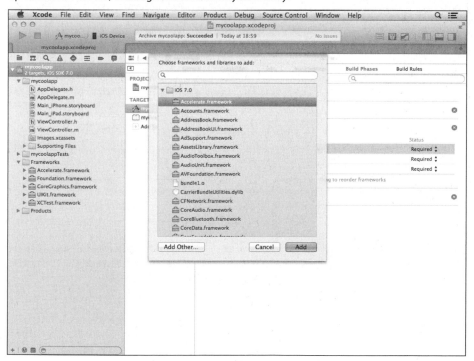

Note that the list of frameworks is filtered by platform, so you can't add an iOS framework to an OS X project (or vice versa).

CROSS-REFERENCE
You also can add an external non-Apple framework by selecting the Add Other option and navigating to the framework files. Use this option to add frameworks or libraries created by other developers. For more information, see Chapter 14.

Technically, you *link against* a framework. There are two options: Required and Optional.

A Required library must be present on the target platform and is loaded at launch with the rest of the application or product. If it isn't present, the application refuses to load.

Optional libraries are loaded only when they're referenced at runtime. This saves memory and creates a smaller initial product. But if the library isn't available, the application stalls or crashes. You can use the techniques introduced in the previous section—tests for classes and methods, conditional compilation, and so on—to create code that can handle optional libraries robustly.

Always remove frameworks from a finished project if they're not being used. For example, you might add one of the audio or graphics frameworks to experiment with it, decide that another framework is a better solution, but leave both in the build. Although this is an obvious point, it's easy to overlook it. When you finish development, check to see that every framework listed under Link Binary with Libraries is essential.

TIP
You can also add Apple frameworks from Finder. Open the Frameworks group, right-click any of the existing frameworks, and select Show in Finder to view the default list of Apple frameworks. Each framework appears in a folder. To add a framework, drag its icon from Finder and drop it in the Link Binary with Libraries area. This option is quicker for adding and selecting multiple frameworks. (Don't forget to add `#import` directives to include the headers in your code!)

Selecting a compiler and C/C++ dialect

In Xcode 4, you could choose either the GCC (Gnu Compiler Collection) or LLVM (formerly Low Level Virtual Machine, now officially acronym-free) compiler.

Xcode 5 uses LLVM only. However, you can still choose various dialects for the C elements of your code, and for C++, if you use it. The dialect switches tell the LLVM compiler to expect one particular standard of C/C++. Keywords and syntax that work in one dialect may not work in another.

This is particularly important if you are working with code created by other developers, or if you need to use specific language features. The differences between C++98 and C++11 are marked. There are also differences between the GNU C++ library (libstdc++) and the Apple C++ libraries (libc++) and between the various C dialects.

If you are seeing unexpected compiler errors, check these settings. In the Target Build Phases page, scroll down to the Apple LLVM 5.0 – Language and C++ boxes, as shown in Figure 13.5. You can then select various dialects using the highlighted switches.

Figure 13.5

Select a C Language dialect.

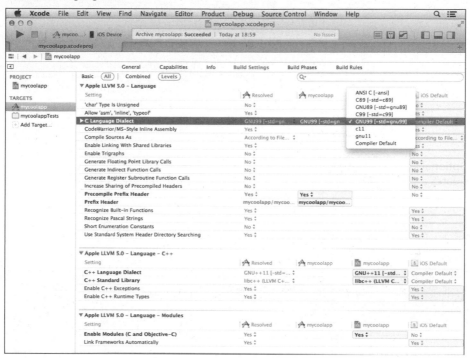

NOTE

If you only use Cocoa, you can ignore these settings. Xcode supports exactly one dialect of Objective-C, and you can't switch versions. If you're an advanced C or C++ developer, you can set some of the more obscure expert-level language options in these sections. Note that some dialects have better cross-platform compatibility than others. If you're creating a multi-platform project, you need to research which dialect to use.

Controlling warnings

You can use the Warnings section toward the bottom of the full list of build settings to enable and disable specific warning messages, as shown in Figure 13.6.

The master switch is called Inhibit All Warnings. When this is enabled, the compiler ignores the other warning switches and suppresses all warnings, without exception. This is a dangerous option.

Most of the other options are self-explanatory, to varying degrees. For example, unused variables and unused values produce warnings by default. Unused functions don't. It's worth exploring the list to fine-tune the options to match your programming style.

Figure 13.6

Select warning messages.

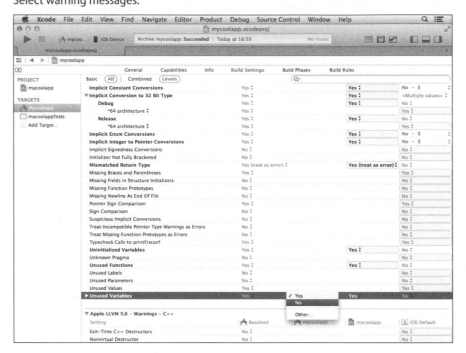

Disabling iOS PNG compression

By default, when you include PNG (Portable Network Graphics) image files in your project, the build process runs the art files through a PNG compression stage.

Unfortunately, Xcode's PNG compression isn't outstandingly efficient and may add unwanted transparency artifacts. You can minimize the size of the files by compressing them manually in an editor such as Adobe Photoshop. You can then tell Xcode to disable its compression and use the files as they are. (If you don't, you may find it makes precompressed files bigger.)

The compression setting is labeled Compress PNG Files. You can find it at the top of the Packaging heading in the Target Build Settings.

Selecting an architecture

At the time of this writing, Macs use Intel 64-bit processors, and iOS devices use 32-bit and 64-bit ARM processors. The default iOS build settings create a combined 32/64-bit binary that runs on a selection of ARM processors, including the armv7, armv7s, and arm64. The default Mac build setting creates an "i386 x86-64" binary for 64-bit processors.

For current versions of iOS and OS X, you shouldn't usually need to change the Valid Architectures setting in the Architectures section of the Target Build Settings. It's possible that future versions of iOS and/or OS X will use some other processor architecture, and you may need to select a valid architecture manually. So be aware of this setting.

CAUTION

One exception to this rule is when a project uses an open source library. Many libraries aren't 64-bit clean. You can either lose the benefits of 64-bit and build the project as 32-bits for backward compatibility, or pick through the library and try to fix any word length issues. You can find a 32-bit to 64-bit converter tool in the Auxiliary Tools for Xcode, described in Appendix B.

Changing an app's name before shipping

It's often useful to change the final production title for an app, to customize the name string that appears under the app icon in iOS or above the Dock in OS X.

There's no easy way to change the project's filenames or the project name as a whole. But you don't need to, because you can set the name independently using the Product Name setting in the Build Settings. You can find it halfway down under the Packaging header.

The default is a macro called $ (TARGET_NAME). You might assume this means that the target name is copied from the Target name. This is true, up to a point. But it's easier to edit the name directly, as shown in Figure 13.7. You can single-click twice on the product name to edit the name in place. Or you can double-click to display the floating edit box shown in the figure.

Figure 13.7

Edit the product name. This setting changes the name that appears under/over the app in the Dock and in Springboard.

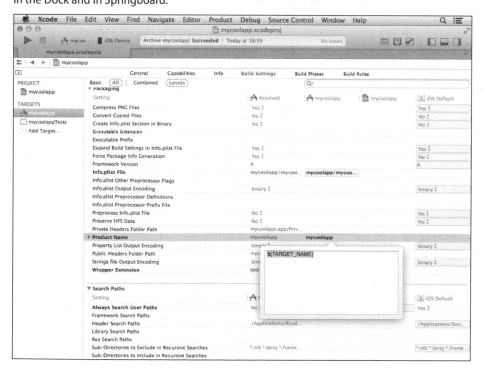

Note that changing the name here changes the display name *only*. It has no other effect. Use this option when you have created matching bundle IDs and provisioning profiles that use them, but you want to change the name for marketing reasons at the last minute.

TIP
You should keep iOS app names short, because Springboard truncates longer names with ellipses (...). Ten characters is a realistic maximum, but you may occasionally be able to squeeze in 11. You can test the truncation in the Simulator.

What if you want to edit the target name instead and force the product name to follow it? You can edit the target name by double-clicking it next to the icon in the gutter area to the left of the settings. If you leave the product name set to the default macro, it will follow suit. Use this option if you haven't yet created a distribution profile. Changing the name here changes the Bundle ID of your app, which can confuse the provisioning process.

Creating an App Store Submission

Now that you're familiar with the build system and with build customization, you can start to create builds for the App Store. If you haven't yet set up certificates and identities, work through Chapter 11. It's a prerequisite for this chapter.

Uploading marketing and support materials

iTunes Connect works in almost exactly the opposite way you'd expect. Instead of uploading a binary and then adding marketing text and images for it, you upload the marketing materials first to create an *application record*. You then build your app as an archive, validate it, and submit the archive. The archive becomes the binary associated with the record. After some basic checking, the application record goes live in the App Store, and customers can view your sales information and either buy the app or download it for free, depending on the price you set in the record.

The way iTunes Connect works may seem counterintuitive, but it has a valid purpose. If your binary is rejected, the application record remains in place, and you don't have to reenter it when you resubmit. Similarly, when you upgrade your app to a new version, you can reuse the details you entered when you first submitted the app. You can also change most marketing and sales details, including the text, images, and prices that appear in the App Store, without having to create a new binary. A few items, including keywords, require a version change.

CAUTION
You must give iTunes Connect information about your bank account and tax details before you begin uploading a paid app. Work through this process well before you submit an app. International tax law is outside the scope of this book, but be aware that you may need to supply extra paperwork for certain territories; otherwise, income is taxed at the source, although it may be possible to reclaim deductions later. Non-U.S. individuals require an ITIN (Individual Taxpayer Identification Number) or EIN (Employer Identification Number) from the U.S. IRS to avoid deductions. It can take between three months and a year to obtain one.

The complete list of information for an application record is long. You should collect all the information before you begin. If you spend too much time entering the information, iTunes Connect logs you out and you have to start again. It doesn't always generate an error message when it does this; the upload process simply stops working.

You need the following details:

- **The app name:** This should match the name string you set in Xcode.

- **The app bundle-ID:** You can create a new ID when you begin creating a record, but then you need to change your app in Xcode to match the ID.

- **An SKU number:** This is number or string unique to the app. SKU numbers are used to identify individual products for stock control, inventory, and accounting purposes. The exact contents don't matter, but if you have more than one app for sale, you should create a standard system. If you can't think of one, use the date backward, possibly prefixed with the app name.

- **An availability date:** You can set immediate availability, or you can delay the date to allow for a marketing run-up or for seasonal sales.

- **A pricing tier:** You can select one of Apple's standard pricing tiers, which are converted automatically into local currencies in the various international App Stores.

- **Discount options:** If you don't uncheck a box, educational institutions get a discount on bulk purchases of your app. You can't set the discount. This may seem like a good way to increase sales—and sometimes it is. But it may not be a good way to increase income.

- **Territory options:** Unless you specify otherwise, an app goes on sale everywhere. You can limit this by selecting specific territories.

- **A version number:** This doesn't have to match the number you set in Xcode— you get a warning if it doesn't—but it's a good idea to make the two numbers match.

- **Copyright information:** This sets a copyright notice that appears in the App Store.

- **Primary and secondary categories:** Selecting the correct category can have a big influence on sales. Be sure to research competing apps in your selected category.

- **Ratings:** Age-ratings limit the customers who can buy your app. Unless you're aiming for an adult audience, check as many None boxes as possible.

- **Metadata:** The App Store uses this when users search for apps. Spend some time thinking about the keywords and description that are most likely to appear in searches.

- **Contact information:** This includes the obvious details, but you can also include review notes, which are read by Apple when reviewing your app, and an optional demo account, which an Apple reviewer can use to access any app features that need a login. The App Store Contact Information details appear only in the South Korean App Store.

● **EULA:** The standard End User License Agreement is fine for most applications. If you have special requirements, you can specify a custom EULA, but you should ask a lawyer to draw one up for you rather than trying to do it yourself.

● **Graphics and other uploads:** These images appear as the large app icon and screenshots in the App Store. Supported file formats include TIFF, JPG, and PNG. The large app icon needs to be 1024x1024 pixels. The screen shots should be, but don't have to be retina-resolution. Routing apps can include an optional GeoJSON file that specifies the geographical area covered by the app. Follow these steps to create an application record:

1. **Log in to the iOS Developer Portal, and select iTunes Connect from the list of items at the top right of the screen.** You can also access iTunes Connect directly at `itunesconnect.apple.com`.

2. **Select Manage Your Apps.**

3. **Click Add New App at the top left.**

4. **Work your way through the "paperwork," the first page of which is shown in Figure 13.8.** Fill in all the fields, upload artwork, and copy and paste your marketing information and contact details.

Figure 13.8

Note the Bundle ID menu on the first page of the "paperwork."

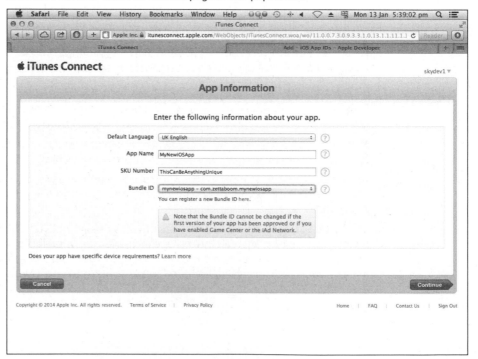

5. **Click Save on the last page.** You now have an application record. You can click the Edit button to edit it. The Status field should show Prepare for Upload.

6. **Click View Details and Ready to Upload Binary.** Answer a question about encryption. You *must* perform this step to change the Prepare for Upload status to Waiting for Upload. Otherwise, the Prepare for Upload status never changes, and you cannot upload your app.

7. **Build and upload your binary.** Figure 13.9 shows the Waiting for Upload status. You can use this page to edit the app details and set up optional features such as Game Center and In-App Purchases. You can also click the Transfer App button if you want to give or sell your app to another developer.

Figure 13.9

Here's the final state of the "paperwork," with the Waiting For Upload status.

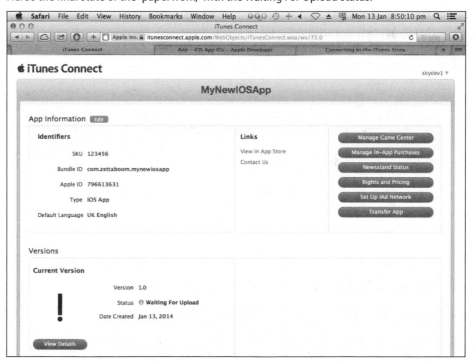

CROSS-REFERENCE
See Chapter 11 for a reminder about App IDs.

You can repeat the process to create multiple app records in a single session. In fact, you can create as many records as you want. They aren't visible on the App Store until you upload a binary for each, and the record and binary are approved for sale.

Building and packaging an iOS project for the App Store

After completing your Application Record, you can build and upload the app it advertises. Xcode 5 includes a simplified building and packaging process that makes it easier to submit apps to the App Store and to create and distribute beta versions for testing. The process is simpler than it was in Xcode 4, but some assembly is still required.

The submission process isn't simple. It becomes easier with experience, but the best way to guarantee a successful first upload is to work through the stages carefully and methodically.

CAUTION

Don't try to build a submission using a beta version of Xcode. Everything seems fine until you get to the end of validation and discover you can't upload the finished archive. You *must* use a production version of Xcode for App Store submissions.

The packaging process has six steps:

1. **Create an Application Record.** Follow the steps in the preceding section. You *must* do this before you try to upload the app.

2. **Add icons and start-up screens.** You must include at least a minimal set of icons before Xcode allows you to submit an app.

3. **Customize build settings and capabilities.** These added features control access to Apple services and add optional special features to your app.

4. **Set up the code signing identity, and create and select a provisioning profile.** This usually means a visit to the Member Center to set up a profile.

5. **Build the archive.** Select a device scheme—the device doesn't have to be connected—and select the archive build option.

6. **Validate and distribute.** These options appear in the Organizer. The validate option checks the app and makes sure the app ID, distribution provisioning profile, and distribution ID all match. The distribute option uploads the binary.

After you upload the archive, Apple reviews it to check for unacceptable content and basic reliability. If the review is successful, the app goes live in the App Store within a few days after upload.

Getting started with artwork

At the time if this writing, a fully specified iOS app needs 15 different image files: the app icon, a start-up image in various orientations, and optional icon images for Settings and Spotlight, all in PNG format, and in various resolutions to support retina and non-retina devices.

Preparing these files isn't a trivial job; even if you have good design skills and aren't attempting a complex design, it can take a few hours to create every required file. Developers often outsource this work to graphic designers. Creating a striking and professional source file takes time and talent.

TIP

The flatter, simpler look used for iOS 7 has simplified icon design. It's no longer obligatory to add polished time-consuming glossy/glassy 3D effects to your icons. Icon design is still harder than it looks, but it's not quite as difficult as it used to be. To save even more time, search online for "iOS icons" for various free or cheap ready-made options.

In Xcode 5, images are stored in an .xcassets file that includes both app icons and start-up images. To define images, select the .xcassets file in the Project navigator. The editor loads the default contents of the file, which includes AppIcon and LaunchImage placeholders for each kind of image. Each placeholder includes a number of empty slots, as shown in Figure 13.10. Click either AppIcon or LaunchImage in the gutter between the Navigator and the Editor area to select the corresponding slots.

Figure 13.10

Find asset sizes for artwork.

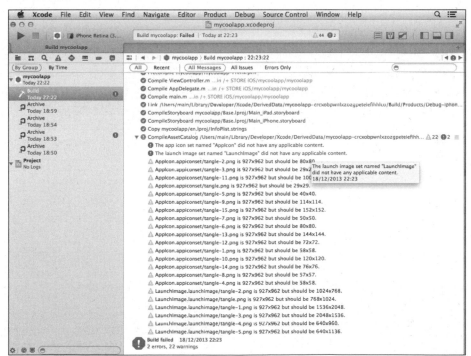

Unfortunately, the slots are only partially labeled with explicit image dimensions. Because the Apple product line changes regularly, the image dimension requirements change regularly too.

The easiest way to find the most up-to-date list of dimensions is to drag a temporary image of any size—a 1x1 test image will do—into each of the image slots. Then build the project, and open the Log navigator, and you see a list of the required dimensions for each slot, as shown in Figure 13.10. You can then use the list to prepare the images.

T I P

If you are using Adobe Photoshop, the quickest way to create suitable icon images is to create a single image at the largest size, and then create an action that resizes and saves versions of the image at all the required dimensions. Don't forget to undo the resize operation after each save. Launch screens usually have to be prepared manually because they include rotated and unrotated content at various dimensions and resolutions.

T I P

If you're confused about which image size fits in which slot (you probably will be), open the Log navigator in the Navigator area and either the AppIcon and LaunchIcon collections from xcassets in the Editor area. Click each issue in the log to highlight the corresponding slot.

Setting capabilities

Capabilities, shown in Figure 13.11, are a new feature in Xcode 5. To work with them, select the Capabilities tab in the target build settings.

Figure 13.11

This is where you set Capabilities.

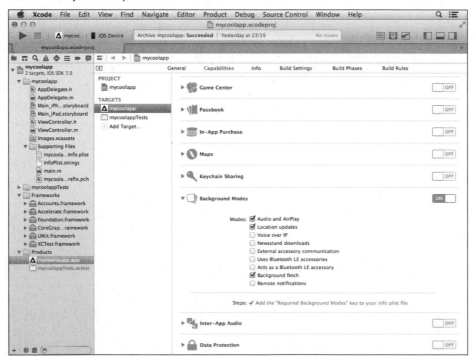

They're much easier to use than the equivalent entitlement settings in Xcode 4. To add a capability, click any switch to turn it on, and then check any further options that appear, as needed. Xcode and the Developer Center communicate with each other and add the features you select to the corresponding app ID.

CAUTION

The capabilities themselves don't "just work." The switches simply tell Apple's app support infrastructure that your app would like to use these extra services, by baking their settings into the app ID. You must still add supporting code to your app.

CAUTION

If you rename your app's target to match a bundle ID (for example, if you develop your app, decide to change the name, create a bundle ID for the new name, and then rename the app itself), don't set the capabilities *until you change the name*. Xcode and the Developer Center can get confused if the app's target name and the bundle ID don't match.

Using the Info tab

The Info tab, shown in Figure 13.12, includes a list of key app options. iOS uses these options to manage your app as it launches and runs. Some options change as you set capabilities, and others are set by default or managed by Xcode. Still others are truly optional, and you can only add them by hand.

Figure 13.12

Set custom plist keys.

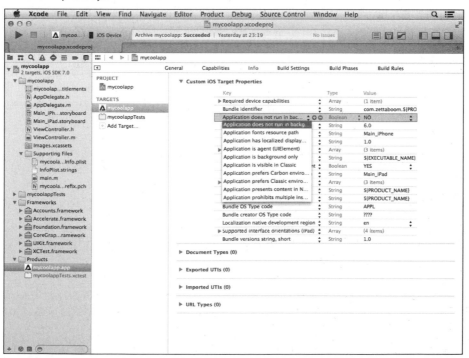

For a first app, you can ignore the options here. Your app should run without them. For more advanced projects, you can set the following:

- **Custom plist keys:** Click any item in the Key column, click the + (plus) icon, click the up/down arrows to the right of the new key, and select a key from the menu that appears, as shown in Figure 13.12.

NOTE

You can use the keys to set advanced options, such as custom font paths. For information about the keys and what they do, search online for "Information Property List Key Reference." Note that iOS and OS X apps have separate keys.

- **Document types:** You can add various document type names and standard plist keys here to make your app appear in the Open with . . . list for that document type. You need to know the plist key for each document type. For example, to associate the app with PDFs, the key is com.adobe.pdf, and the name is PDF File.
- **UTIs:** Uniform Type Identifiers are Apple's answer to file extension proliferation. Apple defines a number of standard UTIs, and your app can define its own custom UTIs that other apps can use. For details, search for "Uniform Type Identifiers Reference."
- **URL schemes:** When you click a map reference or phone number, iOS automatically launches the corresponding app. This magic happens through the use of standard embedded URLs. Your app can define its own URL scheme. Other apps can then launch your app and pass it information. For details, search for "Apple URL Scheme Reference."

Renaming an app and managing bundle IDs

In Xcode 4, you had to jump through hoops to create a final App Store build. Xcode 5 makes the process much easier. But there are still a few wrinkles and gotchas.

First, decide if you want to rename your app target. You should begin app development by creating an App ID and then creating an Xcode project with a matching name. But if you're new to development, your first few projects may have names like MyFirstProject, TheGame, or MyOpenGLTest.

If you look at the General tab in the build settings, you see the last part of the bundle identifier is grayed out. You can't edit it here. But you can edit it by double-clicking the app name under the Targets header in the Projects/Targets gutter to the left of the build settings.

If you change the target name, various macros copy it automatically to the Info plist settings, the Bundle Identifier field under the General tab, and the product name field setting in the build settings.

If you haven't already created a matching App ID for the Developer Center, do so. If you want to match the app name to an App ID that you have already created, simply rename it as required.

CAUTION

Be very careful when renaming an app. If you're relying on macros to copy the name to the bundle ID, the new name *must* match the name in the bundle ID. If they're different (for example, if you make a spelling mistake or get the names confused), you get mysterious errors later on.

Managing code signing

Code signing is the most complex part of the submission process, and it's the part where you're most likely to have problems. In outline, you're trying to do the following:

- Build an archive that includes a provisioning profile for distribution.
- Code sign the app with a certificate/identity that matches the one in the profile.

Xcode claims to offer various fixes to problems you may encounter, but for various reasons—some reasonable, some mysterious—the fixes don't always work.

A common problem is that Xcode doesn't understand that if you're building an archive, you probably want to upload your app. Instead, it assumes you're still testing, and it tries to sign a distribution build with an iOS developer identity.

If you don't select any code-signing options, Xcode "fixes" the problem by adding the wrong kind of profile and identity. You can archive your project successfully, but you can't validate it. When you try to validate, Xcode tells you that no identities are available, as shown in Figure 13.13.

Figure 13.13

If you see this error, you haven't set up code signing correctly.

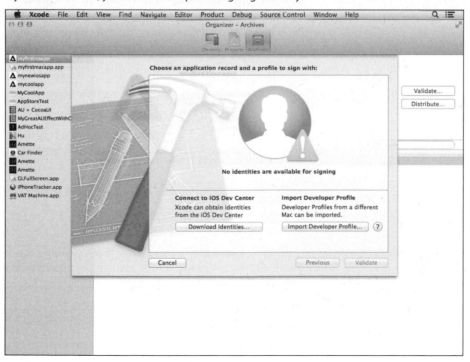

Clicking Download Identities . . . doesn't usually fix the problem. The reliable way to fix the problem is to follow these steps:

1. **Manually create a distribution profile online.**

2. **In Xcode, open the Accounts tab in Preferences, and refresh it to download the profile.**

3. **Select the correct provisioning profile in the Build Settings.**

4. **Select the Automatic option for the Release scheme, to force Xcode to include the correct code-signing certificate with the build.**

Creating a distribution profile

Follow these steps to create a distribution profile:

1. **Log in to the Developer Center, and click Certificates, Identifiers & Profiles from the list of links at the top right.**

2. **Select iOS Apps and Provisioning Profiles.**

3. **Click Distribution.**

4. **Click the + (plus) icon, and select App Store, as shown in Figure 13.14.**

5. **Select the App ID that matches your app's bundle ID.** Ignore the prefix; look for the com.yourname.appname string. You should have set this when you create an App ID.

CAUTION

If you can't find a matching App ID, follow the steps in Chapter 11 to create one. Then return here.

6. **Click Continue and select a certificate to set the distribution ID that's baked into the profile.**

   Note that distribution IDs select a *team,* not an individual. Even if your team name and individual name are the same, the ID you select here is still a team ID. This matters because when you sanity-check the build settings, you'll see the distribution profile prefix matches your team name, and isn't the same as your developer profile prefix.

7. **Click continue again, and give the distribution profile a memorable name.** Use one that includes the word *distribution* or something similar, so you can recognize it easily in a list.

8. **Click Generate.** The distribution profile is now ready for download. But don't click Download, because Xcode can download and install it for you automatically.

Figure 13.14

Create a distribution profile.

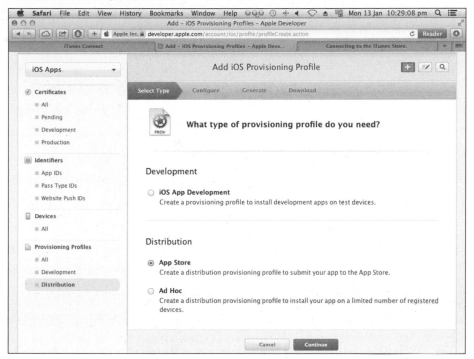

Refreshing Xcode's provisioning profile list

Follow these steps to refresh the provisioning profile list:

1. Select Xcode ⇨ Preferences ⇨ Accounts.

2. Select a team if you manage more than one, and Click View Details.

3. Click the Refresh button at the lower left of the dialog. You may need to do this a few times.

As shown in Figure 13.15, Xcode refreshes the list of provisioning profiles. Your new profile should appear in the list. Adding *distribution* to the name guarantees that you can tell it apart from any development profiles that Xcode may have generated for the same bundle ID.

4. Click Done when you're finished.

Figure 13.15

Refresh the provisioning profiles to download the distribution profile.

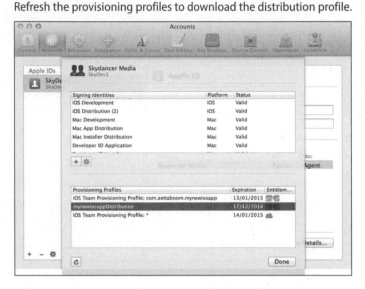

Selecting the distribution profile

Return to the target Build Settings page, and follow these steps to select the distribution profile:

1. **Scroll down to the Code Signing area, and find the Provisioning Profile tab.**

2. **Click the disclosure triangle to show the Debug and Release schemes.**

3. **Select the Release scheme.**

4. **If you haven't already set a profile, click the empty area under the target column. If you already set a profile, click the existing profile.** Figure 13.16 shows how you can select the distribution profile for this field from a floating menu.

CAUTION

Don't forget to change the profile for the Release scheme only. If you don't click the disclosure triangle, you'll set the distribution profile for the debug builds too. If you come back to the project later, you can no longer test it.

Selecting Automatic code signing

Follow these steps to select automatic code signing:

1. **Click the disclosure triangle of the Code Signing Identity field a few lines up.**

2. **Select the Release field.**

3. **Click the field in the Target column, and select Automatic.** Repeat for the Any iOS SDK line.

Figure 13.16

Select the distribution profile in the Provisioning Profile field.

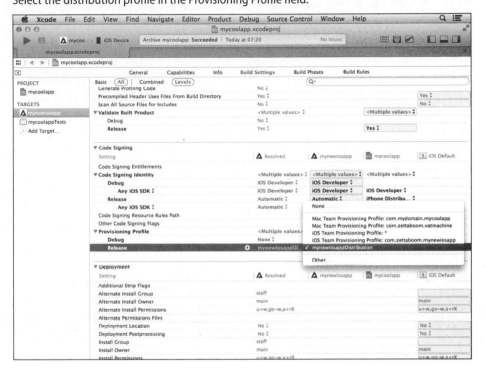

NOTE

Selecting automatic code signing tells Xcode to load the signing identity from the distribution profile. You can click Other to select a signing identity manually, but Xcode may get confused if you do.

Building and validating an archive

You can now try to build an archive with Product ➪ Archive. Note that archive builds take slightly longer than debug builds, because Xcode does more copying and packaging. If you set up everything correctly, the build should succeed without errors and the Organizer window should open.

When you click the Validate button to check the build, you should see the dialog shown in Figure 13.17. If you have more than one application record and/or more than one distribution profile for the given app ID, you can select them here. Typically the menus show single items, so you can leave them unchanged and click Validate. You should see a message telling you that no issues were found, and you can submit the app to the App Store.

Figure 13.17

Select the application and provisioning profile.

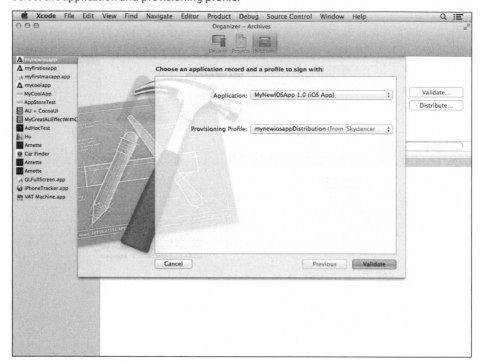

Distributing the archive

Follow these steps to distribute your archive:

1. **Click the Distribute button, and select the Submit to the iOS App Store option.**

2. **Click Next.**

3. **Log in, and select the application ID and provisioning profile, as you did during validation.**

4. **Click Submit.**

Xcode packages your app and uploads it to the App Store. It can take a minute or two to attract the App Store's attention. Eventually, Xcode begins uploading the binary, displaying a blue progress bar as it does so. If there are no network errors, you should see the message shown in Figure 13.18.

After submission, the app is added to the review queue. It typically takes one to two weeks for the app to reach the head of the queue, and the review process may take a random duration of a day to a couple of months. Most apps go on sale within two weeks of submission.

Figure 13.18

This was a successful upload.

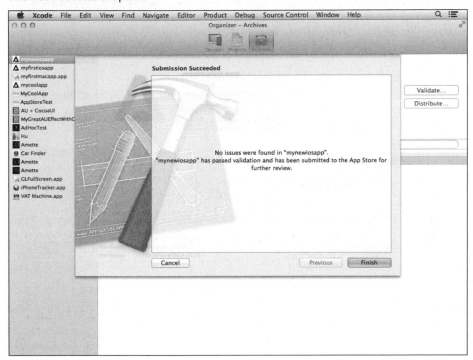

iTunes Connect displays status messages—Waiting For Review, In Review—to let you see where the app is in the review process. When the review is complete, you receive an e-mail with notice of acceptance or rejection.

Troubleshooting

If something goes wrong, load the accounts in Preferences and check that Xcode has a full set of valid identities. Refresh the list if it doesn't.

Occasionally, you need to create a new distribution profile, because the first one you try doesn't work even though it's valid. Give the profile a different name, and use the accounts page in Preferences to download it. You should then be able to select it and its signing identity in the Build Settings.

Deleting or hiding apps after submission

If you discover a problem with your binary after submission, select the app on iTunes Connect, select Binary Details, and click the Reject This Binary button at the top right. You can then repeat the submission process with a new binary. Note that you can't delete an app submission record while a binary is awaiting review.

Deleting an app after it has been accepted for sale is a complicated process. It's usually easier and quicker to remove an app from sale than to delete it completely. Select the app, click Rights and Pricing, select the Specific Stores link, and click the Deselect All button at the top right of the Rights and Territories list. This leaves its application record on iTunes Connect so you can update it with a new version at a later date, but it hides the app from buyers on iTunes.

Creating a Mac App Store submission

A Mac submission is similar to an iOS submission, but somewhat simpler. Begin by creating an App Record on iTunes Connect, filling in the "paperwork" to create a binary slot. You then customize the app's settings, build it as archive, validate it, and distribute it to upload the binary.

Currently, there's no device registration or support for device-limited Ad Hoc distribution for testing. (This may change in the future.)

Finding iTunes Connect

At the time of this writing, there's no direct link to iTunes Connect on the front page of the Mac Dev Center. To open iTunes Connect, select the Member Center link near the bottom right of the page. You can then click a link to iTunes Connect, as shown in Figure 13.19.

Figure 13.19

There's no direct link to iTunes Connect from the Mac Dev Center front page; you must go through this intermediate page.

CAUTION

The design of the Mac Dev Center changes regularly. If you can't see a link to the Member Center or to iTunes Connect, you have to do some exploring.

Customizing the build settings and capabilities

Click the project at the top of the Project navigator, select the target, and click the Build Settings tab to open the settings editor. These are the critical settings:

- **Architectures:** For apps that are 64-bit only, including those that run under OS X 10.7 Lion and later, set this to 64-bit Intel. Optionally, you can select Universal to build a 32/64-bit binary that can work on older Macs.

- **Product Name:** If you need to change this, double-click the name under the Targets heading. Don't change it directly in the Build Settings.

- **Capabilities:** These work as they do under iOS, although the list of capabilities isn't identical. The same caveats about renaming apply.

- **Deployment Target:** Set the lowest supported version of OS X, as described earlier.

Creating marketing and support materials

The "paperwork" for a Mac submission is very similar to an iOS submission. The promotional screenshot must have a resolution of 1280x800 or 1440x900 in `.jpeg`, `.jpg`, `.tiff`, or `.png` in the RGB color space with a resolution of 72dpi or better. In practice, this means that you can run the app, set your Mac's display resolution to the required dimensions, and use the Grab utility in `/Applications/Utilities` to capture the art as a `.tiff` file.

TIP

The artwork doesn't have to be an unedited screen grab. You can create custom promotional artwork that captions or highlights important features of your app. This is pushing against the guidelines, but if the artwork isn't too heavy-handed and promotional, there's a good chance it will be accepted.

Creating app icons

Mac app icons use the same xcassets system as iOS apps. You can create them in Photoshop or some other graphics package and drag and drop them into the slots in the xcassets editor, as shown in Figure 13.20. You need six images, sized in powers of two from 16x16 to 1024x1024. Note that there are five slots and no 64x64 icon, but you still need a 64x64 image for 2x32x32 slot.

TIP

Because of the large range of sizes, simple rescaling from 1024 pixels down to 16 pixels loses most of the detail in the image. You'll get sharper results, at the cost of extra effort, by creating two versions of the image—one at 1024x1024 and one at 64x64.

Creating an App ID

For iOS apps, the most reliable way to manage App IDs and certificates is set them up manually.

Figure 13.20

Drag and drop the app icons.

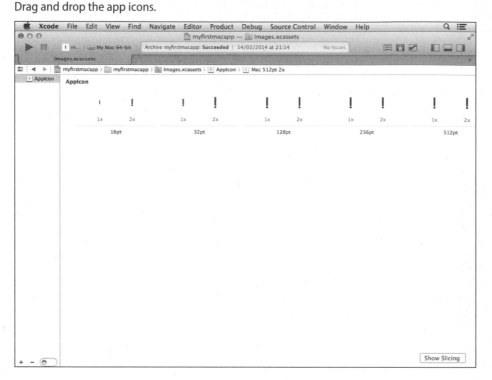

Follow these steps to create an App ID:

1. On the Certificates, Identifiers & Profiles page, select Mac Apps and then select App IDs under the Identifiers tab.

2. Click the + (plus) icon.

3. Add a description for the ID, and scroll down to App ID Suffix.

4. Type the full bundle ID into the relevant field, including the reverse domain name, as shown in Figure 13.21. Optionally, you can enable various special features, including access to Maps, iCloud, Game Center, and so on, by checking the boxes under the App Services heading.

The bundle ID you enter should match the Bundle ID shown in the Identity tab on the General Page of the Target build settings, shown in Figure 13.22.

Figure 13.21

Create an App ID.

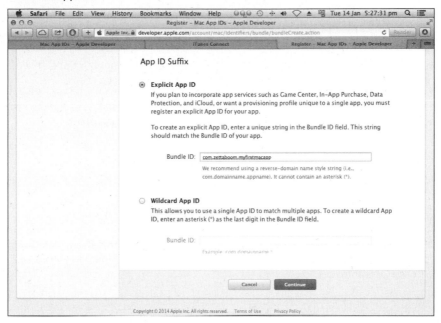

Figure 13.22

Read the bundle ID you need to use when creating an App ID.

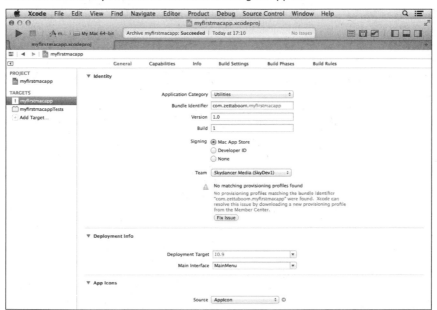

NOTE

OS X apps support wildcard/suite IDs. But if you want to use any Apple services, you need to use a unique ID.

Selecting a team

The General tab has a signing field, which manages code signing for your app. The default setting is None. Click Mac App Store to enable code signing, and select a team.

Ignore the Fix Issue message; currently, the fix doesn't work because Xcode tries to set up a development provisioning profile and not the distribution profile you want.

Creating a distribution profile

Follow these steps to create a distribution profile:

1. **Back on the Certificates, Identifiers & Profiles page, click the Distribution item under Provisioning Profiles.** Click the + (plus) icon near the top right.

2. **Click Mac App Store under the Distribution heading, and then click Continue.** Select the App ID you created in the preceding steps, as shown in Figure 13.23, and click Continue.

Figure 13.23

Bake the App ID you created into a distribution profile.

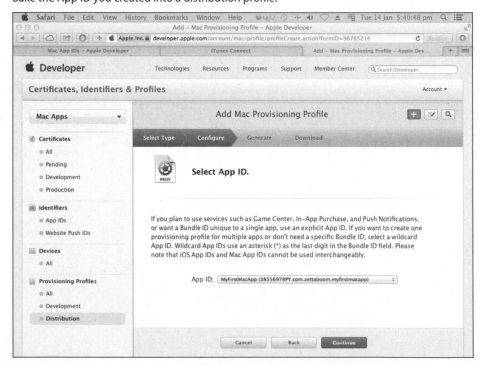

3. **Select your team name (if you are a solo developer, you see one option), and click Continue again.** Type a profile name, preferably using the word *distribution* so it's obvious what the profile is for, and click Generate. Don't click Download.

4. **Back in Xcode, open Accounts in Preferences, and click the Refresh button at the lower left.** You may need to repeat this several times. Eventually, Xcode downloads and displays the profile you just created, as shown in Figure 13.24.

Figure 13.24

Force Xcode to download the new distribution profile.

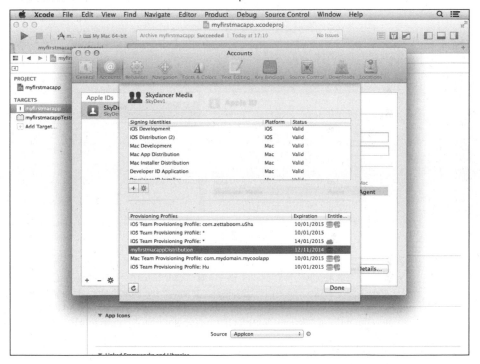

5. **Open the Build Settings for the Target, select the new provisioning profile under the Code Signing heading, and then select Automatic to read the signing ID from the provisioning profile, as shown in Figure 13.25.** For an iOS project, set the Automatic option for the Release scheme only.

You should now be able to validate the app and upload it to the App Store.

Figure 13.25

Select the distribution profile and the automatic signing identity.

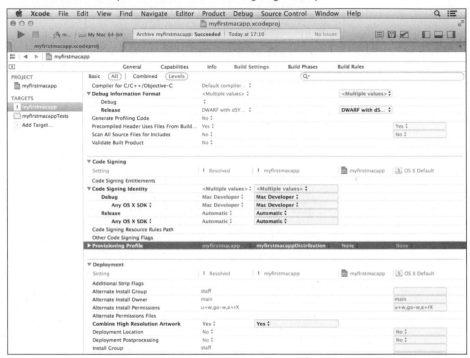

T I P

If validation fails because of an App/Bundle ID error, Xcode suggests that you need to create a completely new Application Record. This is true only if the app has already been accepted for sale. If you haven't yet uploaded it, you can open the app record in iTunes Connect, click Edit, and select a new Bundle ID from the menu. You can even go through the entire bundle/App ID/distribution profile process in full and return to this dialog to select the new bundle.

Handling receipts

When a user buys an app from the store, iTunes generates a receipt file that locks it to one specific Mac. As of iOS 7, iOS apps also support this feature.

To minimize piracy, your app can include code to validate a receipt. This feature isn't included in the build process, so you must add your own code. Unfortunately, the code and the underlying cryptographic concepts are complex, obscure, and poorly documented. Fortunately, the developer community has created its own solutions. Search online for "App Store Receipt Validation."

Note that you should customize or obfuscate any code you use, to make it harder to bypass. This helps prevent automated piracy: If everyone used the same code, it would be easy to create an automatic tool to strip it out.

Working with iOS Ad Hoc builds

The build process for an Ad Hoc build that you can share with beta testers is similar to an App Store build, but there are differences. Before you create an Ad Hoc build, you must create an Ad Hoc distribution profile.

Creating and installing an Ad Hoc provisioning profile

To create an Ad Hoc profile, open the Certificates, Identifiers & Profiles page, and select Provisioning Profiles. Click Distribution, and then click the + (plus) icon. Instead of App Store, click Ad Hoc and then click Continue.

Select an App ID. You can use the same ID you use for a distribution profile. Select a certificate/ID to sign the app, and click Continue.

Ad Hoc profiles include an explicit list of supported devices. You can select only those devices in your Devices list. When you add new beta testers to your testing program, add their devices to the Devices page before creating a profile.

You can then check the boxes that appear on the Select Devices page to choose the devices supported by the profile. The app won't run on device IDs that aren't baked into the profile.

You can now name and generate the profile as you did for an App Store distribution. Be sure to include *AdHoc* in the profile name to identify it clearly.

Creating an Ad Hoc build

Use the refresh feature in Accounts Preferences to download and install the profile. Click it repeatedly until the profile appears in the list. You can now select the profile in the Provisioning Profile in your app's Build Settings and select Automatic to sign the app with the certificate/ID it contains.

Note that you can't validate an ad hoc build. Instead, click Distribute and check the Save for Enterprise or Ad Hoc Deployment box. Click Next.

Select the Ad Hoc provisioning profile from the menu, as shown in Figure 13.26. The default is usually wrong, so you need to double-check that you have selected the Ad Hoc profile.

Figure 13.26

Select the correct Ad Hoc distribution profile.

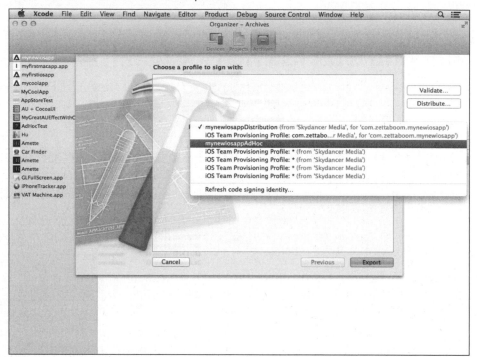

Distributing an Ad Hoc build

You can now save the app as a file or a pair of files. If you leave the Save for Enterprise Distribution box unchecked, Xcode creates a standard IPA file. You can e-mail this file to beta testers, and they can install it using iTunes by dragging and dropping it onto their app library and syncing their device.

If you check the box, as shown in Figure 13.27, you can save the file with an optional manifest plist. Although this option is labeled Enterprise Distribution, anyone can use it to distribute the app using OTA (Over The Air) distribution, which bypasses iTunes and allows users to download the app by clicking a link.

Figure 13.27

Create an Enterprise Distribution with OTA support.

From the user's point of view, OTA just works. The user must use Safari on her device. But if you set up the distribution web page correctly, Safari downloads and installs the app. The application URL should match what you set when you created the Enterprise build. Optionally, you can specify large and small image URLs, but this isn't essential.

To create the link, create a simple HTML file with the following content, changing the links, app name, and link text as needed. Optionally, you can add extra text, graphics, and styling to make the page more attractive.

```
<a href="itms-services://?action=download-manifest&url=http://
    linkto/yourapp.plist">Click here to download the beta. </a>
```

Creating Mac Developer ID Builds

If you don't want to distribute your Mac app through the App Store, you can still choose to sign it with a developer ID. This bypasses a security dialog that appears in OS X Mavericks and later, which keeps users from installing unsigned apps unless they manually override a per-app setting that is buried deep in the System Preferences.

You don't need a provisioning profile to distribute a Developer ID build. You can simply sign the build with your standard developer ID.

Setting up a Developer ID build

Start by opening the General tab in your target's build settings. Click the Developer ID radio button in the Signing section of the Identity header, as shown in Figure 13.28. Check that your team is selected in Team menu and select it if it isn't, or pick the team ID you want to use if you have created more than one team.

Figure 13.28

Prepare for a developer ID build.

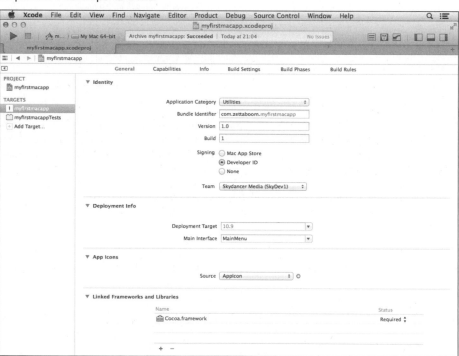

Open the Build Settings for the target. If a provisioning profile is selected under Code Signing, remove it by selecting None.

Click the disclosure triangle under Code Signing Identity to reveal the Release scheme. Click the Release and Any OS X SDK fields under the target, and select the Developer ID Application identity. It should match your team name, as shown in Figure 13.29.

Figure 13.29

Select the Developer ID application identity.

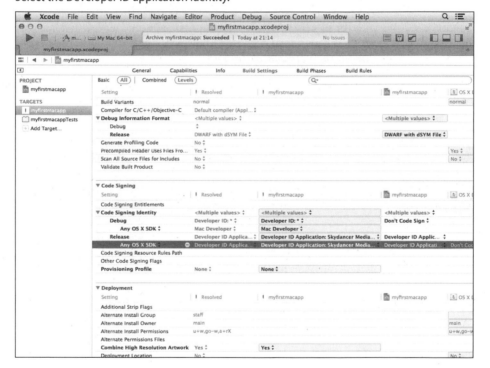

NOTE

If the identity is missing, see Chapter 11 for information about creating a set of Mac developer identities.

Build and archive the app. Click Distribute, and select Export Developer ID-signed Application. Click Next, and select the Developer ID you set in Figure 13.28. Click Export, and Xcode builds an app package.

Users can install the app package by dragging to `/Applications`. Traditionally, the app is packaged into a folder with an alias for the `/Applications` folder and an arrow graphic showing how the user can grab the app package and drop it on the alias. The folder is then packaged as a `.dmg` file in Disk Utility.

Creating installer packages

You can create installer packages for Mac App Store distribution and for direct distribution. Unlike plain vanilla apps, packages can run scripts that copy and install further resources such as fonts, images, sound files, and so on.

To be compatible with the installer, apps must be signed with the Third Party Mac Developer Installer ID for the App Store, and the Developer ID Installer for direct distribution. You may need to adapt your provisioning profile accordingly.

Xcode cannot build a package. You must download and install the optional Package Maker tool. Select Xcode ➪ Open Developer Tool ➪ Further Developer Tools, and download Package Maker from the Apple tools list.

Package Maker is famously quirky, so expect to spend some time building a package that works. Further details and tutorials are available by searching online for "Package Maker."

Summary

With Xcode 5, setting up distribution is simpler than it used to be. But the various distribution modes mean that initial setup can be time-consuming and occasionally frustrating. Allow at least a day or two to work through the process the first time you do it.

You should test it with a dummy app that does nothing, so you gain some experience with it. You can always delete the binary after upload so it never reaches review, and leave the application record in place—perhaps for further experiments.

And you should NOT leave it to the last minute before a deadline.

Advanced Workspace and Build Management

So far, the build process has been treated as a "black box" that does its job after it's initialized with a standard list of build settings. This is adequate for simpler apps, but for more complex projects, it can be useful to break apart the build process and customize it further. This is particularly true after you start trying to include external code from free and/or open-source libraries and frameworks in your projects.

Understanding the Build Process

In outline, the build process has four stages:

1. Preprocessor
2. Compiler
3. Linker
4. File copier and processor

The preprocessor makes working copies of the original source files, expanding `#include` directives to include the original headers, expanding macros (low-level reusable code snippets and definitions), and implementing *conditional compilation*. Conditional compilation uses directives such as `#if` and `#ifdef` to test compiler and system settings and select code according to their values.

Internally, the preprocessor is more complex than this simple description suggests, but a full introduction is outside the scope of this book. The key practical point is that you can use preprocessor directives to include and exclude code automatically according to various system, platform, and build settings.

The compiler converts the files generated by the preprocessor into machine code—a file with the `.o` (object) extension. Each source file in the project creates a separate object file. The linker combines them all into a single executable binary, resolves symbol references to a specific location in the binary, and checks that all references are present and correct. For example, if your code calls a framework, the linker checks that the framework is included. If it can't find the framework or the specific symbol in it, it can't complete its task and the build fails.

The file copier processes supporting files. Different file types are processed in different ways, according to set rules. For example, nib files are compacted, image files may be compressed, plists may or may not be compressed depending on their function, and so on. All processed files are copied to the target's product folder. Some may be handed to the linker, so the point at which files are processed may vary.

The Xcode build system implements this scheme inside a customizable build manager. Each stage runs multiple shell scripts. You can add your own scripts to the default build sequence. Potentially, you can even replace the default scripts with your own custom-written alternatives, although this isn't something you want to consider doing without a very good reason.

In practice, Xcode manages the build process through a combination of two elements:

- Build phases select and process files of a given type. You can add phases that run arbitrary scripts. Build phases define *when* files are processed and when other scripted build events happen.
- Build rules define the scripts that control what happens to a file with a specific extension. They define *how* files are processed.

To customize a build fully, you must know how to do the following:

- Access the standard build settings and environment variables in your code, so you can add conditional compilation features.
- Create your own custom build settings for use in conditional compilation.
- Create and manage build phases.
- Create and manage build rules.

You can use an external compiler for some other language to create .o files. You can do this from the command line using whatever command-line compiler tool works for that language, or you can include a custom script in your build system that generates the .o files. You can then use the project build settings to tell the linker to add them manually.

NOTE

You can use an external compiler for some other languages to create .o files. You can run the appropriate compiler manually from the command line, or you can include the compiler commands in a custom script in your Xcode project. You can then use the project build settings to force the linker to link the files to your project. Xcode's LLVM compiler can compile the standard C-family languages (C, Objective-C, C++). Other languages need an external compiler, which you must find, download, and install separately. (Note that LLVM does not compile Microsoft's C#, which is more of a C++/ Java hybrid than a true C-family language.)

NOTE

Many popular languages, such as Python and Ruby, are *interpreted*. The interpreter runs the source code one line at a time and never produces a separate binary. You can still compile these languages, with varying degrees of success, efficiency, and LLVM compatibility, if someone has written a compiler for them. A full discussion of the current state of interpreted, compiled, and Just In Time (JIT) on-demand compilation for each popular language would fill an entire book. Practically, you can find what's available for any language with some diligent web searching.

Creating Custom Builds

You need to learn these key skills and options to work with custom builds:

- Conditional compilation
- Custom build phases
- Custom build rules
- Custom build scripts
- Header and library management

Introducing conditional compilation

Conditional compilation is an automated process that literally includes and excludes lines of code from your source files. You create conditional code by surrounding it with preprocessor directives, which look similar to conventional C code but are prefixed with the # character.

Table 14.1 lists the standard conditional and unconditional directives.

Table 14.1 Conditional Compilation Directives	
Macro	*Meaning*
#define	Sets the value of a token.
#if	Includes the following code if a conditional test is true. Conditional comparisons work only with integers. There's no way to compare a macro with a string or with the numeric value of a string.
#ifdef	Includes the following code if a token is defined.
#ifndef	Includes the following code if a token isn't defined.
#else	Includes the following code when the preceding test is false.
#elif	Combined #else #if for nested conditionals.
#endif	Ends the conditional test. Code after #endif is always included, in the usual way.
#include	Includes the following code unconditionally.
#import	The Objective-C equivalent of #include.
#pragma once	An alternative way to tell the preprocessor to avoid duplicated includes. Not considered standard, but works as stated—usually.
#warning	Prints a C string warning to the console. (Because this is a C directive, don't prefix the string with the Objective-C @ objectifier.)

TIP

You can use #pragma mark to add a divider line to the list of methods that appears in the menu in the jump bar. (This is more useful than perhaps it sounds.)

Using conditional compilation

In theory, conditional compilation is very simple. A typical example looks like this:

```
#ifdef <some token>
        ...code to include...
#endif
```

The *token* is a general catch-all name for all the available settings, macros, environment variables, and user-defined flags and values. The challenge with conditional compilation is finding which tokens are available.

Compilers include a range of settings that are defined by the language, platform, compiler, and build. Some tokens are defined as macros and use a special format: Their names are prefixed with a double underscore, and they may end with another double underscore. Users can define their own custom tokens as absolute values, references to other settings, or logical combinations of two or more settings.

CAUTION

Note that you can't compare strings in an #if directive, but you can compare tokens with numerical values. You can also check whether a specific token has been defined.

Table 14.2 lists a small selection of useful macros and platform settings.

Table 14.2 Useful Macros and Conditional Compilation Tokens	
Macro	*Meaning*
__FILE__	The name of the current file as a C string constant
__LINE__	The current line number in a source file as a decimal integer
__DATE__	The date as a C string constant
__TIME__	The time as a C string constant
__OBJC__	True for an Objective-C project
TARGET_IPHONE_SIMULATOR	True when compiling for the Simulator
TARGET_OS_IPHONE	True when compiling for iOS, false for OS X

Having a single source for these tokens would be useful, but they're scattered across many different locations. For compiler-specific tokens, search online for "LLVM preprocessor macros." For some of the Apple-specific tokens, search in Finder for the file TargetConditionals.h.

Creating custom tokens

Creating your own tokens is often useful; for example, you can add a token that's only defined when you select a custom configuration.

Note that it's a good idea to give your tokens a custom prefix; your initials are a popular option. Developers often add tokens to their code. If code is shared, simple names such as DEBUG and IPHONE can be defined in multiple locations, creating conflicts.

1. **Open a project. Open the target build settings, and scroll down the Other C Flags entry under the Language settings, as shown in Figure 14.1.**

2. **Double-click under the target name.**

3. **Type** -DMY_TOKEN=0 **into the value field at the right to define the name and the value of the token.**

If you select a specific build configuration—for example, Release, Debug, or a custom configuration you added yourself—the token is defined only for that configuration.

4. **If you need to add more tokens, repeat the process.**

You can define a value for the token by adding = (equal sign) followed by the value. The critical element that "tokenizes" your entry is the -D prefix.

You also can simply #define tokens in your project's -Prefix.pch file. They're available to every file in the project, and they override existing definitions.

Figure 14.1

Add a custom token. Clicking the Other C Flags field shows a pop-over. You can add and remove tokens using the +/- (plus/minus) icons at the lower left.

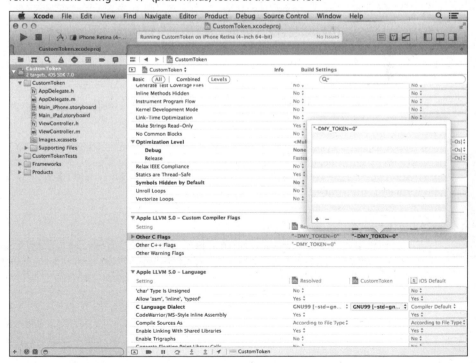

TIP

If you add `#define NSLog` to your project's `-Prefix.pch` file, all instances of `NSLog` are stripped from your code. This is a quick way to eliminate log messages when you no longer need them.

After you've defined MY_TOKEN correctly, you can use this conditional directive to include when the token is valid:

```
#ifdef MY_TOKEN
        <...code included if MY_TOKEN is defined...>
#endif
```

NOTE

You can also add tokens to the Preprocessing section. Add them in the same way, but don't prefix them with `-D`.

Converting build settings into tokens

You can convert any build setting into a token by wrapping it in a dollar sign and either brackets or curly braces. For example, to read the value of the SDKROOT build setting into your own custom SDK_ROOT token, use the following:

```
SDK_ROOT = $(SDKROOT)
```

You see that Xcode substitutes the real value immediately, so, for example, you may see this:

```
SDK_ROOT = iphoneos
```

Unfortunately, you can't do much with this because the value isn't treated as a C string. If you use SDK_ROOT anywhere, iphoneos is substituted by the preprocessor. The compiler then looks for a symbol called iphoneos and doesn't find it, because it isn't a true symbol.

You can, however, use this technique to read numerical build settings into your code. But don't forget (again) that these values are valid at compile-time only.

Conditional compilation is useful for language-, platform-, and target-dependent compilation, but using compile-time build settings to select runtime code is somewhat eccentric. A more useful alternative is to create scripts in the build phases and build rules to define how a build proceeds internally.

TIP

To find the name of any build setting, select it in the Build Settings editor, select Edit ⇨ Copy from the main Xcode menu, and paste the string into TextEdit. You can select multiple settings at the same time, as long as they don't take multiple configuration values. For a full list of build settings, see the Xcode Build Setting Reference in the documentation.

NOTE

When you create a new C++ class, Xcode automatically adds conditional definitions around it. This is standard practice for C++; adding conditionals guarantees that each class is compiled only once. Without them, the compiler can get lost in recursive redefinitions.

Working with Build Phases

It's worth repeating that Xcode is simply a UI for a set of command-line scripts. The Build Phase and Build Rules tabs in the build editor define which scripts are run and what they do.

You can view the details of the build—the commands given at the command line and the output they generate—by selecting the Log navigator, selecting a completed build, and choosing All and All Messages in the toolbar at the top of the window. The default terse view shown in Figure 14.2 displays the commands in the order they were given. This project is part of a workspace that builds a target combing a custom source file with two simple static libraries. As you can see, the sequence in practice isn't quite as neat as the Preprocess ⇨ Compile ⇨ Link ⇨ Copy template given earlier.

Figure 14.2

This lists what happens during a build in the Log navigator.

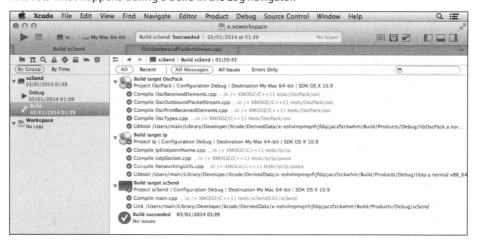

If you right-click anywhere in the list and select Expand All Transcripts, you see the scripts for each stage, as shown in Figure 14.3. The long list of paths, steps, and compiler switches is difficult to read. In theory, you could copy and run each step in Terminal to create a complete build for related source files.

In practice, you can't, because each new project uses a randomized file path for the build directory, which is in the project's derived data folder. You can find the location of this folder in the Projects page of the Organizer.

Setting up build phases

The build phase system can seem complex when you encounter it for the first time, but in fact it's surprisingly easy to work with. To view the build phases editor, select the target build settings and click the Build Phases tab, as shown in Figure 14.4.

Figure 14.3

Look at the detailed commands in each step.

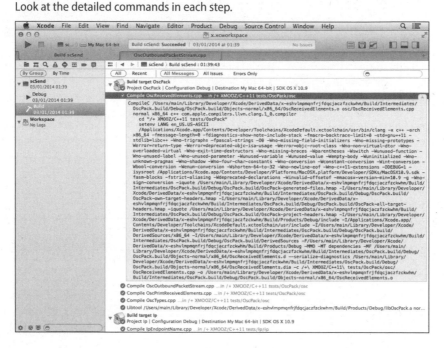

Figure 14.4

Explore build phases.

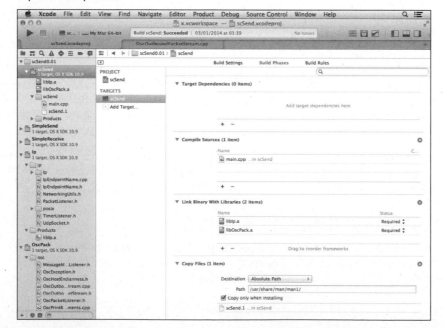

You can do the following:

- Manage target dependencies. (Use this option to control the order in which targets are compiled, so the targets are built in the correct sequence.)
- Add more files to the compile sources list.
- Add more libraries and frameworks to the Link Binary with Libraries list.
- Copy resource files to a product bundle.
- Add a *custom build phase* to do one of the following: copy files to the product, copy headers to the product, or run an arbitrary script.

You have already used the build phase pages when adding Cocoa libraries to a project. In fact, you can use them to add any library, including your own—and more besides.

Build phases are often useful when working with multiple targets. For example, if your project has two targets, such as an app and one or more libraries, you typically add the libraries to the app's Link Binary with Libraries list, as shown in Figure 14.4. Xcode automatically treats libraries as dependencies. If you edit them, Xcode builds them before it builds the final target that depends on them. Optionally, you can choose to specify further dependencies manually.

CROSS-REFERENCE
You can find a practical example of a workspace that builds libraries and a final target later in this chapter.

Getting started with the Run Script build phase
You can add custom build phases by selecting the Build Phases tab, then choosing Editor ➪ Add Build Phase in the main menu. You can then select one of the three options—Run Script, Copy Files, or Copy Headers—from a sub-menu.

CAUTION
In Xcode 4, you could add a build phase by clicking a button at the bottom of the Build Phases window. This button is no longer available in Xcode 5. You can add a build phase only from the main menu.

You can use the Run Script option to add customized scripted processing or support. Scripts can be written in any language that works from the command line, including AppleScript, Perl, Python, Ruby, and the standard UNIX bash shell, all of which are built into OS X.

Scripts can make use of build setting macros to read Xcode's own internal build variables. The two very simple examples in Figure 14.5 show how to read the source and destination directories.

Figure 14.5

Start a build phase script. The input and output directories are defined by macros and added automatically when you click the + (plus) icon for each option.

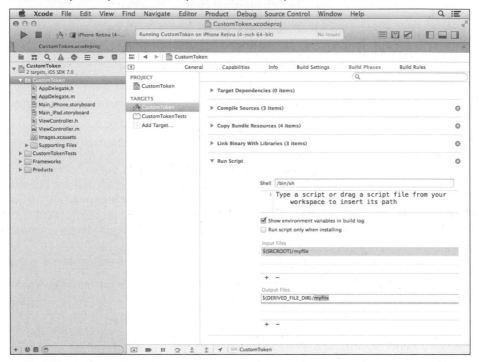

A full-featured script might loop through every file in the source directory or select files with a specific extension and process them. Because scripts have access to environment variables and to other commands and processes, the potential of custom scripting is almost limitless. For example, if you don't want to use bots, you can add command-line access to source code management here, or back up the files in your build to a remote server. You can also implement a build number script to keep track of build progress—a feature that is missing in Xcode.

To remove a script or build phase, click the cross icon at the right. You can rearrange the order in which build phases are run by dragging them up and down the list. The Target Dependencies are fixed, but every other phase can be moved. Note that you can add more than one scripted build phase and more than one Copy Files build phase, and you can place them in any sequence in the build.

CAUTION

Rearranging build phases can create nonsensical results; for example, placing the compile phase after the link phase is rarely useful. Note also that deleting a custom build phase removes it permanently; there is no Undo option.

Copying files or headers

You can use a Copy Files build phase to copy files to various destination. As shown in Figure 14.6, Xcode includes a comprehensive menu of destinations.

Figure 14.6

Select a destination for a Copy Files build phase.

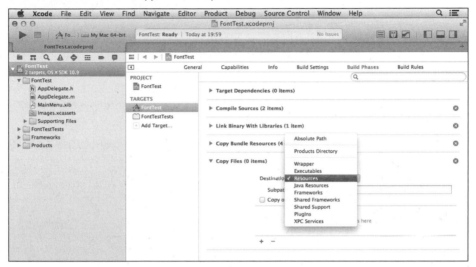

Copying files to a target bundle is an essential option. By default, Xcode copies resources by adding them to the Copy Bundle Resources build phase, which is included in every project. But you can customize this process with a Copy Files build phase, to copy files of various types to custom resource sub-folders.

You can also copy files to an absolute path, to a framework, and so on. Depending on the design of your project and its various dependencies, you may want to copy files to a folder before you build the rest of your app.

TIP

Note that you can combine the Run Script and Copy Files build phases. For example, you may want to collect a set of files in a specific directory with Copy Files and then run a compile and link script to create a custom binary. You could also use a Copy Headers phase to include the headers to make a library you can distribute to team members or online. The possibilities are almost endless.

Creating build rules

Build rules specify a build action for each file type in a project—or more specifically, for each file with a given extension. To view the default build rules, select a target and click the Build Rules tab at the top right. The list shown in Figure 14.7 is the same for every target. It includes a list of file types and names the commands that can process them. The commands are at the lowest level of the Xcode build system; they're utilities that copy, compile, and process various files in various ways.

Figure 14.7

These are the default build rules.

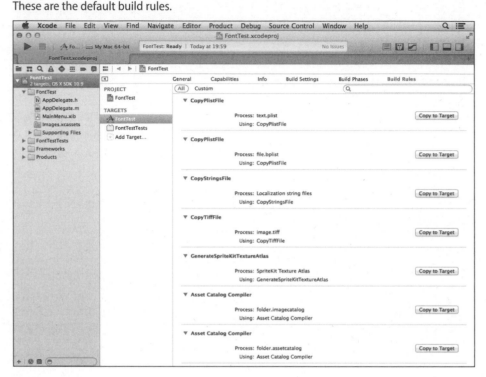

NOTE

Because only targets are built—projects are collections of targets—only targets have build rules. You can't define build rules for a project. Each target has its own rules, and there's no easy way to copy rules between targets.

You can customize the existing rules by clicking the Copy to Target button. This opens the pane shown in Figure 14.8. Use the Process menu to select a file type. You can choose from a standard selection of types, or you can select "Source files with names matching:" and type the extension in the box to the right. Each of the standard rules defaults to one type. If you select a custom script, the default script stub includes a relevant build setting that points you to the directory holding the associated files. You can modify any of these default options in your script, as needed.

Use the Using box to select a processing action. You can select from another list of standard options or select the Custom script option to create your own scripted processor. The script editor is identical to the one for build phases, and it can use the same selection of languages supported by the shell.

Figure 14.8

The build rules use the same scripting options as the build phases. (You can get as creative as you want here.)

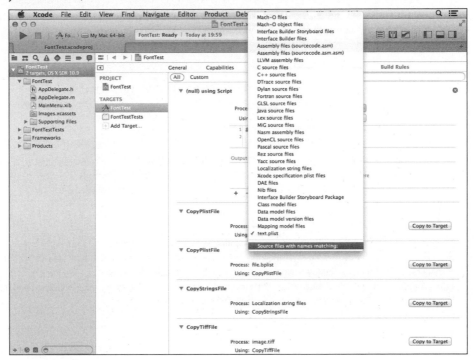

NOTE

You may be unfamiliar with some of the file types and processes in the menus. Many are highly specialized, and you're unlikely to use them.

Customizing command-line builds

Xcode is designed to make it easy to build apps. It's less effective as a build system for imported projects that use a command-line build system. Many libraries and open-source projects use alternative standard build tools such as `make` and `cmake`.

The easy way to work with these projects is to use Xcode purely as a source editor and run the alternative build script as a custom build phase. You can remove the compile, link, and copy bundle phases from a project by opening the Build Phases tab and clicking the cross next to each phase. You can then add a custom script to run the build commands, or—more usually— to launch an existing script supplied with the project.

This system typically requires additional setup. It's usual to have to define extra environment variables, fix permissions, and perform extra housekeeping before you can get a build to work reliably.

A key point is that you can waste lots of time attempting to convert a project with a custom build system into a project that you can build exclusively inside Xcode. As a general rule, if you're using external code as a "black box," you may as well build a binary once and link your project to it using its standard headers.

If you think you may want to modify or extend the source and the project isn't particularly complex, it can be worth attempting a conversion. Simple libraries can be worth the time. As a library gets more complex, the amount of time you can spend on it increases and the chances of success decrease.

With scripted building, you can keep some or all of the main benefits of Xcode—built-in source control, automated testing, symbol sharing and code completion, explicit dependencies, and automated building and uploading with bots—while also using external build tools.

TIP

Many open-source projects can be installed using popular package manager and build systems such as MacPorts and Homebrew. If you're trying to build an open-source project or library, it's a good idea to check whether either of these managers already includes a build system you can use. For example, building the Boost C++ library is challenging, even using the standard Boost build system. But you can download a Boost package using Homebrew, and it more or less just works, as long as you remember to add the Boost headers to your project.

CAUTION

Another key advantage of Xcode is that you can easily work with a variety of Apple architectures. Under the hood, there are huge differences between building an app for the App Store and building it for the Simulator. Xcode hides these differences, so the same code just works on both. If you use a command-line system, you can't ignore the differences and must manage architecture customization yourself. There's no quick fix for this, although if you're lucky, you may find that someone else has already done the work and posted the details on a blog or uploaded them to GitHub.

Working with Libraries and Headers

So far, you have learned how to use the standard Cocoa/Carbon/Darwin libraries and headers. They're described in the Apple documentation, and you can use them as is, without worrying how they work.

If you want to use an external library or framework, you need to understand how Xcode works with libraries, binaries, and header files. You also need to tell Xcode to include the binaries, source code, and headers in your projects.

The most efficient way to demonstrate this process is with a practical example. oscpack is a free C++ library that you can use to send and receive messages using the OSC (Open Sound Control) network protocol. oscpack is a lightweight implementation of OSC that works for basic applications.

This section demonstrates how to use a workspace to build two simple libraries for oscpack—a low-level networking library that sends and receives information over a network, and an OSC library that packs OSC messages, sends them, receives them, and unpacks them. It includes two very simple applications—one that sends messages, and one that receives them and logs the results.

The oscpack source code is available as an SVN repository at `http://code.google.com/p/oscpack/source/checkout`. You can also download it directly from the site of Ross Bencina, the author, at `www.rossbencina.com/code/oscpack`.

Figure 14.9 shows the unpacked directory. As is usual, there are various source files, plus readme and other text files, and supporting files for a cmake build. The network library code is in `/ip`, the osc library is in `/osc`, and the send and receive applications are in `/examples`.

Figure 14.9

Look at the oscpack source folder.

For this example, we don't use the build system supplied with oscpack, because it's relatively easy to convert it to an Xcode project. Instead, we add various library files to a workspace and use them to build the two test applications. In a real project, we could then extend the workspace to create a custom project that uses the oscpack libraries in a larger application.

NOTE

For a build, only source and header files matter. Readme files, notes, web pages, help documents, and other nonessential information are for your benefit as a potential user, but they are irrelevant to a build. If you want to keep your source folders tidy, you can delete them if you don't need them. But note that it is customary *not* to delete these extra items, especially if you go on to share your project online. Someone else may find the files useful, even if you don't.

Working with workspaces

To begin the project, select File ⇨ New ⇨ Workspace to create a new empty workspace. Save it as oscpack, as shown in Figure 14.10. An empty workspace has no content of any kind. It's simply a blank placeholder for new projects.

Figure 14.10

Create a new workspace.

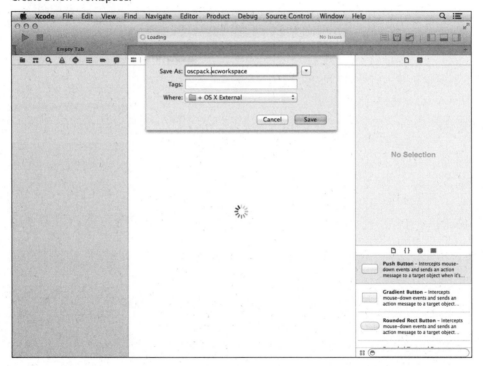

Although you can add projects to a workspace by dragging and dropping, you get more consistently useful results by creating new projects inside the workspace and adding files to them. Right-click in the Navigator area, and select New Project. Select the C/C++ library option, as shown in Figure 14.11. Select the Static library type in the bottom menu, if it isn't already selected. Save it as lp. Make sure you select the oscpack workspace from the Add to . . . menu as shown in Figure 14.12.

Adding a library creates a target and automatically prefixes it with *lib*. The target has a complete set of build settings, build phases, and build rules. Unlike an app, it has no source files, so we have to add them to the project before we can build it.

Figure 14.11

Create a new library in the workspace . . .

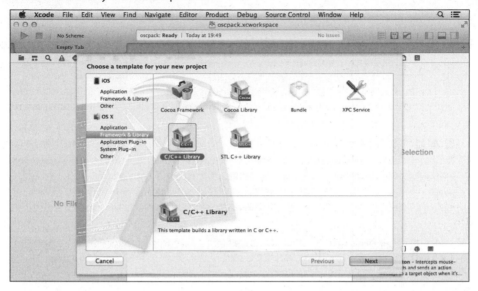

Figure 14.12

. . . and add a project to the workspace.

NOTE

The target has the .a extension because it's a UNIX binary archive file. If you were curious why packaged apps are called archives—this is why.

To add the files, right-click the Ip target at the top of the Navigator window, and select Add Files to Ip . . . . Navigate to the location where you downloaded the oscpack source, and select the ip folder. Check the Copy items into destination group's folder (if needed) and the Ip target boxes, as shown in Figure 14.13. Select the "Create groups for added folders" radio button. Note that Xcode capitalizes target names, even if the original source folder has a lowercase name.

CAUTION

You may think it's wasteful to copy the source files. Unfortunately, Xcode doesn't always set up links to header files correctly if you don't. This can cause the infamously baffling "file not found" error, which appears even when files that are clearly visible in the Project navigator. You can sometimes fix this manually, but it's extra work. Generally, it's easier to let Xcode manage the project files automatically by copying them than it is to set up the correct references.

If you build the project now, you get a slightly mysterious error telling you a file called `winsock2.h` isn't found. This is because the source includes files for Windows and for POSIX— the technical name of the UNIX variant used by OS X. Winsock is part of the Windows networking system and is included automatically in Windows build systems.

Because this is an OS X build, you can right-click the Win32 folder in the Project navigator and select Delete to remove it. It's fine to move all the files to the trash. The target should now build correctly, creating a finished binary called `libIp.a`.

Figure 14.13

Add files to the project.

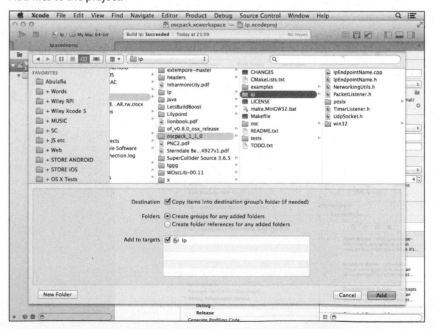

TIP

You can also set a flag called `-EXCLUDED_SOURCE_FILE_NAMES` and follow it with a list of the files you want Xcode to ignore. Deleting the file can be simpler and clearer, but if you use a flag you can exclude different files in the debug and release versions of your project.

You can now repeat the same steps for the contents of the osc folder to create another library called libOsc.a. To recap: Create a new library project, copy in the source files from the osc folder, create groups and add them to the Osc target, and build.

NOTE

It's not unusual for open-source projects to include OS X, Linux, and Windows sources in the same distribution. It's less usual for the code to include all the conditionals needed to make sure only the right code is selected. Expect to have to do some hand-editing and perhaps some deletions before you can get a project to build. Developers often make some attempt to make sure builds work correctly on all platforms, but creating a bullet-proof multi-platform build is far from easy.

This time there's no Windows content, so you don't need to delete any files. However, you need to be careful to make sure Xcode creates a separate osc project. By default, Xcode adds the project to the previous project. This is not what you want, so you *must* create a new group to keep the projects separate.

When you create the new project, select the oscpack workspace group, as shown in Figure 14.14. This creates a new group at the top level of the oscpack workspace, instead of adding it to the ip group.

You should now be able to build `libOsc.a`. Don't forget to select the osc scheme next to the build button before you try to build it.

Figure 14.14

Add a new project and make sure Xcode puts it in a new group.

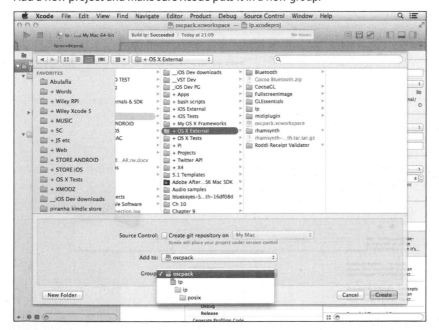

Static versus Dynamic Libraries

A static library is always linked into your finished binary. This is a good thing for a stand-alone self-contained application, because the library is guaranteed to be available—it's literally baked into the app itself. For iOS projects, this is the only option.

A dynamic library exists as a single copy of the binary and can be loaded on demand by applications that need it. This saves space: Only one copy exists, so the same library file can be shared by multiple applications. But dynamic libraries can cause installation issues. If it's lost from the application suite, or isn't included in the installer, or there's a file path issue, the entire suite can stop working. There can also be issues with versioning, if the library isn't updated on the same schedule as the apps it supports.

Generally, static libraries are easier to manage. You have less to worry about, and if you're building a single app, there's no reason not to build everything into one file. Dynamic libraries are useful for complex applications where there's no good reason to duplicate the same code over and over. But you need to pay more attention to installation.

Linking libraries with apps

We now have two libraries we can use in our projects. The oscpack source includes two simple command-line applications that we can use to check the libraries are sending and receiving messages. (It also includes a full testing suite. You may want to build that after you've explored unit testing in Chapter 18.)

Building apps from source files is very similar to building libraries, with a couple of differences. The first is that you must tell Xcode to link in the binaries. The second is that you must tell Xcode where to find the headers used to access the libraries.

UNIX build systems typically install headers and binaries in various semi-standardized locations. `/usr/bin/local` is a popular choice, but alternative locations are sometimes used.

Whether you use Xcode or an external build system, you must tell Xcode where to find the headers and binaries that make up a library when you want to link it to an application by adding some search paths to the Build Settings. This is a critical step, but it isn't well-documented, and it's easy to miss the correct settings among the hundreds that are available.

For this example, the headers are in the library source folders. For an Xcode-only project, there's no reason to copy them to another location. But we still have to tell Xcode where to find them.

NOTE
If you decide to package a project into a non-Xcode build system, you should copy headers and binaries to one of the standard locations and set up your build scripts accordingly.

Creating an application in a workspace

We need to create the SimpleSend application first. Follow these steps:

1. **Right-click anywhere in the Project Navigator, and select New Project . . .**

2. **Select OS X Application and Command Line Tool.**

3. **Click Next, and type** SimpleSend **into the Product Name field.**

4. **Select C++ in the Type menu if it isn't already selected.**

5. **Add the project to the oscpack workspace and the oscpack group, as shown in Figure 14.15.**

   This creates a separate project with its own target in its own group.

6. **Right-click the SimpleSend group, and select Add Files . . .**

Figure 14.15

Create a new command-line application for the project.

7. Navigate to the /examples folder in the downloaded source, and select
SimpleSend.cpp.

8. As before, make sure the Copy items . . . and the SimpleSend target are both
selected, as shown in Figure 14.16.

CAUTION

In this example, SimpleSend is a single source file. To add multiple source files inside a folder, select the entire folder.

You won't be able to build the project without making a few more changes. The first is
to delete the default main.cpp file. SimpleSend.cpp file includes a replacement for
main. You can't include both—if you try to, the linker will complain about a duplicated
symbol.

Figure 14.16

Add an application to the project.

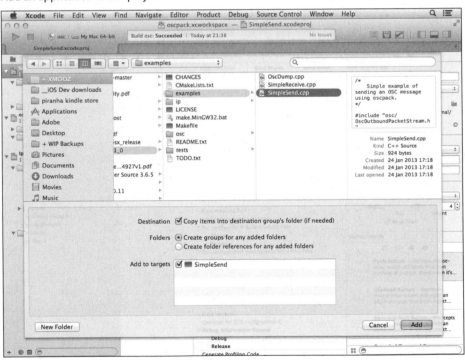

9. So right-click main.cpp, and select Delete and Move to Trash.

10. Next, add the library files to the link list.

11. Select the SimpleSend target, click Build Phases, and click Link Binary with Libraries.

12. Click the + (plus) icon.

Figure 14.17 shows that Xcode automatically displays the libraries in the workspace at the top of the list.

13. To add them, highlight them and click Add.

Figure 14.17

Add the libraries in the workspace.

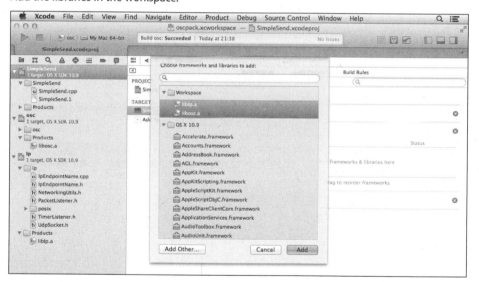

NOTE

If you add more libraries to the workspace, they appear in the libraries dialog automatically. Of course, you still have to tell Xcode to link them for each target. Note also that added libraries automatically count as dependencies. If you change their code, Xcode rebuilds them before it builds and links any project that uses them. You don't have to add them as explicit dependencies.

Finally, you have to tell Xcode where to find the library headers. This step seems counterintuitive. After all, for this project, the headers are right there in the workspace. Unfortunately, this doesn't mean Xcode can find them. For whatever reason, headers only work as headers when you tell Xcode where to look for them. This is a two-stage process.

14. Click the SimpleSend project, and then select the SimpleSend target.

15. Click Build Settings.

16. Scroll down to the Search Paths sub-pane, and find Always Search User Paths.

17. Click the No item, and select Yes from the menu, as shown in Figure 14.18.

It doesn't matter if you do this for the target or the project: In this example, they're identical.

Figure 14.18

Tell Xcode to search the header search paths you specify.

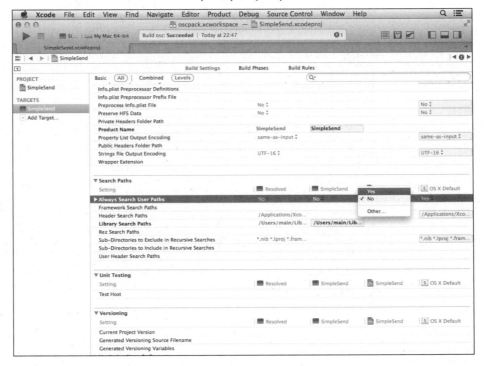

18. Double-click the blank Header Search Paths item under either the target or the project.

This displays Xcode's default header search path.

19. Click the + (plus) icon, and add the full path to the two library folders, as shown in Figure 14.19.

Figure 14.19

Tell Xcode which header paths to search.

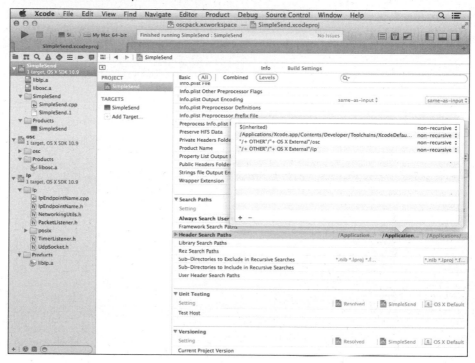

This part of the process can go very wrong, because Xcode has problems dealing with spaces in paths. The reliable answer is to put straight quotes around each path element. If you quote the entire path, the internal spaces are escaped to backslash/space pairs that don't work. Alternatively, you can try to remember not to use spaces in the paths of any of your development folders.

The non-recursive/recursive switch at the right of the dialog tells Xcode whether or not to flatten the folder hierarchy. Selecting the recursive option removes all path information from headers. This breaks any header includes that use a sub-path and is usually a bad thing to do.

However, note that if you copy headers to a project, you should include the top level of each copy. The headers are actually in a sub-folder below the top level. This is why the paths in this example work, even though they don't match the structure of the original source files.

Generally, path management is not very intuitive. You need to remember to do it in the first place, and you need to do different things depending whether you use the original source files or copy them to your project.

TIP

You can use the detailed error reporting in the Log navigator to see how Xcode is interpreting your path settings. Look for items beginning with "–I".

If you have followed the steps correctly, the SimpleSend application should build and run. It quits almost immediately, because it sends a couple of short OSC messages and terminates.

To check if the messages are being sent correctly, follow similar steps to build the SimpleReceive application. You need to make one edit to a file called `OscPacketListener.h` in the osc library. The include path for `PacketListener.h` assumes it is one level down the folder tree. Remove the unnecessary dots and the slash, shown in Figure 14.20, to fix this.

Figure 14.20

Fix an include path. It's not unusual to have to do some of this.

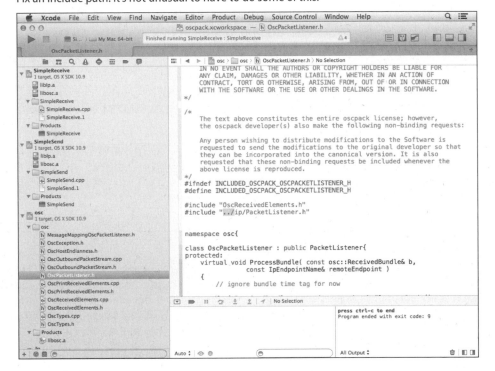

CAUTION

Unfortunately, there is no simple way to duplicate or copy settings between projects in a workspace. Because SimpleSend and SimpleReceive run as separate applications with a separate version copy of `main`, you can't link them into a single project. You could, however, create a single combined project by copying and combining the code from both projects into a single test file with a single version of `main` that runs both sets of code in a useful order.

If everything is working as it should, SimpleReceive should work as shown in Figure 14.21. You can launch it using the build/run command in the usual way and then click the SimpleSend project in the workspace to build/run it too. Note that a single project can run only a single application at a time, but projects in a workspace run independently—which makes them ideal for testing.

Open the debug window for SimpleReceive before running Simple Send. The messages should appear as shown in Figure 14.21. You can now use oscpack to send OSC messages to other OSC-compatible applications on your network by editing the port number and IP address in SimpleSend.

Figure 14.21

Check that SimpleReceive is receiving the messages sent by SimpleSend.

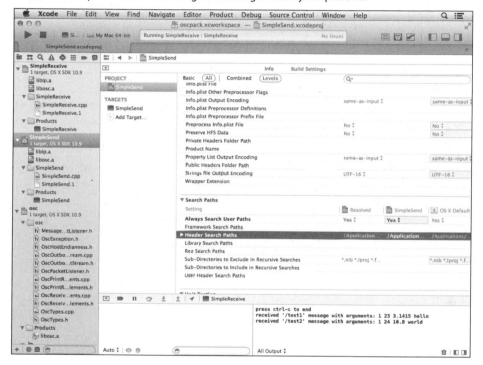

Summary

Adding external libraries and code to Xcode projects can be relatively easy, or it can be very complex. Because there's more than one way to do it, you can save time by exploring the various build/install options that are available and working out which does the job with the least effort. Trying to include everything in an Xcode project may not be the easiest option.

At this level, you've moved beyond the relatively simple skills needed to assemble apps out of Apple-standard components into the wider world of collaborative software development. Expect to spend some time setting up projects that use external code.

The up side is that working with others opens you to different ideas about coding and development, and can dramatically increase your developer skills.

Using Version Control

Development isn't always a smooth process, and sometimes it's necessary to abandon code that isn't working and restore a project to a previous state. It also can be useful to compare older and newer versions and to use tools that manage development across a team.

Managing code in these ways is known as *version control* or *source control management* (SCM). Several version control tools are built into Xcode. They're not obligatory, so you can ignore them, but this isn't recommended. At a minimum, you can manage versions manually in Finder. But you also can use the more powerful tools that are new to Xcode 5.

Using Manual Version Control

The easiest way to manage versions is to duplicate and rename project folders in Finder, as shown in Figure 15.1. Each folder should contain stable or nearly stable code with a consistent set of features. The code should build cleanly.

Create a copy before you begin to add new versions. If it's obvious that the next version must be abandoned, you can mark it by giving the folder a unique name—perhaps one that includes the word "abandoned"—and starting again with a new copy.

Manual version control is ideal for simple, self-contained projects, such as apps. It's not recommended for more complex projects, such as frameworks. And it should never be used for a collaborative development. You can rely on manual management if you're a solo developer. Don't use it if you need to share your work or if your code must be linked into another project.

The advantages of manual control include the following:

In This Chapter

Using manual version control

Using snapshots

Working with Git source control

Using Xcode with GitHub

- **Simple and clear no-fuss management:** Each version is separate and clearly marked. If you need to backtrack, you can.

- **Easy backups:** You can copy folders to a backup server manually or allow Time Machine to manage them.

- **Robust persistence:** Combined with backups, multiple copies mean that your work is less likely to be lost if a disk crashes. Files in a project are discrete and easy to access.

Figure 15.1

Manual version control is simple and easy to use, but limited.

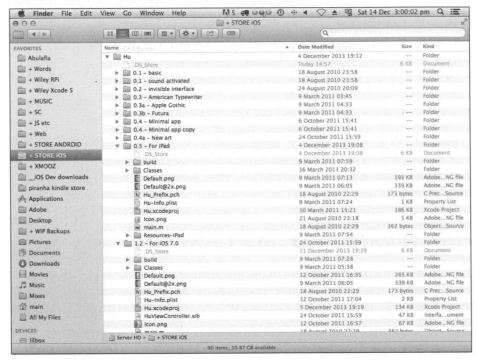

The disadvantages include the following:

- **No change logs:** You can use the Unix `diff` family of command-line utilities to compare files manually. But you can only do this manually in Terminal, not in the Xcode editor.

- **Limited support for constant file locations:** If your files are accessed from another project, you won't be able to move the files without telling Xcode you've moved them.

- **Possible errors:** It's surprisingly easy for either you or Xcode to get file paths confused and to edit files in an old folder when you mean to edit files in the most recent copy.

- **No simple rollback:** You can't see a record of edits, and you can't compare different versions of a file or restore it to a previous state.

- **No collaborative development:** Although it's possible to use informal schemes to check out code for editing, there's no easy way to integrate changes created by a team into a single code base.

Although manual version control is primitive, it can be worth considering if you're new to Xcode development and don't yet want to learn how to use a professional solution such as Git, described later. It's a practical solution for simple projects, and it won't distract you with further learning while you're trying to master the rest of Xcode and Cocoa.

Using Snapshots

A snapshot is a simple semi-automated solution for source control. You can take a snapshot of your project at any point with the File ➪ Create Snapshot menu option in the main Xcode menu. A snapshot records the state of the files in the project, and snapshots are listed in the Organizer. You can restore a project to an earlier state by restoring the snapshot.

As an example, create a new OS X Cocoa application following these steps:

1. **Save your new OS X Cocoa application as SnapshotExample.**
2. **Use the Create Snapshot option to save a snapshot of its initial state.**

   Figure 15.2 shows the new snapshot dialog.
3. **You can give each snapshot a title and an optional description.**

Figure 15.2

Create a new snapshot, with a name and description

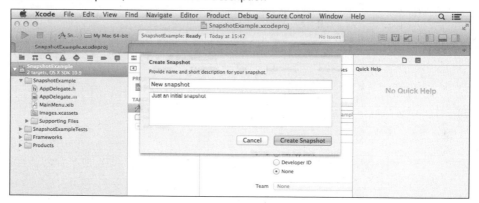

NOTE
In a real project, you don't usually need to save the initial default state of the application, because you can always re-create the default as a new project. But occasionally, it can be useful to keep the initial state as a starting point when you're experimenting.

4. **Add some code.**

   For an initial demonstration, it can be as simple as a single comment line.
5. **Create another snapshot, and give it a different title and description.**
6. **Open the Organizer window.**

   You open the Organizer window by selecting the filing cabinet icon near the top right of the Xcode window.

7. **Select the Projects icon at the top of the window.**

You should see a display similar to the one shown in Figure 15.3. The new Snapshot Example project appears at the top of the list at the left of the window. A list of snapshots for the projects appears in the pane at the bottom of the window.

Figure 15.3

View a project's snapshots.

The snapshot list can become cluttered, so you can delete individual snapshots by selecting the Delete Snapshot icon at the bottom right of the window. You also can restore a project to an earlier state by selecting a snapshot and using the Restore Snapshot option. You'll see a preview window, shown in Figure 15.4, which highlights the changes between the selected snapshot and the preceding snapshot.

CAUTION

There's no undo option for deleted snapshots; after they're gone, they're gone. And note that changes are incremental. The preview window doesn't show the changes between the first version of the project and the snapshot. Instead, it shows the changes between the current and previous snapshots.

Figure 15.4

View the restore options.

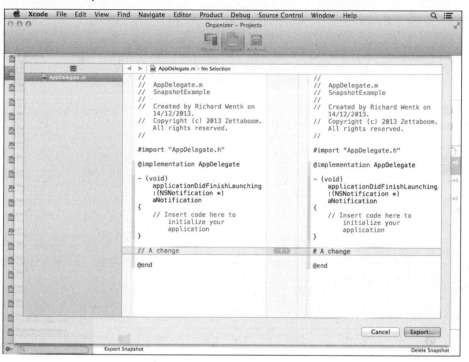

TIP

Xcode can create snapshots automatically before every bulk edit, such as a refactoring operation or a find-and-replace. Select File ⇨ Project Settings or File ⇨ Workspace Settings to open a preferences dialog, click the Snapshots tab, and check the "Create snapshot of project before mass-editing operations" box. You can also define a custom location for the snapshots. Note that this feature is *on* by default.

You might expect the snapshot to restore the project to its earlier state, but it doesn't. Instead, a Restore dialog appears and asks you to specify a folder on disk. The old state of the project is written to the folder. To reload the state, close the current project and reload the old version from the folder you specified. This separate save requirement makes the snapshot option clumsy. It implements minimal version control, but it's not very elegant or sophisticated.

Working with Git Source Control

Xcode supports two source control systems—Subversion and Git—which can track changes to files and support collaborative development. Source control adds the following features to Xcode:

- **Open development:** You can allow other developers to work with you on projects.
- **Edit logging:** You can see how files have developed over time and how code has been added, changed, or removed.

- **Change control:** You can accept or discard changes made by you or by other developers.
- **Blame logging:** Changes are tagged with the ID of the developer who made them.
- **Project branching:** You can create parallel projects to support independent development of different features or split projects to allow branches to develop in different directions.
- **Remote server backup:** Server-based source control stores code on a remote server, so you're less likely to lose it in an accident.

Subversion and Git have significant differences. Although Subversion is supported in Xcode, Git is integrated more tightly. You can create and manage a project that supports Git from the Xcode UI without using the command line. Certain advanced Git features are available only at the command line, but you can use Git successfully without them.

In contrast, you must use command-line access to set up Subversion for a project. After setup, many basic features are also available in the UI. Subversion requires an external server. Git can be used locally, and it can support server-based development.

CAUTION

Git and Subversion are part of the command-line utilities that are installed with Xcode. To use them, check the System Tools box when you install Xcode. If you don't do this, they're not available.

Understanding Git

Source control tools work with a repository or repo—a database configured to manage the files in a project. A key benefit of professional source control is that the contents of a repo can be kept on a single Mac or shared, either on a private server or online.

It's possible to copy, or clone, repositories to duplicate them across multiple Macs. Online storage with a service such as GitHub (github.com) gives you "free" backups—a remote copy of your source code is always available—and supports collaborative development.

In Xcode 5, you can also link source control with the new bot testing and integration system, which is introduced in Chapter 18. You can host a Git repo on the same server you use for integration and testing. This is a good way to keep private projects private; GitHub development is public, unless you pay a fee. A private Git server offers many of the remote access and version control benefits of GitHub, without the fee.

Repositories can store either incremental changes to files or complete files. Subversion stores incremental changes. Git stores complete files; in fact, it always works with a complete local version of the entire project. This makes it more robust than Subversion, at the cost of extra disk space and download/upload times. Because code files are usually small, the time penalty isn't usually significant. Because Git doesn't need to merge and update files, it can feel more responsive.

To use Git, you create a repository, either locally using Xcode or manually on a remote server, and then add and edit files in the usual way. After each significant edit, you commit the changes. This creates a complete snapshot of the project and adds copies of any modified or added files to the repository.

Commits don't have to proceed in a linear order. You can create a new branch to experiment with code or work on certain features independently. Branches can develop independently, or they can be merged together.

If you work with Git locally, version control is automatic. Git tracks your commits, and you can use a new Xcode feature called the Version Editor to view and compare the changes to each file as the project develops.

CAUTION

When you make commits, you're updating multiple files at the same time. There's no automated way to revert a single file to an earlier state without also changing other files that were committed at the same time. However, you can use simple manual copy/paste to copy an old version of a file from the Version Editor into the main code editor and then create a new commit with the old contents of the file.

If you use a remote server, the process becomes more complex. To use Git remotely, collaborators need to supply a name, an e-mail address, and a public key for security. If you are managing a Git project, you can review and accept or decline commits supplied by other developers.

When you work with an online repo, you can clone a project—copy the current version from the server to your Mac—to work on it independently and then perform a push to merge your changes back into the source. The lead developer can then review the changes and accept or delete them. When you work collaboratively, Git and Xcode include author information with all commits, making it easy to see who is responsible for changes. You can also update a project to refresh the version you're editing with the most recent changes without creating a new copy.

NOTE

Git is a complex system with many features and options, but it's well documented. This chapter introduces Git in Xcode, but it isn't a complete Git primer on collaborative development with GitHub. For full documentation, see the free ProGit book available at `http://www.git-scm.com/book`, the official command summaries at `gitref.org`, and the GitHub help at `help.github.com`.

Using Git locally

You can use Git locally for simple project versioning. Simple versioning doesn't require a remote server, advanced Git skills, or command-line management, and it uses GUI features that are built into Xcode. This example demonstrates how to create a local repository and how to use the Version Editor to review changes to the files in a project. The edits in this sample project are trivial, but they're sufficient to illustrate how you can use the Version Editor to manage code as you work.

CAUTION

The Xcode implementation of Git leaves out many of the features and concepts that are used when working with the command line. If you've used Git from the command line in other contexts, you'll find that the Xcode implementation is simpler and less powerful, but still adequate for basic SCM.

Creating a project with Git support

Git support is optional and available for both OS X and iOS projects. Use the File ➪ New Project option in the main Xcode menu to create a new project (this example uses an OS X project called GitExample), and check the Source Control box, as shown in Figure 15.5. By default, My Mac appears in the adjacent menu to show that you're creating a local repository.

Figure 15.5

Create a project with Git support.

CROSS-REFERENCE
You can also create a repository on a server. For information about creating repositories on OS X Server and performing automated testing and integration with bots, see Chapter 18.

CAUTION
In Xcode 4, you could see a list of repositories in the Organizer. Apple removed this feature in Xcode 5 to make the Git experience "more project-centric." If you want to see a list of repositories, use a remote server with Git. You can also look in the Account Preferences pane, which now links repos with accounts.

Xcode creates the project in the usual way. If you open the project's folder on disk, you see the standard collection of files. However, if you click Source Control in the main menu, you see that Xcode has created a master branch for the project, as shown in Figure 15.6.

Figure 15.6

Here's a first look at the Source Control menu.

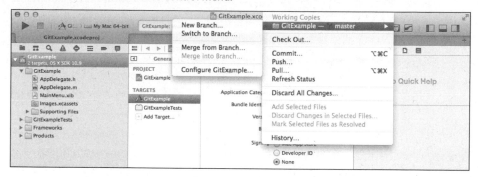

In outline, this is what the menu commands do:

- **Check out:** Copies the project from the repository so you can work on it.
- **Commit:** Copies the project to the repository, adding a note on its current status.
- **Push:** Copies the project to a remote repository. This option is available only after you set up a remote repository server for the project. The server can be a site like GitHub (github.com), or it can be a Git server on your local network.
- **Pull:** Copies the project from a remote repository.
- **Refresh status:** Compares the project with the local repository and marks files that have changed.
- **Discard all changes:** Reverts to the last committed version.
- **History:** Displays a list of commits, with associated notes.

The Branch sub-menu includes options for managing *branches*—independent versions of the project. It's standard practice to create a new branch before you make any significant changes and then *merge* the branch back into a main "production" branch when you're happy that the new code works. This keeps your main production branch safe, while making it possible to edit and test the development branch without breaking anything important.

TIP

If you decide to never use version control, you can turn it off with Xcode ⇨ Preferences ⇨ Source Control. Uncheck the Enable Source Control box. You can also change a few useful settings here.

Editing a project with Git support

Git support is transparent, so you can develop a project in the usual way while Git is active.

Try this example:

1. Add an extra Objective-C class to the project by right-clicking the <ProjectName> group in the Project navigator and selecting New File.

2. Create a new subclass of NSObject, and save it with the default MyClass name.

3. **Make a small, but obvious, change to the original `AppDelegate.m` file.**

   The example shown in Figure 15.7 has been extended with a single comment.

4. **Wait a few seconds.**

   Note the icons that appear next to certain files after you save them. The M stands for "modified" and indicates that a file has been changed since the last commit. The A stands for "added." These icons are added by the Git system and appear only when a project uses Git. Table 15.1 has a comprehensive list of the other icons displayed by Git.

Figure 15.7

When you modify a project with Git support, modified files are tagged automatically.

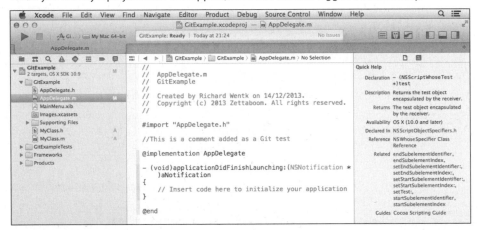

Table 15.1 Source Control Status Icons

Icon	Comments
M	Modified locally
U	Updated in repository
A	Added locally
D	Deleted locally
R	Replaced in repository
-	Mixed status (applies to folders)
?	Not under source control

CAUTION
The update tags can take a while to appear. They're not as speedy as the build error markers, which appear almost instantly as you type. Note that you don't have to save the files for Git to recognize your changes.

CAUTION
Git is a source control system, not a build management system, and it doesn't care if your project builds successfully. It tracks changes to the project source files only. You can make edits that break a build, and Git tracks them faithfully.

Committing changes

To create a new commit, select File ➪ Source Control ➪ Commit from the main Xcode menu. You see the dialog shown in Figure 15.8. It shows a list of modified or added files at the top left and a comparison window called the Version Editor—the new Xcode tool for exploring and comparing different versions of a file.

Figure 15.8

Create a commit. Xcode's new Version Editor displays and compares current and previous versions of a file.

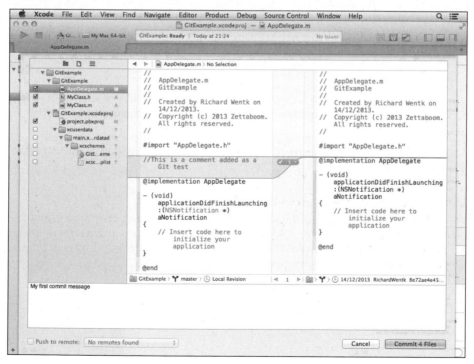

At the bottom of the window is a blank line for descriptive text about the commit. Note that *Xcode forces you to add a comment for each commit.* If you don't edit this line, you can't complete the commit.

CAUTION

If you don't have the main editor selected—which is likely, if you're looking at the Organizer—the source control menu options are grayed out.

In this example, the changes in each file are trivial, but in a working project, the highlighted areas are more extensive. Added files don't yet have changes, so the same version is shown in both views.

You have some control over when and how changes are added to the commit. You can do the following:

- **Omit any file:** Uncheck any modified file in the list at the left if you do not want to include it in the commit.
- **Omit any edit:** Edits appear as numbered check marks in the gutter between the two file versions. Click each mark to toggle it and include/exclude the change.
- **Cancel the commit:** Click Cancel at the lower right. Otherwise, click the Commit . . . Files button to save the changes.
- **Push the commit to a remote repository:** If you set up a remote repository, you can select it in the bottom-left corner and push the files to it.

TIP

You can use the icons above the file list to list the files in the project in three different ways—with groups, like the Project navigator, as files in the project directory and the project file, or as a flat list of files.

After a commit, the M and A icons disappear from the Project navigator until you make further changes.

Using the comparison view in the Version Editor

Version comparisons are one of the key features of the Git system. They're so useful that they're built into the main Xcode editor. Click the Version Editor button near the right of the toolbar to load the Version Editor and begin reviewing your changes. The editor displays a double comparison pane for any selected file, as shown in Figure 15.9.

Figure 15.9

Load the Version Editor to compare versions.

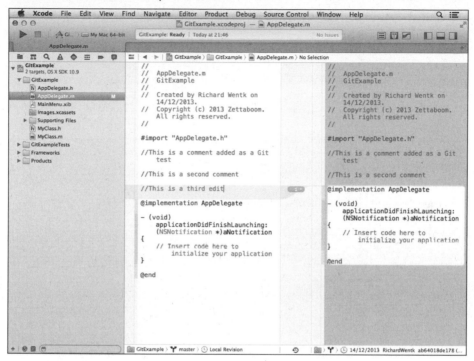

You can view the state of the file at any commit in either window. By default, the editor shows the most current version of the file in the leftmost pane and the last committed version in the pane to the right. You can change this default in the preferences.

There are various ways to view a commit. If you click the jump bar near the bottom of the window, you see a pop-up menu with a list of commits arranged in chronological order, as shown in Figure 15.10.

It's important to understand that the most recent edit is at the *top* of this list and the oldest initial commit is at the *bottom*.

The nomenclature for revisions isn't intuitive, so it's explained below:

- **Local revision:** The version has been edited, but not committed. Note that Xcode 5 no longer makes a distinction between saved and unsaved versions.
- **<Entries with time stamp, name and hash>:** These versions have been committed.

Figure 15.10

Select commits from the jump bar menu.

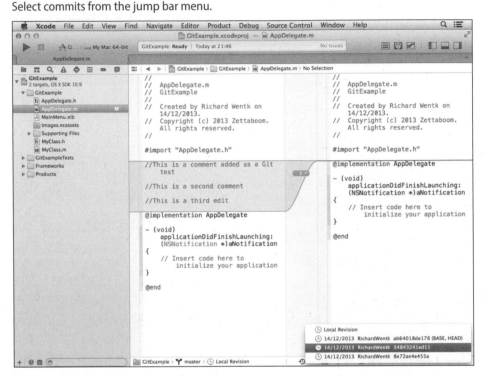

CAUTION

It's worth repeating that the most recent version is at the top of the list, marked (BASE, HEAD). You might think this tag describes the initial commit. In fact, it's critical to remember that the initial commit is *at the bottom of the list.*

Selecting any commit loads the corresponding state of the file into the viewer window. The left and right windows use an identical system, so you can view any commit in either. This system makes it possible to compare any version of a file with any other version. Any differences are clearly marked.

To view the commits for a different file, select it in the Project navigator in the usual way.

Using the timeline view

Instead of a list, you can display a timeline—similar to a Time Machine timeline—with a list of commits between the two views. Select the clock/curved arrow icon in the gutter between the two jump bars. You see the display shown in Figure 15.11. Each "button" in the timeline indicates a commit. Older versions appear at the top of the list, so the initial commit is always the first one from the top. Empty commit slots at the top of the list appear in a darker gray.

Figure 15.11

Select versions using the timeline feature.

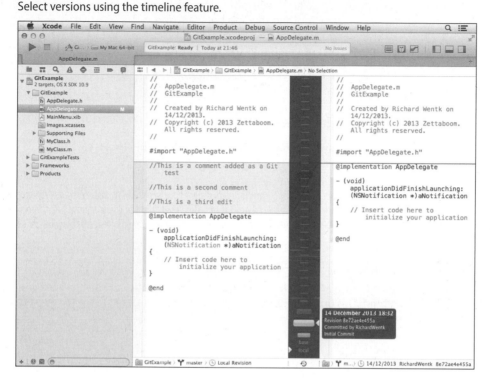

The buttons are animated and expand as you mouse over them, displaying a floating pop-over with a timing tag, hex hash, and comment. To display a commit in a window, click the corresponding triangle in the gutter. The buttons are there to distract you, so ignore them. (In fact, you can click either side of a button too. But it's simpler to ignore the buttons and work with the triangles.)

The triangle indicator for that window moves to the commit you selected, and the corresponding version of the file is loaded and displayed. The base version at the bottom of the list is the last commit. The local version is the last version after editing and is identical to the Local Revision in the jump bar menus.

CAUTION

Arguably, the timeline list is upside down. The initial commit is the top item, and the most recent edit appears at the bottom of the timeline. It's important to understand that the *timeline lists commits in the opposite order to the jump bar menu.*

Reverting to an earlier version

You can revert specific edits in a file, or you can revert the entire file to an earlier version. Make sure the jump bar view is showing, and then do the following:

1. Select the most recent version in the left pane.

2. Select the version to revert to in the right pane.

3. Find the edit.

4. Click its numbered icon in the central gutter.

5. Click Discard Change in the floating menu, shown in Figure 15.12.

CAUTION

Note that when you compare files, the change icons indicate differences between the two versions. If you make a sequence of changes in one location in a file and commit them, the Version Editor doesn't show the differences as a discrete list of commits. It only shows the differences between the two files you selected. All the changes are grouped together.

Discarding all changes

If you select Source Control ⇨ Discard All Changes, Xcode removes all the changes you made since the last commit. This option ignores the Version Editor. You can't use it to revert to any one version of a file.

Using the Blame view

The Version Editor includes two further views. You can select them by clicking the Version Editor icon and waiting until the three icons appear under it, as shown in Figure 15.13.

Figure 15.12

Reviewing changes, and using the Discard Changes option to revert them.

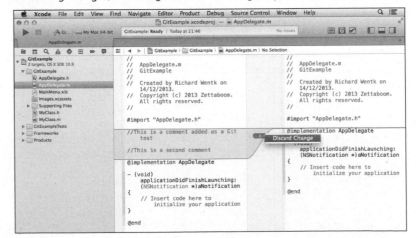

Figure 15.13

Use the Blame view to list changes to a single file, with the name of the author of each change.

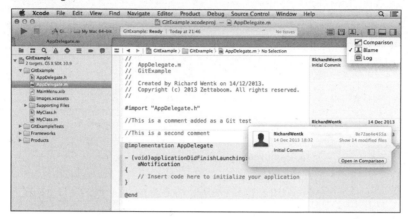

The Blame view, also shown in Figure 15.13, is primarily used for team development, but if you're working solo, you can use it to view a list of changes to a file. Each commit is listed in order at the right of the file in a view that includes time, date, and author information. Commits are linked to one or more lines of source at the left. If you select a commit with one of the small gray info buttons—mouse over the commit, and click the Open in Comparison button in the pop-over—the commit is loaded into the left window of the Version Editor, and the preceding commit is loaded into the right.

Using the Log view

The Log view, shown in Figure 15.14, is a blend of the code view and the commit list in the Organizer. The code editor appears at the left, and a simple list of commits appears at the right. You can load a commit into a Comparison view by selecting the "Show . . . modified files" text under each hash.

Branching a project

Most commits include multiple changes in multiple files. Although you can roll back files individually, this is really useful only for minor reversions. The simplest way to roll back an entire project is to create *branches* as you go.

NOTE

You can roll back an entire project from the command line using `git reset --hard <commit-id>`. This is a dangerous command . . .

A branch is a parallel development track. When you create a branch, Git copies the current project and creates an independent version. Editing one branch leaves other branches unchanged. When you select a branch, Xcode loads the files from that branch and displays them for editing.

Figure 15.14

Use the Log view.

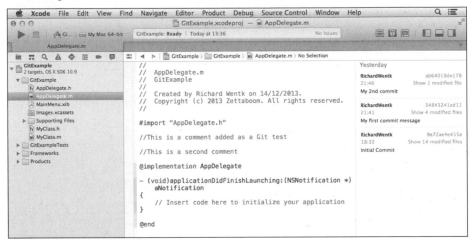

It's important to understand that you can edit only one branch at a time. When you select a different branch, Xcode loads *all* the files from that branch. Changing branches can literally switch the contents of every file in a project.

In a team context, branching is often used for independent development of unrelated features. Branching allows each team or individual to work with a fixed version of the code that surrounds the feature they're working on.

As a solo developer, you can use branching for version management. If you create a branch for each version instead of using the commit system to manage versions, you can restore every file in the project to an earlier state quickly and easily, by selecting its branch.

For a simple example, follow these steps:

1. **Add a few more lines of comments or code to the project App Delegate.**

2. **Select Source Control ⇨ <Project Name> Master ⇨ New Branch.**

3. **Type a branch name into the dialog, as shown in Figure 15.15.**

NOTE

The branch name cannot include spaces or special characters.

4. **Switch to the Version Editor, and click one of the branch selectors in the jump bar.**

You can see there are now two branches, as shown in Figure 15.16. If you make a new commit, it applies only to the currently selected branch. The code in the other branch remains unchanged.

Note that selecting a branch from the jump bar loads it into the Version Editor. But it doesn't load it into the main code editor. The code editor always shows the currently selected branch.

5. **To change that branch, select Source Control ⇨ <Project Name> <Branch Name> ⇨ Switch to Branch. Select a branch from the dialog, and click Switch.**

Figure 15.15

Create a new branch.

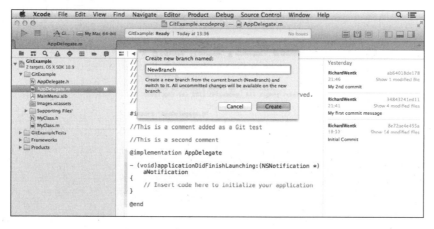

Figure 15.16

Check the commits for the currently selected branch.

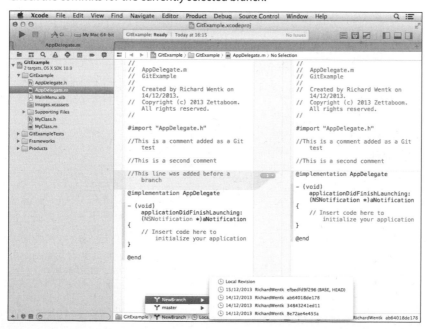

Merging branches

You can merge *from* the current branch or *into* the current branch. These options work as you expect. You usually want to merge files into a single master branch, so select Merge From if you have the current working branch selected, and select Merge Into if you have the master branch selected.

You can select and confirm individual changes, as shown in Figure 15.17. A preview of the merged code is shown at the right.

Every difference in every file is highlighted. The gutter area includes a switch icon. You can use the switch buttons at the bottom of the window to select the differences. The switches are on by default, but you can turn them off to exclude a change. You can also use the switches to resolve conflicts.

Note that you can't toggle the switches by clicking them directly in the gutter. You can only change their state by clicking the button bar at the bottom of the window.

Figure 15.17

Use switches to enable merging for individual changes.

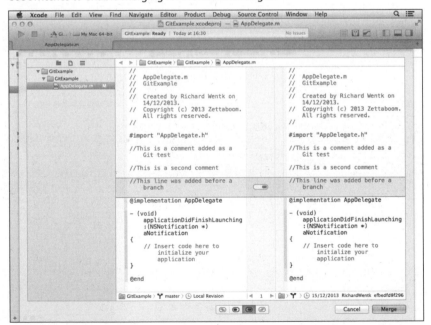

 CAUTION

Branching and merging are not completely robust in the current version of Xcode. If you attempt an operation and nothing happens for a few minutes, quit and restart Xcode. You may need to do this more than once.

Using Xcode with GitHub

Source control is most useful when set up to work with an external repository server. Local source control is ideal for solo developers. Server-based source control is ideal for collaborative development. It also gives you the added security of off-site backups. If your laptop melts because your house burns down, your code should still be available on the remote server.

Although it's possible to create a custom remote server for use with Git, the GitHub website at `github.com`, shown in Figure 15.18, has become a popular choice for development teams and solo developers who use Git. In theory, the differences between local and remote development should be minor, because Git handles both situations in a similar way. In practice, remote development requires significant extra effort when creating a new project.

Figure 15.18

Here's your first look at github.com.

GitHub is optional. If you're working solo, you can develop locally without using GitHub at all. But it's a simple and accessible solution for team development. GitHub includes these features:

- **Free public collaborative development:** By default, GitHub projects are open and public, so anyone can download your code and add his own commits. This is a good thing for open-source projects, but unhelpful for proprietary development.

- **Monthly payment plans for private team development:** Privacy on GitHub, which includes the ability to hide your projects from the public and open them only to select developers, costs from $7 to $200, depending on the number of repositories and developers. Accounts have unlimited disk space, although for practical reasons, it's a good idea to keep less than 1GB of files in each repository.

- **Easy online access:** You can exchange commits and updates wherever there's an Internet connection. You also can work offline and upload changes when you reconnect.

- **Easy downloads:** Your projects can be packaged automatically into a single archive to make it easy for third parties to download them.

- **Project support tools:** These include a Wiki server for documentation, a bug tracker for bug reporting, and the ability to link to a separate project web page.

- **"Free" backups:** Code is stored securely on commercial servers, with a robust backup policy.

These are the chief practical differences between local and GitHub development:

- **Security:** You must set up a username and password. Optionally, you can also create an SSH (Secure Shell) key for command-line access.

- **Updates:** You should update (download) a file or a complete project before you change it. This guarantees that your version of the project includes the latest commits from other developers.

- **Push commands:** You must use the command line to update local commits to the GitHub server.

- **Location:** Instead of a disk location, the project is referenced using a remote server URL.

TIP

Technology employers increasingly treat GitHub accounts as a living CV. You can use GitHub to show off your work ethic and demonstrate your coding skills. Potentially, you can also use it to highlight your project management skills.

Creating a GitHub account

Creating a new free GitHub account is easy. GitHub asks for a username, an e-mail address, and a password. You don't need to give any other details.

On GitHub, your username, e-mail address, and password are essential parts of the online access process. They do more than log you in to the site, so you need them later when you create a user identity for Git on your Mac.

Optionally, you can add public contact information and other personal information to your account, but these details aren't necessary for basic repo management.

Using the GitHub Mac app

Although you can use GitHub from the command line, the free GitHub Mac app, shown in Figure 15.19, simplifies basic code sharing and repository management, and fills in some of the features missing from Xcode. The app is very easy to use and should be considered an essential timesaver if you use GitHub with Xcode.

Figure 15.19

Here's a first view of the GitHub Mac app.

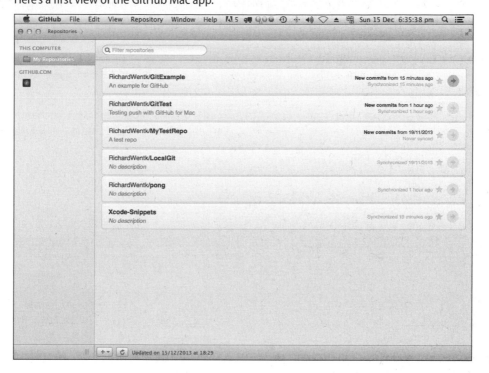

If you access the site with a Mac, GitHub suggests you download it. To set it up, enter your username and password. You can now view files in the app, create commits and branches, and view a history.

In practice, you'll rarely want to edit in the app, because you can edit, build, and test in Xcode. The app is most useful for creating and managing repositories on GitHub and synchronizing them with Xcode.

Understanding HTTPS and SSH access

In the past, Git communicated with GitHub via SSH. SSH access is still available, but it's necessary only if you want to access GitHub using the command line in Terminal.

For most applications, secure web access (https) is adequately secure and much easier to work with, especially if you use the Mac app. To set up the Mac app for secure https access, enter your GitHub username and password.

If you decide you need SSH, you need to generate a binary key on your Mac and upload it to GitHub. For details, see the Set Up Git instructions in the Bootcamp area of the Help section.

Cloning a local Git repository to GitHub

To clone a repository, launch the Mac app and select File ➪ Add Local Repository. Navigate to the project folder that you want to copy to GitHub, select it, and click Add. The Mac app automatically creates a new repository on GitHub and uploads the project files.

If your app is already under local Git control, all your commits and branches appear in the new online repository. If your app was under manual control, the upload creates a new initial commit that you can use as a starting point for further edits.

As you make further commits and branches in Xcode, the Mac app monitors the changes, as shown in Figure 15.20. To upload the changes, click the Push to GitHub button in the top-right corner.

Figure 15.20

Get ready to synchronize an Xcode project with GitHub.

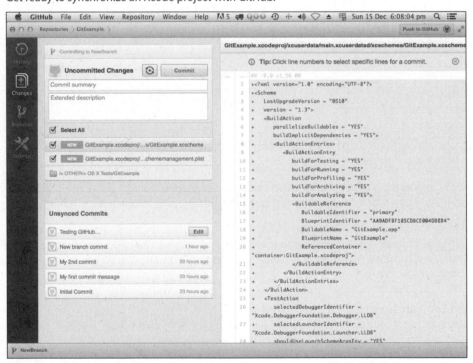

After you push to GitHub, the online repository is added automatically to your project as a remote. Select SourceControl ➪ <ProjectName><BranchName> ➪ Configure <ProjectName> ➪ Remotes, as shown in Figure 15.21.

Figure 15.21

Between them, Xcode and the Mac app set up a remote repository for you.

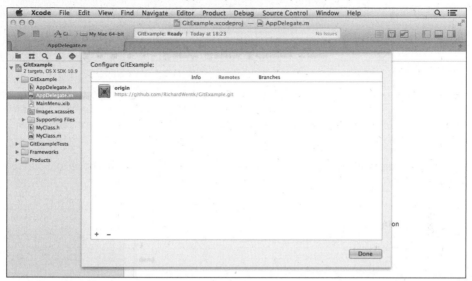

When you push a commit, Xcode automatically logs you in to GitHub—you need to enter your username and password the first time you do this—and pushes the commit to the GitHub servers.

CAUTION

Source control can get confused if you try to include dependent files in a build. If your project uses a collection of files in a framework, it's better to keep the framework and your project in separate repositories.

Cloning a repository to your Mac

To clone an existing repository to your Mac, open the repository page on GitHub and click the Clone in Desktop button near the lower right. This launches the Mac app automatically, copies the files to a folder you nominate, and adds the repository to the list in the app. You can now work on the files in Xcode in the usual way.

Using Git from the command line

Git includes a selection of extra features that can be accessed only from the command line. You don't need them for basic source control, especially if you also use GitHub. You may need them for more advanced projects or for projects that use a different remote server. A full list of Git commands is outside the scope of this book. man pages are available at `www.kernel.org/pub/software/scm/git/docs/git.html`. There are also plenty of command-line tutorials available online.

Summary

Understanding source control systems like Git has become a basic skill for developers. If you only work solo, manual source control may be all you need. But if you work with others, you need to master Git and GitHub and know how to integrate them with Xcode. Eventually, you may want to work other editors and development systems on other platforms, and you'll find that Git and GitHub remain constant while everything else changes.

However, it's a good idea not to rely too much on any one product or solution. The developer community has worked through a couple of other code management solutions over the last decade or so. Those other solutions are rarely used now, and it's possible a competitor to Git and GitHub will have a similar effect by the end of the decade.

If you understand the principles of source control, you'll find it easy to move to a different system if you ever need to.

Creating Fast and Reliable Code

Getting Started with Code Analysis and Debugging

The Xcode toolchain includes a powerful suite of code analysis, code correction, and debugging tools. Some run outside the main Xcode editor and are introduced in the following chapters. This chapter discusses features that are built into Xcode itself: the code analyzer, tips and issues, the debugging area, and a selection of other options in the Project navigator that are dedicated to debugging.

With these features, you can perform the following tasks:

- Check your code for issues as you type
- View tips that can help you correct issues
- Analyze code to reveal more complex issues
- Log messages to a window called the *console* while your application is running—typically to provide live diagnostic information
- View the console output from previous runs
- Pause execution at any point in the code with one or more *breakpoints*
- Add *conditional breakpoints* that pause the code when a specified condition is true
- Step through the code line by line or method by method
- View object properties and list their contents at a breakpoint
- Monitor the state of active threads
- Trigger external events at breakpoints, including sounds or scripts

The Xcode debugging tool is a windowed frontend to an open-source command-line debugger called LLDB. LLDB adds extra low-level options such as direct hex dumps of memory, object listings, in-line compilation and code modification, and hundreds of other features. You can access these features by typing commands into the Console window or by running the debugger manually in Terminal.

LLDB is a huge, complex tool, and these advanced features are optional. You can be productive and efficient without them, but it's useful to know that they're available.

NOTE

LLDB and the Debugger support very advanced options, such as remote debugging, that are outside the scope of this book. The definitive guide to the debugger's features is at `http://lldb.llvm.org/`.

CAUTION

Previous versions of Xcode used an alternative debugger called GDB (Gnu Debugger.) GDB is no longer included in Xcode 5. From the Xcode GUI, LLDB and GDB are very similar. But if you're working at the command line, the command sets are significantly different.

Checking and Analyzing Code

It's more productive to get code right as you type than it is to fix it later. To help you achieve this, Xcode 5 checks code and reports issues as you edit.

Checking code as you enter it

This feature is enabled automatically. It begins working as soon as you start typing. Questionable code is underlined or marked with a tiny arrow, and warning or error icons appear in the gutter to the left of the code. If you open the Issue navigator, you can see longer descriptions of each issue, as shown in Figure 16.1.

Figure 16.1

Xcode has flagged two errors in this line of code—a missing delimiter and a misspelled class name.

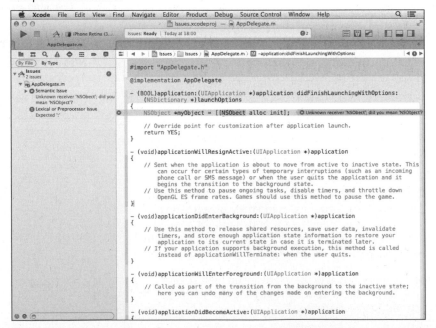

NOTE

The issues checker is identical to the code parser used during a build. It flags the same errors and generates the same error messages, but it runs in the background and parses your code as you edit. In practice, code completion means you rarely make spelling mistakes in class names, but you can make them in method names.

The issues checker is reasonably intelligent, but it can be slow. A lag of a few seconds isn't unusual. It doesn't understand partial edits, so it reports errors that exist only because you haven't finished typing a complete line of code. It may not find errors in literals—for example, in listings of keys and values—because it doesn't know what they mean.

The faster your Mac is, the more you can rely on this feature. It's less useful on slower hardware. Because of the lag, issues can continue to be flagged after you've fixed them. In extreme cases, you can waste time trying to fix code that's correct, as the parser plays catch-up with your most recent edit. Xcode can also miss errors because of lag.

This is a powerful feature, but you should treat it with care. Don't assume it's infallible—it isn't.

CAUTION

Xcode 5 displays a warning whenever you call a method before it's defined. This is a feature of Objective-C—the compiler does a single pass and always flags unresolved method references, even if they're resolved later. Unfortunately, this makes it difficult to tell the difference between bad code that attempts to call a nonexistent method and calls to valid methods that are defined lower in the implementation. You can avoid these messages by adding valid method names to a category declaration at the start of an implementation, but this isn't often done.

Using Fix-It code tips

If you click an issue flag in the gutter, Xcode may suggest a possible fix, as shown in Figure 16.2. To accept the fix, double-click the blue fix-it suggestion. The Fix-It feature is good at catching obvious errors, but it isn't a full expert system and lacks awareness of certain common code idioms.

Experienced developers find it easy to tell the difference between helpful and misleading fix-it suggestions. Newcomers should be aware that this feature isn't a substitute for writing good code and that some of its suggestions may not fix code that isn't working. It's ideal for fixing various minor issues, but it isn't a comprehensive teaching or training tool.

NOTE

If Xcode can't suggest a Fix-It tip, it displays a short issue summary instead. Fix-It tips are available only for a sub-set of all possible issues. Don't be surprised if Xcode doesn't offer one.

Figure 16.2

Use the Fix-It feature for obvious errors in code.

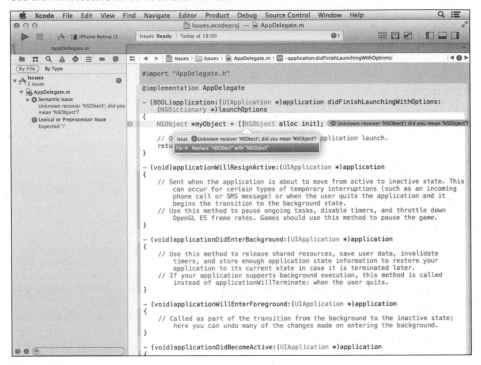

Using the Static Code Analyzer

Xcode 5 includes a Static Code Analyzer designed to flag deeper issues, such as errors in code logic and memory management. It's particularly useful for the latter, and it's very good at finding and highlighting code that's likely to leak.

To analyze your code, select Product ➪ Analyze in the main Xcode menu. Xcode builds the project and adds an extra analysis pass. Issues are reported in the code and in the Issues navigator with blue highlights, as shown in Figure 16.3. The highlighting is sophisticated enough to display execution logic and variable dependency chains.

NOTE

The Analyzer displays likely issues. It doesn't suggest fixes for them—but the issue descriptions are often detailed enough to hint at what needs to be fixed.

Figure 16.3

Issues appear with blue highlights.

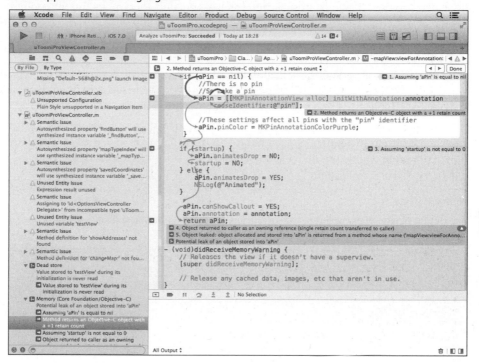

Getting Started with Debugging

The Issues navigator and the Static Analyzer are good for finding basic syntactical errors and simple logical errors. But bugs are often more complex, and some don't appear until you run the code. The Xcode 5 debugger includes a selection of tools for checking code *as it runs*.

The debugger appears in its own area, which is hidden by default. To display it, click the middle icon of the three near the top left of the Xcode window. You also can select View ➪ Show Debug Area in the main Xcode menu. The debug area appears at the bottom of the screen, under the code editor. There are three active panes:

- **A mini-toolbar:** The buttons are used with breakpoints. You can use them to single-step or restart execution after a pause.

- **A hierarchical object viewer called the *Variables View,* in the pane at the left:** The viewer displays an object as a tree that can be expanded to show its contents. Like the toolbar, this pane is used when working with breakpoints to examine objects and check their contents.

- **The *console window*, in a pane at the right:** The console displays messages from the application and the OS.

You can choose to show either or both of these panes with the two buttons in the bottom-right corner under the console. Or you can resize the entire area by clicking and dragging the line under the toolbar—the area is usually too small, by default—and move the split point between the left and right panes by clicking and dragging it.

TIP
You can view the debugger in a separate floating window by opening a new tab, displaying and resizing the debug area until it fills the editor window, and tearing it off. It's useful to have code visible at the same time as you use the debugger. But the split-pane design can feel awkward, especially on a smaller monitor.

Optionally, you can display the navigator area at the left. Figure 16.4 shows a typical combined view of the display at a breakpoint, with the Debug navigator, the code editor showing the location of the breakpoint, and the two debug area panes at the bottom of the screen.

Figure 16.4

The Debug navigator at the left of the debug area is optional. You can hide it to maximize the code view.

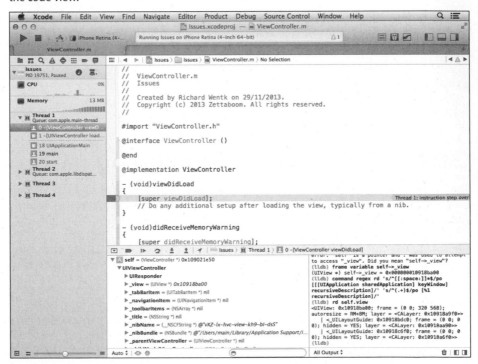

In Xcode 5, the Debug navigator includes a useful summary of app status, including threading details, processor cycles, and memory usage. If your app has a very obvious memory leak, you can often see there's a problem here, without having to load the Instruments developer tool described in Chapter 17.

TIP

If you need to run an application full-screen, you can place a smaller version of the debugger window in front of it by selecting Product ⇨ Window Behavior ⇨ Xcode in Front. When Xcode hits a breakpoint, the window expands to show a larger version of the debugger window.

Using the Console

The console is a text output terminal, equivalent to UNIX's `stdout` (the standard output file), which is typically routed to a display rather than written to disk. It displays four kinds of messages:

- **System generated messages:** Console messages include time stamps and other supporting information that is generated automatically.
- **Custom messages, created with `NSLog` or `printf` statements in your code:** Use custom messages to check program flow, dump information about object properties, and monitor variable values.
- **System generated warnings:** These are rare. A very small number of Cocoa classes generate text to report errors or warnings. Beta OS versions are more likely to generate warnings than production versions.
- **Crash dumps:** These are also known as backtraces and stack dumps, and they list the messages and events that led to the crash.

You can choose some or all of these messages with the output selection menu at the top left of the console. These are your options:

- **All Output:** Displays all messages
- **Debugger Output:** Displays system messages, crash reports, and error messages
- **Target Output:** Displays messages from your application

You also can use the trash icon to clear the console of all output.

Creating custom messages

You can write a message to the console by including a call to `printf` anywhere in your code. For example,

```
printf("This is a message");
```

writes `This is a message` to the console. All the standard `printf` formatting features are supported.

If you are writing Objective-C rather than C or C++, the `NSLog` function is more comprehensive. It includes additional formatting and output options that aren't available in `printf`, at the cost of slightly clumsier syntax. For example, to write a text string, you must prefix it with Objective-C's @ "objectification" feature:

```
NSLog(@"This is a message");
```

NSLog supports the standard `printf` formatting features and adds a new one—the `%@` option, which displays information about an object. Table 16.1 summarizes the most useful options.

Table 16.1 Useful NSLog Format Options

Option	Used for
%i or %d	signed int
%u	unsigned int
%ld	signed long
%lu	unsigned long
%lld or %llu	As above for long long integers
%f	float/double
%x or %X	int as hexadecimal
%p	memory address (similar to %x, with a standard 0x prefix)
%zu	size_t
%@	object
\r	new line

For example, to display the value of an integer use:

```
NSLog(@"Int value is: %i", someInt);
```

To dump information about an object, use:

```
NSLog(@"%@", someObject);
```

Note that the first @ prefixes the format and output string; the second @ selects the format. Be careful to remember the following:

- NSLog has a capital L for Log.
- It's followed by a round bracket.
- The bracket is followed by @.
- The @ is followed by a string, in quotes.

This object logging feature has special properties. It runs a method called `description` on the object being logged. Different objects implement `description` in different ways. For example, data collection objects such as `NSArray` and `NSDictionary` dump their contents as text. For other objects, `description` defaults to the object's class name and memory address.

NOTE

`description` isn't always listed in class reference documentation. The easiest way to discover what this method does is by experimenting.

TIP

Every message in the console appears with a date stamp and time stamp. The time is specified to the nearest millisecond. You can sometimes use this information to check performance. Note that the output from debugger commands doesn't include the time stamp. It only appears when your app generates a message.

Using custom messages

You can add custom messages anywhere in your code. Figure 16.5 shows a log message added to the `application didFinishLaunchingWithOptions:` method in the app delegate of a typical iOS project. This method runs after when the application loads. The console appears automatically, if it is not already visible, and logs the message, as shown in the figure.

Figure 16.5

Add an `NSLog` message to send output to the console.

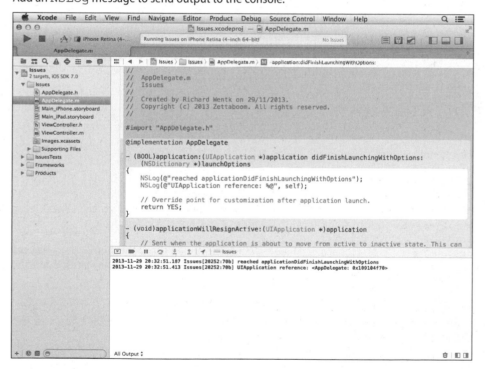

You can use this technique to log events—for example, by writing a message to confirm when a method is called. You also can use messages to list variables and values, display loop counts, and so on.

Unlike breakpoints, messages don't interrupt execution. They're usually faster and more informative than breakpoints when you want to check a sequence of events, but they don't give you the option of exploring memory or checking conditional execution.

CAUTION

Be careful about using messages in loops. There's nothing to stop you from writing a message on every repeat of a loop, but this may generate hundreds or thousands of messages. It's good practice to use messages more selectively. Don't forget that you can surround log messages with custom code to create conditional logging. For example, you might log only every tenth or hundredth iteration of a loop.

CAUTION

NSLog is slow, and you certainly don't want to include it in production code. You can comment out all NSLog statements by hand, but it's easier to include a single line with #define NSLog in the project's .pch file. This redefines NSLog to a null feature and eliminates it from the project. You can comment out this line to re-enable logging if you need to continue debugging.

Understanding crashes

When an application crashes, the console appears automatically and displays a series of diagnostic messages that can help you discover the cause of the crash.

Your projects will crash accidentally often enough. But as an exercise that illustrates how Xcode handles crash event, you can create a crash deliberately. Add the following line to the `application didFinishLaunchingWithOptions:` method of the app delegate of an iOS project, such as the IB project from Chapter 7:

```
int *x = NULL;
*x = 42;
```

This tries to write to a section of memory that is out of bounds.

Figure 16.6 shows the result. The offending line is highlighted, with some basic information about the crash. You can see immediately that the crash occurred within the `application didFinishLaunchingWithOptions:` method of the `AppDelegate` object. Sometimes, this gives you enough information to find the file with the bug and fix it.

In earlier versions of Xcode, a crash automatically opened the Debug navigator. This does not happen in Xcode 5. To find out more about a crash, click the Debug navigator icon. Figure 16.7 shows the result.

The navigator shows a basic *backtrace,* or *stack dump*—a list of methods and functions called, in reverse order. If the cause of the crash isn't obvious, the backtrace can give you some clues about events that could have contributed to the crash.

CAUTION

Many methods and functions in the backtrace are internal to Cocoa Touch or Cocoa. Often, but not always, internal methods and objects begin with an underscore. You won't find them in the documentation. They're unlikely to be responsible for a crash.

TIP

LLDB is somewhat better at basic stack dumps than GDB. OS X apps now produce a backtrace in the Debug navigator. However, the only way to see a detailed backtrace on either iOS or OS X is with a text command, as described later in this chapter.

Figure 16.6

A crash event is displayed.

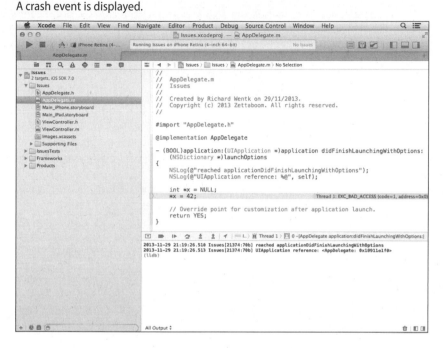

Figure 16.7

Look at an OS X's app backtrace in the Debug navigator.

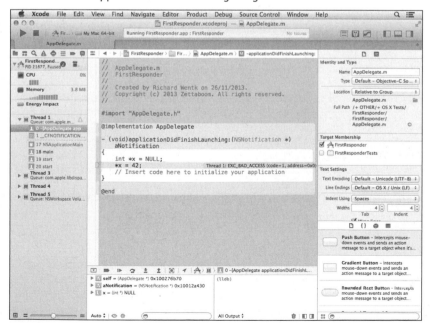

Viewing multiple logs

You can use the Log navigator shown in Figure 16.8 to compare the console output from different runs. Each build and debug run adds a new entry to the list at the left. Clicking a Build entry displays build information, including errors and warnings. Clicking a Debug entry displays the console output from that run.

Figure 16.8

View a list of logs in the Log navigator: Debug logs display console output; Build logs display build results.

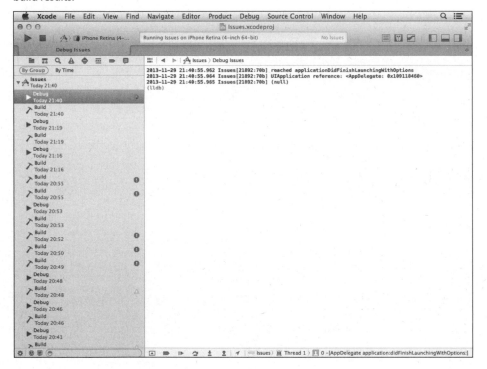

For example, the log message added earlier has been modified, and the most recent Debug entry shows the modified text. Although it's not illustrated in the figure, clicking the earlier Debug entry shows the original console output from the example earlier in this chapter.

Sessions aren't saved with the project, and the list of entries and their contents is cleared when you close a project.

TIP

You can drag-select the contents of the Console and use the right-click context menu to copy them. Unfortunately, you can no longer use the main Xcode File ⇨ Save As . . . menu option to write the entire log to a text file.

Working with Breakpoints

A *breakpoint* is a deliberate pause in your code. When Xcode encounters a breakpoint, it stops and drops into a special breakpoint mode. You can use this mode to view memory, list objects and their contents, and step through the code line by line.

Breakpoint debugging is very powerful, but relying on it can slow you down. For maximum productivity, use breakpoint debugging selectively, and don't assume that it's a reliable solution for every possible problem. For example, if you don't manage memory correctly in an iOS app, memory errors can happen at almost any point in your code. Single-step debugging can show you that an object or property has incorrect or null contents, but it won't show you which line of code released it prematurely.

Working with simple breakpoints

To explore breakpoints, create a very simple application as a test bed. Use File ⇨ New in Xcode to create a new iOS or OS X Cocoa Application and save it as BreakpointTest. Add a simple counter loop to the end of the `applicationdidFinishLaunchingWithOptions:` method in the App Delegate:

```
for (int i = 0; i< 10; i++) {
        NSLog(@"Count: %i", i);
}
```

The code counts from 0 to 9 and logs each increment to the console. Open and resize the console window, and then build and run the application. The result should look like Figure 16.9.

Figure 16.9

Log a very simple counter to the console.

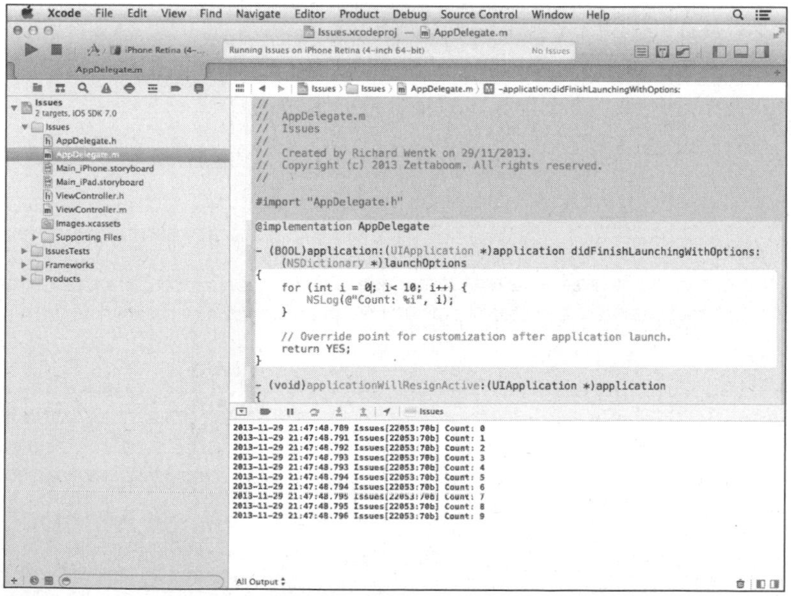

When you run the code, the count completes almost instantly. With a breakpoint, it's possible to step through the loop manually and check what happens at each repeat.

Inserting a breakpoint

To insert a breakpoint, click in the gutter area to the left of the `for . . .` line, as shown in Figure 16.10. An arrow indicator appears in the gutter. This tells you that Xcode is running in debug mode and that breakpoints are active.

Figure 16.10

Insert a breakpoint.

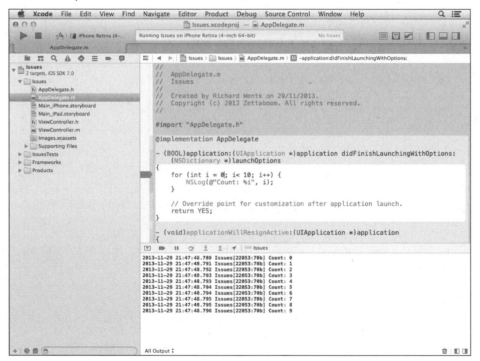

CAUTION

Be careful not to click in the shaded area to the right of the gutter. The shaded area controls the code folding feature described in Chapter 10. It hides the code instead of adding a breakpoint, which isn't what you want here.

Build and run the application again. This time, the run pauses automatically at the breakpoint, as shown in Figure 16.11. The breakpoint is highlighted in the code editor, the Debug navigator appears at the left, and the Variables View appears at the bottom of the screen. You can now use the Variables View, described in more detail later, to examine objects, or you can continue to step through the code by hand.

Figure 16.11

Examine the state of the application at a breakpoint.

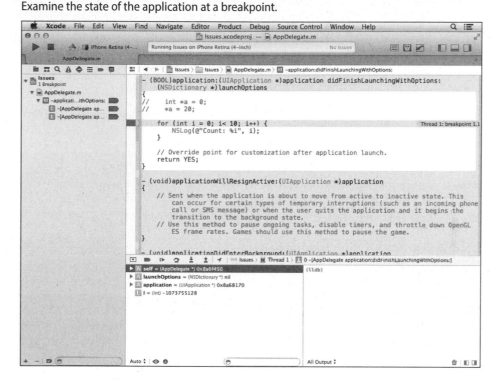

Continuing after a breakpoint

When Xcode pauses at a breakpoint, you can use the toolbar to control how execution continues. The buttons have the following functions:

- **Show/Hide Debug area:** Click this to show or hide the debugging area at the bottom of the screen. This option is equivalent to the Show button in the toolbar at the top right of Xcode.

- **Toggle Breakpoints:** Click this to enable or disable all breakpoints from a single location. Effectively, it turns debugging on and off.

- **Continue:** Click this to run the application from the point at which it paused. It continues to run until it's terminated or it encounters a breakpoint.

- **Step Over:** This executes the current line and stops at the next. This is equivalent to the single-step option in other debuggers.

- **Step Into:** This steps into a method or function. By default, Xcode runs a method or function without stepping into it; you see the result, but you can't step through each line of the code. Use this option when you want to examine what happens inside the method or function.

- **Step Out:** This steps out of the current method or function—in other words, it runs to the end or returns—and then it steps in the calling function or method. If there is no calling function or method, this option steps out to an assembly listing of the OS internals.
- **Simulate Location:** This simulates a location for MapKit and other code that uses GPS in a real device.
- **Select a Stack Frame:** Use this option to select the thread and stack frame. This duplicates the information available in the Breakpoint navigator.

In this example, use the Step Over button to continue the count manually. You see the code cycling between the first line of the for... loop and the second line. The value of the i loop counter increases with each repeat.

When i is 9 on the last repeat, the final Step Over takes you to the end of the method. If you keep stepping over, you eventually see an assembly listing of the method dispatch code in the Objective-C runtime. This is iOS internal code. Although you can continue stepping through it statement by statement, this isn't usually a useful thing to do.

Enabling and disabling breakpoints

You can disable an individual breakpoint by clicking its gutter arrow, which becomes translucent. A disabled breakpoint remains in place but is ignored by Xcode. It keeps its settings, which are described later.

You can also disable all breakpoints by clicking the main Debug arrow at the top left of the debug area. This turns off debug mode globally. As before, all breakpoints remain in memory, and they are saved as part of the project. But when Debug Mode is disabled globally, Xcode ignores them.

TIP

You can click any breakpoint and drag it to move it.

Using the Variables View

Figure 16.12 shows the Variables View expanded to full screen size. The view shows a list of objects in the application, with disclosure triangles next to each. Clicking a triangle reveals an object's contents, including named properties. Where relevant, properties may have associated memory addresses or literal values. The current object—the one in which the breakpoint was triggered—is labeled self.

Standard system objects such as the app delegate, windows, and views have very complex hierarchies. In the figure, you can see that the app delegate's window object includes a long list of properties. Many of the items in this list are objects in their own right and have further subproperties that you can explore.

Figure 16.12

Explore the contents of an object with the Variables View.

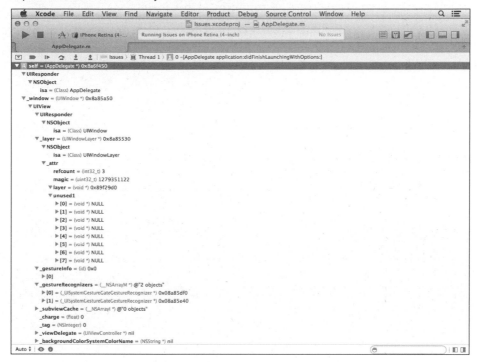

Because the view is unfiltered, it can be difficult to find useful details. As a general rule, you can ignore internal properties and objects unless you have a good reason to check them. In this example, all the properties of `window` are irrelevant. But in a more complex project, you might want to check the `delegate`, `initialFirstResponder`, or `frame` properties to see if `window` is being initialized correctly.

TIP

If you hover over an object, Xcode 5 displays a pop-up summary view with basic information and a disclosure triangle you can click to drill down through the object's contents. You can also click an eye icon at the right of the pop-up to display a value and name, and an information icon to print a description in the debug window. It's a good idea to practice with this feature because it can be easy to miss.

NOTE

System object instance variables are typically prefixed with an underscore character. They may not be listed in the documentation. Examining them can give you useful insights into how system objects are organized and how they work with each other.

If you scroll down through the list, you can see the `i = (int)` entry at the bottom of the window. This is a placeholder for the `i` loop counter. It hasn't yet been initialized. There may be any number after `int`, depending on the existing memory contents.

Use the Step Over button to step through the loop. You see the value is initialized to 0 and incremented on each repeat. Figure 16.13 shows how the value is updated in the Variables View before the log message prints it to the Console.

Figure 16.13

A typical combined debugging session combines information from the Variables View with messages on the console.

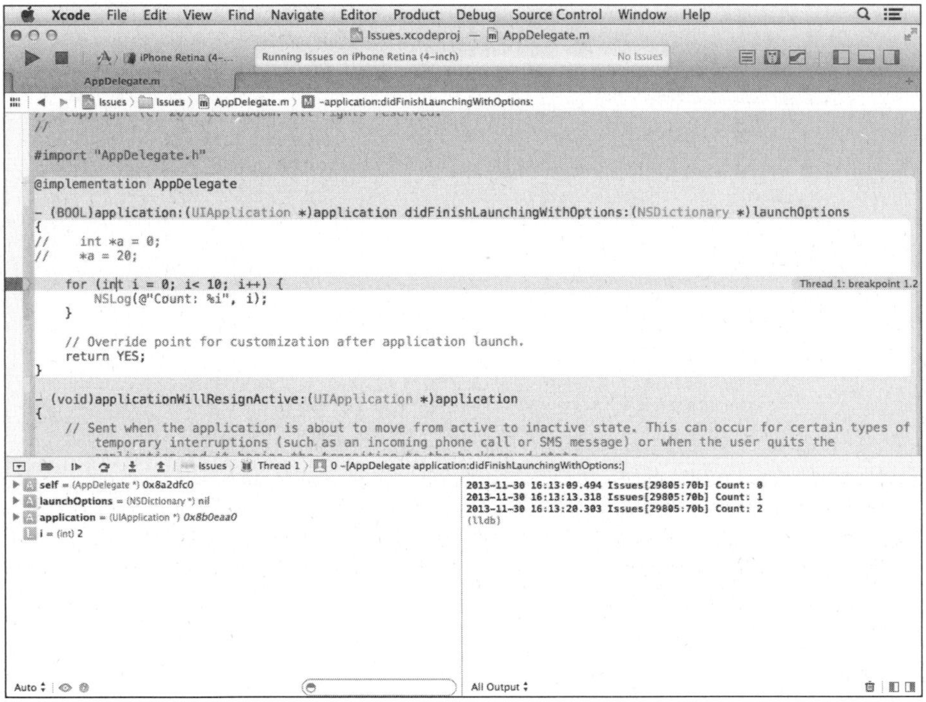

Working with values

The Variables View isn't just a passive display. Right-click a variable to show the menu illustrated in Figure 16.14. You can use the options here to enable and disable data formatting and type information and to edit values by hand. For example, select the Edit Value option as shown in the figure, and type **0** into the box that appears next to the `i` variable. This resets the counter without restarting the application. You can now repeat the count from the beginning.

Figure 16.14

Use the right-click menu to edit a value "live" after a breakpoint.

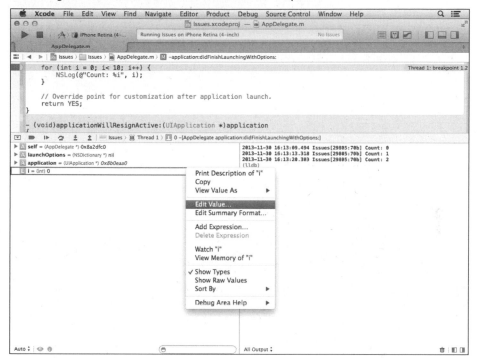

Using expressions

You can add your own items to the Variables View using *expressions.* An expression is an extra customized listing of an object, property, or variable. You can use expressions to extract properties and values from objects, so you don't have to drill down the hierarchy to find them. Expressions can contain standard C, C++, and Objective-C code, but they don't require the semicolon terminator. Expressions must be prefixed with a cast to define the type.

Figure 16.15 shows a sample expression. Right-click anywhere in the Variables View, select Add Expression, enter the following string, and click Save.

```
(NSString *) [self description]
```

You see a new entry in the view, which shows the result of running the `description` method on the object currently in scope in the debugger window.

Expressions can be challenging but powerful. The syntax required to display a certain value or property can become complex, and you often need to rely on trial and error before you find the correct answer. But if you can master expressions, you can make your debugging sessions significantly more productive. You can review the most important properties and variables at a glance, without having to open other objects to reveal them.

Figure 16.15

Create a custom expression to display a value of interest.

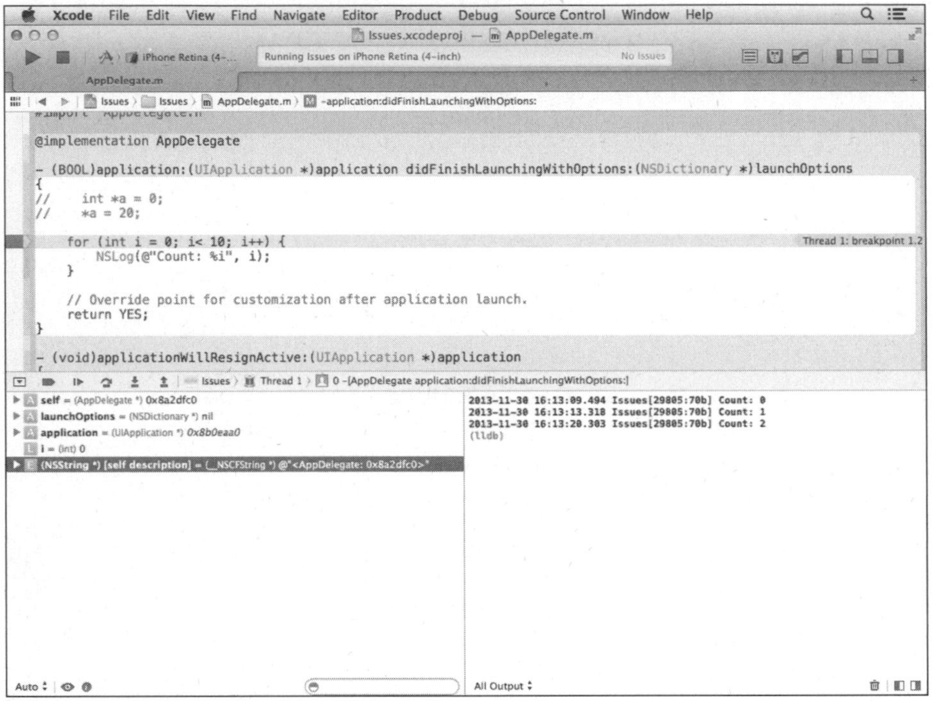

Using data formatters

Every item that appears in the Variables View is formatted, and the formatting information is set by a *data formatter*. All the standard data types have predefined formatters. In practice, these define extra details that may be unnecessary. Uncheck the Enable Data Formatters option in the right-click contextual menu to hide these details, leaving a shorter summary of the key information.

You can also customize the formatting for certain data types. Use the Edit Summary Format option to display a dialog with an editable field that defines the formatting. Formatters are similar to expressions, but the syntax is more complex and more general. A formatter is enclosed between curly brackets and usually includes a type cast. It may also include one or more macro placeholders to represent input data and a format reference that selects one of four display options. Table 16.2 summarizes the key options.

Table 16.2 Variable View Reference Options and Macros

Option	Used for
n	Shows the variable name
v	Value
t	Type
s	Summary
%apath.to.avalue%	Dot syntax key path for apath.to.avalue
$VAR	Variable value
$ID	Variable identifier
$PARENT	Structure or object containing the variable

For example, this line of code runs the standard Objective-C `sel_getName` function on the selected variable and outputs the description as a summary string:

```
{(char *) sel_getName($VAR)}:s
```

Data formatters can create some very sophisticated effects. You have almost total freedom to select and combine data from any object in your application and to display it as you choose. However, the programming cost can be substantial. Custom data formatters are best reserved for more complex projects where Xcode's other features can't display data in a useful way.

TIP

You can define your own custom data formatters and import them into Xcode. The process is moderately complex, but you need to do it only once. You can then reuse the formatters in any project. For details, see the Viewing Variables and Memory section of Xcode Debugging Guide in the documentation.

Adding watchpoints

A watchpoint is loosely related to a breakpoint, but it's triggered when a variable is modified. Use the Watch Address of . . . option in the right-click contextual menu to create a watchpoint, as shown in Figure 16.16. There's no way to add a watchpoint using the code editor.

When the watchpoint is triggered, Xcode logs a message to the console and highlights the line of code that modified the variable in the code editor. Messages list the values of the variable before and after the watchpoint was triggered.

CAUTION

There's no way to delete a watchpoint manually. A watchpoint is deleted automatically when execution moves beyond the scope of the watched variable. This is strange behavior and not entirely helpful; for better or worse, watchpoints are only loosely related to breakpoints. Internally, they modify the stack. This means that system calls are likely to crash if you set a watchpoint for a local stacked variable, because this operation modifies the stack.

Figure 16.16

Create and use a watchpoint.

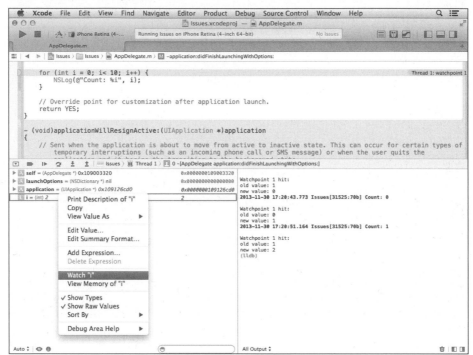

Viewing and editing memory

You can use the View Memory of . . . option in the menu to display a hex memory dump, as shown in Figure 16.17. The dump appears in the editor area and starts with the address of the selected variable. You can rearrange the display to show various byte groupings and dump lengths. Hex dumps can be useful when working with text or with byte-level buffers. But unless you can read raw hexadecimal and convert it to code in your head, other applications are limited.

TIP

Click in the left column to change the address format from decimal to hex.

Figure 16.17

View raw hex in memory.

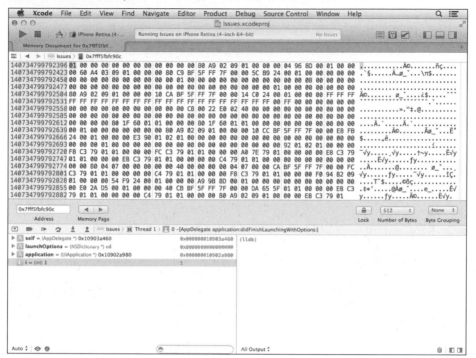

Using advanced breakpoint features

Breakpoints include a selection of optional advanced features. You can use these to create conditional breakpoints, which are triggered selectively, and to trigger actions (external events).

Editing breakpoints

To access the more advanced features, right-click a breakpoint to display a right-click contextual menu. The following options are available:

- **Edit Breakpoint:** This displays the dialog described later in this chapter.
- **Disable Breakpoint:** This is equivalent to clicking a breakpoint to disable it, as described earlier.
- **Delete Breakpoint:** This removes the breakpoint, with all existing settings.
- **Reveal in Breakpoint navigator:** This opens the Breakpoint navigator and highlights the breakpoint.

Creating conditional breakpoints

You can create a conditional breakpoint in two ways. Follow these steps for your first option:

1. Delete the original breakpoint at the loop initialization point.

2. Add a new breakpoint at the line with the `NSLog` statement.

3. Right-click the breakpoint, and select the Edit Breakpoint option.

4. Set the Ignore value to 5, as shown in Figure 16.18.

5. Build and run the application.

The breakpoint is ignored the first five times the code runs through the loop, and it isn't triggered until the sixth repeat. This option is ideal for simple delayed breakpoints where you know in advance how many times a loop or method will be executed.

Figure 16.18

Create a delayed conditional breakpoint.

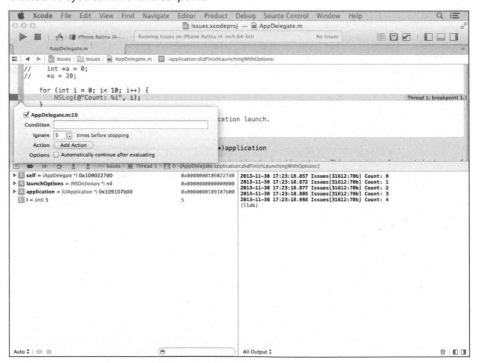

You can create a similar result by resetting the ignore count to zero and entering `i == 5` into the Condition box. In this simple example, this creates exactly the same outcome. (You could also set i >= 5 if you want the breakpoint to be triggered on all subsequent repeats.) But the Condition box is far more flexible. You can reference any variable that is in scope and use any valid code as a conditional. For example, you can set a breakpoint at the start of a method and test any parameter value to make sure that the method is getting the values it should be getting.

TIP

You can check whether notifications or other messages are being passed to the method by checking for `nil` or 0.

Triggering actions at breakpoints

The Actions feature is one of the more powerful options in the debugger. You can use it to trigger almost any event at a breakpoint. For example, you can:

- Run an AppleScript
- Send the debugger a text command
- Log a message to the console or speak it as text
- Run a UNIX shell command
- Play a sound

You can combine actions without limit, adding and deleting them with the +/- (plus/minus) buttons. You can also run multiple scripts simultaneously or run a script at the same time as you run a shell command.

For example, select the AppleScript option from the Action menu and type the following:

```
display dialog "Breakpoint %B, Count: %H "
```

Check the "Automatically continue after evaluating actions" box. Select Done, and then build and run the application.

NOTE

The `%B` option lists the breakpoint location, which is typically the method name and a line number. The `%H` option lists the number of times the breakpoint has been triggered.

CAUTION

OS X Mavericks has an infuriating habit of replacing plain quote marks with open and close quotes, whether or not you want it to. This reliably destroys all kinds of scripts and creates mysterious syntax errors in code that looks correct. You may need to prepare small scripts in a dummy Xcode project before copying and pasting them into place. TextEdit is no longer suitable for script editing.

On OS X, you won't see the breakpoint update shown in Figure 16.19, because your application has focus. This is a drawback of the action system; some features don't work unless you can force focus or the action doesn't need it.

Figure 16.19

Use simple scripting to create a custom breakpoint alert.

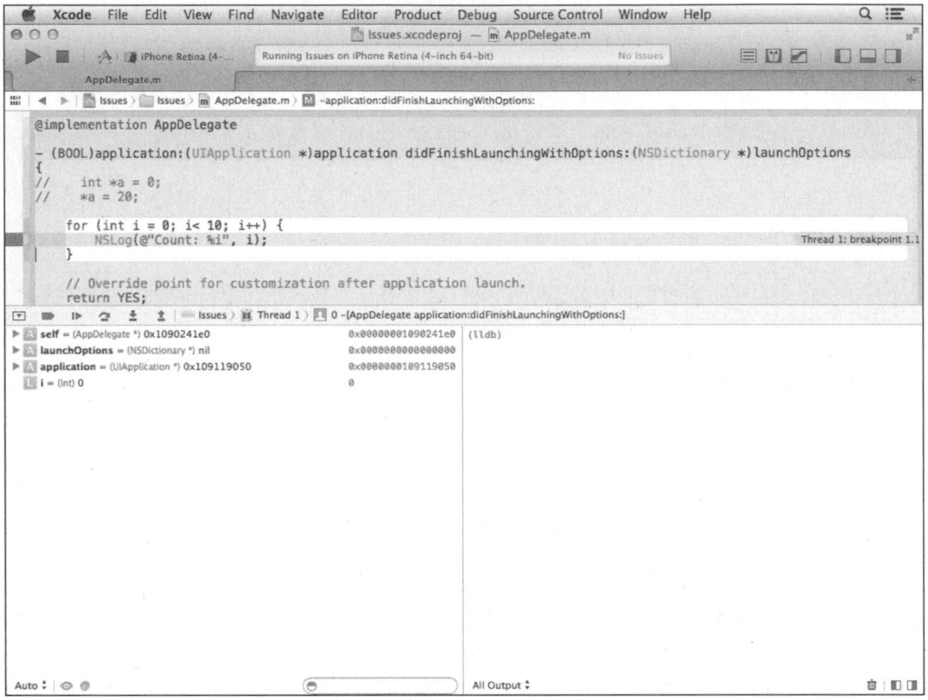

For this simple example, force focus manually by clicking anywhere in the Xcode window to bring the alert to the front. Click OK or Cancel, and watch the count increment. With a more sophisticated script, you could force focus from the script code and create a delayed loop that displayed the alert for a short period before continuing execution.

Actions are almost infinitely customizable. They're limited only by your imagination and scripting skills. A key point is that you don't have to use them for manual debugging. You can use actions to create complex automatic testing tools that can respond to external events, log code paths, and list variable values to log files. You can run tests remotely, posting the results by e-mail or uploading them to a web server. These advanced options are specialized, and describing them in detail is outside the scope of this book. But it's important to understand that after you include actions, your debugging options become much more open-ended and creative.

Using the Breakpoint navigator

The Breakpoint navigator, shown in Figure 16.20, displays a list of all breakpoints in the project. You can use this list to simplify breakpoint management. You can enable, disable, and delete breakpoints in a single window without having to find and edit the corresponding file. The options in the right-click menu are similar to those available for a single breakpoint, with a couple of additions:

● **Move Breakpoints To:** Use this to group breakpoints. You can enable and disable every breakpoint in a group with a single menu selection. There are two groups: <project name> and User. By default, all breakpoints are in the <project name> group. There's no way to create further custom groups. But you can command-click any number of breakpoints to create a single manual multiple selection.

● **Share Breakpoints:** Use this option to share breakpoints with other developers who may be working on the file. By default, breakpoints are unique to each user and are not shared. Shared breakpoints appear in a shared group in the Breakpoint navigator.

Figure 16.20

Work with the Breakpoint navigator to manage breakpoints.

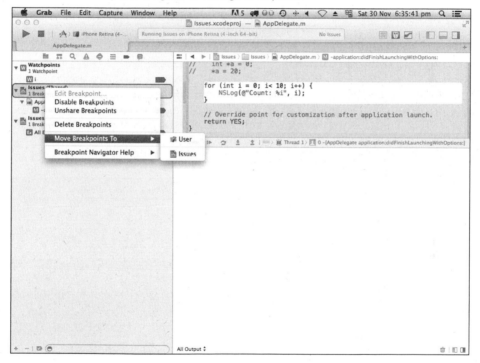

Using advanced breakpoints

You can create a selection of advanced breakpoints with the + (plus) and – (minus) icons at the bottom left of the Breakpoint navigator. Click the + (plus) icon to see the following options:

● **Add Exception Breakpoint:** Break on Objective-C, C++, or all exceptions.

● **Add Symbolic Breakpoint:** Add a breakpoint when a named symbol, such as a variable, property, method, or library, is accessed. This is a quick way to test for references in a complete app, without having to add them by hand.

- **Add OpenGL ES Error Breakpoint:** Break on errors in OpenGL ES code. This is helpful for debugging graphics code, which is notoriously difficult to test.

- **Add Test Failure Breakpoint:** Break on a unit test failure. You can use this option to log failures or to run a script when a test fails.

Advanced breakpoints don't have a specific code location, so you can work with them only in the Breakpoint navigator. Typically, you use them to perform one of the standard actions or to run a custom script. You can also use them to specify a default debugger command. They can be powerful timesavers, so it's worth taking the time to explore them.

TIP

The two icons adjacent to + (plus) and - (minus) are also useful—and they're not tied to advanced breakpoints. Use the breakpoint arrow with a check mark to hide unselected breakpoints. Use the search box to find breakpoints by filename.

Debugging multiple threads

Debugging becomes more complex when an application has multiple parallel threads. Breakpoints suspend execution in a single thread, but other threads continue to run. It can be useful to suspend them so other events don't interfere as you step through your application. Figure 16.21 illustrates the Debug navigator's thread display. To suspend a thread, right-click it and select the Suspend Thread option from the menu.

Figure 16.21

Suspend a thread in the Debug navigator.

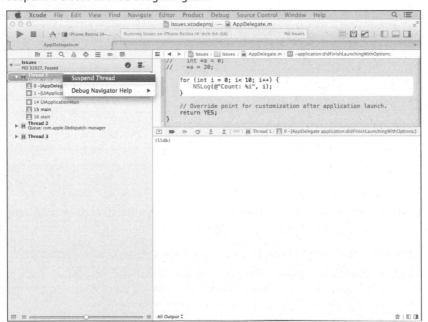

CAUTION

The lowest few threads in the display are usually system threads. Xcode lets you suspend system threads, but unless you have a very good reason for stopping OS threads, it's better to leave them running.

Advanced Debugging

Xcode includes a couple of less-direct debugging options. Although the basic GUI features of Xcode are powerful enough for most jobs, you can use command-line debugging for even finer control. LLDB includes a Python API and can be run directly from the command line in Terminal, so you can script and automate debugging sessions for regression testing.

You can also import crash dumps from iTunes Connect, to find out more about how your app is failing when it's used live by real users, as opposed to beta testers.

Getting started with command-line debugging

The (lldb) text at the bottom of the console window is a command-line prompt. You can enter text commands to the LLDB debugger to reveal details that can't be accessed with the standard debugging tools.

The complete list of LLDB commands includes hundreds of entries, and it's unlikely that any Xcode user has ever memorized them all. Table 16.3 shows a small selection.

Table 16.3 Selected Useful LLDB Commands

Command	Used for
help	Lists the main LLDB command groups. You also can use help <command> to get information about a specific command.
po	An abbreviation for "print object." Runs the `description` method on a specified object and displays the result in the console.
bt	Displays an extended backtrace with a long list of events and messages.
frame info	Lists information about the current stack frame.
expression . . .	Evaluates any valid Objective-C or C++ expression. You can use this option to change variable/property values as you debug. But note that it's not limited to simple assignments; any valid code of almost any complexity is acceptable.
print	Lists the result of evaluating any expression.
command history	Lists the debugger commands used in this session.
command alias	Creates an alias—for example, if you want to set up LLDB to use older GDB commands.
memory read/ write	Reads or edits memory directly.

Figure 16.22 shows an example of LLDB command-line control. The help command lists the main command groups, and the backtrace command displays a stack dump. Note that standard breakpoints support LLDB commands. You can type in a command as a breakpoint action, and LLBD prints the output to the console. Use this feature to print extra information about objects without using NSLog or to modify test conditions. For example, one breakpoint can set or delete another automatically.

Figure 16.22

Use the LLDB command line.

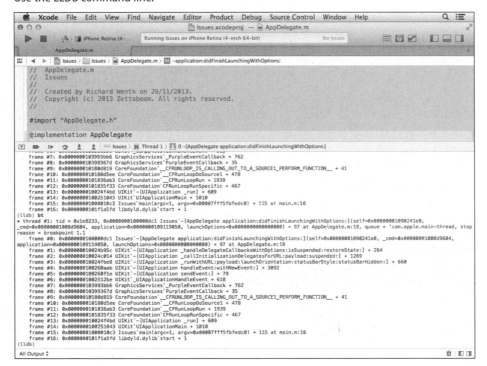

TIP

You can use the up and down arrows to scroll through a list of typed commands. For example, to repeat a command without retyping it, tap the up-arrow key followed by the Return key.

TIP

LLDB includes full access to the Clang compiler. So it includes code completion and hinting, and it can handle any expression the compiler can.

Using LLDB outside Xcode

If you download and install the Xcode command-line tools, you can use LLDB from the command line in Terminal. This is an advanced topic and a detailed description is outside the scope of this book. To find out more, see the various LLDB view presentations in the Xcode help in the documentation.

Command-line debugging is cumbersome for basic testing of a single app, but it can be very useful when you're developing a complex environment with assorted libraries, code components, and other elements. LLDB has been designed to avoid redundancy, so it can work with multiple targets and threads without duplicating binaries unnecessarily.

LLDB also includes an API that works with the Python language, for scripted and automated testing. For details, see the reference at `http://lldb.llvm.org/python-reference.html`.

Working with crash reports

You can find crash report files in iTunes Connect under Manage Your Apps ➪ <App Name> ➪ View Details ➪ Crash Reports, as shown in Figure 16.23.

Figure 16.23

Find crash reports in iTunes Connect.

The ideal is to make apps that don't crash. If for some reason that isn't possible, you can download the files and drag them to the Devices page in the Organizer. Xcode can then symbolicate the reports, which gives you some clues about possible bugs that may have caused the crash.

Summary

The Xcode debugging system is simple and productive, but it has hidden depths that you can use to speed up debugging and give a more detailed insight into why your code isn't working—or sometimes into what your code is really doing, even when it's working as it should.

Although it's possible to build powerful scripted debugging and testing rigs around the LLDB command line, the basic built-in debugging features should be more than adequate for most app projects. It's worth taking the time to explore breakpoint settings, symbolic breakpoints, and exception breakpoints. These are simple features, but they can save you lots of time.

Testing Code with Instruments

D ebugging is ideal for low-level line-by-line fault finding. But it's often useful to take a wider view of application performance—for example, to identify performance bottlenecks, monitor processor loading, and check for memory leaks.

The Xcode toolchain includes a powerful and comprehensive helper application called Instruments, used for general testing and profiling. Instruments is a general purpose timeline–based test rig that supports a selection of instruments—plug-in test probes that monitor some feature or performance metric.

NOTE

The name of the test application is Instruments, with a capital *I*. The individual test plug-ins are instruments, with a small *i*.

You can combine multiple instruments to create a custom test rig, save the rig for use with other applications, and save the results of every test run for comparison with other runs. Instruments supports both iOS and OS X applications, but each OS supports a slightly different selection of instruments.

These are the key benefits of Instruments:

- **A timeline:** You can graph and compare the output of multiple instruments simultaneously and watch supporting charts and tables.

- **Live testing:** You can interact with an application and monitor how user events affect its performance.

- **Overall system profiling:** Some instruments monitor how an application affects system resources as a whole and how other applications or processes compete with it.

- **A comprehensive library of instruments:** You can monitor performance in almost every possible way.

- **Automated testing:** You can play back scripted events to drive your application.

- **Simultaneous parallel testing:** You can track and monitor multiple instruments in the same application; on OS X, you can monitor multiple applications simultaneously.

- **Test recording:** Instruments creates a record of each run on separate tracks. You can save the record and reload it to compare it with other runs.
- **Customized instruments:** Advanced developers can create their own instruments.

Beginning with Instruments

Instruments runs in an independent window, as shown in Figure 17.1. You can launch it in two ways:

- Select Product ➪ Profile in the main Xcode menu to build a project and load it into Instruments. By default, Instruments is automatically attached to (set up to profile) the current project. The monitored application is called the target.
- Launch Instruments independently from Finder or the Dock. Select Xcode ➪ Open Developer Tool ➪ Instruments. When you launch Instruments manually, you must attach it to a target yourself. Usually, the target is your project, but you can monitor any running process—with some limitations, which are described later in this chapter.

Figure 17.1

This first view of Instruments shows one instrument out of the many that are available.

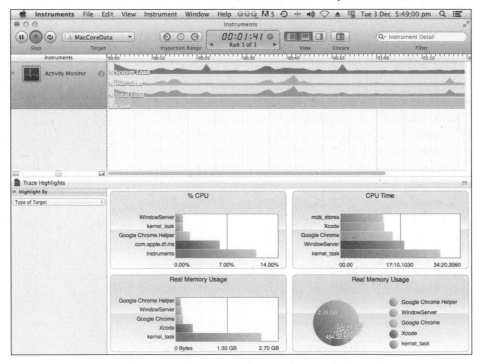

Understanding Instruments

Instruments is a multi-track recorder for system events and statistics, similar to a music or video recorder.

Each instrument records data of one type—object allocations, processor load, user events, and so on—on a separate lane or data track. When you start a test run, Instruments initializes each lane and begins to fill it with statistics collected from the target. Instruments remembers the results of each test run, and you can review each recording while Instruments is paused.

Many instruments include filters, and you can use them to include or exclude certain event sub-types. For example, when monitoring object and memory allocations, you can exclude all low-level `malloc` events to simplify the display and make it easier to monitor object-level events of interest.

In addition to the timeline view, most instruments display various statistics as they're collected. Statistics may appear as tables, charts, lists, or other summaries.

NOTE

Instruments is huge and complex, almost as complex as Xcode. A detailed breakdown of every element would fill this book. Most features can be understood with educated guesswork and experimentation. This chapter doesn't list every feature, but it does outline how you can get started with Instruments so you can begin to explore it for yourself and start working with the tools that you're most likely to find useful.

CAUTION

Instruments works with Cocoa and Carbon apps. You can't use Instruments to profile C++ command-line apps.

Exploring the Instruments UI

Figure 17.2 shows a more typical working view of the Instruments UI, this time showing the Allocations instruments, which monitors objects in memory. The design follows the standard OS X guidelines, with a selection area at the top left, an active area in the middle, and a view at the right that can display supporting information. The active area is split into a timeline view at the top and a detail pane at the bottom. A toolbar at the top of the window controls the main application features.

The selection area is called the instruments pane and includes a list of all instruments used in a trace. Each instrument has a reveal triangle that shows the results of previous runs and an information icon that reveals extra options for fine-tuning a recording.

The timeline view is called the track pane. You can use a slider at the bottom of the instruments pane to expand the scale of the track pane.

The detail pane fills the bottom of the display. It includes a selection area at the left that can fine-tune and filter the information that's displayed and a display pane in the bottom middle that displays the information that has been selected.

Figure 17.2

Look at the detail available in the Allocations instrument.

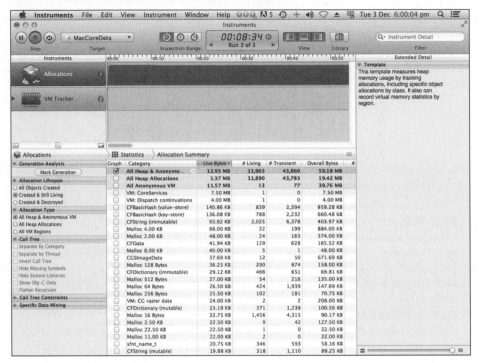

The extended detail pane at the right shows optional further detail that supports the information in the detail pane. In the figure, the extended detail pane shows information about the template. In other contexts, it can show details about specific events, including a stack frame for every `malloc` event.

You can see an immense amount of detail in the display. The Allocations instrument (refer to Figure 17.2) literally lists every object in memory. You can monitor the creation and destruction of specific class instances and view stack traces for each creation event. You can also get more general statistics about created and destroyed objects, the total memory footprint of the application, and so on. Not all instruments display this much detail; others are simpler summaries of less complex application states.

CAUTION

Some features work at a low level, so you need a basic understanding of Cocoa and OS X/iOS internals to get the most from certain instruments. You can use Instruments without this knowledge, but you will miss the more powerful and productive features.

NOTE

Because some instruments literally modify the OS kernel as it's running, you may be asked for your OS X username and password before they grant low-level access. The kernel changes are transparent and temporary.

Introducing the toolbar

The toolbar includes the most important controls and is visible unless you hide it using the button at the top right. The features in the toolbar are described in the following sections.

Record, pause, and loop control

The large Record button begins and ends recording. While recording, the label changes from Record to Stop. If you're recording an instrument that manages UI events, the label changes to Drive and Record.

CAUTION

When you profile an application, you first select one or more instruments for a run, as described later in this chapter. Instruments then pauses while the instruments are loaded, and eventually it begins recording automatically. If you're profiling your project from Xcode, don't click the Record button while nothing seems to be happening. Instruments begins recording when it's ready. If you're profiling some other existing process, you need to start the recording manually.

The Pause button pauses recording. The timer shown in the main time indicator stops, and Instruments stops collecting data. In fact, the timer continues to run, and if you click the Pause button again, you see that a gap has appeared in the recording, as shown in Figure 17.3. This isn't an essential feature, and typically you can ignore it. But occasionally, you may want to change application settings or interact with the application without recording the results.

Figure 17.3

Create gaps in the recording with the Pause button.

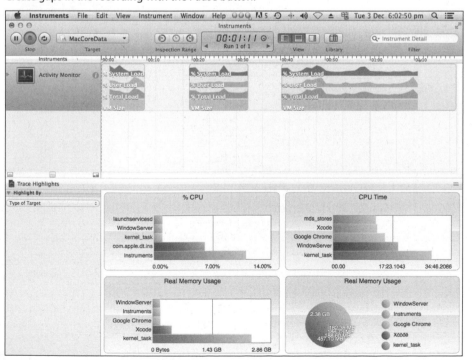

The Loop button toggles between playing a track once and repeating it. You can use this feature with recordings of UI events to create multiple test runs from the same user actions.

The target menu

Use the target pop-up to select the process or processes to be recorded. When you profile a project from Xcode, your project is preselected for you here. But you can profile any running process by attaching Instruments to it, as shown in Figure 17.4.

Figure 17.4

When you are attaching to a process, the pop-up shows all running processes, including ones you won't usually want to profile.

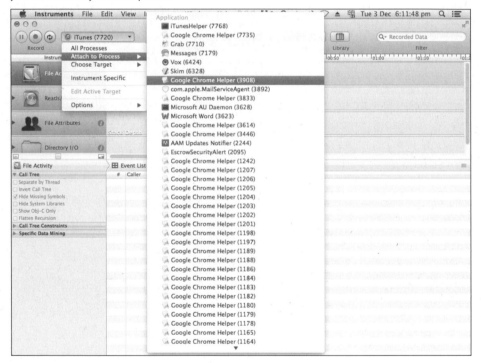

Manual attaching is more limited than project profiling. For example, system applications such as iTunes, Front Row, DVD Player, and QuickTime are deliberately cloaked from Instruments, and you can't collect data from them. Some instruments rely on debug symbol tables. Most applications don't include these, so you can't profile or test them at a low level.

Like many features in Instruments, the target menu has hidden depths, and you can make very specific selections. Figure 17.5 shows the Edit Active Target sub-option in the target menu. You can define the environment variables for the target, add new variables and launch arguments, and select one of the possible consoles for the application.

Figure 17.5

Work with target settings.

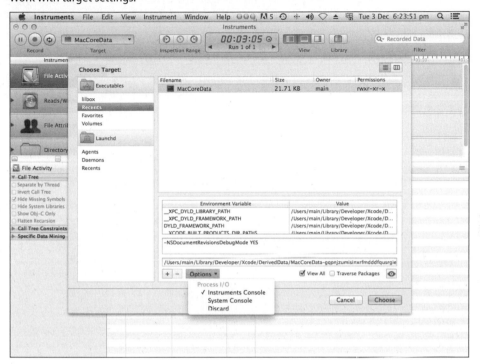

TIP

The Agents and Daemons views are useful because they collect default plists for each system item in a single, easily accessible location. To view the defaults, select a daemon or agent from the list and click the eye icon at the bottom right of the dialog. You see a text XML dump of the plist, with the keys and values in the dictionary. To edit the plist, double-click it. Xcode opens a new plist editor window. For more about editing plists, see Appendix B.

The inspection range

Use the three inspection range buttons to set the start and end time of the display. To set the start time, drag the position cursor in the timeline (described later) to your chosen start point and click the leftmost range button. To set the end time, repeat for the rightmost button. To clear the range, click the middle button.

The inspection range doesn't affect the timeline. It doesn't zoom to fill the screen, and it doesn't modify the position cursor. However, it sometimes affects the statistics that are chosen and displayed elsewhere in Instruments.

The time/run control

This shows the elapsed time in a recording. You can use the arrows under the time display to select different runs. The clock/run icon to the right of the time digits toggles the display between the current recording position and the current cursor time.

The view selector

The three view buttons display and hide the various possible panes. You can view as much detail as possible, or you can hide the lower panel, as shown in Figure 17.6. It's more usual to run Instruments with the left and lower panes showing.

Figure 17.6

Use the view selector to hide the bottom panel. This isn't often useful, but occasionally you may want to maximize the number of visible tracks, to simplify multiple comparisons.

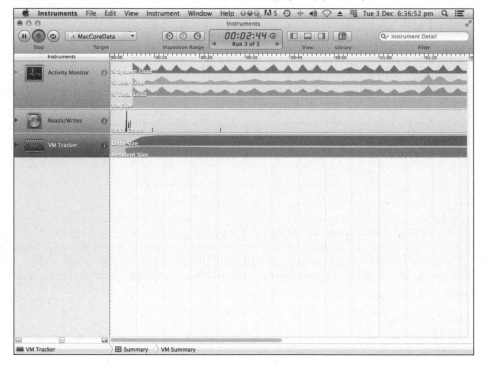

NOTE

In Xcode 4, you could hide the Instruments list at the left of the display. In Xcode 5, you can't. Even if you click the left panel button, the list remains on the screen.

The library button

This button toggles display of the instrument library—a floating window that lists all available instruments, as shown in Figure 17.7. You can use the gear icon at the bottom left of the window to show a menu with various display options. The Library menu at the top of the window displays a list of instrument groups. You can use the library to create your own instrument collections, saving them as *templates*—instrument collections that profile related application elements.

Figure 17.7

Use the Library's view options to save space on smaller monitors. The large icons are impressively detailed, but they waste space on a smaller monitor.

NOTE

Only instruments that match the current project platform are shown; in other words, only Mac-compatible instruments appear for an OS X project, and only iOS-compatible instruments appear for an iOS project. There are significant differences between the instruments supported on each.

The search field

You can use the search field at the top right of the main toolbar to add another set of filters to the information in the detail pane. Search operations depend on the data produced by an instrument, so searches are context-dependent.

Figure 17.8 shows how you can filter the output of the allocations instrument to show only CFArray items. In your own projects, you can use this feature to monitor your own custom objects while hiding all other activity. It's easy to overlook the search field, but it can be a very powerful way to filter a flood of data to a trickle of precisely targeted useful statistics.

Figure 17.8

Use the search field to filter the output of the Allocations instrument, reducing hundreds of items to just three.

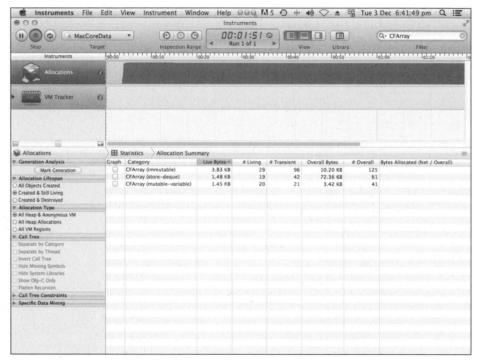

Getting Started with Instruments

Instruments has some quirks, and the easiest way to become familiar with them is to experiment with a practical profiling project—one that monitors memory events in an iOS app.

Memory management in iOS can be challenging, and Instruments includes tools that can monitor memory and report on crashes. Although Instruments has many possible applications, memory profiling is one of the most useful. If you develop for iOS, Instruments can save you time and help you create apps that are robust and don't leak memory.

Creating a leaky test app

To demonstrate this in practice, you need to create an app that deliberately leaks memory. Instruments monitors the leak so you can see how allocations and leaks are graphed and summarized as statistics. Follow these steps:

1. **Create a new Window-based iOS project in Xcode with File ⇨ New Project.**

   Don't include unit tests or Core Data.

2. **Save the project as MemoryLeak.**

3. **Modify the start of `AppDelegate.m` so it matches the following listing:**

```
@implementation AppDelegate

char* buffer;

-  (BOOL)application:(UIApplication *)application didFinishLaunch
   ingWithOptions:(NSDictionary *)launchOptions
{
    NSTimer *theTimer =
    [NSTimer scheduledTimerWithTimeInterval:1.0
                                    target:self
                                  selector:@selector(timerDo)
                                  userInfo:nil
                                   repeats:YES];
    return YES;
}

- (void) timerDo {
   buffer = malloc(1000);

   }
```

   This code creates a timer that repeats once per second. The `timerDo` timer handler method grabs a new block of memory on every repeat. The memory is never freed and becomes a leak.

If you build and run the project, as shown in Figure 17.9, the app appears to work. The view has no UI elements and does nothing. But the app doesn't crash, and there's no indication that it's leaking memory. If you leave it running for long enough, it eventually causes an iOS memory error. But because the memory leak is small, it's difficult to distinguish the leak from other possible crash events, unless you monitor memory directly.

CAUTION

iOS and OS X ARC (Advanced Reference Counting) is good at preventing memory leaks in Cocoa objects. ARC does nothing to prevent leaks in code that uses C language memory management. Instruments will usually find C language leaks, but some instruments are Cocoa-specific, and leaks may not show up correctly.

Figure 17.9

There's no way to tell from the Simulator or from the build messages in the editor that this app is leaking memory.

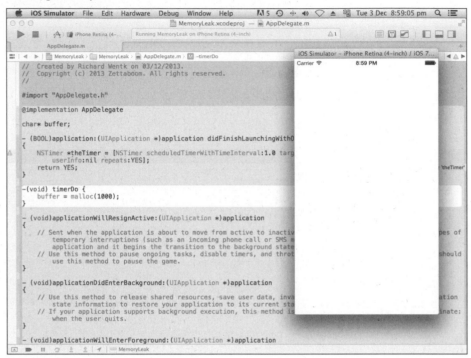

Profiling an app with Instruments

Loading a project into Instruments is known as *profiling*. The process is the same for OS X and iOS projects. The simplest version has the following steps:

1. Make sure the project builds with no errors.

2. Select the Product ⇨ Profile option in the main Xcode menu.

3. Wait while Xcode creates a special profiling build.

You see the usual Build Succeeded message at the end of this step.

4. Wait again while Xcode loads and launches Instruments automatically.

You don't need to launch Instruments manually when profiling.

5. Select a trace template.

A template includes one or more instruments with predefined settings, and it's designed to collect and display information about specific issues or runtime values.

6. **Wait while Instruments initializes the instrument.**

7. **Optionally, authenticate with your standard OS X user password if asked to.**

   Not all instruments require this step.

8. **Wait again while Instruments completes its initialization.**

   This can take a few seconds. Instruments appears to do nothing, and your Mac may become slow or unresponsive until initialization completes.

9. **Begin monitoring the app, using the instrument you selected.**

   The timeline begins scrolling with a graphical display, and the detail pane shows dynamic statistics. Depending on the instrument, you can modify the display to zoom in or out, select or hide certain statistics, reveal further details, and so on.

10. **At the end of a run, select the Stop button at the top left.**

    You can now scroll through the timeline to review the graph.

This process seems simple, but there are a few hidden complications. Not all templates are available on all platforms. When Instruments launches, it offers a slightly different selection for OS X, iOS Simulator, and iOS hardware projects.

Note also that the start-up delay is variable and inconsistent. When you load Instruments for the first time, it can take up to a minute before the timeline displays useful information. iOS projects usually take longer than OS X projects, because it can take a while for the Simulator or a device to load and run an app. Instruments needs extra initialization time on top of this delay. Generally, start-up isn't an instant process, and there's an ambiguous period after launch where it may not be clear if everything is running correctly. (It usually is.)

TIP

You can delay recording and timeline updates by selecting File ⇨ Record Options in the main Instruments menu. The options dialog includes a start delay option, a time limit option, and a deferred display check box that disables data processing and display until the end of a run, minimizing the live processing overhead. Delay times can be set in seconds, milliseconds, microseconds, or nanoseconds. (You won't often use the last option.)

CAUTION

In the first release of Xcode, Instruments sometimes fails to attach itself automatically to the iOS Simulator if you select Product ⇨ Profile. If this happens, attach manually instead.

Note that although you can scroll along the timeline graph manually, Instruments doesn't necessarily keep a record of the statistics gathered at every point. Typically, the statistics remain frozen with the values they had at the end of the run. Although it would be useful to replay statistics manually, Instruments doesn't support this.

Selecting a trace template

To explore this process in practice, select the Project ⇨ Profile menu option in Xcode to create a profile build and launch Instruments.

Figure 17.10 shows the Trace Template selection dialog. Because this project is running in the iOS Simulator, Instruments has preselected the relevant iOS Simulator Instruments. The All option at the top left displays all available templates. You can filter them by selecting the Memory, CPU, and File System groups.

Figure 17.10

Select a template from the standard list.

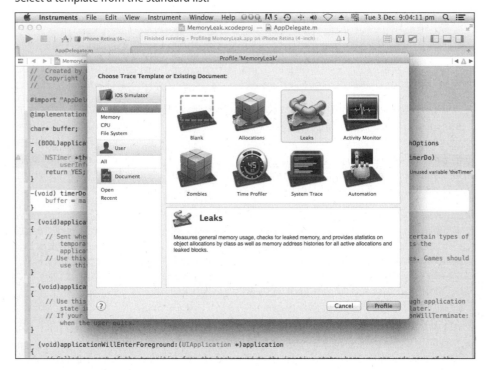

For this example, select the Leaks template. Click Profile. Wait while Instruments launches and initializes. Eventually, you see the display in Figure 17.11. The Leaks template includes two instruments: Allocations and Leaks.

Understanding the timeline

After the display is updating regularly, you can begin reviewing the output to see how it offers insights into the behavior of the app.

There are two areas of activity. The timeline area shows an initial flurry of allocation events when the app launches and a steadily increasing series of events in the Leaks lane. The statistics show a much more comprehensive—and difficult to understand—list of information, which is described in more detail later.

Figure 17.11

Take a look at the Leaks template.

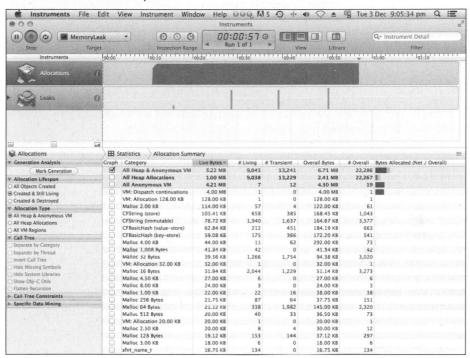

The Leaks graph provides a clear indication that the app is leaking. But note that the graph doesn't exactly mirror the leak activity. You might expect the leak count to grow steadily, but by default, the graph is sampled every ten seconds, so the leaks timeline displays a summary view.

TIP

In fact, you can change the sampling time to force the graph to update more frequently. For smaller apps, the cost is a small performance hit. Select the Leaks instrument, and change the Snapshot Interval value in the box in the Snapshots configuration under the Instruments list. The initial ten-second default is excessively long for many applications. As apps use more memory, the performance hit becomes more obvious, so use this feature with care.

Generally, the timeline is best used for quick broad-brush overviews of app activity. It's not a precise diagnostic tool, but it does give you enough information to check whether more detailed investigation is necessary.

Getting started with the statistics

The statistics in the detail pane are the key to using Instruments productively. Where the timeline provides an overview, the statistics provide extremely detailed information.

At first sight, the Allocations statistics may look complex, but the display is simply a list of all objects created by your app, with an associated instance count, and the instrument is literally monitoring and counting every object in memory.

A combined All Allocations summary at the top of the list counts the total number of objects and lists the total memory used. You can click each column header (Category, Live Bytes, # Living, and so on) to sort the list in various ways and to highlight aspects of the data.

N O T E
If you can't see the display shown in Figure 17.11, select the Allocations instrument at the top left of the timeline pane and select Statistics and Object Summary using the menus under the timeline.

N O T E
Allocations displays all objects and all low-level memory allocations. Many of the objects in the list aren't documented, because they are internal to the OS and are created and released at a low level. Typically, when you create a standard Cocoa object, the allocation code runs a number of low-level allocations and creates various other low-level structures and objects. Allocations lists them all separately.

As the app runs, you see that both the # Living and the # Overall counts for the All Allocations summary increase by one every second. The # Living column counts objects that are allocated and active. The # Overall column is a running total for the app, and it includes objects that have been released.

C A U T I O N
Occasionally, you find that Apple's own iOS and OS X objects are leaking memory. When this happens, Instruments shows it clearly. But don't forget that in the application, the objects are organized in a hierarchy and not a linear list, and OS objects may leak memory at the `malloc` level. If your code is doing nothing while memory allocations are increasing, you're likely dealing with a genuine OS bug. You may not be able to see which object is causing the problem, because Allocations is reporting the problem as a low-level leak.

Monitoring specific objects

The unfiltered object list includes objects created behind the scenes by the OS. You don't usually need to monitor these, so instruments includes a powerful selection of filtering options that can help you focus on some objects while hiding others.

Use these options to show objects with specific names. Functionally, the various filters overlap, and there's usually more than one way to pick out individual objects from the list. It's up to you to choose the approach that works for you.

Selecting objects with the category list

Select the Category column header to sort the object list alphabetically. Scroll down to find the `Malloc 1,008 bytes` entry, as shown in Figure 17.12. If you monitor this entry while the app is running, you see that its # Living and # Overall counts both increase steadily. It also climbs the Live Bytes and Overall Bytes columns as its memory footprint increases.

Figure 17.12

Use the Category column to list objects alphabetically.

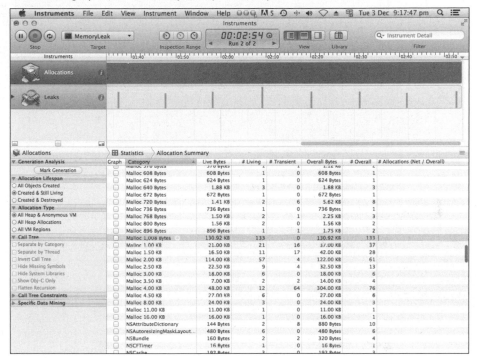

NOTE

`malloc` adds a few extra bytes for maintenance, which is why the leak is 1008 bytes, not 1000 bytes.

Selecting objects with the search field

Figure 17.13 shows an alternative solution. Type one or more class or function names into the search field at the top right of the Instruments window, select the magnifying glass icon, and choose Matches Any. The main list is filtered to show the object names you entered. Use this approach when you want to monitor a small number of related objects that you suspect may be leaking memory.

CAUTION

There may be a difference between internal system object names and official documented object names. For example, if you search for `NSArray` you'll find the objects that implement it won't find it behind the scenes. Depending the class you're looking for, you'll see extra underscores at the start of the class name, extra trailing letters, and/or names that begin with CF instead of NS—among other possibilities. These objects aren't mentioned in the documentation, but ideally you should know enough about Cocoa to understand what they do from the search context. This applies only when you're monitoring Cocoa and other system objects. Your own custom objects should have unique and unambiguous searchable names.

Figure 17.13

Select objects with the search field.

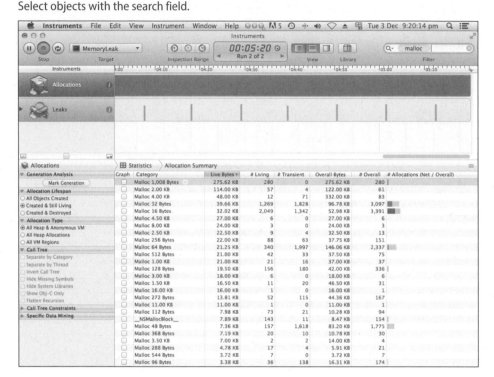

Listing object allocation events

When you select an object, you can click the detail arrow that appears to its right to reveal a list of allocation events, as shown in Figure 17.14. The list includes an address, time stamp, and context for every allocation.

You can see from this list that the app is generating multiple `malloc` allocations. Because all of them are live, it's not releasing them. All of them are created in the `timerDo` method in the app delegate.

In a real project, this kind of information can give you useful debugging hints. But you can also use the Leaks instruments to find leaking objects and functions directly. Click the instrument to see the display shown in Figure 17.15.

Leaks does a good job of listing suspected leaks. It's not infallible, but it can find and list most kinds of memory leaks. If you click the disclosure triangle to the left of a leaky object, you can see the list of leak events that appeared in Figure 17.14.

This can be a lifesaver on projects with memory issues, because it gives you an X-ray of the app's memory events. You can interact with the app while it's running and monitor an object to check whether it's being allocated and released correctly.

Figure 17.14

List objects of a single class with their associated allocation times, addresses, and the application/library and method in which the allocation occurred.

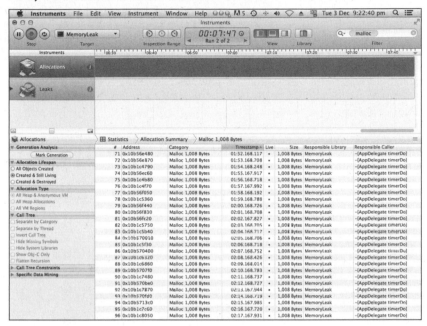

Figure 17.15

Look at Leaks to find leaky objects.

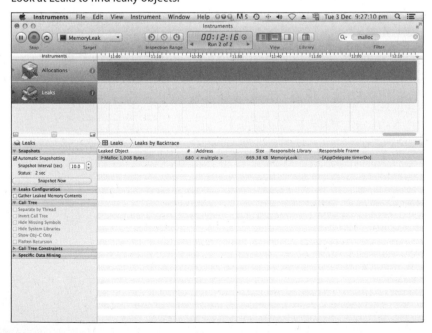

Viewing an allocation event stack trace

A related powerful option gives you precise information about the event that created an object. Select an allocation event, click the disclosure arrow to the right of the address, and click the extended detail icon in the toolbar—the one at the right of the group of three labeled View.

You should see the display in Figure 17.16. The stack trace lists the events that preceded the allocation. You can display further information in the trace; for example, you can list the Cocoa and OS libraries by name, highlight user and system events with different icons, and display file links to your source code. The Description sub-pane also lists the size of the memory used and the retain count. With Cocoa objects, the latter provides a useful double-check to make sure you are using ARC correctly.

The stack frame display includes some very useful features. System code is shown in light gray to distinguish it from your code, which appears black. You can use the options shown in the menu to give items a number, reverse the stack order, show the associate library and file, and even the exact line. Use the menu (refer to Figure 17.16) to enable every display option. Scroll down to item 2—the item that lists the allocation event in your code, marked with the head-and-shoulders user icon. Double-click anywhere on the entry.

Figure 17.16

View an allocation event stack trace and reference count.

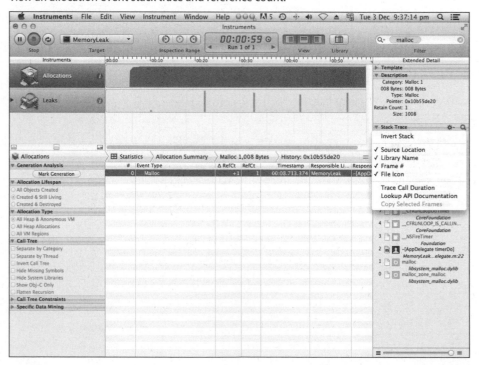

Viewing code from a stack trace

Instruments loads the source code and highlights the line associated with the event, as shown in Figure 17.17. You can immediately see where the object was allocated.

Figure 17.17

Bring it back to the source code.

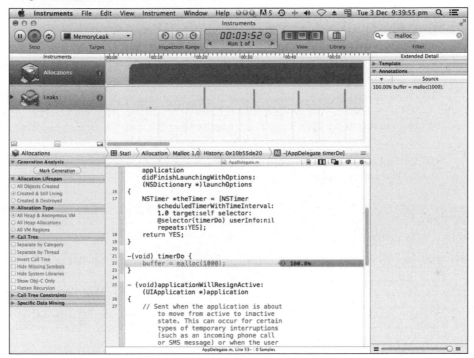

For an object that's still active—one with a retain count greater than zero and that hasn't been released from memory—the reference count display in Figure 17.15 shows the most recent memory management event. You can use the source code link feature in Figure 17.17 to find the code associated with that event.

N O T E

You can use this feature to monitor system objects. But if you try to jump into the source code, you see a short assembly listing, because naturally you cannot view or change the original system files.

Comparing Allocations and Leaks

The Leaks and Allocations instruments have identical drill-down features. The only difference is that Leaks shows leaking objects, while Allocations shows all objects. The Allocations view is useful to see objects in context—for example, to check their relationships. For quick leak-finding, use Leaks.

The Allocations instrument can display even more information in the detail pane. The default view in the detail pane is called the Statistics view. But the pane can display allocation data in other ways. You can select the other options, described later, using the menu above the detail pane, as shown in Figure 17.18. Here's what's available:

- **Call Trees:** This displays a complete list of nested function and method calls. Use it with the Mark Heap feature, described later, to display a calling context for an active method. You also can view the complete call tree of the entire application. This gives you a very detailed view of the events in your app, but it's so detailed that it's rarely useful.

- **Allocations List:** This is a simple linear list of objects that can be sorted by memory address, category (name, for example), creation time, size, library, and calling context. It's identical to the object list introduced earlier.

- **Generations:** Formerly known as *Heapshots*, this creates a simple summary snapshot of heap (total memory) use. Click the Mark Generation button at the left to save the state of the heap. Click it again to measure the new state. The instrument lists the growth between generations in KB or MB, and in objects.

- **Console:** This displays a console window to monitor text output and accept text input for the current target.

Figure 17.18

You can select other types of displays in the detail pane.

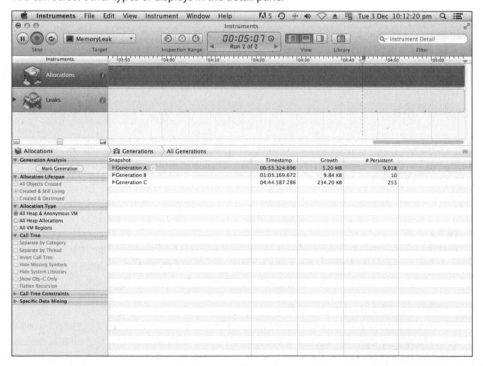

Managing zombies

Zombies—dangling pointers to released objects—are considered a solved problem with ARC. From iOS 6 and OS X 10.8 onward, you should not have to use the old Zombies instrument. If you need to debug older code, you may find the instrument useful. It lists possible zombie events and generates a stack trace for each one.

Modifying instrument settings

When you load a template, the instruments it contains are initialized with default settings. You can modify these settings before or after a run by clicking the small information (i) icon at the right of the instrument to show an Inspector dialog, as shown in Figure 17.19. Each instrument displays a different set of options. Some options are available for many instruments.

Figure 17.19

You can change instrument settings with the inspector.

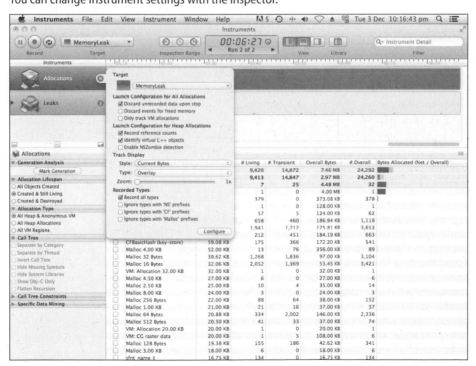

The settings inspector is easy to overlook, but it includes powerful features. Some common settings include the following:

- **Target:** By default, this matches the process or thread that Instruments is monitoring. Some instruments allow you to select a different process or thread with this menu, to enable simultaneous monitoring across multiple applications. You cannot change the target while Instruments is collecting data.

- **Launch Configuration:** These are general settings for the instrument.
- **Track Display - Style and Type:** The Style and Type options can show cumulative or activity-summary views of the data. The Overlay type displays different runs on a single graph, while the Stacked type (which is preferred) displays a series of strips with the same vertical scale.
- **Track Display - Zoom:** The Zoom option changes the vertical height of the timeline. You can use it to emphasize the data from one instrument or to highlight activity at the lower scale of the display.
- **Recorded Types:** Use this to filter out certain kinds of objects or events. In outline, you can show/hide Cocoa (NS), Carbon and Foundation (CF), and basic C (Malloc) events.

For the Allocations instrument, the remaining settings are unique. The Launch Configuration options for the Allocations instrument include a selection of check boxes. Most are self-explanatory. For example, the Record reference counts option does what you'd expect it to; if you uncheck the box, the instrument doesn't record reference counts.

TIP

Note that Enable NSZombie detection turns on the zombie monitoring feature introduced earlier. There is no separate Zombies instrument; zombie detection is built into the Allocations instrument, and you can enable or disable it here. It's important to remember this if you create your own templates; otherwise, you'll look for a Zombies instrument and wonder why there isn't one.

CAUTION

Your custom objects are considered Cocoa objects. If you don't record NS objects, Instruments ignores them, even though their names may not begin with NS. But on iOS, objects that begin with UI *aren't* ignored. Also, you can set the Recorded Types options to filter out everything. If you do this, you see an empty yellow timeline with a warning message.

If you click the Configure button at the bottom right of the inspector, it spins around to show the view in Figure 17.20. By default, this dialog repeats the record/ignore options from the previous view, but you can use the add/remove icons under the table to add your own prefix strings for customized filtering. Most instruments include the Configure option, but as with the main settings, every instrument displays a different set of features on the flip view.

Comparing different runs

To monitor a new run, click the Record button to stop a run, and click it again to begin recording. By default, you see a new set of tracks in the timeline, and the description string under the main time counter changes to "Run *N* of *N*", where *N* is the total number of runs.

To compare different runs, click the disclosure triangle at the left of an instrument. The timeline displays each run on a different track, as shown in Figure 17.21. Selecting each run in the timeline displays its final statistics in the detail view. You can also select runs by clicking the forward/back arrows on each side of the "Run *N* of *N*" text in the time counter.

Figure 17.20

On the other side of the inspector, each instrument displays different options. Not all instruments implement this flip view feature.

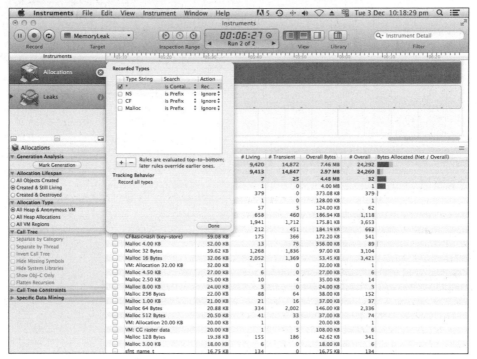

CAUTION

Although each run in this example is identical because they all use the same zombies test app, you can see from the graphs how different the timing can be. Instruments must share Mac resources with other applications, including Xcode and the Simulator. The time taken to launch an app and begin recording events can vary dramatically. Generally, you can't rely on profiling for interactive time-critical monitoring, at least not for the first minute or so of each run.

CAUTION

After Instruments launches, use the Record button to record runs. Do not use the main Run button in Xcode.

Saving and loading runs

To save a run, select File ⇨ Save As from the Instruments menu. The current run is saved to a .trace file, with all the current settings and data. You can reload a trace with File ⇨ Open. After loading, you can record further runs. They're added to the data in the usual way. The original runs aren't deleted or modified. You can then resave the new file with a new name or overwrite the original.

Figure 17.21

Compare different runs.

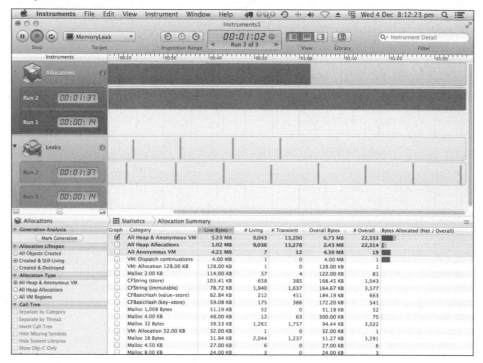

Working with Instruments and Templates

You can use the templates to get started with Instruments. But to customize the testing with your own preferred mix of instruments, you must understand the difference between instruments, documents, and templates.

Understanding templates

The standard templates have three elements:

- One or more instruments
- Default settings for each instrument
- An appealing graphic that appears in the standard template list on launch

The default templates are designed to create a selection of standard useful profiles. But you can create custom templates, with your own selection of instruments and settings. When you save a template, it's added to the user library. You can select one of the standard icons for the template when you save it.

Creating a template

To create a new template, select File⇨New in Instruments and select the Blank template. Click the Library button, and drag and drop one or more instruments from the list onto the Instruments column at the left of the Instruments window, as shown in Figure 17.22.

Figure 17.22

You can create a custom template.

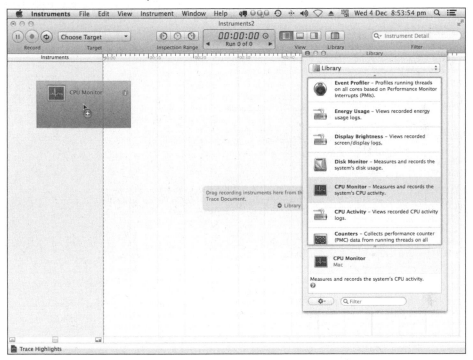

Go through each instrument, and change the settings to useful defaults. You can add multiple copies of the same instrument to the template with different settings. For example, you might add two copies of the CPU Monitor instrument and use the Configure options to display two different statistics in the timeline, such as PhysicalMemoryUsed and PhysicalMemoryFree.

CAUTION

Make sure you select only the instruments that match your target platform. The info panel at the bottom of the Library window specifies "Mac" for OS X instruments. It's blank for iOS instruments.

If you want to monitor different threads and processes in each track, set the Target menu in the toolbar to Instrument Specific. You can then select the targets for each instrument when the template loads.

Finally, use the File ⇨ Save as Template option in the main Instruments menu to save the new template. Click the triangle at the bottom right of the Icon box to select one of the standard icons. Give the template a memorable name.

As shown in Figure 17.23, when you create a new Instruments document, the saved template appears in the User section of the template list. To delete a custom template from the list, navigate to the path shown in the template description in Finder and delete the file by hand.

Figure 17.23

You can load a custom template.

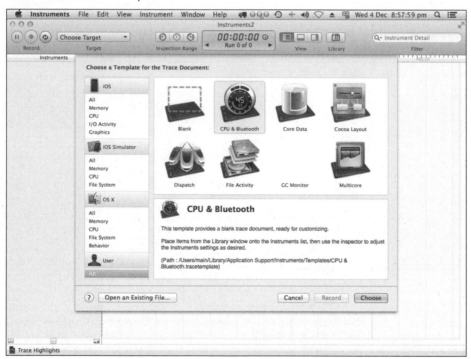

TIP

The Library window includes a terse description for each instrument in the list. You can find more information about each instrument, with selected extra details about parameters and settings, in the documentation under Tools & Languages ⇨ Performance Analysis Tools ⇨ Instruments User Guide ⇨ Built-in Instruments.

Creating custom instruments

You can create custom instruments to monitor OS features and other events that aren't included in the standard library. Instruments uses a technology called DTrace, which is outlined later. But you can create simple custom event monitors without understanding DTrace.

Select Instruments ⇨ Build New Instrument to display the custom instrument dialog, shown in Figure 17.24. If you understand DTrace and the D scripting language, you can fill in the DATA, BEGIN, and END fields with custom code.

For a simple event monitor, you can enter a library and function name in the probe fields and select one or more parameters to monitor in the "Record the following data:" box. A more detailed primer on creating custom instruments is beyond the scope of this book. You can find more details by searching the documentation for Instruments. Details of custom instruments are under Tool Guides ⇨ Creating Custom Instruments.

Figure 17.24

Use the custom instrument dialog to create custom instruments.

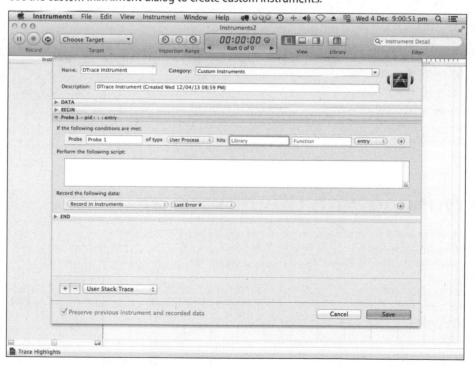

DTrace and Instruments

Internally, Instruments is based on a technology called DTrace. Originally developed by Sun Microsystems (now Oracle) to help debug kernel and application issues in Solaris, DTrace was made available under a free Common Development and Distribution License (CDDL) and ported to various Unix systems. Instruments, effectively, is a GUI for DTrace, with a selection of prewritten scripts for monitoring useful performance features. Because DTrace works at the kernel level and modifies running code, it requires kernel-level privileges.

DTrace scripts are written in a custom programming language called D. The syntax of D is very similar to C, but the program structure has more in common with the acronymically named AWK language invented by Alfred Aho, Peter Weinberger, and Brian Kernighan.

Internally, DTrace uses a selection of providers, or access points, that are patched into key parts of the kernel. For example, a provider called `objc` reports information about Objective-C objects in user space. `syscall` reports on system calls in the kernel. `fbt` (function boundary tracing) reports kernel functions. Each provider can be monitored by one or more probes that report on provider-level events.

You can access DTrace from the command line in Terminal with the `dtrace` command. For example, the following dumps a list of active probes:

```
sudo dtrace -l
```

Instruments works by adding a custom action to each probe, which runs when the probe "fires"—in other words, when some relevant event triggers it. You can script your own actions, although you need to have some understanding of each probe and its options.

You don't need to use or understand DTrace to use Instruments, but it can be useful to incorporate DTrace features into command-line development. A full introduction to the scripting syntax is outside the scope of this book. Default scripts are available in /usr/bin. In Terminal, type the following to see a list of scripts that you can reverse-engineer:

```
grep -l DTrace /usr/bin/*
```

More information is available at `wikis.oracle.com/display/DTrace/DTrace`.

Although this kind of low-level exploration of DTrace is better suited to experienced programmers than beginners, it can give almost everyone some insights into how DTrace can be used to monitor application and process activity.

Working with UIAutomation

It's often useful to send a sequence of test events to an app to check the UI for various possible errors and fail states. Instruments includes an Automation script player that can read a set of automation and test events from a file and send them as actions to an iOS app.

Test scripts are written in JavaScript and use the `UIAutomation` class. UIKit objects have a library of associated `UIAutomation` objects that can receive automation events. You can find the full list of objects in the UI Automation Reference Collection in the Xcode documentation.

Test scripts can be simple or extremely complex. It's up to you to decide how you want to test your UI. The following example is very simple indeed, but it illustrates the process of testing and can be expanded to create a more sophisticated test suite.

It's tempting to leave testing to the end of the development cycle, but it can be more productive to develop your test script as you develop. Testing adds some overhead, but if you combine automated testing with the unit testing described in Chapter 18, you can create a useful test suite that exercises the key features of your project and helps ensure that features aren't broken by updates and bug fixes.

TIP

Most UI objects are subclasses of `UIAElement`. The documentation for `UIAElement` lists the messages you can send to objects as you test them. It's a good place to start when you begin using `UIAutomation`. (If you look at the object subclasses themselves, you won't find much of interest.)

NOTE

The Automation instrument is available only on iOS. For OS X, Instruments includes a simple UI recorder that can capture and replay user actions.

Setting up objects to support automation

The UI automation system doesn't use outlets or links. Objects are referenced in two ways:

- Views can be accessed through the application's view tree. With the correct code, views "just work."
- UI elements should be named in IB.

To include an object in testing, select in IB and modify it as listed here and shown at the right of Figure 17.25:

- Make sure the Accessibility box is checked. (For many objects, Accessibility is on by default.)
- Give the object a unique name in its Label field.

The figure shows a very simple example with a single text field. A real UI is likely to have a longer list of UI elements, and you must repeat both steps for all of them.

TIP

If you have an extremely simple UI with one of each kind of element, you can access it directly through the [0] index without naming it in IB. This is recommended only for quick and lazy testing. You get more reliable results if you name objects and access the names explicitly in your code.

CAUTION

Don't enable accessibility for container views. If you do, automation can't find the UI elements inside them.

Figure 17.25

This is how you set up a UI object to support test automation.

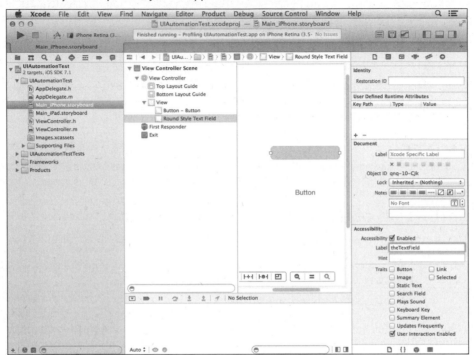

Creating a test script

The easiest way to create a test script is to create an empty file with a .js extension using any text editor. You can save the file anywhere. Your project directory is a good location because it guarantees you can find it later. Optionally, you can include some test code in the file, but you'll be editing this file later within Instruments, so it's convenient to leave the file blank until you do that.

NOTE

Even though Automation files can be loaded into Instruments and saved in a project directory, they're not part of the project's code base. If you add them to a project, they're copied into the final build, which is probably not what you want. You can fix this by not adding them to a target when you import them.

Launching the Automation instrument

Select Product ➪ Profile and choose the Automation instrument, as shown in Figure 17.26.

Figure 17.26

Select the Automation instrument.

At the time of this writing, this launches the instrument and immediately begins recording—nothing. No script is selected, so Automation simply fills the timeline with a blank rectangle.

Click the Stop button to stop the run. Wait while Instruments resets itself. Click the Add button on the Scripts sub-pane, as shown in Figure 17.27. You can create a new script and edit it in the instrument, import an existing script, or click a previous script from a list at the bottom of the floating menu—assuming you have loaded at least one script already.

Editing an Automation script

Select Product ➪ Profile, and choose the Automation instrument (refer to Figure 17.26).

Click the Edit button and an edit window appears, as shown in Figure 17.28. This window is part of the Dashcode widget editor described in Appendix A. It includes keyword highlighting for JavaScript and a script selection menu. But it's less sophisticated than the Xcode editor and lacks most of Xcode's features, including code completion, syntax checking, and automated indentation.

Even though it's limited, it's built into the Automation instrument; this makes it more convenient than an external editor.

Figure 17.27

Load an automation script.

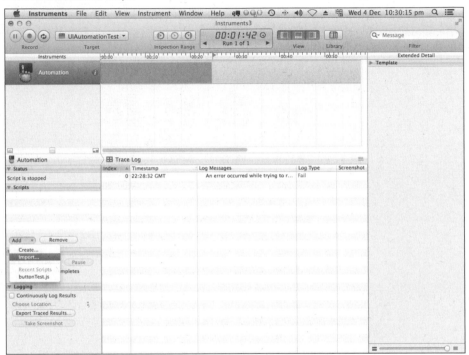

CAUTION

It's a good idea to use the built-in editor after you create or import a script. If you try to edit in an external editor while the script file is open in the instrument, both will get confused and you can lose changes. If you prefer to use an external editor, the instrument prompts you with a dialog after every edit. Select the Revert option to load the changed file.

Getting started with Automation scripting

Automation scripting is related to the Document Object Model (DOM) used to access the features of web pages. Like Objective-C, it uses objects and accessors, but the syntax is somewhat different. You don't need to create classes in your code, because they already exist.

Initializing the script

Scripts typically start with the following boilerplate code:

```
var target = UIATarget.localTarget();
var thisApp = target.frontMostApp();
var thisWindow = thisApp.mainWindow();
```

Figure 17.28

Editing an automation script.

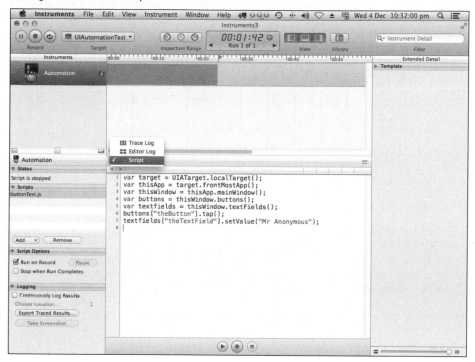

You can then use the object types listed in the documentation for `UIAElements` to return arrays of UI elements. For example,

```
var textfields = thisWindow.textFields();
```

returns an array of text fields. You can then access the text fields by the name you set in IB

```
textfields.["aNameSetInIB"]...
```

or by the standard numerical subscript

```
textfields[0]...
```

The `length` function returns the number of items in an array.

TIP

`mainWindow()` includes all the controls in your app. You don't need to be more specific about selecting sub-views.

Generating input events

You can set values for UI events by accessing their value property:

```
textFields["username"].setValue("Mr Anonymous");
```

You can also automate button taps using the `tap()` function:

```
buttons["theButton"].tap();
```

An extended version of the same code can tap buttons on the built-in keyboard. For example,

```
app.keyboard().elements().["go"].tap();
```

taps the Go button.

If your application needs to wait after an event, use this:

```
target.delay(timeInSeconds);
```

Logging output

To log events and values, use calls to `UIALogger`, which displays messages in the script log window under the timeline. `UIALogger` has various message levels, which force messages to appear in different colors. For example,

```
UIALogger.logFail ("Something bad happened.");
```

appears on the console in red.

Creating test scripts

Testing typically follows these steps:

1. Preset some UI elements with test values.

2. Perform an operation, sometimes using a button tap.

3. Pause if necessary.

4. Read return values and generate messages for pass/fail conditions or general reporting.

You can, of course, include various paths through the test sequence, depending on the test results.

Figure 17.29 shows a trivial example running a very simple test. In this example, the code is unlikely to fail, because the number of text fields is fixed. But in a more complex test, it can be useful to report the number of items in a UI. For example, you can report the number of cells in a table view after loading data from a remote source.

Figure 17.29

This is the output from a very simple test script. The script has changed the contents of the text field and logged the UI events.

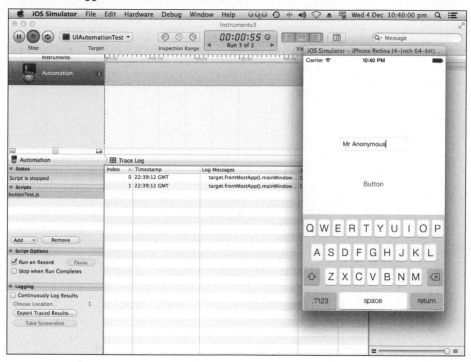

CAUTION

Scripts can be unpredictable, and features may not work as expected. It's a good idea to review the many online examples of scripting created by other developers before you begin creating your own. At the time of this writing, scripting remains somewhat buggy.

Summary

Instruments can be useful for tracking down subtle low-level errors that are difficult to find with simple debugging. The Instruments UI is fairly straightforward, and being able to watch allocations in real time is a very powerful feature.

However, Instruments really needs a good, fast Mac. The initial launch and setup time can be long on slow hardware, especially if memory is limited. To get the best from Instruments, you need at least 16MB of memory and a recent quad-core processor.

Working with Testing and Integration

Unit testing is a powerful software engineering technique that's supported in Xcode. This chapter outlines the technique so you can understand the theory behind unit testing, and it explains how to use unit testing in practice.

Introducing Unit Testing

You can test software in many ways, and software engineering has evolved formal processes that can simplify design and improve project efficiency.

Software can fail in five ways:

- The conceptual model for the user interface is misleading, incorrect, or inconsistent. If typical users make wrong assumptions about the software, the developer has made wrong assumptions about how users think and how they expect the software to work. Failures at this level may not be critical, but they frustrate users and waste their time.

- The UI is fragile. Common and inevitable user errors—such as whitespace in text, null entries, misspellings or invalid characters, or accidental mouse clicks—cause the application to fail.

- The UI or underlying model isn't secure. Deliberate hacking attempts can open an application's internal features to outsiders in an uncontrolled way.

- The underlying logic is flawed. Code may contain incorrect assumptions about interfaces, contracts, and processing requirements.

- The underlying logic is fragile. Memory or file errors, API inconsistencies and bugs, threading issues, and other method-driven issues create crashes or other problems. Failures can be complex and cumulative; a feature works until a problem occurs, and then a dependent feature appears to fail at some point later. The dependencies may not be obvious.

In This Chapter

Introducing unit testing

Creating a simple unit test project

Using bots for testing and integration

NOTE

In software engineering, a *contract* is an explicitly defined interface between two elements. The two elements are designed to exchange information in a certain way, and the contract defines the details of the exchange—specifically the data format sequence and sometimes the precise timing of the exchange.

Unit testing is designed to help with some of these problems, but it isn't a solution for all of them. Philosophically, unit testing is closer to method and function testing than sequence testing. To use unit testing successfully, code should have clearly defined interfaces and predictable outputs.

A key benefit of unit testing is that if a bug is easy to reproduce, it's easy to test for it. Creating a test guarantees that future bug fixes don't reintroduce problems. Unit testing can help make these *regression errors* less likely.

Another benefit is that with minor modifications, test code can be used as example code in documentation, to illustrate how features are designed to work.

Unit testing can also be used to stress test applications. The same code can be run over and over. Memory errors and obscure timing issues are more likely to show up in repeated testing than in sporadic beta exploration. You also can use unit testing as a design aid. If you test as you go, you can catch logical inconsistencies and overly complex contracts before you implement them. Some developers create test code to sketch how a feature should work before writing the code for the feature.

In spite of the advantages, unit testing remains controversial. There's an approximate consensus that unit testing is most effective in collaborative projects with a well-defined API. Solo programmers are more likely to have an overview of their project than group developers, so objective testing of elements can sometimes be more of a distraction than a benefit. As interaction becomes more GUI-driven and open-ended, unit testing code can become so large that it rivals the size of the main application, and the return on the time and effort invested becomes smaller.

For all applications, unit testing is most effective when combined with intensive beta testing and formal bug tracking. The most robust production regime combines beta testing, unit testing, and aggressive defensive coding that anticipates and codes around likely input errors.

TIP

Larger collaborative projects can benefit from a commercial bug tracking application such as FogBugz (`http://www.fogcreek.com/Fogbugz/`). GitHub and other source code repositories include alternative bug management tools. Even solo developers can benefit from formal bug reporting and management.

Understanding Unit Testing in Xcode

In outline, you can do the following with unit testing:

- Compare returned values from a method or function with expected values.
- Check that objects are created and initialized correctly.

- Confirm that error conditions throw an exception.
- Repeat tests any number of times.
- Create composite test sequences that run various tests in order.
- Select tests depending on the results of previous tests.

When you create a new iOS or OS X project, you can choose to add unit testing features. Xcode automatically adds the features—in fact, it adds a separate target that implements unit testing—and initializes them. However, the initialization isn't comprehensive, and extra work is required before you can begin adding test code. The work isn't described in the official documentation, but it is listed below.

In detail, the unit testing package includes the following:

- **A framework called XCTest:** The framework manages the testing and creates error reports. You must add custom code for each feature or case you want to test.
- **A set of test macros:** The macros are part of the testing framework. They can check for possible error conditions and report them during a build, but they do nothing until you add them to your code.
- **A separate test bundle:** To run your tests, build the bundle. Errors are reported during the build.
- **A test class, which is part of the bundle:** You add custom test code to this class and include macros to check for error conditions and report them. This custom code runs automatically during a build. Each test method in the class is called a *test case*.

If you're new to unit testing, you may find the process counterintuitive. You might expect unit testing to be a runtime process, like debugging. But it isn't. In fact, you run unit tests by selecting a special test build option for testing. The build process runs your test code, and errors appear in the Issue navigator and Test navigator. Supporting output appears in the console. But unlike conventional debugging, the Issue navigator and Test navigator display the main results.

You must understand that the test build is independent of the standard release/debug builds. It's possible for a release/debug build to complete with no errors, even though a test build reports multiple bugs. It's also possible for a test build to work even though a release or debug build doesn't.

A standard build reports basic compilation and linking errors. Your test build adds further checks for logical consistency, predictable output, and other error conditions. It's up to you to decide what you want to test and how you want to test it, to add code to implement the tests, and to define the format and content of any error messages generated by tests that fail.

The testing framework gives you the tools to build tests, but it doesn't recommend specific tests, include any default tests, or suggest useful testing strategies. Until you add test case code, a test build fails by reporting that a default test method hasn't been implemented. It's up to you to decide which features should be tested, how they should be tested, and how complex and exhaustive the testing process should be.

CAUTION

If your test code includes logical errors, the testing process itself fails. Keep tests as simple as possible, and build more complex tests from simple tests that are known to work. This won't guarantee that your tests are valid, but it's more likely to be useful and manageable than a complex, intricate test system that's difficult to understand.

Creating a Simple Unit Test Project

To create a project that includes unit testing, follow these steps:

1. **Use File ⇨ New Project to create a new project.**

   Xcode automatically creates unit test classes for iOS and OS X apps.

2. **Develop your project, modifying the standard project classes and adding new classes in the usual way.**

3. **For each feature that you want to test, add test case code to the test class file.**

   Each test method must begin with `test`.

4. **Optionally, you can use standard debugging tools to verify the test code.**

5. **Whenever you need to test the project, select the test build and build it.**

   If the test build fails, correct the bugs in the project code.

6. **When the project is complete, build a release version in the usual way.**

   Because the test code exists in a separate bundle, it isn't linked into a standard release build.

Because unit testing is open-ended, the example described in the rest of this chapter illustrates how to create a single simple test case for a single trivial class; it's a very basic math operation in a math framework. Although the framework and the test code are trivial, you can easily expand this example to meet the needs of a real project.

NOTE

This example illustrates how to create a unit test for an iOS project. The unit testing process for iOS and OS X projects is similar enough to be considered identical.

Creating a new project that supports unit testing

In Xcode 4, you had to choose to include tests when you created a new project. You also had to enable testing in the Build Settings.

In Xcode 5, all app templates include a test class with stubs for setup and teardown and a basic test case that fails by default.

When you create a new app, the test target and test class are included. Figure 18.1 shows the default test code in the . . . Tests.m file in a sample iOS project called UnitTesting, which was created with the SingleView template.

iOS and OS X apps include the same code. The `setUp` method is called before testing begins, and the `tearDown` method is called when testing ends. To work through the rest of the examples later in this chapter, create your own version of the UnitTesting project.

Figure 18.1

Review the code in the test class.

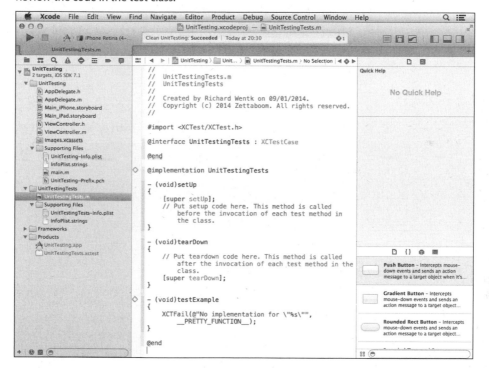

NOTE

The test class as a whole and individual test methods have small gray diamonds next to them. When you run a test, these either become green check marks for tests that pass or red crosses for tests that fail. `__PRETTY_ FUNCTION__` displays a human-readable formatted version of a function or method name.

To run the default test, select Product ⇨ Test from the main Xcode menu. The initial build takes significantly longer than usual, because Xcode must compile the test framework.

Figure 18.2 shows the result. The test class and the `testExample` method both fail, as shown by the red crosses in the code and in the Test Navigator window.

The failed function is also marked with a red asterisk. This looks like a code error, but don't allow this to confuse you. In this context, it's a test error.

Figure 18.2

Here's the result of running the default test.

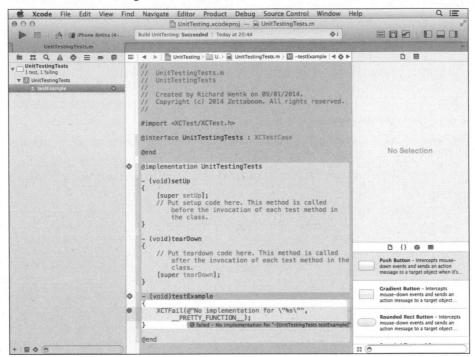

Creating a class for testing

Testing doesn't modify your main source code. It's an external process, and it leaves your main build code unchanged. For this example, create a new class called `MathMachine` to hold some basic math code. Right-click the UnitTesting group in the Project navigator, select New File, choose the Objective-C class option, and set it to be a subclass of `NSObject`. Save the file as `MathMachine`. Xcode adds a header and implementation file to the Classes group in the usual way.

NOTE

Because this project is called UnitTesting, the UnitTesting group holds the main source code. The unit testing code is in the UnitTestingTests group. In a project with a different name, such as ProjectX, the unit testing code would be in ProjectXTests, and so on. Put simply, the test code always lives in a file with "Tests" at the end of the name, in its own group.

NOTE

In spite of appearances, you don't need to add test classes to the test target. As long as you import the correct headers at the start of the `...Tests.m` file, Xcode should be able to find your code.

MathMachine unleashes the power of multi-gigahertz computing by adding together two integers—`inputA` and `inputB`—and storing them in a property called `sumAB`, which is set when a class instance is created.

Add the following code to the header file, as shown in Figure 18.3:

```
#import <Foundation/Foundation.h>

@interface MathMachine : NSObject {

    int inputA;
    int inputB;
    int sumAB;
}

@property int inputA;
@property int inputB;
@property int sumAB;

-(id) initWithSum: (int) inA and: (int) inB;

@end
```

This defines the `MathMachine` class with some supporting properties. It also creates a single method called `initWithSum:`.

Figure 18.3

Create a new class to add a pair of integers.

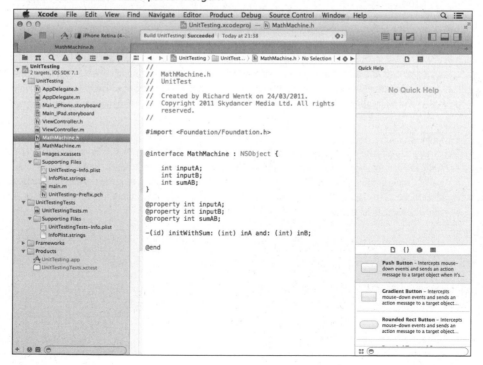

Add the following code to the implementation file, as shown in Figure 18.4; see if you can spot the mistake:

```
@implementation MathMachine

@synthesize inputA;
@synthesize inputB;
@synthesize sumAB;

-(id) initWithSum:(int)inA and:(int)inB
{
    if (self = [super init]) {
        self.inputA = inA;
        self.inputB = inB;
//Deliberate error!
        self.sumAB = inA - inB;

//Correct version
//        self.sumAB = inA + inB;
    }

    return self;
}


@end
```

NOTE

If you're new to Objective-C and Cocoa, this may seem like lots of code for a simple operation. In fact, most of this code creates a new class and defines one possible custom initialization method. Although this is a long-winded idiom, it's standard for Objective-C and Cocoa classes. In a real math framework, the class would be extended with many more properties and many other initialization and processing methods.

NOTE

Technically, you can also use the new auto-synthesize feature and skip the @synthesize directives. But note that if you do, Xcode requires an underscore in front of auto-synthesized variable names. Production code would also use NSInteger instead of C-style ints to create code that's 32-bit and 64-bit clean, and probably wouldn't explicitly declare the instance variables in the @interface section of the header, because LLVM can add them automatically. This example has been left as explicit as possible for clarity.

Figure 18.4

Implement the initialization and (buggy) addition method.

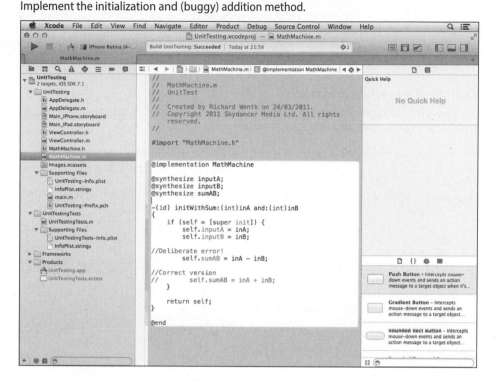

Creating a test case

Now that the project includes something to test, you can add the extra code you need to test it. Tests are defined as individual methods in the `<ProjectName>Tests` class.

The name of each method *must* start with `test`. These methods are run automatically by the testing framework. Methods that begin with any other string are ignored.

Each method is called a *test case.* As explained earlier, it's up to you to create test code that exercises the features of your target class in the most logical and comprehensive way. In practice, this requires three steps:

1. **Define the inputs to the test and the results they should generate.**

2. **Add a test case method to the `Tests` class header.**

Depending on your test code, you may need to define the inputs and expected results as constants.

3. **Implement the test method in the Tests implementation file.**

Use *assert macros,* described below, to implement the tests and report errors.

4. **Optionally, add setup and teardown code around the test.**

The Tests implementation file includes predefined `setUp` and `tearDown` methods to hold this optional code. Typically, you use `setUp` to create any objects you want to test and `tearDown` for any cleanup. But this approach isn't obligatory; the best solution depends on the test requirements.

Defining test inputs and results

Figure 18.5 shows the interface of the test class. Note that there's no separate header file: The default test code includes an interface section at the top of the .m file.

You can see two predefined inputs, `kA` and `kB`, and a predefined expected sum, named `kExpectedSum`. The `testMathMachineSum` method runs the test that compares them. Here's the code:

```
#import <XCTest/XCTest.h>
#import "MathMachine.h"

@interface UnitTestingTests : XCTestCase

#define kA 1
#define kB 1
#define kExpectedSum 2


-(void) testMathMachineSum;

@end
```

The `#define` statements and the `testMathMachineSum` method have been added. The other parts of the file are created with the project. Note that the method doesn't take parameters, and there are no semicolons after the #define directives.

This example is trivial. In a more realistic test case, the relationship between the expected result and the inputs would be less obvious. It might rely on a series of object allocations and other complex operations. Potentially, you could predefine an array holding a sequence of input events in the `setUp` method and sequence through the array in the test code implementation. Inputs and expected results might be downloaded as a file from a remote server and created by other members of a development team.

The key point isn't that the test is simple, but that the relationship between the test inputs and the expected output is well defined and predictable. The point of testing is to confirm that this relationship is reliable and that the code being tested reproduces it on demand.

The test code itself can use any standard Cocoa/Cocoa Touch and OS X/iOS features in any combination. You can even generate inputs and results dynamically using independent code that is known to work.

Note that you usually must be this explicit during testing. The XCTest framework adds no intelligence of its own. You must define the inputs, define the correct outputs, and create the code that compares one against the other. It's perfectly possible to create nonsensical tests that do nothing of value. XCTest runs them just as reliably as it runs any other test.

TIP

There are various ways to minimize developer error. A popular approach on larger projects is pair programming. Two developers sit next to each other and discuss code. One developer types it, and the other checks it. Between them, they're more likely to spot logical errors than a developer working alone.

Figure 18.5

Define test inputs, an expected value, and a test method.

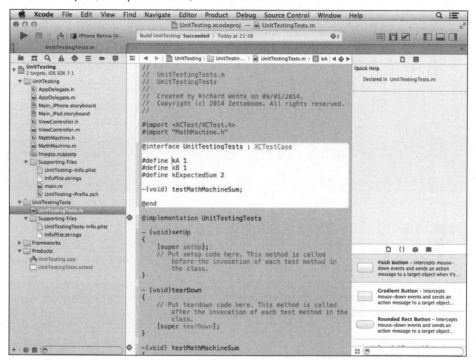

Creating test code

By default, the test implementation file includes a single `testExample` method that prints a "No implementation for this test method . . ." message.

To create a test, delete this method and add the code shown in Figure 18.6 and listed below it. The code creates an instance of the `MathMachine` class, initializing it with the `initWithSum:` method. It runs an assert macro to check whether the expected sum is the same as the sum returned by the method. Finally, it releases the instance. The two `%i` parameters are part of the macro. The first displays the expected value, the second the value returned by the test method.

Figure 18.6

Implement a test method.

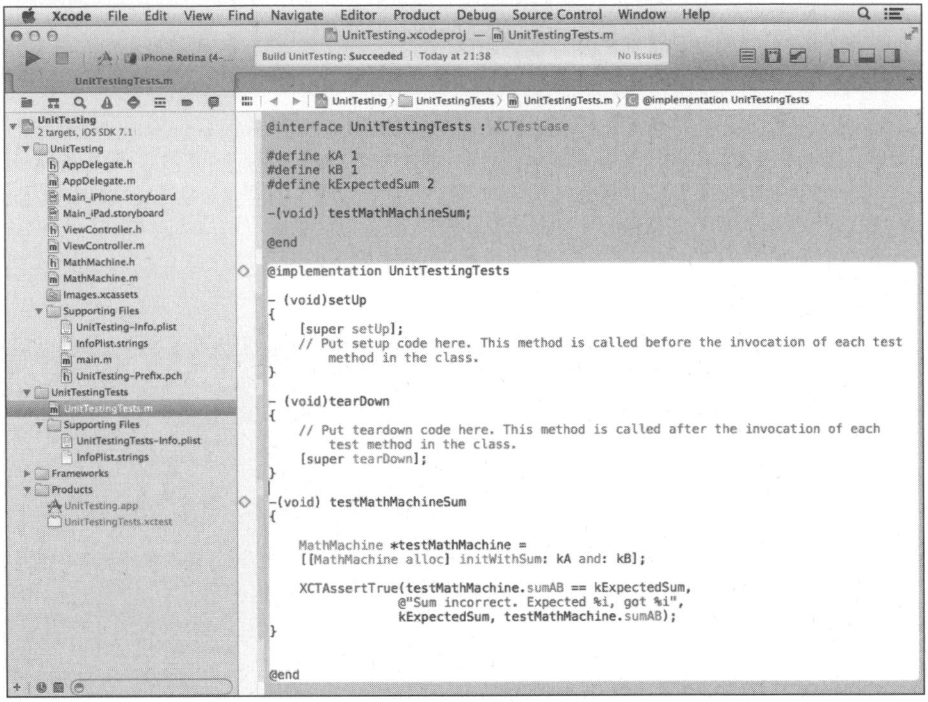

```
@interface UnitTestingTests : XCTestCase

#define kA 1
#define kB 1
#define kExpectedSum 2

-(void) testMathMachineSum;

@end

@implementation UnitTestingTests

- (void)setUp
{
    [super setUp];
    // Put setup code here. This method is called before the invocation of each test
        method in the class.
}

- (void)tearDown
{
    // Put teardown code here. This method is called after the invocation of each
        test method in the class.
    [super tearDown];
}

-(void) testMathMachineSum
{
    MathMachine *testMathMachine =
    [[MathMachine alloc] initWithSum: kA and: kB];

    XCTAssertTrue(testMathMachine.sumAB == kExpectedSum,
                  @"Sum incorrect. Expected %i, got %i",
                  kExpectedSum, testMathMachine.sumAB);
}

@end
```

NOTE

The `alloc` code could go into the `setUp` method. This example is deliberately self-contained for simplicity. In a more complex example, you can often improve clarity by keeping setup, test, and teardown code separated.

```
@implementation UnitTestingTests

- (void)setUp {
    [super setUp];

    //Set up code here
}

- (void)tearDown {
    // Teardown code here.

    [super tearDown];
}
```

```
-(void) testMathMachineSum
{

    MathMachine *testMathMachine =
    [[MathMachine alloc] initWithSum: kA and: kB];

    XCTAssertTrue(testMathMachine.sumAB == kExpectedSum,
    @"Sum incorrect. Expected %i, got %i",
    kExpectedSum, testMathMachine.sumAB);

}
@end
```

Understanding XCTAssert macros

The core of the test is in the line that begins XCTAssertTrue. This is one of the special macros included in the test framework. The full list is shown in Table 18.1. You can find more information about the macros by looking in XCTestAssertions.h in the XCTest framework.

Table 18.1 XCTESTAssert Macros

Macro	Reports an error if . . .
XCTestFail(message, <parameters>)	Always
XCTAssertNil(a1, message, <parameters>)	a1 is not nil.
XCTAssertNotNil(a1, message, <parameters>)	a1 is nil.
XCTAssert(expression, message, <parameters>)	expression does not evaluate to true.
XCTAssertTrue(expression, message, <parameters>)	expression does not evaluate to true.
XCTAssertFalse(expression, message, <parameters>)	expression does not evaluate to false.
XCTAssertEqualObjects(a1, a2, message, <parameters>)	a1 is not equal to a2. Both must be Objective-C objects that support the isEqual: method.
XCTAssertNotEqualObjects(a1, a2, message, <parameters>)	a1 is equal to a2. Both must be Objective-C objects that support the isEqual: method.
XCTAssertEqual(a1, a2, message, <parameters>)	a1 is not equal to a2. Both must be C scalar values.
XCTAssertNotEqual(a1, a2, message, <parameters>)	a1 is equal to a2. Both must be C scalar values.
XCTAssertEqualWithAccuracy(a1, a2, accuracy, message, <parameters>)	a1 and a2 are not within the stated accuracy. Used to compare floats and doubles, allowing for small rounding errors.

continued

Table 18.1 Continued

Macro	Reports an error if...
XCTAssertNotEqualWithAccuracy(a1, a2, accuracy, message, <parameters>)	a1 and a2 are within the stated accuracy. Used to compare floats and doubles, allowing for small rounding errors.
XCTAssertThrows(expression, message, <parameters>)	expression does not throw an exception.
XCTAssertThrowsSpecific(expression, specificException, message, <parameters>)	expression does not throw an exception of the specificException class.
XCTAssertThrowsSpecificNamed(expression, specificException, aName, message, <parameters>)	expression does not throw an exception of the specificException class with aName.
XCTAssertNoThrow(expression, message, <parameters>)	expression throws an exception.
XCTAssertNoThrowSpecific(expression, specificException, message, <parameters>)	expression throws an exception of the specificException class.
XCTAssertNoThrowSpecificNamed(expression, specificException, aName, message, <parameters>)	expression throws an exception of the specificException class with aName.

The macro syntax is unusual compared to standard Objective-C, so it's worth breaking it apart element by element. To create a test using the macro, you must include the following:

- An XCTAssert macro from the table
- A conditional expression to implement the test, which may take multiple parameters
- An error string, which optionally can contain standard printf/NSLog parameter placeholders with formatting codes
- The parameters to be logged, if there are any

In the example code, the elements look like this:

- **XCTAssertTrue:** Test if the following conditional evaluates to true. Write an error to the build log if it doesn't.
- **testMathMachine.sumAB == kExpectedSum:** This is the conditional that implements the test. It checks whether the expected sum constant matches the sum returned by the initWithSum: method in the previous line.
- **@"Sum incorrect. Expected %i, got %i":** This is the text of the message that appears in the build log when the test fails. It takes two integer parameters.
- **kExpectedSum, testMathMachine.sumAB:** These two parameters are reported in the message. If the test fails, the current value of the parameters is logged as part of the message.

When you create test code, you must select a macro from the table, add a suitable expression, and fill in the message and parameter details as needed. Without a test macro, your test code does nothing.

You can test for multiple error conditions by including multiple macros in a single test method. You can and should include multiple independent test methods. In a real example, each test case method should test a specific feature in your code. When you add a new feature or correct a bug, add a corresponding test case. You can also use these macros to generate messages that confirm when tests have been passed.

TIP

The `Assert` macro syntax is used throughout development in many environments. If this is your first encounter with it, it can seem unintuitive because `Assert` assumes negative logic and does the opposite of what you expect it to in English. It checks a condition and logs an error if the condition *isn't* true. When you use these macros, it can be helpful to think of "Assert" as equivalent to "Check if."

Running tests

Build the test, and you should see the output shown in Figure 18.7. The test case for the sum operation reports that the sum is incorrect. The error message uses the text and parameters you added to the test code.

Figure 18.7

The test failed. The unit testing code generated an error message to tell you which test raised an error.

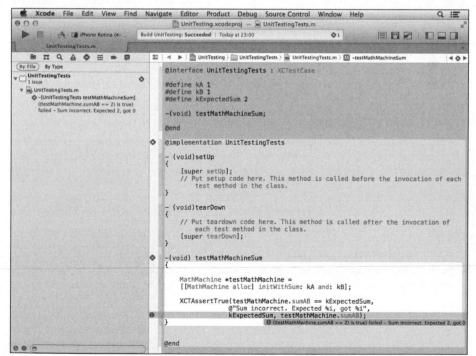

Note again that testing isn't like a normal build or debug session. The error appears in the test case code, not in the class that is being tested. In fact, it appears—with some redundancy—under the code that defines the error. And it's reported in the Issue navigator as an issue with the test bundle, not the main target. This shouldn't be surprising, but it is unusual compared to a standard Xcode build, and it's worth keeping the differences in mind when you work with the XCTest test framework.

To repair the damage to MathMachine, change the subtraction in the `initWithSum:` method to an addition. Select Product ⇨ Test again, and you should see the output in Figure 18.8. This time, the code passes the test, and Xcode displays green check marks next to the test method and the test class.

Figure 18.8

The test succeeded. Xcode displays green check marks when there are no `assert` errors.

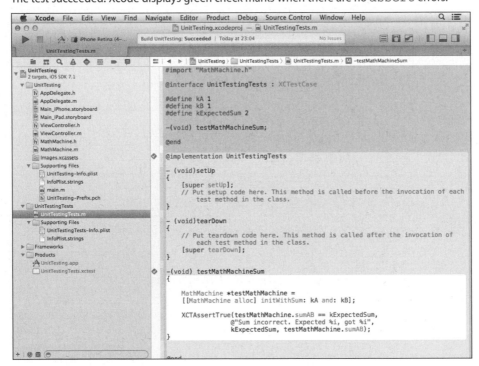

TIP

XCTest is ideal for Objective-C tests, but alternatives are available. For C++, it's worth exploring the alternative googletest framework available from `code.google.com/p/googletest/`. The framework isn't trivially easy to integrate into Xcode, but it offers expert developers a richer feature set and wider community support.

TIP

Don't forget that you can use the UI Automation feature in Instruments to exercise a UI. UI Automation is a different system, but the two test systems can work well together. You can use unit tests to check basic code logic and then exercise the UI to ensure that it manages user events correctly.

Using Bots for Testing and Integration

Bots are a new feature in Xcode 5. A bot can do any combination of the following:

- Static code analysis (See Chapter 16.)
- Unit testing (See the previous section in this chapter.)
- Archiving for distribution (See Chapter 13.)

Bots can run at regular intervals. You can also set them up to run whenever someone on a team makes a commit, or you can run it manually on demand.

To use bots, you must do the following:

- Buy and install OS X Server, preferably on a separate server Mac.
- Set up user accounts for your development team on the server.
- Set up a repository for your project, and enable source control.
- *Share* a build scheme with the server. Optionally, you can control what a bot does by creating a custom scheme.

Bots are designed to support team development. As developers commit changes, bots can check the code for basic errors, run unit tests, and build an archive. The last option is dual-purpose: Not only does it create a product that can be uploaded to the App Store, but it also reports basic build errors that may not appear during static analysis and unit testing.

If any step fails, a lead developer or other team member can see which commit broke the build. The developer responsible can then fix the issues.

For iOS, steps can build and run in all the available device emulations. Optionally, they can also run on various connected devices. This helps simplify the testing process. Tests don't catch subtle logic errors, but they do confirm that a project builds correctly on as many real devices and versions as you care to buy and connect.

TIP

You can set up OS X Server and bots on your development Mac. This may be a bad idea for solo manual development, because bots take time and resources to run, and you can typically get results that are just as useful by performing analyze/test/archive steps manually. However, it can be worth considering for large projects that take a long time to build, because you can set up a build and testing system that runs autonomously overnight.

CAUTION

Bots don't support UIAutomation, as described in Chapter 17. So there's no way to add automated UI testing to a bot—at least , not without creating custom UI testing code with specialized unit tests or custom scripting.

Getting started with OS X Server

OS X Server, shown in Figure 18.9, is an optional web server, Wiki server, user management, and network support add-on for OS X. It has two elements: `Server.app`, which is a UI for server management, and a selection of scripts and processes that run behind the scenes to create, manage, and support various network services.

Figure 18.9

Here's a first look at OS X Server.

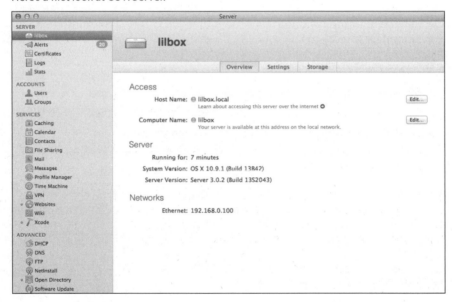

The Xcode element, shown in Figure 18.10, appears as a module with its own web service, accessed using a special port. The web element is really just a basic UI that displays reports generated by analyze/test/archive builds. The bot service runs behind the scenes and generates the web reports.

CAUTION

OS X Server has a patchy history. It's not known for bulletproof reliability, and the simplified UI presented by `Server.app` can disguise the fact that it may need some extra setup using commands typed into Terminal. It will *probably* work as described here. But if it doesn't, expect to spend some time in the Apple forums and elsewhere online looking for answers to low-level problems.

Figure 18.10

Here's the Xcode service in OS X Server.

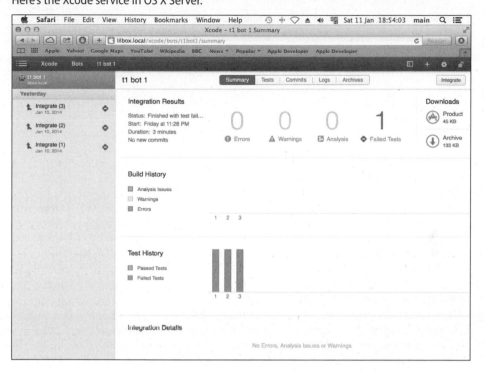

If you are in the Mac Developer Program, you can download and install OS X Server for free. Log in to the developer center, scroll down to the OS X Server link, and click the Download button to see a code that you can redeem in the App Store.

Click the button again to launch the App Store and redeem the code. OS X Server appears in your Purchases, and you can install it in the usual way, as a download of approximately 280MB.

If you are not enrolled in the Mac Developer Program, you can buy OS X Server from the App Store. OS X Server for OS X Mavericks costs $19.99 (£13.99 in the UK).

Setting up OS X Server

A full guide to setting up OS X Server would require a separate book (such as *OS X Server Portable Genius*). But for use with Xcode, you can ignore most of the features.

These are the three key elements to set up:

- **Users:** Each Xcode user with access to the bot server needs a network account on the server.

  Note that a network account is not the same as a conventional Mac user account. One logs you into the network services available on the server, and the other gives access to a single Mac.

● **Xcode Settings:** The Xcode module needs to know details of the developer team and to set up permissions to control who can use bots and view the results of bot runs.

● **Xcode Repositories:** Although you can set up the server to work with external repositories, the server can also host team repositories on the network.

Optionally, you can also set up the e-mail service, so team members can be notified of bot reports. This isn't obligatory, but—after you get it working—it can be convenient.

NOTE
You *don't* need to set up the Websites service to use the Xcode web front end.

TIP
Private team development on GitHub costs money. If you set up a local server, you can host your repositories on your network with optional Internet access for off-site work and optional Time Machine backup. Creating completely secure external access to your server can be challenging. But if no one knows your server's Internet IP address, and you install added authentication, you can have a reasonable expectation of security and privacy for less than the cost of an annual GitHub account.

Setting up user accounts and e-mail

Setting up user accounts and e-mail accounts can be a very simple process or a very complex one, depending how the server integrates with existing web servers, account management systems, domain name and IP address servers, and other network infrastructure. Full details are outside the scope of this book.

In outline, the easiest and simplest option is to set up the server as a stand-alone system on your network and give users local e-mail addresses. This avoids much of the complexity but still creates a useful working service. Users won't be able to access the server from the Internet, but this is acceptable for many offices.

More complex solutions typically require some combination of Open Directory setup (Open Directory is a popular networked user management technology), port forwarding to allow external Internet access, and local/Internet address translation and management using either or both a local DNS (Domain Name Service) or DHCP (Dynamic Host Configuration Protocol) service. For added security, you can also set up the server to work with a VPN (Virtual Private Network).

Setting up the Xcode service

After creating users and setting up e-mail, click the Xcode item in the list at the left. Click the big toggle button at the top right to the ON position. Then click the Edit button next to the Permissions item under the Access header to set up bot permissions, as shown in Figure 18.11.

Use the two menus to restrict access, in increasing order of security, to anyone on the network, to logged-in users, or to a specific list of named users. The last option is useful if you want to limit bot management to a team leader and perhaps a sub-set of senior developers.

Use the top menu to set bot creation and viewing privileges. Use the second menu to restrict who can view the web reports generated by the Xcode server. For small trusted teams, it's efficient to give everyone full access unless there is a very good reason not to.

Figure 18.11

Manage user access to bots and reports.

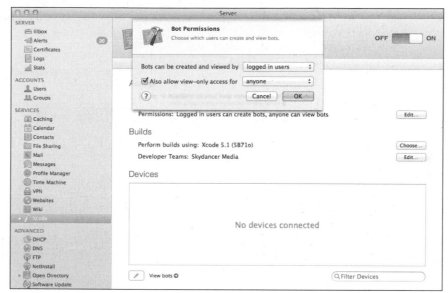

Next, click the Choose button under the Builds heading. Navigate to your production installation of Xcode on the server, and select it. (If you haven't yet downloaded and installed a version of Xcode on the server, do that first.) The server then uses the binary you select to build and test your apps.

Note that this option selects a version of Xcode *on the server*. It has no relationship to versions you have installed on a separate developer machine. The server doesn't know, or care, which versions you use on your developer Mac, but for practical reasons, it's a good idea to make them the same.

Note also that there's no way to run two different copies of the Xcode service with different versions of Xcode. It would be useful to build and test the same code on different SDKs to allow for future and/or backward compatibility, but in the current version of server, this isn't possible.

NOTE

Virtualized copies of OS X Server running on a single physical machine are beyond the scope of this book.

Finally, click the Edit button next to the Developer Teams item. Click the + (plus) icon, and enter the Apple ID and password you used to create a developer account, as shown in Figure 18.12. This adds the corresponding team to the Developer Teams list.

Optionally, you can also plug in one or more physical devices. Note that you must launch the server copy of Xcode to register the devices in the Organizer before you try to use them for testing. The server doesn't know about devices you register on your development machine.

After devices are registered, you can build/run projects on them automatically and create bots that report on the success or failure of a run.

Figure 18.12

Set up a team.

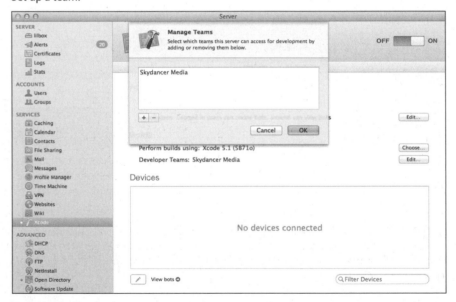

Setting up repository access

To set up repository access, click the Repositories tab in the Xcode window of the server module. Note that you don't need to create repositories here. You can do that later from within Xcode.

But you do need to set up access. Click the top Edit . . . button. If your server is on a private local network with no Internet access, enable all three options, as shown in Figure 18.13.

If the server is on the Internet and you want to limit external access, you may want to disable HTTP and HTTPS access. This limits repository access to SSH, which is a secure system protected by a password.

Figure 18.13

You control repository access here.

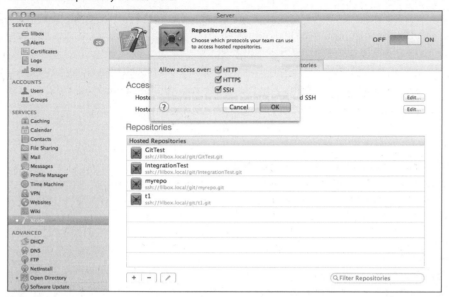

Finally, click the second Edit . . . button, and choose which users can create repositories. You can limit this to all users with a network account or to a specific list of users. Or you can leave access open to everyone.

More about security

Network security is a complex topic, and the correct security choices for your environment depend on whether you use Xcode exclusively or whether you also allow command-line Git access to local repositories. It also depends on whether you have an *SSL (Secure Sockets Layer) security certificate* installed on the server.

If you don't, HTTPS access won't work. OS X Server does not include an SSL certificate. If you want one, you have to buy one from an issuing authority and install it on the server. Users usually still see a warning when they access the Xcode server. They have to manually set up their Mac to trust the certificate.

In general, these kinds of issues become a problem only if you try to put the server on the Internet. If you are using it locally on a private network, security is much less complex. You can check all the options, and between your developer version of Xcode and the server, the process should just work.

By default, Xcode uses SSH to communicate with the server and logs in to the server using your network login. HTTP and HTTPS access work with curl and wget. Although you can copy the web address of a repository and prefix it with either protocol, you get a blank page in a web browser—not a stylish download page, as you might expect.

Working with repositories

Repository support on the server is very flexible. You can also do the following:

- Create a server repository automatically when you create a new project on your development Mac. (This option assumes you have user access to the server and are on the list of users allowed to create repositories.)
- Set up a repository on another server, including a public hosting site such as GitHub.
- Create an empty repository on the server and add files to it.
- Clone an existing repository on your Mac to the server.
- Manage repositories manually from the command line.

Creating a server repository from Xcode

You can now use your developer version of Xcode to create a repository on the server. When you create a new project, check the Source Control box and select the server name from the list, as shown in Figure 18.14.

Figure 18.14

Create a server repository directly from Xcode.

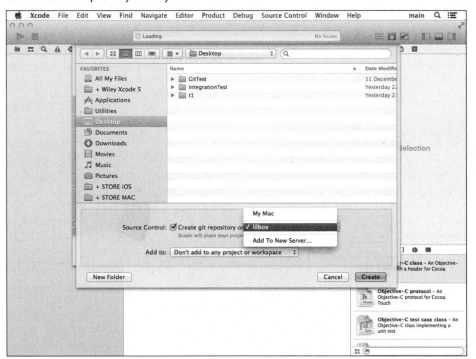

Make a trivial edit, and commit the project. Check the Push to Remote check box, and give the commit a name. Your local version of Xcode communicates with the server and creates a repository on it. The repository appears in the Repositories list on the server.

Using a remote repository

To use a remote repository, click the + (plus) icon in the Repositories tab, select either the Git or Subversion repository option, and enter a useful name; the name is for your reference only. Enter the repository URL, select an authentication option, and enter your credentials, if needed. Click Create, as shown in Figure 18.15.

Figure 18.15

Set up the server so it communicates with an existing repository.

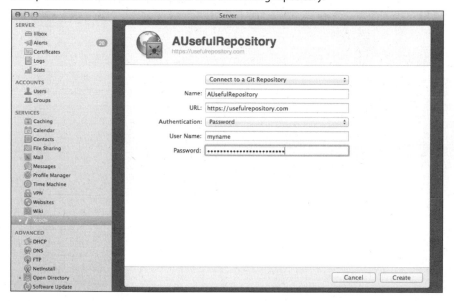

Note that when you set up a remote repository, the bot process copies the files in the project to the server and then runs the bot build sequences. Your developer Mac, meanwhile, commits files to the remote server in the usual way. The files don't pass through the server when you commit them. Access from your Mac and the server is independent and unconnected.

This matters because if you haven't done so already, you must set up the remote repository on your development Mac before you can exchange files with it. Click Xcode ➪ Preferences, select Accounts, and click the + (plus) button at the bottom right of the window to enter your credentials for the repository.

You can skip this step when you create a new repository on the server, because Xcode sets up your credentials automatically.

Creating an empty repository on the server

To create an empty repository, open the Repositories tab in the Xcode item of the server and click the + (plus) icon. Leave the default Host a Git Repository item selected in the top menu. Give the repository a useful name.

You can now set up a list of users allowed to access the repository using SSH. The default limits access to logged-in users. Optionally, you can also allow users to access the repository over HTTP by checking a box, as shown in Figure 18.16.

Figure 18.16

Create an empty repository.

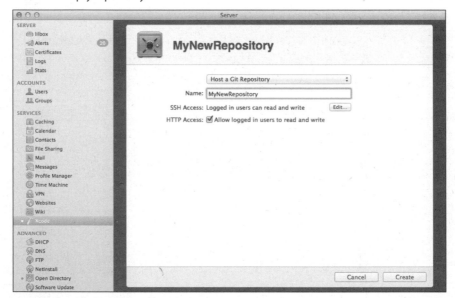

Cloning an existing repository to the server

If you have an existing repository, you can clone it to the server to simplify bot creation. Select Source Control ⇨ <ProjectName> ⇨ Configure <ProjectName>. Click the Remotes tab, and + (plus). Select Create New Remote. You can now select the server in the top menu and set up a remote name for the repository in the lower text field, as shown in Figure 18.17.

CAUTION

Don't click Add Remote, because it adds a repository that already exists on the server. Create New Remote creates a repository on the server using your local data.

Figure 18.17

Clone an existing repository to the server.

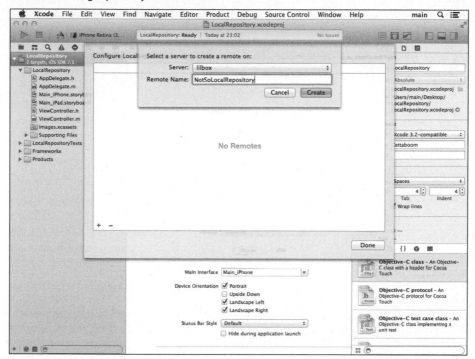

Managing repositories manually

Repositories on the server are Git-compatible, and you can use the standard Git commands to manage them. Potentially, you can create your own specialized scripts for complex source control applications. You don't need to drop down to low-level access for basic source control or for bot creation. But if your project is unusually complex, the option is available if you need it.

Creating bots

You can now open a web browser to view the bots page, as shown in Figure 18.18. The URL is `<local server name>/xcode/bots`. If you get an Apache error message, something has gone badly wrong. The simplest way to fix this is to take drastic action—format the server hard drive, and reinstall OS X and OS X Server. If you're a networking expert, you may be able troubleshoot subtle networking problems. If not, you can waste lots of time trying to fix complex issues that require expert skill.

Figure 18.18

View the bots page.

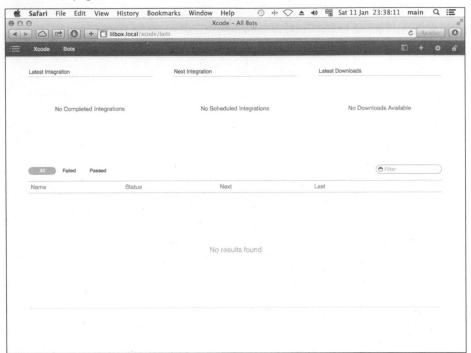

TIP

OS X Server is far more likely to work from a clean install. If you have an older version of OS X Server installed on your server Mac, you can try gambling on a successful install. But if there were any issues with the old installation, OS X Server may not work, and you should reformat and reinstall anyway.

Although you can create bots directly on the server, it's easier to set up a bot from Xcode on your developer Mac. Select Product ⇨ Create Bot, and type a name into the Name field, as shown in Figure 18.19. Make sure the Server menu is showing the name of your server and that the Share scheme box is checked. Click Next.

CAUTION

If you check Share scheme and click Cancel, you won't see the Share scheme check box again. Xcode has marked the scheme as shared already. You can un-share it again in the scheme editor.

Figure 18.19

Create a bot.

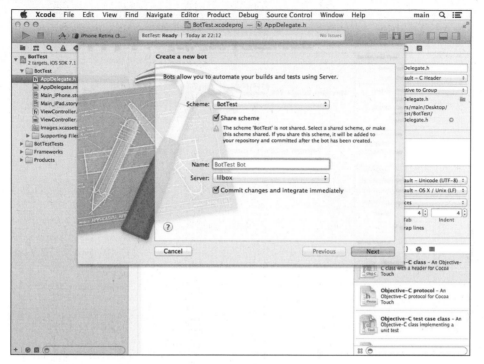

Figure 18.20 shows the bot scheduling options. You can run bots hourly, daily, or weekly, on every commit, or manually. You can use the check boxes to enable analysis, unit testing, and archiving separately. You can also turn cleaning on or off. It's common practice on larger projects to schedule a daily integration build to check that new commits don't break a build.

For the most accurate results, enable cleaning always. This slows down the build process by a significant factor and makes each build take much longer than an uncleaned build, because each build starts from scratch with no pre-compiled headers or other items. But it also gives each build the same fixed starting point. Because you are running the builds on a server, you can leave them to take as long as they need to.

CAUTION

If you're running the server on your development Mac, you want to build as rarely as possible. Xcode takes significant memory, and two separate instances with the server running take even more. If you don't have powerful, fast hardware, the server slows down your development builds. Similarly, if you're using the server for some other application, such as web development, you should monitor performance carefully to make sure it doesn't become too slow to be usable. However, if you're using the server purely for Xcode and build performance becomes less critical, you can usually afford to wait for a bot to complete, even if it's resource-intensive.

Figure 18.20

Schedule a bot.

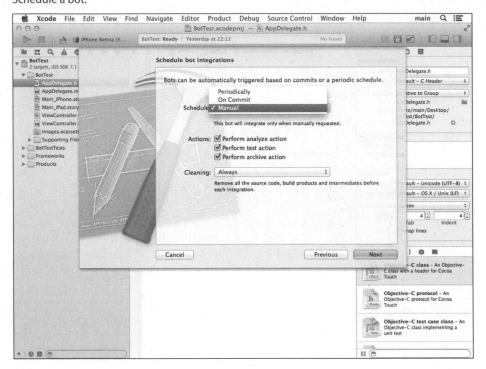

Next, you can choose a list of devices for iOS testing. You can build for all simulators, all devices, or selected devices. This option looks simple, but it can have a big impact on performance.

Building for all simulators can take a long time and may not be very productive unless you've included UI testing within your unit tests. It's usually more efficient to test a small and carefully selected stable of devices. Not only can you test special hardware features in full, but you can also set up different versions of iOS on different devices.

Finally, you can use the dialog shown in Figure 18.21 to set up a list of e-mail addresses. The bot can send e-mail notifications on success and/or failure. If you don't want to use notifications, uncheck the On Success and On Failure boxes. You may sometimes want to leave bots running overnight and receive error messages so you can fix issues immediately. More usually, you can leave the process to run as slowly as it needs to and check the web reports for details.

Click Create Bot to make your first bot. If you set it up to integrate immediately, it begins running on the server within a minute or two.

Figure 18.21

Set up bot notifications.

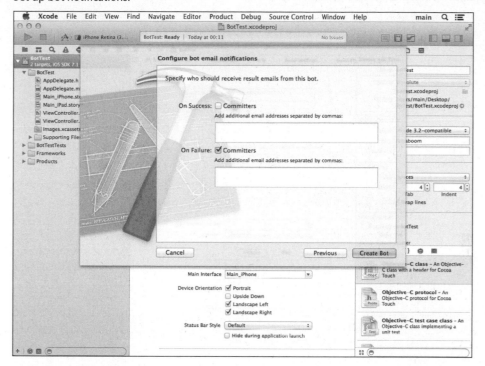

Monitoring bots

You can view bot results from within Xcode or on the web reports page. The Log navigator, shown in Figure 18.22, includes a list of bot-related information. The list at the left shows source control activity and bot integrations.

If you select a bot, the editor window shows the results of the last integration. In the figure, the build failed the test because it included the default unit testing error, described earlier in this chapter. Note how the unit testing is integrated. You don't need to do anything else to run it or set it up. After the server is working, unit tests can run automatically, and any errors appear with the bot report.

Additionally, the report includes a build history. Errors, warnings, and analysis issues are listed. If you click the download arrow near the top right, you can download a zipped version of the project and an ipa-packaged app version. To edit or delete the bot, click the gear icon. You can also click the Integrate Now button to begin a manual integration.

The integration summary, shown in Figure 18.23, shows the current integration state for all bots. You can click an individual bot to see more information about an integration.

Figure 18.22

View an integration report in Xcode.

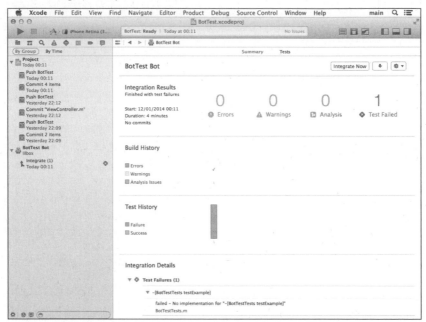

Figure 18.23

View an integration summary on the server.

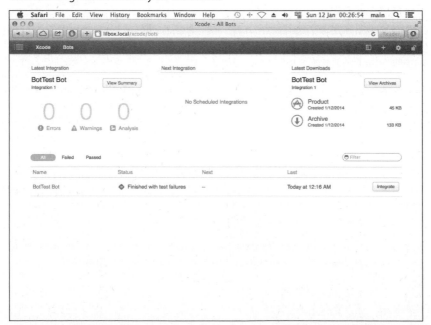

The key benefit of the web view is access to the detailed logs of the build. Click the View Summary button next to an individual integration to see the details, and click the Logs tab to see a complete list of all Git and build events that contributed to a build, as shown in Figure 18.24. The logs are very, very detailed. You don't need all the information they hold. But they can occasionally reveal build errors that are hard to find elsewhere.

Figure 18.24

View an integration log.

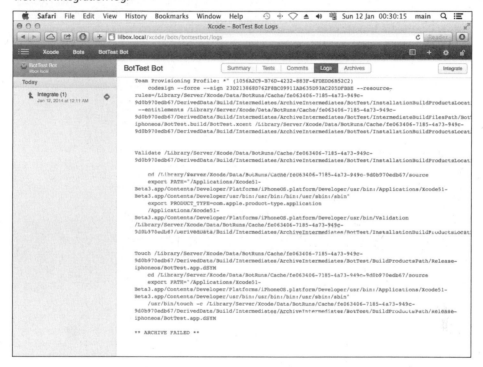

Bots have a few other interesting features. If you click the Screen icon in the bar at the top right, the server displays a full-page summary view of an integration, with pass/fail information about specific devices and/or simulators. You can click the gear icon to change bot settings or to delete a bot. And when you have multiple bots, you can click each bot's name in the integration list to view integration details.

Summary

Unit testing works best when combined with continuous integration. But it's most useful on moderately complex projects where the development team needs to exercise the code with standard tests to make sure updates don't break anything. Put simply, it's useful for industrial production-line testing, where a sequence of operations has a predictable result.

Stand-alone apps that use iOS hardware features and rely on UI interactions are more difficult to test. For the best results, spend some time mastering the UIAutomation features introduced in Chapter 17. When combined with bots and unit testing, you can build an app production system that's almost bulletproof—if you can spare the time to set it up.

Using Developer Tools

Xcode 5 includes a small selection of extra developer tools. Some tools, including the Application Loader, the Simulator, and Instruments, are described in detail in the rest of this book. The remaining tools are a grab bag of extras that are worth exploring. They are specialized rather than essential, but for certain applications, they can save significant time and effort.

NOTE
Early versions of Xcode 4 included a more extensive range of developer tools. Many are still available. They are no longer included in Xcode 5, but you can still download them from Apple's developer site. For details, see Appendix B.

Finding the Developer Tools

The built-in tools appear under the Xcode ⇨ Open Developer Tool menu, shown in Figure A.1. Selecting an item launches the tool. Most run as separate applications.

Understanding the Tools

The Instruments tool is described in detail in Chapter 17. The Simulator and Application loader are described throughout this book. The remaining tools are introduced in this Appendix.

Introducing the Printer Simulator

The Printer Simulator, shown in Figure A.2, makes it possible to test iOS app printing features without needing a real printer. The Load Paper pane, shown in the figure, displays a list of virtual printers. You can select the available paper size for each printer and even simulate printing to a large-format commercial roll printer.

Figure A.1

Find Xcode's Developer Tools.

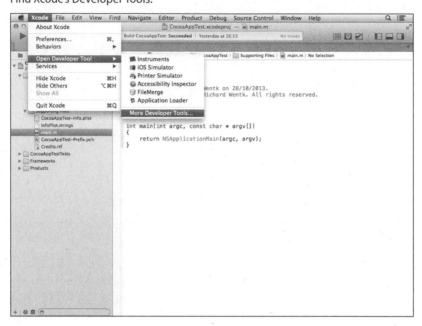

Figure A.2

Test your app's printing features with the Printer Simulator.

If your iOS device and your Xcode machine are on the same local network, the simulated print-ers are added to the list of printers available to the app. A print operation automatically creates and displays a PDF of the printed output on your Xcode machine. You can also view information about the print job in the log window. The simulation works smoothly and transparently, and it doesn't waste paper.

Working with the Accessibility Inspector

The Accessibility Inspector, shown in Figure A.3, displays information that you can use to enhance the accessibility of your applications. Details appear as a hierarchy in the application's main window. The details change as you mouse around the screen; the inspector displays the hierarchy for the element under the mouse pointer. You can also open a Verifier window that runs accessibility tests on any application in memory.

Figure A.3

The Accessibility Inspector works with the NSAccessibility class.

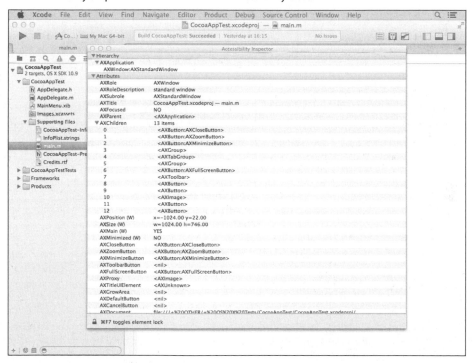

The accessibility features in OS X still have remnants of the old Carbon API, which is why the fea-tures in the inspector start with the AX prefix. To learn more about developing for accessibility, search for NSAccessibility in the online developer documentation.

Comparing and Merging Files

In spite of the name, the FileMerge tool, shown in Figure A.4, offers file comparison as well as file merging. The comparison tool is similar to a visual version of the UNIX `diff` command.

Figure A.4

The first part of a merge identifies file differences.

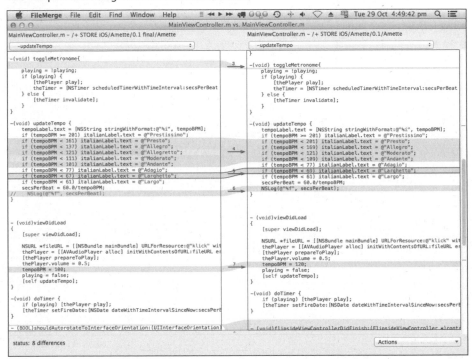

FileMerge is more powerful than it looks, and it's easier to use than any of the standard UNIX command-line tools. You can compare directories and files, merge directories and files, and compare two files or directories to a common ancestor, merging the differences into a separate merge target.

Differences are highlighted, as shown in the figure. You can use the Actions menu at the lower right to manage differences, choosing to combine files in either direction or to leave specific differences unchanged.

Summary

This appendix listed the tools built into Xcode that aren't described elsewhere in this book. It introduced the Printer Simulator, the Accessibility Explorer, and FileMerge tool and included brief usage notes for each application.

Getting Started with Optional Tools and Utilities

M any of the utilities that were bundled with earlier versions of Xcode are now available only as optional downloads. This helps minimize the overall Xcode package size, but it also means the tools are easy to miss. It can also be difficult to understand what they do, because documentation is perhaps not as comprehensive as it could be.

A full user guide for every tool would double the size of this book, so this appendix summarizes the key features of each tool. Interested readers can find more detailed information in Apple's official documentation and in online discussions.

Finding the Tools and Utilities

To find the download area, select Xcode ⇨ Open Developer Tool ⇨ More Developer Tools . . . Xcode loads the location of the download area in your default browser, as shown in Figure B.1. You may need to log in to your developer account before the page appears.

NOTE
You can access the download area directly from `http://developer.apple.com/downloads`. When you access the page from Xcode, the URL includes a default search term to filter out downloads that are not relevant to Xcode.

In This Appendix

Finding the tools and utilities

Understanding different versions

Understanding the tools

Figure B.1

Look at Xcode's optional tools and utilities in the Apple developer downloads area.

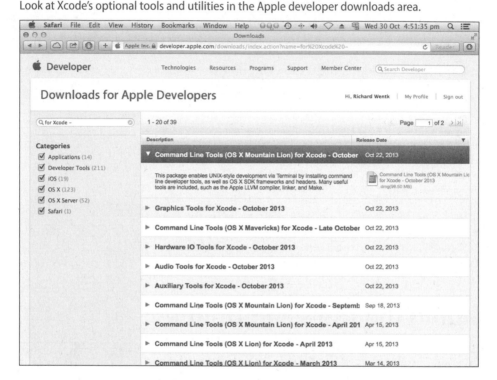

Understanding Different Versions

Apple regularly updates the tools for each new version of OS X and iOS. Apple may also issue intermediate updates. Some downloads are compatible with a specific version of iOS or OS X.

As a general rule, always download the most recent version that matches your development system. You may occasionally need to work with older versions if you are targeting an older version of an operating system, or because Apple sometimes removes features from the tools and you can only work with those features if you download an older version.

CAUTION

Some tools are no longer updated. For example, at the time of this writing in Fall 2013, the Accessibility Tools were last modified in February 2012. However, even if the tools haven't changed for a while, they may still be useful and current. Or they may not be; Apple sometimes abandons tools that are no longer useful. For example, at the time of this writing, the Dashcode widget creation tool has not been updated for OS X Mavericks.

Understanding the Tools

The tools are bundled into categories. Each category is supplied as a single downloadable dmg file. After you open and mount the dmg file, you can select the tools you want to install by dragging some or all of them to /Applications.

● **Command-line tools:** Download this bundle if you want to build applications from the command line. Many open source projects available on GitHub and other repositories are not packaged as Xcode projects and can be built only with the command-line tools.

● **Graphics tools:** This bundle includes tools for working with OpenGL graphics, the Quartz graphics framework, and Core Image filters.

● **Audio tools:** This bundle downloads optional extras needed to Apple-format Audio Units.

● **Hardware tools:** This bundle includes the IORegistryExplorer tool (for exploring a Mac's hardware registry) and a selection of connectivity and network diagnostic monitoring tools.

● **Auxiliary tools:** This bundle includes a collection of miscellaneous tools, including a clipboard viewer, crash reporter, and so on. A full list appears later in this appendix.

Exploring the command-line tools

OS X is based on BSD (Berkley Software Distribution) UNIX. You can access the OS X command line using the Terminal app, in /Applications/Utilities, as shown in Figure B.2. All the standard UNIX command-line tools are available, with support for shell scripting, pipes and redirection, and access to the full UNIX file system. You can also use other scripted languages such as Python, which is bundled with OS X.

Figure B.2

Use the Terminal application to perform a simple UNIX command.

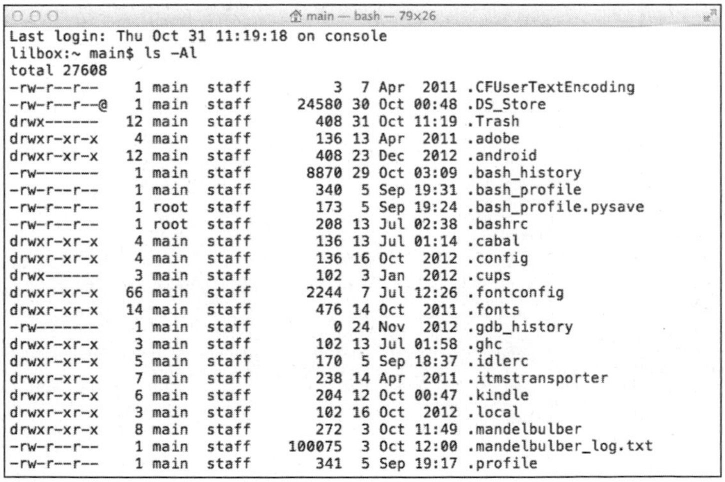

```
                            main — bash — 79×26
Last login: Thu Oct 31 11:19:18 on console
lilbox:~ main$ ls -Al
total 27608
-rw-r--r--    1 main   staff        3  7 Apr  2011 .CFUserTextEncoding
-rw-r--r--@   1 main   staff    24580 30 Oct 00:48 .DS_Store
drwx------   12 main   staff      408 31 Oct 11:19 .Trash
drwxr-xr-x    4 main   staff      136 13 Apr  2011 .adobe
drwxr-xr-x   12 main   staff      408 23 Dec  2012 .android
-rw-------    1 main   staff     8870 29 Oct 03:09 .bash_history
-rw-r--r--    1 main   staff      340  5 Sep 19:31 .bash_profile
-rw-r--r--    1 root   staff      173  5 Sep 19:24 .bash_profile.pysave
-rw-r--r--    1 root   staff      208 13 Jul 02:38 .bashrc
drwxr-xr-x    4 main   staff      136 13 Jul 01:14 .cabal
drwxr-xr-x    4 main   staff      136 16 Oct  2012 .config
drwx------    3 main   staff      102  3 Jan  2012 .cups
drwxr-xr-x   66 main   staff     2244  7 Jul 12:26 .fontconfig
drwxr-xr-x   14 main   staff      476 14 Oct  2011 .fonts
-rw-------    1 main   staff        0 24 Nov  2012 .gdb_history
drwxr-xr-x    3 main   staff      102 13 Jul 01:58 .ghc
drwxr-xr-x    5 main   staff      170  5 Sep 18:37 .idlerc
drwxr-xr-x    7 main   staff      238 14 Apr  2011 .itmstransporter
drwxr-xr-x    6 main   staff      204 12 Oct 00:47 .kindle
drwxr-xr-x    3 main   staff      102 16 Oct  2012 .local
drwxr-xr-x    8 main   staff      272  3 Oct 11:49 .mandelbulber
-rw-r--r--    1 main   staff   100075  3 Oct 12:00 .mandelbulber_log.txt
-rw-r--r--    1 main   staff      341  5 Sep 19:17 .profile
```

TIP

By default, Finder hides the UNIX system directories and certain other files. You can change this by launching Terminal and typing `defaults write com.apple.Finder AppleShowAllFiles YES`. Option+right-click the Finder icon in the Dock, and select Relaunch to restart Finder. This has the disadvantage of revealing `.DS_STORE` and other "housekeeping" files, but it also makes it possible to see /Library in your main user folder.

The command-line tools install a full version of the LLVM compiler and LLDB debugger for scripted and command-line building. They don't give you any of Xcode's visual features, but they are useful if you are more comfortable working with text commands or custom scripted builds, or if you are working on projects with raw source code that does not need Xcode's UI design features and is not packaged as an Xcode project.

Many open-source projects fall into the latter category. The command-line tools are also useful if you want to develop projects using popular cross-platform frameworks such as Qt. Finally, note that some kernel and I/O level tools can only be accessed from the command line.

CAUTION

The command-line tools include a version of the `make` utility. You may need to download and install further utilities such as `cmake` from other non-Apple sources before you can build some projects.

Getting started with the graphics tools

The graphics tools, shown in Figure B.3, include the following options:

Figure B.3

The graphics tools.

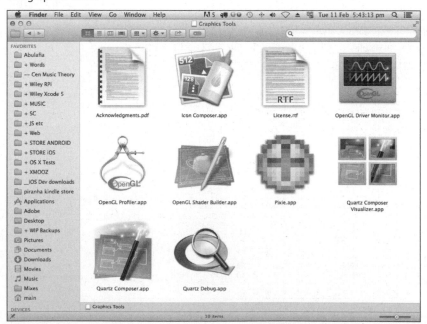

- **CI Filter Browser:** This is a Dashboard widget that previews the standard Core Image filters, either singly or in combinations.
- **Icon Composer:** This tool is now redundant, because equivalent functionality is included in the xcassets editor in Xcode.
- **OpenGL Profiler:** This app monitors OpenGL activity. You can attach it to a running application or launch a new one. Note that on some versions of this app, you need to copy a plug-in to /Library before it works correctly.
- **OpenGL Shader Builder:** This app creates new shader files and allows you to preview them before using them in an Xcode project.
- **Pixie:** Pixie is a floating magnifying window. Anything under the window is magnified by a factor between 1X and 12X, depending on Pixie's settings. You can lock movement horizontally or vertically. Pixie is useful for general magnification of app windows and includes a capture feature that can save the magnified image to disk.
- **Quartz Composer:** This app is like a music synthesizer for visuals. You can patch together various modules to generate and modify video content and to create music visualizers, screen savers, and custom Xcode views. Composer is powerful, fun, and poorly documented. It is much easier to use than raw OpenGL code, but it has never been as popular as perhaps it could have been.
- **Quartz Composer Visualizer:** This tool previews Quartz Composer projects in a separate window.
- **Quartz Debug:** You can use this tool to monitor the graphic performance of an app. It includes a frame-rate checker and a CPU meter.

CAUTION
Apple regularly adds and removes tools from all the collections mentioned in this appendix. The version of the toolsets you download may not include every tool listed here.

Introducing the audio tools

The audio tools, shown in Figure B.4, include two apps: HALLab and AULab. HALLab (Hardware Abstraction Layer Lab) displays information about audio hardware and drivers. You can use it to test audio drivers and report on the status of the default system drivers.

Figure B.4

The audio tools.

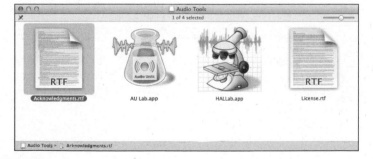

AULab (Audio Unit Lab) is a host application for audio units. If you don't own a separate sequencer application such as Logic, you can use AULab to host and test AU plug-ins.

TIP

Earlier versions of Xcode 4 included an AU plug-in Xcode template, with associated headers and libraries. Xcode 5 makes AU development much more complex. The AU headers are no longer available in the audio tools bundle, even though the package note states that they are. In fact, they have been moved to the Developer Library. See Technical Q&A QA1731 for a download link.

Investigating the hardware tools

The hardware tools, shown in Figure B.5, make it possible to explore and investigate your Mac's hardware options and network environment.

Figure B.5

The hardware tools.

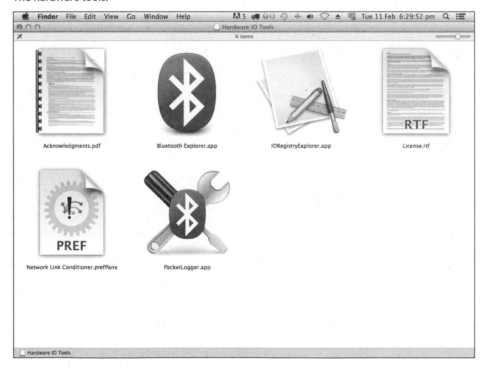

- The IORegistryExplorer app lists all the hardware devices listed in your Mac's registry, with a complete list of keys for each one.

- The Network Link Conditioner installs as a Preference Pane. You can use it to test your app's response to poor network connections, deliberately introducing DNS (Domain Name System) and packet latencies, and losing a set percentage of network packets.

- The Bluetooth Explorer app, shown in Figure B.6, provides extremely detailed information about Bluetooth operation, including device lists, packet logs, WiFi coexistence errors, and many other options.

- The Packet Logger app collects and lists raw Bluetooth packet information.

Figure B.6

Viewing Bluetooth Status and Bluetooth throughout with the Bluetooth Explorer tool

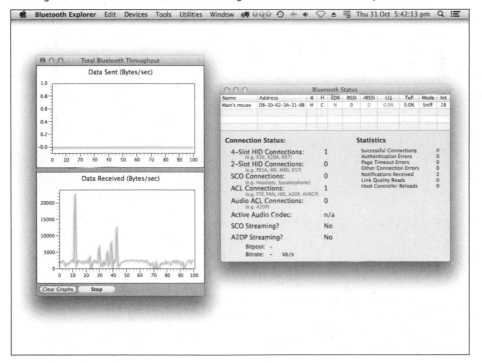

TIP

OS X includes a WiFi diagnostic utility that complements Bluetooth Explorer. You do not need to install it. However, the location is not obvious. The simplest way to launch it is to Alt-Click the WiFi icon and select Open Wireless Diagnostics. Note that WiFi must be on; otherwise, the utility is not listed in the menu.

Exploring the Auxiliary Tools

The Auxiliary Tools, shown in Figure B.7, include a miscellaneous selection of useful but non-essential extras:

Figure B.7

The Auxiliary Tools

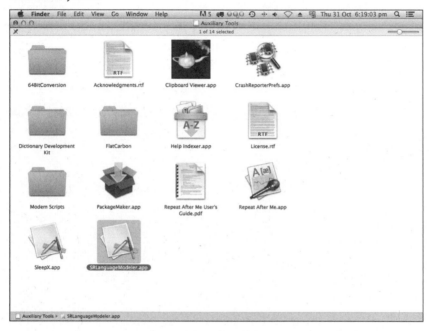

- **64BitConversion:** This folder includes a selection of scripts that you can run to convert 32-bit source code to 64-bit source code using the Darwin `tops` command.

- **Clipboard Viewer:** This app displays current and former clipboard contents as ASCII, HEX, or both.

- **CrashReporterPrefs:** This is not a complex app. It switches the Unexpectedly Quit dialog on or off.

- **Dictionary Development Kit:** You can use the tools in this folder to create your own dictionaries for the standard OS X Dictionary app.

- **FlatCarbon:** This is a collection of header files for developers who want to build legacy Carbon-compatible applications.

- **Help Indexer:** Use this tool to build help files. See the Apple Help Programming Guide in the Developer Library for details.

- **Modem Scripts:** This is a selection of CCL (Communication Command Language) scripts for modems. See the Introduction to CCL Modem Scripting Guide in the Developer Library for details.

- **Package Maker:** This legacy tool is used to build packages for older versions of OS X. This tool is no longer used for modern apps.

- **Repeat After Me:** With SRLanguageModeler, this app helps improve accessibility. It increases the performance and legibility of the standard OS X speech synthesizer. With diligent searching, you may be able to find a manual online.

- **SRLanguageModeler:** In theory, you can use this app to build custom models for the speech synthesizer. In practice, it hasn't been updated since 2005.

- **SleepX:** Test your apps or your Mac configuration with programmable wake/sleep cycles. As shown in Figure B.8, you can specify a script or command to run every time your Mac wakes.

Figure B.8

Put your Mac to sleep with SleepX.

CAUTION

Unfortunately, you can't use SleepX for general Mac automation. So you can't make it wake at a set time on different days, nor can you set it up to record a radio show from the Internet.

Summary

This appendix listed the tools and utilities that are bundled with Xcode but aren't built into the main application. It explored Dashcode and Quartz Composer and listed the audio, graphics, and hardware monitoring tools. Finally, it introduced the set of Auxiliary Tools and briefly summarized each one.

Working with Other Editors

X code includes a number of other built-in editors and supports links to external editors.

Editing plists

Plists (or property lists) define application settings. When you create a new iOS or OS X app, Xcode automatically creates a file called `info.plist`, prefixed with the app name—for example, `myApp-info.plist`.

This file includes important app settings—the name of the nib file loaded on launch, the application icon, version number, and so on—which were discussed in Chapter 13.

You can also create your own separate custom plists for your own use—for example, to define application preferences.

Plist editing is more complex than it looks. Xcode 5 has a number of non-obvious features that can simplify the editing process, if you know they exist and understand how to use them.

Understanding plists

Internally, a plist is an XML file saved with the `.plist` extension. The content is a standard Cocoa `NSDictionary`. It holds a hierarchy of named key objects that either store a single value or hold an array or dictionary object with its own contents.

If you're new to iOS and OS X, think of a key/value pair as an entity with two components: a key, which is a name string, and a value, which can be a simple or complex object.

Simple values are one of the following: a string, a number, a date, a Boolean, and a general data field.

Container objects are arrays or dictionaries.

An array stores values in strict sequential order and can be accessed with either a numerical or enumerated index. Array items typically appear with a number, such as Item 0, Item 1, and so on. Non-contiguous numbering isn't allowed.

In This Appendix

Editing plists

Editing Core Data model files

A dictionary is more free-form and is used as a more general, but slower, key/value container.

Container objects can be nested. An item in an array can be a string, a Boolean, and another array. This second array can contain a date and a dictionary. The dictionary may contain one or more further collections and so on, creating a hierarchical data structure.

Plists are typically used for application initialization of launch settings and user preferences. Although they can be arbitrarily complex, they're not designed for generic data storage. Some plists are standardized with specific keys and content formats. When you edit these in Xcode, you can only add keys from a fixed set of options. The formatting of the key values is preset.

Other plists are optional and freeform. It's up to you to design their formatting and content.

It can take some time to master plist editing, so it's good practice to experiment with it before you need to use it professionally.

Getting started with plist editing

Although Xcode includes a general purpose plist editor, it also includes features that simplify the editing of certain kinds of plists.

Three options are available:

- To edit any plist included in a project bundle, select it in Xcode, as shown in Figure C.1. This loads the file into Xcode's plist editor window.

Figure C.1

The plist editor in Xcode is the easiest way to work with plists.

- For simplified access to the main application settings plist—the `info.plist` file—you can use two editors built into the project build settings. These editors can be used only to modify this one file.

● To edit any other plist—for example, one of the standard OS X plists used to define the preferences for other applications—double-click it in Finder. After you install Xcode, it becomes the default editor for all plists. A floating editor window appears, as shown in Figure C.2. This editor is identical to the plist editor in Xcode. If the plist is part of an Xcode project, the project isn't loaded.

Figure C.2

Loading a plist into the Xcode editor as a stand-alone file launches Xcode, if it isn't already running. If the plist is part of a project, Xcode loads the project files.

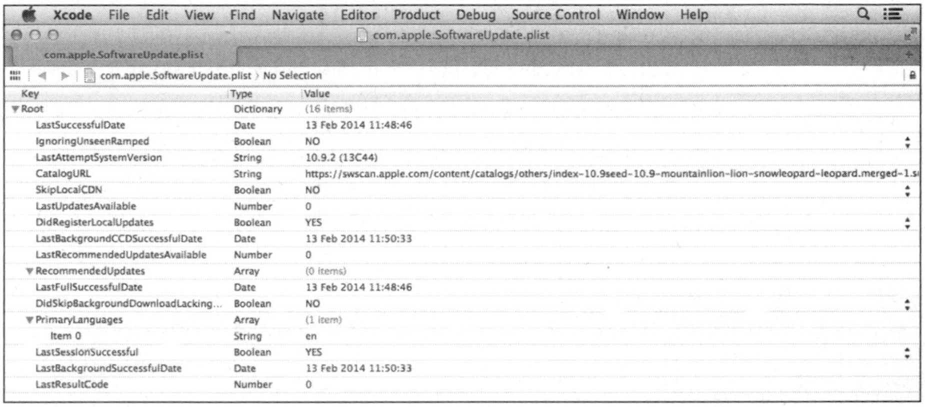

CAUTION

In Xcode, you don't need to save a plist file by hand. If you edit the same file in multiple Xcode editors, you see that any change in any editor is instantly duplicated in every editor. The file is saved automatically when you build or quit a project, like a source code file. This applies only to Xcode. Edits made in TextEdit must be saved in the usual way. It's a bad idea to open a file in Xcode and TextEdit at the same time.

NOTE

In Xcode 4, loading a plist file from an Xcode project didn't load the project. This has changed in Xcode 5. If you double-click a project plist, Xcode loads the entire project. In previous versions of OS X, TextEdit was available for simple plist editing. This is no longer possible in OS X Mavericks and later.

Editing info.plist project settings in Xcode

Every project includes a `<projectname>-info.plist` file that stores application settings. The settings are chosen from a list of standard keys. When you create a new Xcode project, the `info.plist` file appears in the project's Supporting Files group. (In very old projects, the `info.plist` file may appear in the Resources group.)

Understanding the application settings

When your app launches, one of the first things it does is load this `info.plist` file. It reads the keys and values from the file to find paths to the app's initial nib file and other support resources, to define runtime features such as the OS platform and multitasking options, to enable or disable graphics options such as anti-aliasing and the gloss look on iOS springboard icons, and so on.

The full list of keys that can be included in the file is long. In the plist support documentation, Apple groups keys into five main groups. The groups don't appear in the editor—they're simply a handy way to help you understand that different keys are used for different applications.

- **Launch Services:** These keys define low-level architecture-specific options.
- **OS X:** These miscellaneous keys are specific to OS X apps.
- **UIKit:** These miscellaneous keys are specific to iOS apps and the iOS UI.
- **Core Foundation:** These keys for either or both platforms define application house-keeping and setup features.
- **Cocoa:** These keys define Cocoa initialization options and Cocoa support features.

NOTE

A brief introduction to each key is available in the documentation in the Information Property List Key Reference document.

By default, the `info.plist` file includes a minimal selection of essential keys. You won't usually need to set the essential keys by hand. Keys that may need editing are accessed through the Capabilities editor, which is really just a GUI included to simplify plist editing.

The other keys are less critical. If they're included in the default `info.plist`, you can leave their settings unchanged. If they're not included in the default file, you can usually ignore them.

Occasionally, you may want to add a key by hand to enable a non-standard feature. For example, you can use the optional `UIFileSharingEnabled` key to allow a user to access files created by the app through iTunes. To do this, click the Info tab in the target build settings and follow the instructions below.

Editing application settings with the plist editor

To view and edit the application settings directly, find the `<project-name>.plist` file in Supporting Files and click it. Xcode displays the keys, as shown in Figure C.3. Note how the capabilities, supported orientation options, and other app settings appear in one easy-to-read list.

Figure C.3
Review and edit keys with the plist editor.

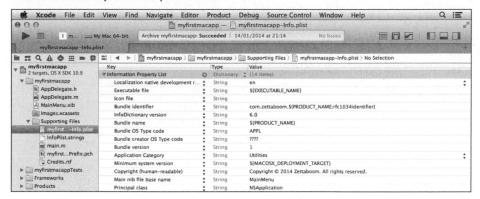

Changing settings with the Info editor
Although the meanings of the settings may not be obvious, the UI features are Mac-standard and simple enough to be self-explanatory. Changing any setting immediately updates the corresponding value in the app's `info.plist` file. The settings you are most likely to edit are listed in Table C.1.

Table C.1	Key Application Settings	
Setting	**iOS/OS X**	**Notes**
Localization native development region	Both	Sets the default locale for language support
Icon file	OS X only	(Replaced by icon content in Images.xcassets)
Main nib file base name	OS X only	The default nib file loaded on launch
Application does not run in background	iOS only	Set to YES if you do not want your app to continue multitasking after the user quits
Main storyboard . . .	iOS only	Sets the name of the storyboard file loaded on launch on the iPhone and iPad
Supported interface orientations . . .	iOS only	Sets the supported orientations for the iPhone and iPad
Application Category	Both	The App Store category for the app. The default setting is blank for iOS, and "Utilities" for OS X.

Editing applications settings with the Build Info editor
You can also edit these keys using the Build Info editor, which appears under the Info tab in the target build settings. Confusingly, the same keys appear *but the order is different.*

The Build Info editor also includes extra fields for Document Types, UTIs, URL Types, and Services, as shown in Figure C.4. These options are discussed in Chapter 13. They modify the plist directly without requiring hand-editing of specific key/value pairs.

Figure C.4

View the same keys, with further settings, in the Build Info editor.

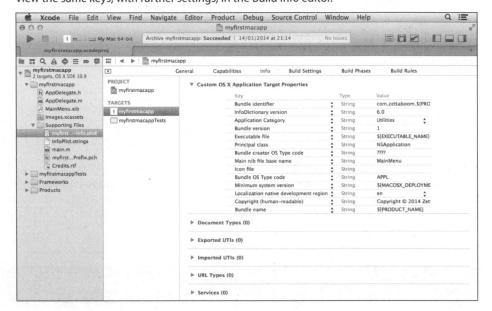

Adding optional keys

To add an optional key, follow the steps below:

1. Right-click an existing row.

   You can select any row as long as it isn't a multi-valued type; for example, the Type field isn't Array or Dictionary.

2. Select Add Row from the floating menu.

3. Select a key from the floating list, as shown in Figure C.5.

4. Click the Value field to edit the key.

   Value editing depends on the value type and is described later in this chapter, in the description of the general plist editor.

Figure C.5

Add one of the optional keys to the `info.plist` file.

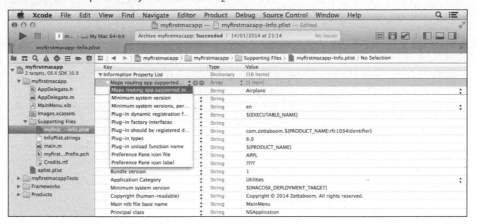

To remove a key, select its row and click the - (minus) icon to the left of the Type field.

A few caveats apply to key editing. Some keys are valid only on one platform; for example, it makes no sense to specify the "Application requires iPhone environment" key for an OS X app. But the key list is the same for iOS and OS X projects, and there's nothing to stop you from adding an invalid key to the project settings. Results are unpredictable; the OS may ignore the key, or it may crash your app.

Don't assume that the keys work as advertised, because some don't. It's good practice to experiment with a key to make sure that it works as you expect.

Finally, do read the Information Property List Key Reference. This reference is buried in the docsets, and it's difficult to find unless you know it exists. Without it, you won't know which keys are available or what they do, and the start-up options and settings will remain forever mysterious.

Creating new plists

The app's `info.plist` file is created for you and its keys are fixed and standardized, but you can add further custom plists for your own use and add arbitrary keys to them to suit the needs of your app. Here's how:

1. **Right-click the Supporting Files group, and select New File.**

   For iOS and OS X, select Resource and then Property List.

2. **Select Next, and save the file with a useful name.**

On iOS only, you can create a unique kind of plist known as a *settings bundle*. This is identical to a standard empty plist, but you can use it to store and manage application preferences. The iOS preferences system is complex and outside the scope of this book. But in this context, the `settings.bundle` file can be edited in the plist editor in the same way as a standard plist; the editor ignores the unusual name.

Using the general Xcode plist editor

The main Xcode plist editor is similar to the Info editor in the build settings, but it lacks the UTI, document, file type, and services options.

In fact, the `info.plist` is just one of a number of default plist file types. In the Summary and Info editors, the plist file type is fixed. In the general plist editor, you can select an alternative plist type. This doesn't change the contents or the format of the file, but it does replace the standard list of optional keys with one of a number of other lists.

Depending on the application, you can use these alternative key lists to save time when entering new keys. Or you can ignore them and create your own unique key list.

To select a file type, right-click anywhere in the edit area, and select Property List Type, as shown in Figure C.6. Select one of the options from the sub-menu. For a customized key list, Unique is the best choice.

Figure C.6

When you set the plist type, this doesn't modify the file type; it selects between the different sets of default keys that appear while editing.

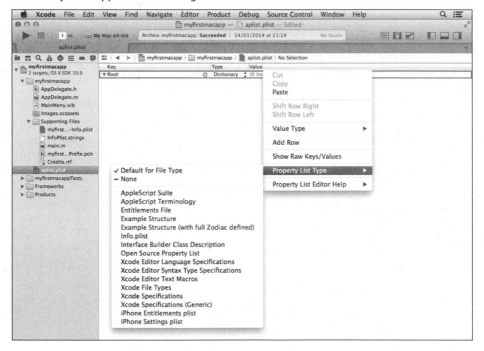

NOTE

These options are not all properly documented. The easiest way to find out what each file type does is to select it, select one or more of the default keys, and search for them in the documentation. Most options are aimed at intermediate to expert developers.

After you set the type, you can edit the list in the following ways:

- **Add a new key:** Right-click an existing single-value key, and select Add Row. Either select the key name from the default list or edit the default New Item name.
- **Change or select the key type:** Right-click the key, and select one of the types from the Value Type sub-options.
- **Delete a key:** Select the key, and use the Cut option in the right-click menu or press the Delete key.
- **View the raw key name:** For keys associated with Cocoa and other OS constants and parameters, you can view the key names by right-clicking and selecting Show Raw Keys/Values. This shows the key as a name—for example, `CFBundleIconFile`—instead of a text description. This can be useful when you're looking for key names in the documentation.
- **Edit a value:** Value editing depends on the key type. See Table C.2 for details.

Table C.2 Key Value Editing

Key Type	Single/ Multi-Value	Editing Operation
Boolean	Single	Double-click and use the menu to select YES or NO.
Data	Single	Double-click and enter an XML data value—for example, a string with arbitrary contents—between the angle brackets. The format and meaning of the data type is context-dependent.
Date	Single	Double-click and enter a date and time string. Dates are checked for validity before the edit is confirmed.
Number	Single	Double-click to enter an integer or floating-point number in string form. Invalid entries (text) are set to zero.
String	Single	Double-click value to enter a new string.
Array	Multi	Use the + (plus) and - (minus) icons to add and remove key/value pairs. Set the type for each and edit as above. Use the reveal triangle to view the hierarchy.
Dictionary	Multi	Use the + (plus) and - (minus) icons to add and remove key/value pairs. Set the type for each and edit as above. Use the reveal triangle to view the hierarchy.

Note that if you're creating a completely customized plist, it's up to you to decide if arrays or dictionaries are the best containers for the data. If you're editing any of the standard pre-defined key lists, the type is defined by the standard values and can't be edited.

CAUTION
Note that if there are no single-value keys in the list, if you try to add a new key, you get a new key/value pair in one of the multi-value items. The work-around is to make a copy of the multi-value item and edit it as needed, rather than trying to add it from scratch.

Editing Core Data Files

Xcode 5 also includes a Core Data Entity editor. Core Data is an optional data management framework included in both iOS and OS X. Although the concepts used in Core Data are simple, the English words used to describe them are complicated, and elements of the API are also more complex than they need to be. This can make Core Data seem more intimidating than it really is.

Understanding Core Data

Core Data has three main elements, supported by three optional elements:

- **A managed object context:** This is a complicated way to say "a container for objects."
- **One or more entities:** An entity is an object that holds data.
- **One or more attributes in each entity:** An attribute is a key/value pair. The key is a name string, and the values are one of a set of standard supported types: integers of various lengths, decimal numbers, floats, doubles, strings, Booleans, and so on.
- **Optionally, entities can have relationships:** A relationship references one entity from another. References can be bidirectional. They can be one-to-one, linking entities directly, or one-to-many, with multiple cross-links. Core Data's support for one-to-many relationships is limited.
- **Optionally, entities can include one or more predefined fetch requests:** A fetch request is an operation that returns objects or selected object attributes, such as the highest or lowest value.
- **Optionally, each fetch request can include one or more predicates:** These are specific search filters.

Although Core Data isn't a full relational database, it's often used for general data management. Typical applications include media collections and contact databases. For example, to manage a library, you might create a Book entity and add attributes to store the title, year of publication, author, and so on. You can then call standard Core Data code to add an instance of the Book entity for each book in the library, call other code to list all books with a specific author, and so on.

Entities, attributes, relationships, and other details are defined in a data model file, with the `.xcadatamodel` extension.

When you create a new project, you can include Core Data by checking the Use Core Data option, as shown in Figure C.7. This option generates a blank data model file that you can expand with your own entity designs.

Figure C.7

Create a Core Data project for OS X. iOS projects include the same feature.

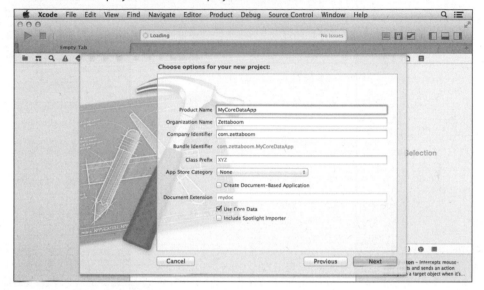

The data model becomes "live" with only supporting code. The Core Data templates include minimal setup and teardown code, but you must add further code to access and modify the data.

NOTE

This section is a brief practical introduction to the Core Data model editor but isn't a complete guide to Core Data development. For an introduction to practical Core Data programming and more information about creating and using entities, relationships, fetch requests, and predicates in practice, see the companion *Cocoa* Developer Reference title.

Introducing the data model editor

The data model editor appears when you select a data model file in the Project navigator, as shown in Figure C.8. The default file is empty.

Figure C.8

Take a first look at the Core Data editor, with an empty default data model file.

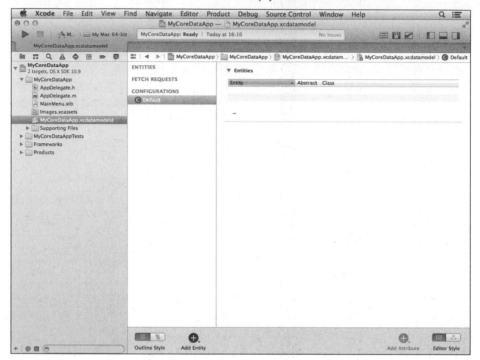

A key feature of the editor is the Editor Style option at the bottom right of the window. You can use this feature to toggle between the default table view and a graph view.

The table view is designed for quick summary overviews of the entities in the file. The graph view shows entities and relationships visually. The table view is easier to work with when the data model is busy, with many entities. The graph view is better suited for simpler models with a smaller number of entities, and it provides a more intuitive visual guide to entity relationships.

CAUTION
In Xcode 5, you can no longer select the graph editor if the data model is empty.

Creating a simple data model

As a very simple example of a data model, you'll add a couple of entities with a handful of attributes and create a relationship between them.

To create an entity, follow these steps:

1. **Begin in the table editor, and click the Add Entity button near the bottom left of the window, as shown in** Figure C.9.

   A new entity appears in the Entities list at the top left.

2. **Double-click the entity name to edit it. In this example, the entity name is changed to Entity1.**

NOTE

When you create an entity, Xcode displays options for Attributes, Relationships, and Fetched Properties. Note also that you can click the Default item under the Configurations header to view a list of entities, with associated class names. By default, each entity is an instance of Cocoa's `NSManagedObject` class. In a complex project, you can subclass entities to customize them with special features. You can also use Core Data successfully without subclassing.

Figure C.9

Create a new entity.

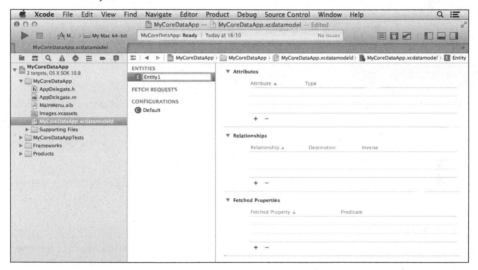

CAUTION

Entity names cannot contain spaces or special characters. Only letters, digits, and underscores are allowed. Names must begin with a letter.

To add attributes, follow these steps:

1. **Click the + (plus) button at the bottom of the Attributes pane, and type a name.** In Xcode 5, entity names must be lowercase.

2. **Left-click (not right-click) in the Type column to set the type.**

3. **To remove an attribute, click the – (minus) button.**

Figure C.10 shows an entity with three attributes.

Figure C.10

Add attributes.

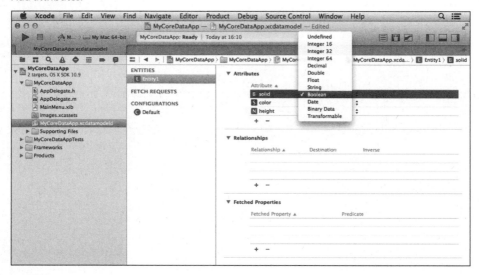

CAUTION

Although you can modify entities and attributes at any time, if your project has a data collection, you need to *reversion* the data. Reversioning is a complex topic outside the scope of this book; in outline, you must create a new extended data model and then merge the existing data with it. If you change the data model and re-import an existing data collection, Core Data crashes. It's good practice to finalize the design of the entities, attributes, and relationships in a data model before you begin working with live data.

To create relationships, follow these steps:

1. Add another entity, and add an attribute.

Name them Entity2 and usefulAttribute.

2. Select Entity1 again, and click the + (plus) button in the Relationship pane.

You'll see a new relationship called "relationship."

3. Left-click under the Destination header to select Entity2 as a destination, as shown in Figure C.11.

Figure C.11

Create relationships.

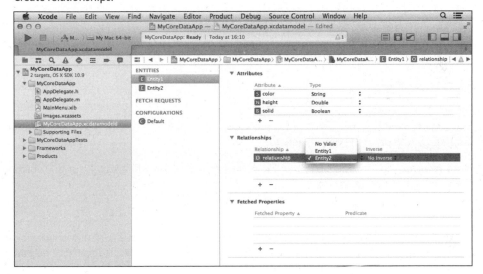

4. Select Entity2, create a relationship, and select Entity1 as a destination.

This creates a double relationship between Entity1 and Entity2.

5. Select No Inverse under the Inverse column, and select relationship.

These steps create a mutual two-way link between Entity1 and Entity2. In your code, you can use the relationship to share data between Entity1 and Entity2.

Using the graph editor

Select the graph editor to view the entities and their relationship visually, as shown in Figure C.12. Object positions aren't important. Only the contents of each entity and the arrows indicating relationships are significant.

Figure C.12

View entities and relationships in the graph editor.

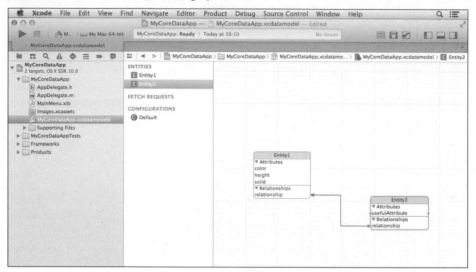

You can drag entities to move them. (In fact you may need to—it's not unusual for entities to overlap by default in the graph view.)

Note you can add attributes by selecting an entity and clicking the Add Attribute button near the bottom right of the editor.

TIP

Arrowheads include information about relationships. A one-way relationship has a single arrowhead at one end. Two-way relationships have an arrowhead at each end. To-many relationships have double arrowheads. Note that you can have a one-way to-many relationship; this appears as a double arrowhead at one end, while the other end of the link has no arrowhead.

Using other options

You can add fetched properties in the Fetched Properties by clicking the + (plus) button. To add a predicate filter rule, click twice under the Predicate header and type the predicate as a string.

When the data model editor is selected in Xcode, a number of menu items become available under the main Xcode menu Editor header. Some options duplicate the buttons in the main editor; for example, the Add Entity menu item duplicates the Add Entity button.

However, this menu also includes unique options you cannot access elsewhere:

- **Add Configuration.**
- **Add Fetch Request:** This defines a fetch request used to read data from records that match a selected entity type and also match an optional list of attribute conditions. Figure C.13 shows an example.

Figure C.13

You can define arbitrary fetch requests in code, but it can be easier to define standard requests in the model editor. You can then load them and use them as needed.

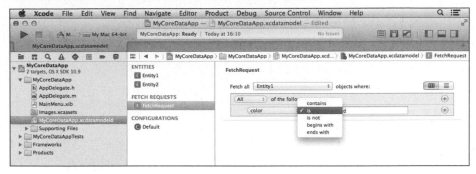

- **Create NSManagedObject subclass:** Use this option to create a customized version of one or more of your entities, with extra code features. By default, each entity is an instance of NSManagedObject. This class provides basic read, search, and write options for an entity. If your entity needs to do more—for example, it might need to interact with the rest of your application whenever data is accessed—this option creates code files for a subclass.
- **Import:** Use this option to import an existing data model from a saved file.
- **Add Model Version:** Use these options to manage multiple versions of a model file.

Summary

Core Data is a moderately esoteric skill. You do not have to use the Xcode Core Data Editor to create working Core Data code. But the editor makes it much simpler to set up a working Core Data project. If you need to use Core Data for a project, it's worth taking the time to familiarize yourself with its features.

Plist editing is more common. For basic app development, you can largely ignore direct plist editing of app properties and settings. Xcode includes simpler, indirect tools for managing the properties that are most likely to matter.

However, if you use custom plists in your app, the editor is invaluable. You can manage data in other ways, but plists are a standard Apple technology. Advanced users expect to be able to find custom settings in custom plists, so you'll find it useful to spend some time understanding how to use this editor.

Index

W

X

Z

Office

InDesign®

Facebook®

THE WAY YOU WANT TO LEARN.

HTML

Photoshop®

DigitalClassroom.com

Flexible, fast, and fun, DigitalClassroom.com lets you choose when, where, and how to learn new skills. This subscription-based online learning environment is accessible anytime from your desktop, laptop, tablet, or smartphone. It's easy, efficient learning — on *your* schedule.

- Learn web design and development, Office applications, and new technologies from more than 2,500 video tutorials, e-books, and lesson files
- Master software from Adobe, Apple, and Microsoft
- Interact with other students in forums and groups led by industry pros

Learn more! Sample DigitalClassroom.com for free, now!

We're social. Connect with us!

facebook.com/digitalclassroom
@digitalclassrm